Internet Computing: Technologies, Frameworks and Applications

Internet Computing: Technologies, Frameworks and Applications

Edited by **Anthony Rocus**

WILLFORD PRESS

New York

Published by Willford Press,
118-35 Queens Blvd., Suite 400,
Forest Hills, NY 11375, USA
www.willfordpress.com

Internet Computing: Technologies, Frameworks and Applications
Edited by Anthony Rocus

International Standard Book Number: 978-1-68285-074-9 (Hardback)

The publisher's policy is to use permanent paper from mills that operate a sustainable forestry policy. Furthermore, the publisher ensures that the text paper and cover boards used have met acceptable environmental accreditation standards.

Trademark Notice: Registered trademark of products or corporate names are used only for explanation and identification without intent to infringe.

Printed in the United States of America.

Contents

Preface

This book has been an outcome of determined endeavour from a group of educationists in the field. The primary objective was to involve a broad spectrum of professionals from diverse cultural background involved in the field for developing new researches. The book not only targets students but also scholars pursuing higher research for further enhancement of the theoretical and practical applications of the subject.

Internet computing is an emerging concept in the field of information technology and computer engineering which is related to creating and providing on-demand access to various computing resources like networks, servers, etc. This book aims to elucidate novel techniques and applications of internet computing. It is a compilation of various topics that focus on diverse concepts of network architecture, software engineering, network security, etc. It will prove to be an excellent guide for students and professionals engaged in this field.

It was an honour to edit such a profound book and also a challenging task to compile and examine all the relevant data for accuracy and originality. I wish to acknowledge the efforts of the contributors for submitting such brilliant and diverse chapters in the field and for endlessly working for the completion of the book. Last, but not the least; I thank my family for being a constant source of support in all my research endeavours.

Editor

A data infrastructure reference model with applications: towards realization of a ScienceTube vision with a data replication service

Morris Riedel[1*], Peter Wittenburg[2], Johannes Reetz[3], Mark van de Sanden[4], Jedrzej Rybicki[1], Benedikt von St. Vieth[1], Giuseppe Fiameni[5], Giacomo Mariani[5], Alberto Michelini[6], Claudio Cacciari[5], Willem Elbers[2], Daan Broeder[2], Robert Verkerk[4], Elena Erastova[3], Michael Lautenschlaeger[7], Reinhard Budig[7], Hannes Thielmann[7], Peter Coveney[8], Stefan Zasada[8], Ali Haidar[8], Otto Buechner[1], Cristina Manzano[1], Shiraz Memon[1], Shahbaz Memon[1], Heikki Helin[9], Jari Suhonen[9], Damien Lecarpentier[9], Kimmo Koski[9] and Thomas Lippert[1]

Abstract

The wide variety of scientific user communities work with data since many years and thus have already a wide variety of data infrastructures in production today. The aim of this paper is thus not to create one new general data architecture that would fail to be adopted by each and any individual user community. Instead this contribution aims to design a reference model with abstract entities that is able to federate existing concrete infrastructures under one umbrella. A reference model is an abstract framework for understanding significant entities and relationships between them and thus helps to understand existing data infrastructures when comparing them in terms of functionality, services, and boundary conditions. A derived architecture from such a reference model then can be used to create a federated architecture that builds on the existing infrastructures that could align to a major common vision. This common vision is named as 'ScienceTube' as part of this contribution that determines the high-level goal that the reference model aims to support. This paper will describe how a well-focused use case around data replication and its related activities in the EUDAT project aim to provide a first step towards this vision. Concrete stakeholder requirements arising from scientific end users such as those of the European Strategy Forum on Research Infrastructure (ESFRI) projects underpin this contribution with clear evidence that the EUDAT activities are bottom-up thus providing real solutions towards the so often only described 'high-level big data challenges'. The followed federated approach taking advantage of community and data centers (with large computational resources) further describes how data replication services enable data-intensive computing of terabytes or even petabytes of data emerging from ESFRI projects.

Keywords: Reference model, ScienceTube, Data infrastructure, Replication

*Correspondence: m.riedel@fz-juelich.de
[1] Juelich Supercomputing Centre, Juelich, Germany
Full list of author information is available at the end of the article

1 Introduction

'A fundamental characteristic of our age is the rising tide of data - global, diverse, valuable and complex. In the realm of science, this is both an opportunity and a challenge [1]. As this quote suggests there are many opportunities and challenges in the steadily increasing amount of scientific data and there are a wide variety of rather high level reports, press releases, or statements given to support this claim. The following other examples are taken from high-level recommendations by the e-Infrastructure Reflection Group (e-IRG)[a] report on data management: *'Encourage the development of non-discipline-specific frameworks and information architectures for interoperable exchange of data...support communities for the definition of their requirements...'* [2] and *'Ensure that besided hardware and services, digital objects deserve infrastructure components in their own right: ... persistent linkage of research data... policies for long-term preservation of data, maybe focused into dedicated centers...'* [2]. Another example from the European e-Infrastructure Forum (EEF)[b]:*'Data archiving and curation is a common need for several of the ESFRI projects'* [3].

But in many cases, less concrete information is given about concrete activities that link to these high-level reports and goals while at the same time have roots with bottom-up activities in order to ensure that solutions are provided that are really needed in science in the next decade. For example, the high level expert group on scientific data puts the following high-level vision towards 2030: *'Our vision is a scientific e-infrastructure that supports seamless access, use, re-use, and trust of data. In a sense, the physical and technical infrastructure becomes invisible and the data themselves become the infrastructure'* [1]. But how will such an infrastructure look like and what would be the first steps towards the implementation of such a vision? How it will work together with the wide variety of existing local, regional, national, or even pan-European data infrastructures? Would it be possible to compare at least roughly these different existing data infrastructures in order to explore synergies and what mechanism is provided for that? How can community centers with domain-specific expertise and data centers with large-scale processing expertise work together to perform data-intensive computing and perhaps even contribute to the avoidance of 'big data' by investigating, for example, data de-duplication approaches?

These are all questions for which the answer is not evident while we need to acknowledge that some fragmented answers exist to some of these questions. This paper provides more consistent answers to the aforementioned questions with bottom-up solutions driven by scientific end-user needs while at the same time being linked to the aforementioned high-level vision. This high-level vision

where *'...data themselves become the infrastructure...'* [1] is broken down into more concrete functionality entities and their relationships that sum up to a *'data infrastructure reference model'* in order to enable comparison with the wide variety of existing solutions in the field as well as providing a more clearer picture of how high-level visions might be realized. The absence of such a more abstract scientific-oriented data infrastructure reference model is diametral to the fundamental design principles of software engineering and has thus lead to numerous different non-interoperable architectures as part of fragmented data infrastructures in the last decade.

In order to advance from the abstract to the more concrete, concrete scientific end-user requirements are analyzed arond a *'data replication service'* use case that drives the design of reference model- derived concrete architectures. This contribution will describe how these concrete architectures are implemented as part of the European Data infrastructure EUDAT project [4] and which data infrastructure integration issues we need to overcome. The approach thus followed in this contribution is *'putting the scientific end-user into the driving seat'* meaning that the architecture is guided by the high-level vision and more clearly defined by using a specific use case around a *'data replication service'* as a driver. Scientific communities that are interested in this use case include members of the European Network for Earth System Modelling (ENES)[c], the European Plate Observing System (EPOS)[d], the Common Language Resources and Technology Infrastructure (CLARIN)[e], and the Virtual Physiological Human (VPH)[f].

This paper is structured as follows. After the introduction, Section "Motivation" provides the motivation for our work and sets it in context to the broader view on scientific data challenges in the next couple of years. Section "Data infrastructure reference model" then introduces the data infrastructure reference model and the high-level goals driving its derived architectural activities. The concrete use case around a data replication service is introduced in Section "Data replication service use case", while Section "Architecture for data replication use case" describes how architectural core building blocks guided by the reference model are derived from this particular use case. After the survey of related work in Section "Related work", this paper ends with some concluding remarks.

2 Motivation

The introduction already provided several examples of high-level recommendations, plans, agreements that motivates a *'real deployment of solutions'* and *'actions from scientific stakeholders and their partners that can make a difference'* within Europe in order to cope with the rising tide of scientific data. This can not be done from scientific communities in isolation from large-scale data centers in Europe, nor are such data centers able to reach out into the scientific communities alone. Instead, the high level expert group on scientific data suggests to *'develop an international framework for a Collaborative Data Infrastructure (CDI)'* [1]. The CDI high-level vision in turn follows a *federated model* that takes advantage of the benefits of community and data centers.

The high level expert group on scientific data report further outlines that data-intensive computing is related to *scientific workflow executions*. Processing-intensive activities such as *data mining* that are considered as common services across scientific domains are required to be available at large data centers. These data-intensive computing activities in many cases requires processing powers that raise the demand for High Performance Computing (HPC) resources. On the other end of the scale, High Throughput Computing (HTC) resources can be also powerful when used with data analysis tools (e.g. MapReduce [5]). Although many community centers (i.e. middle layer) also provide computing power at their centers (e.g. HPC at DKRZ), the larger data centers in Europe complementary offer unique computing capabilities towards the peta-scale performance range (e.g. HPC at JSC). This is the reason why *compute resources* are modelled alongside the 'data replication service' since data is replicated to data centers that enable additional large-scale processing.

3 Data infrastructure reference model

This section aims to provide a *'frame of reference'* in order to systematically approach the high-level challenges listed in the previous section. But these challenges need to be better specified and understood in order to provide concrete solutions for them. A series of workshops [6,7] have been performed with scientific users that face data challenges in order gather requirements for a federated data infrastructure.

A reference model approach is used to understand the requirements in context to each other. Such a reference model is an abstract framework for understanding significant entities and relationships between them within a service-oriented environment [8] such as a service-oriented data infrastructure. The OASIS SOA reference model [8] is taken as the foundation of the work and is illustrated in Figure 1. This illustration shows that a reference model itself is not directly tied to standards, technologies, or other concrete implementation details. A wide variety of user communities lead to many existing concrete data architectures while at the same time these all share common problems that can be expressed with abstract entities on the reference model level. A reference model guides concrete derived architecture work such as the reference architecture that is typically based on standards, profiles, or specifications. Concrete derived architectures and their implementations are expected to

vary from each other, but being described with a reference model enables a better comparison between them.

Figure 1 provides pieces of information how the elements in this contribution are connected with each other by indicating which sections contribute to which reference model elements. The grey parts in this figure have been added to the original from [8] in order to provide even more information how the contributions in this paper on different architectural levels contribute to the overall 'ScienceTube' vision and its derived reference model.

3.1 ScienceTube vision and user requirements

The outcome of the workshops [6,7] held all point to a vision we refer to as *'ScienceTube'* by which we not intend to give it a clear product name. Instead this 'ScienceTube' vision rather stands for a key goal with several aligned activities in this contribution and as being partly implemented in EUDAT.

The requirements expressed by user communities that shaped this vision all sum up to the fact that *'everything is inter-linked data accessible in a lightweight Web-like fashion'* as shown in Figure 2. The vision goes far beyond just 'videos' as data what the 'Tube' might indicate and instead rather connects scientific data and makes it easily accessible to scientific users. The core functionality of the illustrated GUI is a *'scientifc data viewer'* that is able to dynamically switch depending on which data is currently viewed (e.g. scientific datasets, paper, etc.). This viewer needs to understand the different data structures of the scientific data in question.

Figure 2 also illustrates that there are *'recommendation systems'* pointing to the 'most viewed data today' such as papers that are inter-linked with scientific measurement data obtained from a large device (e.g. telescope). Other requirements have been *'rating systems'* in order to encourage trust for users over a long period and to support the reputation of those that share their data. The latter is particularly crucial and addresses a clear challenge by encouraging user communities to share their scientific data with others. Complementary to the data itself, there is a lightweight access to data processing power and available storage resources. All these requirements raise the demand for a strong service backend with various technical functionalities.

3.2 Reference model blueprint and design

Figure 1 introduces the key elements of the reference model parts and this section briefly describes its major design foundations. Figure 3 provides an abstract blueprint via a conceptual view that incorporates key principles of reference models listed in [8]. The reference model is *'abstract'*, because its entities and concepts are an abstract representation of the entities (e.g. data-oriented services) that exist in production data infrastructures.

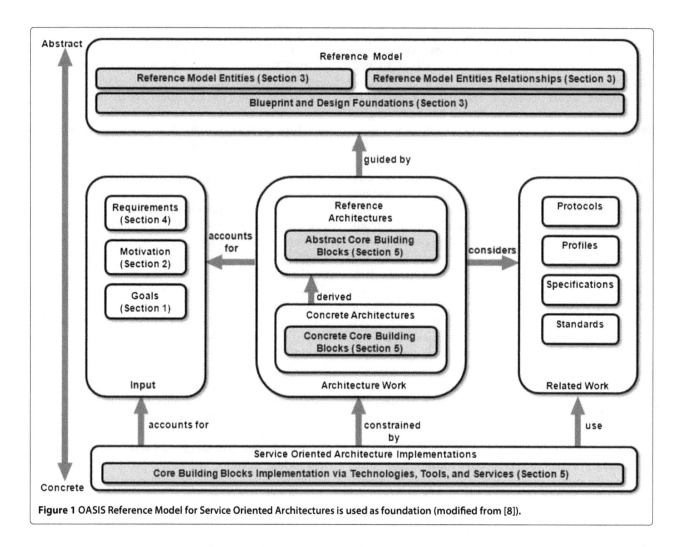

Figure 1 OASIS Reference Model for Service Oriented Architectures is used as foundation (modified from [8]).

The entities follow a service-based approach and actual data services deployed on infrastructures may have certain performance characteristics, but the concept of the individual service types are relevant and not the particular deployment. Figure 3 illustrates not a particular reference installation and also not a concrete deployment of implemented reference architecture core building block services. Instead the focus is on the concept of an abstract service entity and its relationships to other entities. Another principle followed is that the reference defines entities 'within a particular problem domain' that is set as services around the particular high-level 'Science-Tube' vision and the underlying concrete data infrastructure. Another key principle of the reference model design is that it is 'independent of specific standards, technologies, or implementations' making it 'technology-agnostic.

Figure 3 illustrates the major design foundation of the reference model that follows an overall 'federated infrastructure approach' in the blueprint. This means that entities are deployed on community and data centers and that result is a truly 'collaborative infrastructure'. The

infrastructure is thus not created 'for' the scientists but instead together 'with the scientists' that is a major change of views compared to many methods from IT infrastructures applied in the last decade.

3.3   Reference model entities and relationships

The reference model defines entities for key functionality and relationships between them. The major first entity of the reference model are 'virtual workspaces' that represents a kind of 'workbench' where services and resources are conveniently accessed. This entity is illustrated in Figure 3 as a virtual overlay of the backend functionality existing at data centers. It is accessed via lightweight Web-based GUIs as shown in Figure 2.

The 'virtual workspace' maintains a 'list of profiles' to enable scientists to configure different 'workbenches'. This enables scientists with different roles to configure their 'virtual workspace' as needed for each role (e.g. organizational, research project, etc.). 'Pre-configured filters' shows only a limited set of services instead of potentially hundreds of available domain-specific infrastructure services.

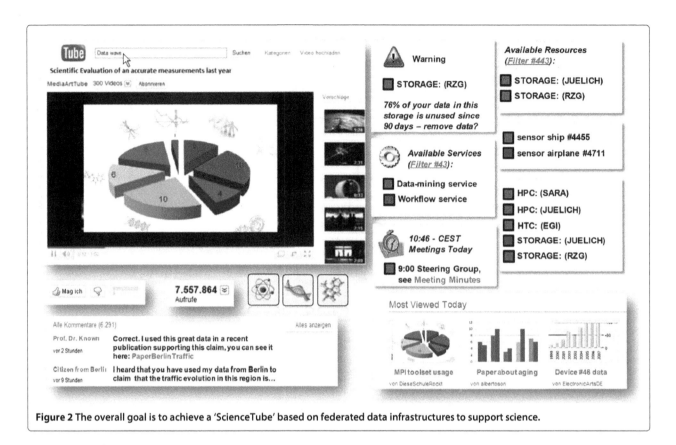

Figure 2 The overall goal is to achieve a 'ScienceTube' based on federated data infrastructures to support science.

Another filter can be applied to scientific measurement devices and to data archives to enable a focussed view on information. The 'virtual workspace' informs about existing 'end-user quota' on data resources. It also informs scientists about their 'community time' on rare resources such as large-scale computational resources on which time is granted after peer-review processes. This includes scheduled time periods as part of large experiments (e.g. collider beam) or devices (e.g. telescope). The elements of the 'virtual workspaces' entity are directly connected to federated security methods based on 'user access policies'. This includes identity management and authentication, but also authorization techniques while at the same time retain a local access control by resource providers.

A large part of the 'virtual workspace' entity are various 'service adapters'. This collectively stands for multiple adapters that bring functionality from services into the workspace. Examples include integrated clients for data-mining services or simple lookup services or integrated APIs for submitting data-intensive computational jobs on different types of compute resources. Domain-specific adapters for scientific workflow services (e.g. WebLicht [9]) can be provided or more general adapter for widespread storage technologies (e.g. iRODS [10]). Other 'service adapters' tackle the 'data wave issues' highlighted in Section "Motivation" such as data recommendation systems or data de-duplication check services. Another

element that visualizes all the previous features is named as 'core functions' with dynamic Web 2.0 functionality or mash-ups.

Table 1 lists elements of the 'virtual workspace' but there are also a wide variety of other entities. The 'Application Server' entity represents the functionality that hosts the virtual workspaces and parts of Web-based Virtual Research Environments (VREs) to make them accessible to scientists. As shown in Figure 3, the 'ScienceTube' features are thus only one element of VREs alongside many other VRE elements (e.g. other services). 'Archives/Repositories' are another entity that collectively represent the broad spectrum of existing scientific domain-specific data. This is deeply connected to data models encoded in the archives or the valuable meta-data assigned to scientific data-sets. The 'storage' technologies entity is also a crucial part of the reference model. This provides access to different types of storage (e.g. tapes, disks, etc.).

Also 'compute resources' are an important entity since data-intensive processing must be conveniently possible using High Throughput Computing (HTC) resources (e.g. with MapReduce techniques) or High Performance Computing (HPC) resources (e.g. for complex climate prediction simluations). Large-scale sources of measurement data are summarized as 'Devices', including ships with sensors or large-scale telescopes.

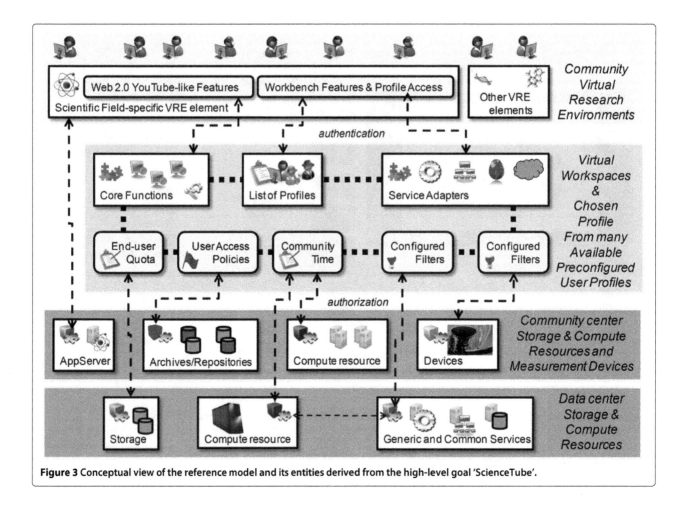

Figure 3 Conceptual view of the reference model and its entities derived from the high-level goal 'ScienceTube'.

The final entity refers to a broad spectrum of services required to run a production data infrastructure with *'Generic and Common Services'*, which in many cases are often also inter-disciplinary in nature. Firstly, infrastructure support services are required such as monitoring of services and resources as well as ticketing system for user help desks and support. Many scientific communities share the demand for a persistent identifier (PID) service such as the European Persistent Identifier (EPIC)[g] service. This service provides the functionality to assign each data object as part of the data infrastructure a unique ID making the data clearly referencable. Services (e.g. Shibboleth Identity Providers) that support the creation of a federated AAI infrastructure model. Accounting services are needed in order to support quotas and tracking the resource usage. Scientific workflow services (e.g. WebLicht [9]) that are of interest for a broader range of user communities are also part of the 'generic and common services' entity.

4   Data replication service use case

The reference model follows a 'federated model' between user community centers and data centers. Each of the

centers have different specialities and boundary conditions leading to questions we need to answer in order to define a more concrete architecture. Hence, in order to derive a more concrete architecture guided by this reference model setup, the requirements from real end user communities need to be more clearly analyzed.

This analysis follows a process in which each of the different use cases drives the architectural design layout thus emphasizing again that end-users decide what services are provided, while the exact how is rather driven by technical constraints. This prevents the creation of big architectures that are not underpinned with user requirements leading to unnecessary services that are not really required. Instead, our approach ensures a slim architecture since the concrete architectures derived from the abstract reference model are underpinned by user requirements of scientific stakeholders.

While this contribution focusses on the *'data replication use case'*, there are other use cases that are tackled in parallel and will be published in other contributions. Examples of other user cases include 'data staging' from one center to another in order to perform computational activities or the 'simple store use case' that aims to work

Table 1 Reference model entities overview

Name	Short Description
Virtual	(VW1) List of Profiles
Workspaces	(VW2) Configured Filters
	(VW3) End-user Quota
	(VW4) Community Time
	(VW5) User Access Policies
	(VW6) Service Adapters
	(VW7) Core Functions
Application	(AS1) Hosting 'Virtual
Server	Workspaces' and Virtual
	Research Environment
Archives	(AR1) Scientific domain-
Repositories	specific datasets including
	different data models and
	meta-data for its description
Storage	(ST1) Storage technologies
	providing convenient access
	to different types of
	storage capacity
Compute	(CR1) Seamless access to HPC
Resources	and HTC resources
Devices	(D1) Large scientific devices
	as sources of measurement data
Generic and	(G1) Infrastructure Support Services
Common Services	(G2) Persistent Identifier Services
(Inter-disciplinary	(G3) Federated AAI Services
Services)	(G4) Accounting Services
	(G5) Workflow Services
	(G6) Other services...

on a dropbox-like functionality. Other use cases is the 'handling of metadata' and 'authorization and authentication infrastructure' that both are needed by end-users. All these use cases will together shape an architecture for a data infrastructure tuned for stakeholder needs following a federated model. One of the goals to create numerous architecture work elements is to better compare the infrastructure architecture with those of others in order to seek synergies (e.g. commonly deployed services) with other data infrastructures (e.g. PanData [11]) and to support the common understanding in the complex arena of 'big data'.

4.1 Scientific community stakeholders

The general stakeholders are projects emerging from the ESFRI roadmap and other larger scientific communities

such as the VPH network of excellence. The stakeholders of the EUDAT task force 'safe data replication' [12] are summarized in Table 2. While a more thorough description is provided in [12], the reason why a data replication service is needed is to improve data curation and accessibility. The added value is thus to replicate data from community data centers to other large data centers to improve the reliability and access to computational resources. Several scientific communities work closely together with large data center representatives in order to understand and implement such a 'data replication service'. In the context of the EUDAT task force, only several data-sets are replicated in order to bring the 'date replication service' towards production meaning that some communities choose to replicate data from some of their specific scientific projects and not all of them.

The ENES community is involved via the Deutsches Klimarechenzentrum (DKRZ)[h] and have interest to replicate data to the Juelich Supercomputing Centre (JSC)[i] in Germany and the IT Center for Science (CSC)[j] in Finland. Another community involved is EPOS represented by the Instito Nazionale di Geofisica e Vulcanologia (INGV)[k]. They aim to replicate their data to the data centers of CINECA[l] in Italy and SARA[m] in Netherlands. Another scientific community is CLARIN with representatives of the Max Planck Institute for Psycholinguistics (MPI-NL)[n]. This community intends to replicate data to Rechenzentrum Garching (RZG)[o] in Germany and SARA in Netherlands. Finally, VPH is involved via University College London (UCL)[p] that want to replicate data to CINECA in Italy, SARA in Netherlands, and Poznan Supercomputing Centre (PSNC)[q] in Poland.

4.2 Use case analysis

Interviews have been performed with the stakeholders in the previous paragraph in order to better understand the demand for a 'data replication service' and a structured analysis of their outcomes is given in Table 3. This use case analysis presented in Table 3 is derived from a method by Malan and Bredemeyer [13] that has proved to be effective as part of our XSEDE infrastructure architectural design process [14].

Table 2 Participating community and data center

Scientific Community	Community Centers	Data Centers
CLARIN	MPI-PL	RZG, SARA
ENES	DKRZ	JSC, CSC
EPOS	INGV	CINECA, SARA
VPH	UCL	CINECA, SARA, PSNC

Table 3 'Data replication service' use case analysis

Use Case I	Data Replication Service
Description	Create and automatically execute a safe replication policy on specified data objects in the infrastructure between community and data centers
References	EUDAT Newsletter April 2012 [12]
Actors	(A1) Scientific Community Center Site Manager (CCSM)
Prerequisites (Dependencies, (Assumptions)	(P1) Federated infrastructure approach (P2) Each data object has unique PID (P3) Data access permissions remain (P4) Federated AAI concepts adopted
Steps	(S1) Create policy P for M replications (S2) Specify the target data centers C (S3) Exclude centers X from policy (S4) Define replicated data lifetime T (S5) Policy is saved and executed (S6) Policy-based replication is done (S7) Data objects are safely replicated (S8) Replicated data stored in local Long-term Archives (LTAs)
Variations	(V1) Existing policy P might be updated by the CCSM (V2) Additional manual data replication if needed by the CCSM
Quality Attributes	(QA1) Reliability of replication (QA2) More optimal data curation (QA3) Better accessibility of data
Non-functional	(NF1) Usability for creating and executing the replication policy
Issues	(I1) Federated AAI concepts work still work-in-progress

Table 3 clarifies the actors that play a role in context and provides a clear step-wise view on the required functionality based on specified assumptions. The variations are listed to have those activities noted that are not directly in-line with the previous described step-wise approach (e.g. manual interventions by actors). Another part of the analysis are the quality attributes that also communicate benefits for the 'safe replication service' users and often related non-functional requirements (e.g. usability, reliability, etc.). Finally, issues in realizing the production setup of the use case are ongoing research activities (e.g. Federated AAI).

4.3 Derived stakeholder requirements analysis

Interviews have been performed with scientific community representatives that are the stakeholders of the 'data replication service' [12]. The summary of the requirements have been analysed and set into context of the reference model and possible derived reference architecture core building blocks. Table 4 lists the identified core building blocks in context of the requirements stated by the stakeholders.

5   Architecture for data replication use case

This section aims to provide more concrete details about various 'architecture work' derived from the 'data replication service' use case guided by the reference model introduced in Section "Data infrastructure reference model" as frame of reference. Figure 1 shows the different levels of architecture work, including a reference architecture with abstract core building blocks and a more concrete architecture. This section will also provide information about implementation activities using technologies, tools, and services. This includes challenges faced while implementing this architecture setup for production summarized as 'data infrastructure integration activities'. The reference model in Section "Data infrastructure reference model" gives the basic blueprint with abstract entities and relationships that are more concrete in this section and focussed on the specific use case of a 'data replication service'. The resulting architecture thus does not describe the whole data architecture nor all services that will be available in EUDAT that provides functionality for many other required service use cases too. Instead, it can be considered as a first step in providing a more concrete architecture description of a reference model with aligned architecture work specifically based on the real 'data replication service' use case. The architecture work accounts for the motivation raised in Section "Motivation", the overall goal described in Section "Introduction" and the specific requirements raised in Section "Data replication service use case". Subsequent activities during the course of the next years will provide more concrete architecture work elements for other service use cases (e.g. data transfer, meta-data search, etc.) and over time produce a more detailed reference architecture.

5.1 Use case derived reference architecture

This paragraph introduces the reference architecture illustrated in Figure 4 being derived from the use case analysis results from Section "Data replication service use case" and being guided by the reference model design in Section "Data infrastructure reference model". The reference architecture provides several abstract core building blocks in order to remain technology-agnostic thus contributing to the software engineering principle that the architecture should be seperated from its implementation

Table 4 'Data replication service' use case requirements

Architecture Core Building Block	'Data Replication Service' Stakeholder Requirements
Mature and Extensible Storage Technology	(R1) The technology required must be mature to guarantee a highly available and robust service. (R2) CCSMs need to have functionality which data objects and collections need replication. (R3) A policy-based feature enables that all centers can be audited (e.g. DSOA) in order to establish trust with clearly described policy rules. (R4) Powerful policy functions are required to enable CCSMs to specify M replicas to be stored for N years.
Persistent Identifier Service	(R5) Each data object in the data infrastructure should have a clearly assigned PID (R6) The use of PIDs for replicated data objects enables CSMs to know whether the replicas are identical with the source.
Monitoring Service	(R7) The infrastructure services must be monitored in order to obtain information about their production status.
Federated AAI APIs	(R8) CCSMs need replicas to be accessible by users while maintaining the access permissions as defined by the originating community center.
Local Long-term Archiving	(R9) The storage technology should require as little changes as possible on the community data organization side that is already established around the local LTAs.
Common Services	(R10) Ticketing service and help desk support should be established for end-users.
Web-based Workbench	(R11) Virtual workspaces making the services accessible to users.

as best as possible. The core building blocks itself are put in context to the reference model entities in Table 5. One of the reference model design foundation is the *federated approach* that is applied to the core building blocks of the data architecture as shown in Figure 4. The positioning of core building blocks is obtained from the use case that aims to replicate data from community centers to data centers.

5.2 Technology assessment

Table 6 provides an overview of the assessed technologies for defining the implementation of a concrete architecture driven by the 'data replication use case'. The listed technologies are either already available at centers including their knowledge or are known to be stable and mature technologies in order to prevent new developments to the most possible degree.

The core building block (RA1) requires some development efforts in order to integrate all the different service functionalities and to make it accessible in a Web-based workbench. The (RA2) data models with meta-data are also existing at the scientific community centers already but are part of the architecture to underline their importance in the data infrastructure and their possible numerous relationships to different storage services. In fact, several investigations in the organization of (RA2) points to the use of file system hierarchies for scientific data (e.g. DKRZ) and there are expected benefits when using a storage technology in conjunction with this organization scheme. Also, (RA4) referring to local long-term archiving solutions are largely already existing at the different centers as well, but needs to work together with the storage technologies of choice.

In terms of (RA3), there are several mature and extensible storage technology systems available in the academic field of infrastructures such as the Disk Pool Manager (DPM) [15], dCache [16], and iRODS [10]. The different involved centers have experience with all of these technologies and all of them seem to be mature and usable. But when taking into account the stakeholder requirements listed in Table 4, in particular the policy-based functionality, the iRODS technology is the most appropriate system. As early evaluations reveal, iRODS also integrates well with existing local LTA technologies (e.g. file systems).

In terms of (RA5), there are two persistent identifier services of interest named as DataCite/DOI [17] and the EPIC service. Several partners of the EUDAT scientific communities (e.g. CLARIN) and centers (e.g. RZG) have already experience with EPIC as part of the REPLIX project [18] and our work is build on top of this approach. Also in terms of (RA6), the NAGIOS system [19] with its extensibility using a probe-based approach was choosen as a monitoring solution, because expertise was existing at the majority of centers. For (RA8), the ticketing

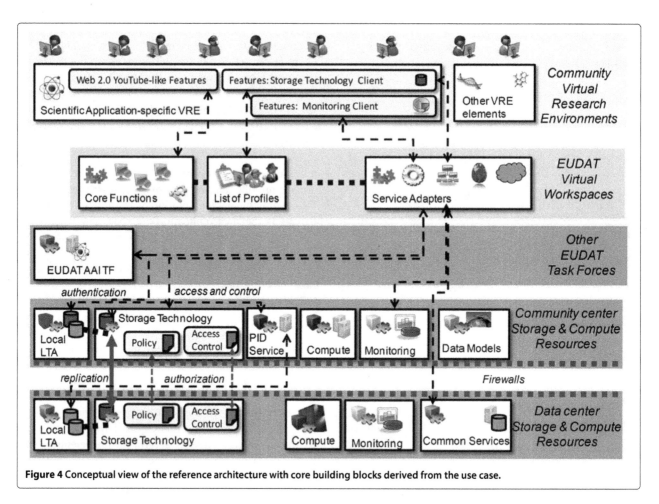

Figure 4 Conceptual view of the reference architecture with core building blocks derived from the use case.

technology of choice is JIRA mostly because it has been also already used as part of the EUDAT project internal tasks. Finally, the (RA7) implementation is most complex since it also affects all other core building blocks. Shibboleth and contrail have been analyzed and so far Shibboleth is the most promising candidate to realize a federated AAI service given its support by educational organizations in Europe.

5.3 Concrete architecture and implementation

Based on the aforementioned reference architecture core building blocks and the subsequent technology assessment, this section aims to describe one possible derived architecture implementation as illustrated in Figure 5. The architecture is described by addressing the concrete stakeholder requirements for the 'data replication service' listed in Table 4.

As Figure 5 reveals, the (RA3) core building block is located in the architecture on the community and data center side by using iRODS. By using this mature technology, the architecture is able to address requirement (R1) and the policy-based mechanisms of iRODS using 'micro-services in rules' [10] (see next paragraph for more details) addresses requirement (R2), (R3), and (R4).

CCSMs are able to specify which data objects need replication and the enormous extensibility of iRODS with user-specific rules enable CCSMs to specify those objects that need M replicas for N years being automatically executed and thus enforced.

Table 5 'Reference architecture core building blocks'

Reference Model Entity	Reference Architecture Core Building Block
Virtual Workspaces	(RA1) Web-based Workbench
Archives / Repositories	(RA2) Data models with meta-data of scientific stakeholders
Storage	(RA3) Mature and Extensible Storage Technology
	(RA4) Local Long-Term Archiving
Generic and Common Services	(RA5) Persistent Identifier Service
	(RA6) Monitoring Service
	(RA7) Federated AAI Service
	(RA8) Ticketing service

Table 6 'Architecture core building blocks with potential technologies that have been assessed for their usage'

Reference Architecture Core Building Block	Potential Technologies
(RA1) Web-based Workbench	Requires development
(RA2) Data models with meta-data of scientific stakeholders	Existing at the community centers
(RA3) Mature and Extensible Storage Technology	DPM, dCache, iRODS
(RA4) Local Long-Term Archiving	Already available at the centers
(RA5) Persistent Identifier Service	DataCite/DOI, EPIC/Handle
(RA6) Monitoring Service	NAGIOS
(RA7) Federated AAI Service	Shibboleth, Contrail
(RA8) Ticketing service	JIRA

The aforementioned architecture element raise the requirement for security functionality in terms of enabling authentication and authorization and keeping identities while replicating data from community centers to data centers. Figure 5 shows that simple Access Control Lists (ACLs) can be used as part of iRODS, but that a use of a federated AAI solution is much more convenient. The related (RA7) is currently defined by the EUDAT AAI task force and the details are kept out of this paper to remain the focus on the 'data replication service'. Using the solution of the EUDAT AAI task force (e.g. a Shibboleth service) addresses requirement (R8) so that replicas are accessible by users while the access permissions as defined by the orginating center is kept. Getting iRODS to work with this security approach is one of the 'infrastructure integration issues' (I1) we found during the implementation of the data infrastructure architecture. Those issues raise the demand for smaller integration developments to get several pieces of the architecture together and are described in more detail in the subsequent paragraph.

The (RA4) architecture core building block in Figure 5 addresses the requirement stated in (R9) in the sense that the iRODS system works seamlessly together with the

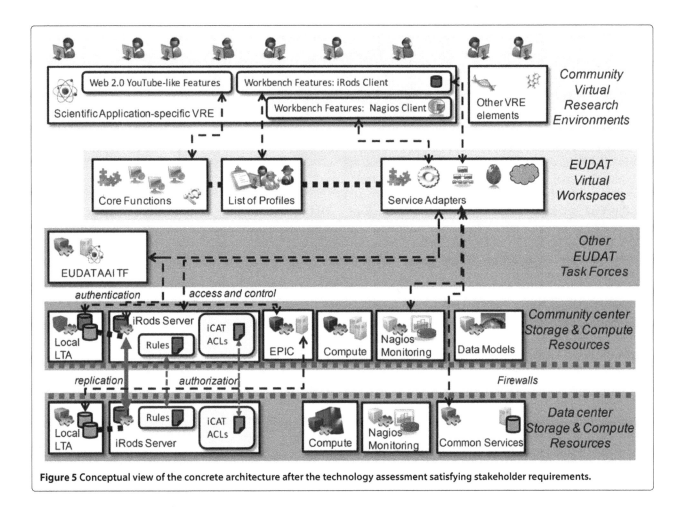

Figure 5 Conceptual view of the concrete architecture after the technology assessment satisfying stakeholder requirements.

local long-term archiving technologies at both the community centers and data centers. The scientific data and their models (RA2) are stored in the local LTAs (e.g. file systems) and are made available in the community centers via iRODS to the data infrastructure. Then, the replication rules automatically replicate this data to iRODS servers at the data center side in order to get stored in their local LTAs (e.g. storage disks, tape robots, etc.).

Another core building block is (RA5) implemented by the EPIC PID service technology as illustrated in Figure 5. It enables the basic functionality to address (R5) by providing the functionality to release PIDs, but still there must be an inter-working with the iRODS server to really get each of the replicated data objects assigned with a PID. Hence, this reveals another infrastructure integration issue (I2) raising the demand to have iRODS working together with the EPIC service. In order to address (R6), the EPIC released PIDs also need to have a mechanism to update or add locations during the process of replication. In both cases, the access of EPIC to have an initial PID for a data object and the update of potentially multiple locations, require a link to the federated AAI setup in order to ensure that the use of PIDs is protected. This points to another issue (I3) again pointing out that production technologies are available, but still need integration development to make it work with the data infrastructure.

The architecture implementation in Figure 5 reveals another core building block on both the community and data center side that is (RA6). The NAGIOS system can be used here to monitor the health status of the underlying storage backend servers, as well as the iRODS service, and the EPIC service. This addresses (R7) and enables that the data infrastructure services are monitored in order to obtain information about their production status at any time. But each of the different NAGIOS probes need a small amount of developments in order to work with the different services that raises another infrastructure integration issue (I4).

The requirement (R10) is addressed by using the (RA8) core building block and JIRA as a ticketing service that is illustrated in Figure 5 as part of the common services hosted by the data centers. This collectively also stands for a help desk support method This service is mature and expected to work well with federated AAI solutions not necessarily requiring security integration-related developments, but in order to emphasize that the security is related also to this service it is part of the infrastructure architecture too.

In contrast, the realization of the core building (RA1) requires more integration development work in realizing partly community-specific Web-based workbenches that we collectively note as infrastructure integration issue (I5).

In order to address requirement (R11), this core building block has numerous parts as illustrated in Figure 5 that

go beyond the aforementioned core functions around the Web 2.0 elements. It firstly needs to work well with the federated AAI solution emerging from the EUDAT AAI task force and secondly needs to offer convenient access to iRODS functionality (e.g. easy writing and monitoring of iRODS rules). The former is specifically important to realize the support for different roles of scientists that need to be configured as different profiles in the virtual workspace. The latter raise the demand for service adapters that are able to work with the backbone services of the data infrastructure (e.g. iRODS, NAGIOS, etc.) and that provides APIs to be used by the used Web 2.0 front-end and lightweight security frameworks.

It is also required to integrate information about the availability of the data services into the virtual workspace that can be realized by using a lightweight NAGIOS client.

5.4 Infrastructure integration challenges

The technology assessment and concrete derived technologies suggests that every technology is already available with a rich set of features and just can be used as production services as is. The implementation of the data architecture, however, reveals several 'infrastructure integration issues' that require smaller developments in order to get the different building blocks of the architecture to work together as one ecosystem. The previous architecture description identified these issues and they are summarized in Table 7 together with potential approaches.

Because of the page limit of this contribution we can not provide detailed information about all of our taken approaches in order to overcome the issues. Instead, we focus here on the issue (I2), because it highlights best how particular key features of iRODS are used and how

Table 7 'Infrastructure integration issues overview'

Data Infrastructure Integration Issue	Potential Approach
(I1) Federated AAI-enabled iRODS servers	Shibboleth-enabled iRODS server
(I2) iRODS and EPIC inter-working	iRODS rules that make callouts to EPIC
(I3) Federatd AAI-enabled EPIC service	iRODS rules that make callouts to EPIC
(I4) Monitoring information obtained from services and underlying storage resources	NAGIOS probes for EPIC and iRODS and hardware storages
(I5) Web-based workbench that makes infrastructure services seamlessly available in a secure manner	Web 2.0 and light security frameworks to integrate NAGIOS and iRODS with federated AAI

in general infrastructure integration issues are connected to development efforts. A more detailed overview of issue (I2) is therefore illustrated in Figure 6.

One of the expected functionalities of the *data replication service'* is to ensure that the digital objects stored within the iRODS service get a persistent identifier known as PIDs. As Figure 6 illustrates, iRODS does not provide a solution for that and development work is needed to achieve an integration of EPIC with iRODS. While there are many solutions for PID, previous sections revealed that in EUDAT it was decided to use PIDs provided by the EPIC service. This service in turn is based on Handle System[r] that defines the format of the PIDs and the protocol used.

Although it might sound trivial to integrate the two services with each other, the development efforts are quite complex and require deep knowledge of both the EPIC APIs and the existing iRODS extension mechanisms around micro-services as part of rules. Hence, for the sake of simplicity we will present a less-detailed overview of our solution. In short, in our case the registration and manipulation of the PIDs boiled down to exchanging Java Script Object Notation (JSON) [20] representations of a PID handle via the HTTP protocol. An example of a handle in JSON format is illustrated in the upper part of Figure 6. The particular challenge is to integrate this message exchange with the Representational State Transfer (REST)-based service [21] API of EPIC within iRODS. We have written a Python-based client software to interact with the EPIC service.

The software firstly serializes a python hash table keyValues into JSON format with help of the SimpleJson library[s]. This library is a simple and fast JSON encoder/decoder for Python. Afterwards, a http client is prepared and we use http authentication with username and password for simplicity while in parallel the federated AAI task force in EUDAT is exploring better options. It is also necessary to set content-type header to inform the server that the PID will be sent in the JSON format. After these preliminary steps, it is possible to issue a http PUT request on a given URI with JSON representation of the new handle in the request body. The URI is composed of service address, handle prefix and handle suffix. It is also possible to delete a PID from the handle system by invoking a HTTP DELETE request.

The aforementioned python-based EPIC client can be easily integrated into data management policies in iRODS as illustrated in Figure 6. This is done by using PyRods and EmbededPython modules provided by irodspython project[t]. PyRods provides a Python API for iRODS (e.g. to access and manipulate data objects in iRODS) and EmbededPython allows to write iRODS micro-services in

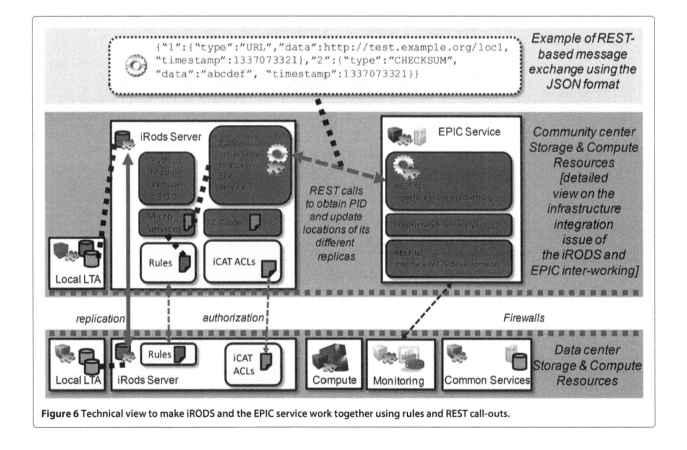

Figure 6 Technical view to make iRODS and the EPIC service work together using rules and REST call-outs.

Python. Our EPIC client presented above provides a set of micro-services for manipulating PIDs that we need to make available in iRODS. In this context, EmbededPython allowed to call Python functions directly from iRODS rules. An example of an iRODS rule that uses createHandle function defined above to register a "testHandle" PID in the PID service currently provided by a data center named SARA is given in Figure 7(a).

We assume that the Python code is stored in the location pointed by the *pyScript variable. As the next step, it is possible to integrate this EPIC call into data management policies of iRODS. An example for a rule which is called each time a new file is ingested in a given collection (i.e. "/zone/monitored/") and then creates a PID for the new data object is given in in Figure 7(b). It is a simplified version which uses fileName of the ingested data object as a PID suffix in order to better undertand the idea and not dive too deeply into the partly complex part of PID prefixes, suffixes, etc. For more information about these details we refer to the information available via the EPIC Website[u].

To sum up, we have presented only a part of our solution but it should be clear to the reader that the solution can be easily extended to define more sophisticated PID manipulation functions in the Python script on one hand, and more sophisticated policies in iRODS on the other. In fact the version used in production in EUDAT is much more complicated but based on the same basic concepts as presented above. Nevertheless, we believe that this already provides insights into the infrastructure integration issues that are commonly overlooked since production technologies are there, but how they seamlessly work together is in many cases still a matter of integration developments.

6 Related work

There is a wide variety of related work in the context of data infrastructures and possible architectural approaches. We set a focus on one particular data infrastructure activity that is relatively close to the ideas of EUDAT but for a smaller set of communities. In contrast to our here described approach that is much based on abstract entities and derived architecture core building blocks, the following data infrastructure activities follow a more standard-based approach within the project.

EUDAT members work on a more broader idea of scientific data infrastructure standardization to order to go beyond one single project that culminated in an Europe-wide activity named as the Research Data Alliance (RDA) [12]. This activity aims to create an open forum for discussing and agreeing on data-related standards, APIs, policy rules, data interoperability covering also those infrastructure integration issues raised earlier in this contribution (AAI, PIDs, etc.) to the semantic and regulatory levels.

One of the most known distributed data infrastructure was established by the High Energy Physics (HEP) community leading to the World-wide Large Hadron Collider Computing Grid (WLCG) [22].

```
testCreateHandle {
        msiPyInitialize;
        msiLocalPython9(*pyScript, "createHandle", "noRecursionTest", *uri, *suffix, *username,
        *pass, "{'URL':'http://test.example.org/loc1', 'CHECKSUM':'abcdef'}", *res2);
        msiPyFinalize;
}
INPUT *pyScript="/srv/irods/current/epicclient.py",*uri="ttps://epic.sara.nl/epic1/9210",
*suffix="testHandle", *username="user",*pass="pass"
OUTPUT null
```
(a) Example of an iRODS rule that uses our createHandle python function to register a "testHandle" PID in the EPIC PID service.

```
acPostProcForPut{
  ON($objPath like "/zone/monitored/*") {
    ... details omitted...
        msiSplitPath($objPath,*collection,*fileName);
        msiPyInitialize;
        msiLocalPython9(*pyScript, "createHandle", "noRecursionTest", *uri, *fileName, *username,
        *pass, "{'URL':'http://myirods.eudat.org/safereplication/*fileName',
        'CHECKSUM':'abcdef'}", *res2);
        msiPyFinalize;
  }
}
```
(b) Example of one possible integration of the EPIC calls into the data management policies of iRODS.

Figure 7 Examples of iRODS rule using EPIC (a) and its integration into iRODS data management policies (b).

PaNdata is a research initiative to realize a pan-European information infrastructure supporting data oriented science. The first step of this effort was PaNdata Europe that aimed at formulating baseline requirements and standards for data policy, user information exchange, data formats, data analysis software, and integration and cross linking of research outputs. After this project has been concluded in 2011, the PaNdata community started the PanData ODI (Open Data Infrastructure) project funded by the EU. This project take the aforementioned requirements and standards as a foundation for providing data solutions, and constructing sustainable data infrastructures, but specifically serving European Neutron and Photon communities. Hence, in contrast to EUDAT, the amount of participating communities is smaller than in EUDAT that aims to offer federated solutions together with all thematic groups of the ESFRI projects. However, it is important to understand that the insights of the aforementioned communities also support a wide range of other disciplines such as physics, chemistry, biology, material sciences, medical technology, environmental, and social sciences. Important applications in context are crystallography that reveals the structure of viruses and proteins and neutron scattering that is used within engineering components, and tomography provides fine-grained 3D-structures of the brain.

The PaNdata ODI will provide their participating scientific facilities with an intuitive and parallel access to the data services which include the tracing of data provenance, preservation, and scalability. It aims to deploy and integrate generic data catalogues within their target communities. Interesting in context of this contribution is that they follow a reference model named as Open Archival Information System (OAIS) [23] that is in contrast to our approach much more focussed on long-term preservation. This also includes the usage of HDF5^v and Nexus^w standards. In order to allow access across different institutions, a federated identity management system will be used that is in-line with the contribution of this paper and the activities performed by the EUDAT AAI task force. In order to provide scalability, the parallelization techniques will be used by developing parallel Nexus API (pNexus) with pHDF5^x. This will enable PaNdata to avoid sequential processing and to manage the simultaneous data inflow from various sources such as X-Ray free electron lasers for instance.

To sum up, the PaNdata activities are highly relevant in the context of EUDAT and provide enormous potential for exploring synergies (e.g. long-term archiving of scientific measurement data). But both projects have a very different focus that is serving the needs of the neutron and photon communities in PaNdata, while EUDAT specifically supports multi-disciplinary science federating approaches from a broader set of communities. Hence,

we need to acknowledge that a common understanding of the projects eventually based on reference models must be first established in order to explore synergies better.

Also many other scientific infrastructures share the demand for data-related services and that is one of the reasons why we conducted the EUDAT User Forum [12]. Other architectural approaches and synergies have been discussed and that will lead to more closer collaboration and new EUDAT service cases beyond those introduced in Section "Data replication service use case". The following examples of related work are based on findings obtained from some of the participating projects to the forum while a complete survey is not possible due to page limits.

The European Clinical Research Infrastructure Network (ECRIN) [24] that works on a distributed infrastructure with services supporting multi-national clinical research. The architectural requirements for such an infrastructure in terms of the registration of clinical trials, the repository for clinical trial data (e.g. raw data and anonymized), and the demand of long-term archiving (i.e. 15 years) all bear the potential for federating these ideas with the ones described in this contribution.

The Integrated Carbon Observation System (ICOS) [25] also shares several of the requirements stated as part of our reference model vision and its derived architectural design. The particular interesting part in terms of ICOS would be the integration of this data infrastructure since it collects data of roughly 60 atmospheric and ecosystem measurement sites and about 10 ocean sites. Requirements include near real time data collection and processing and to achieve the data while ensuring the traceability (and metadata provisioning) of the data.

Another project participating in the EUDAT User Forum was the European Life Sciences Infrastructure for Biological Information (ELIXIR) [27]. Also ELIXIR shares several requirements and approaches with EUDAT such as a wide variety of already existing data collections (repositories, gene ontologies, proteomics data, archives of protein sequences, etc.). The planned biomedical e-Infrastructure services of ELIXIR also aim to follow a federated AAI approach integrating many of the aforementioned already existing data repositories and archives.

Finally, also the data infrastructure for chemical safety diXA and its data pipeline [26] is of interest to EUDAT offering also synergies.

7 Conclusions

This paper was motivated by the high-level recommendations, plans, and roadmaps introduced at the beginning of this contribution and that we formulated more clearly as one potential vision named as 'ScienceTube'. This is not a product but rather a vision of federating the various existing approaches to the most possible degree enabling data sharing across scientific communities. We aim to implement some of these high-level visions with approaches underpinned with bottom-up activities that are scientific user-driven in order to ensure that these solutions are really used in production data infrastructures.

We are able to conclude that this is a quite complex undertaking and this contribution only focuses on one particular shared demand of scientific user communities that is the 'data replication service'. The identified reference model entities, their associated architecture work and the arising infrastructure integration issues already give a glimpse of how difficult it is to create an infrastructure where data itself should be the focus and not underlying compute or storage technologies. Although many people and funding organizations claim that every puzzle piece required for a data infrastructure is out there, we still observe crucial requirements for developments (cf. infrastructure integration developments) in order to bring the individual and eventually already used puzzle pieces together. Further work in this context will be to refine the reference model and its associated architecture work around other use cases such as data-staging or simple store for example.

From the process perspective, we can conclude that we created a working system where the 'scientific end-users are in the driving seats' involving them in architectural decisions whenever possible. We are able to claim that we created a federated data infrastructure part not only 'for' the end-users, but collaboratively 'with' end-users. This is the only chance to get trust and acceptance by user communities to really use the established data services.

The RDA work will be a promising aligned activitiy to increase the role of standards in our reference architecture design process, including emerging standards also from other standardization bodies such as the Organization for the Advancement of Structured Information Standards (OASIS) OData[y]. Also standards used by PaNdata or OpenAire+ [28] are relevant to consider as part of our activities within EUDAT in general and our federated reference model design in particular. It is important to mention that we started this work already by performing the EUDAT User Forum where many other ESFRI projects have been part in order to communicate their demands for a federated pan-European data infrastructure.

Endnotes

[a]http://www.e-irg.eu
[b]http://www.einfrastructure-forum.eu
[c]https://verc.enes.org
[d]http://www.epos-eu.org
[e]http://www.clarin.eu/external
[f]http://www.vph-noe.eu
[g]http://www.pidconsortium.eu
[h]http://www.dkrz.de

[i]http://www.fz-juelich.de/JSC
[j]http://www.csc.fi
[k]http://www.ingv.it
[l]http://www.cineca.it
[m]http://www.sara.nl
[n]http://www.mpi.nl
[o]http://www.rzg.mpg.de
[p]http://www.ucl.ac.uk
[q]http://www.man.poznan.pl
[r]http://www.handle.net/
[s]http://pypi.python.org/pypi/simplejson
[t]http://code.google.com/p/irodspython/
[u]http://www.pidconsortium.eu
[v]http://www.hdfgroup.org/HDF5
[w]http://www.nexusformat.org
[x]http://www.hdfgroup.org/HDF5/PHDF5/
[y]www.odata.org

Competing interests
The authors declare that they have no competing interests.

Authors' contributions
All co-authors worked together in establishing the safe replication service based on interviewed requirements from end users while MR and PW carried out the work of formulating and crafting the ScienceTube vision before the EUDAT project started. All authors read and approved the final manuscript.

Acknowledgements
This work is partially funded by the EUDAT project that is co-funded by the EC 7th Framework Programme (Grant Agreement no: 283304).

Author details
[1]Juelich Supercomputing Centre, Juelich, Germany. [2]Max-Planck-Institut für Meteorologie, Hamburg, Germany. [3]Rechenzentrum Garching, Munich, Germany. [4]Stichting Academisch Rekencentrum Amsterdam, Amsterdam, Netherlands. [5]CINECA, Bologna, Italy. [6]INGV, Rome, Italy. [7]Deutsches Klimarechenzentrum, Hamburg, Germany. [8]University College London, London, UK. [9]CSC - IT Center for Science, Espoo Finland, Finland.

References
1. Wood J, et al (2010) Riding the wave - How Europe can gain from the rising tide of scientific data. European Union, Italy
2. e-IRG Data Management Task Force (2009) e-IRG Report on data management 2009
3. Jones B, Davies D, Lederer H, Aerts P, Eickerman Th, Newhouse S (2010) ESFRI Project requirements for pan-European e-Infrastructure resources and facilities. European e-Infrastructure Forum, Amsterdam, Netherlands
4. Mallmann D, von St. ViethB, Riedel M, Rybicki J, Koski K, Lecarpentier D, Wittenburg P (2012) Towards a pan-European collaborative data infrastructure InSide Magazine. Inside Magazine - Innovatives Supercomputing in Deutschland 10: 84–85. http://inside.hlrs.de/htm/Edition_01_12/article_27.html
5. Dean J, Ghemawat S (2008) MapReduce: simplified data processing on large clusters Communications of the ACM 51(1): 107–113. doi:10.1145/1327452.1327492
6. Wittenburg P, et al (2010) Workshop on research metadata in context. Nijmegen, Netherlands. http://www.mpi.nl/mdws2010. Accessed July 2012
7. Reetz J, et al (2010) Repository and workspace workshop, garching. http://www.mpi.nl/research/research-projects/the-language-archive/events/RWW/program-abstracts. Accessed July 2012

8. MacKenzie CM, Laskey K, McCabe F, Brown PF, Metz R, Hamilton BA (2006) Reference model for service oriented architecture 1.0. Organization for the Advancement of Structured Information Standards: 25–29. Proceedings of the ACL 2010 System Demonstrations

9. Hinrichs E, Hinrichs M, Zastrow Th (2010) WebLicht: web-based LRT services for Germany. In: Proceedings of the 10th ACL system demonstration. Stroudsburg, USA

10. Moore RW, Rajasekar A, Marciano R (2010) Proceedings iRODS user group meeting 2010 - Policy-based data management, sharing, and preservation. CreateSpace. ISBN 1452813426

11. Bicarregui J, Lambert S, Matthews BM, Wilson MD (2011) PaNdata: a European data infrastructure for neutron and proton sources In: Proceedings of e-Science All Hands Meeting 2011 AHM'11, York, UK

12. Riedel M (2012) Secure, simple, sound: data replication on the CDI. http://www.eudat.eu/newsletter. Accessed July 2012

13. Malan R, Bredemeyer D (2011) Functional requirements and use cases. http://www.bredemeyer.com. Accessed July 2012

14. Stewart C, Knepper R, Grimshaw A, Foster I, Bachmann F, Lifka D, Riedel M (2012) XSEDE campus bridging use case descriptions. Year 1. http://www.xsede.org/web/guest/project-documents. Accessed July 2012

15. Alvarez A, Beche A, Furano F, Hellmich M, Keeble O, Rocha R (2012) DPM: future proof storage In: Proceedings of the computing in high energy and nuclear physics. USA, New York

16. Fuhrmann P, Guelzow V (2006) dCache - storage system for the future Proceedings of the Europar 2006, 1106–1113. Dresden, Germany

17. Ball A (2011) Overview of scientific metadata for data publishing, citation, and curation Eleventh International Conference on Dublin Core and Metadata Applications (DC-2011). 2011-09-21 - 2011-09-23, KB, The Hague, The Netherlands. http://opus.bath.ac.uk/26309. Accessed July 2012

18. REPLIX Project. http://tla.mpi.nl/tla-news/the-replix-project. Accessed July 2012

19. Barth W (2008) NAGIOS: System and network monitoring, open source press GmbH. ISBN 1-59327-179-4

20. Crockford D (2006) The application/json Media Type for JavaScript Object Notation (JSON) Internet Engineering Task Force (IETF). RFC4627

21. Fielding RT, Taylor RN (2002) Principled design of the modern Web architecture ACM Transactions on Internet Technology (TOIT). Vol 2(2): 115–150. doi:10.1145/514183.514185

22. World-wide Large Hadron Collider Computing Grid (WLCG). http://wlcg.web.cern.ch. Accessed July 2012

23. Lavoie BF (2004) The open archival information system reference model: introductory guide DPC technology watch report

24. Demotes-Mainard J (2004) Towards a European clinical research infrastructure network: the ECRIN programme Therapie. PubMed - US National Library of Medicine - National Institutes of Health 59(1): 151–153

25. Paris J, Ciais P, Rivier L, Chevallier F, Dolman H, Flaud J, Garrec C, Gerbig C, Grace J, Huertas E, Johannessen T, Jordan A, Levin I, Papale D, Valentini R, Watson A (2012) Integrated carbon observation system EGU general assembly, 2012. Vienna, Austria

26. DIXA Consortium (2012) diXa: A new data infrastructure for chemical safety. http://www.dixa-fp7.eu/home. Accessed July 2012

27. ELIXIR Consortium (2012) European life sciences infrastructure for biological information. http://www.elixir-europe.org/news. Accessed July 2012

28. Manghi P, Manola N, Horstmann W, Peters D (2010) An infrastructure for managing EC funded research output - the OpenAIRE project The Grey. Journal (TGJ): An Int. Journal on Grey Literature 6(1): 31–40

2

Evaluating security and usability of profile based challenge questions authentication in online examinations

Abrar Ullah[*], Hannan Xiao, Trevor Barker and Mariana Lilley

Abstract

Student authentication in online learning environments is an increasingly challenging issue due to the inherent absence of physical interaction with online users and potential security threats to online examinations. This study is part of ongoing research on student authentication in online examinations evaluating the potential benefits of using challenge questions. The authors developed a Profile Based Authentication Framework (PBAF), which utilises challenge questions for students' authentication in online examinations. This paper examines the findings of an empirical study in which 23 participants used the PBAF including an abuse case security analysis of the PBAF approach. The overall usability analysis suggests that the PBAF is efficient, effective and usable. However, specific questions need replacement with suitable alternatives due to usability challenges. The results of the current research study suggest that memorability, clarity of questions, syntactic variation and question relevance can cause usability issues leading to authentication failure. A configurable traffic light system was designed and implemented to improve the usability of challenge questions. The security analysis indicates that the PBAF is resistant to informed guessing in general, however, specific questions were identified with security issues. The security analysis identifies challenge questions with potential risks of informed guessing by friends and colleagues. The study was performed with a small number of participants in a simulation online course and the results need to be verified in a real educational context on a larger sample size.

Keywords: Security; Usability; Online learning; Online examination; E-learning; MOODLE; Challenge questions; Authentication

1. Introduction

This study investigates student authentication in online learning and examinations. Student identification in online learning is largely reliant upon remote authentication mechanisms. The absence of face-to-face identification can make online learning and high stakes examinations vulnerable to a number of authentication threats and therefore, the security of online learning environments is highly important. Online learning offers a number of advantages including availability, reliability, flexibility and reusability [1,2]. Besides the anticipated benefits of online learning, it has some limitations including the security of online examinations as one of the major concerns.

In typical online environments, examination is an integral part of the learning process. In online examinations, face-to-face invigilation is often replaced with authentication systems and therefore, security becomes a critical factor with regard to their credibility. Secure authentication is particularly relevant to the success of high stakes online examinations. Effective authentication approaches are important to ensure secure, reliable and usable student authentication mechanisms in an online learning and examinations context. The implementation of a reliable and secure approach to students' authentication is vital to ensure trust of the stakeholders in the assessment process. It has been an active research area and a number of authentication techniques have been implemented in order to ensure secure online examinations. A diverse set of authentication techniques have been developed in earlier research work, which verify online

---
* Correspondence: abrar.ullah@gmail.com
School of Computer Science, University of Hertfordshire, College Lane, Hatfield AL10 9AB, UK

users' identities based on knowledge or *"What one knows"* [3], possession of objects or *"What one has"* [4] and biometrics or *"What one is"* [5].

In our earlier study [6], we developed the Profile Based Authentication (PBAF) approach for student authentication in online examinations and presented a usability analysis of using challenge questions as a second factor authentication. The results of this study have been presented [7]. In them, we discussed the impact of the clarity and memorability of questions on effectiveness of the PBAF method. The study [7] also analysed participants' feedback through an online survey to determine various usability attributes as well as user satisfaction.

The current paper further explores the strengths and weaknesses of the PBAF method in terms of usability, security and the effect of question design on the overall authentication process. In addition to the above, this paper presents a detailed analysis of the security of the PBAF method in a follow-up guessing authentication attack to risk assess and mitigate any threat. Participants of the follow-up abuse case scenario were selected from the original users group, who participated in the previous phases of the study. The guessing attack was performed to analyse the resilience of challenge questions to informed guessing by friends and colleagues. The findings also contributed to the design and implementation of a traffic light system in the PBAF.

The structure of the paper is organised into 5 sections. The paper starts with an introduction to online learning, examination and authentication challenges in Introduction. The work background and literature review is presented in Background and related work. The research methodology including empirical design, participant recruitment and empirical implementation phases are presented in Study design and methodology. The results, analysis and findings of empirical investigations are discussed in Results. The concluding remarks including work summary and future directions are presented in Conclusion.

2. Background and related work

The online examination is an important feature and critical asset of online learning [8]. A number of previous studies have acknowledged that student authentication in online examinations faces many security threats. Unethical conduct has been growing in online learning due to un-controlled environment in online examinations as a result of use of technology and the Internet [9,10]. Agulla [9] suggests that it can be a real challenge to verify the identity of an individual in an online environment without any physical interaction. Colwell and Jenks [11] argue that online examinations are more vulnerable to academic dishonesty than traditional face-to-face examinations. A large number of authentication techniques

have therefore been developed, which can be implemented to enhance the security of online examinations.

The traditional authentication techniques are classified into three categories:

- Knowledge Based Authentication (KBA) e.g. login-identifier and password, passphrase, challenge questions
- Object Based Authentication (OBA) e.g. smart cards, ID cards
- Characteristics Based Authentication (CBA) or Biometrics e.g. fingerprint, audio or voice recognition, signature recognition and face recognition.

The above authentication techniques have their strengths and weaknesses in terms of cost, usability and security, when applied to online learning environments [6]. KBA are the most prevalent, cost effective and widely accepted approaches [12]. However, KBA approaches can be vulnerable to security attacks including collusion, guessing, lost credentials, dictionary attacks and brute-force attacks [3]. The OBA approaches are widely used in banking, transports, hotels and parking areas, with a potential for use in online learning [13]. The OBA features may be useful to resist adversaries' attacks. However, the authentication objects can be shared, lost or stolen for use in authentication attacks. The OBA features require special purpose input devices, which incurs additional cost. The use of special purpose input devices may limit the implementation of OBA in online learning environments. The CBA approaches free individuals from remembering passwords and carrying cards. An individual's physical or behavioural characteristics are a key to the identification and therefore, CBA (biometrics) are seen as the most reliable authentication features [14]. The CBA features also require special purpose input devices for recording and authentication, which incurs additional cost. The special purpose input devices may limit the scope of CBA implementation in a wider Internet context. The CBA approaches have been reported with algorithm challenges like False Accept Rate (FAR), False Reject Rate (FRR), Equal Error Rate (ERR), Failure to Enrol Rate (FER) and Failure to Capture Rate (FCR) [15].

In light of the above discussion, it is desirable to develop an authentication feature, which is secure, cost effective and accessible to a large online population using standard input devices. The authors designed and developed the PBAF method, which implements challenge questions coupled with login-identifier and password features for authentication purposes. The PBAF approach is chosen for a number of reasons. Primarily, the PBAF integrates learning and the examination process, whereby answers to profile questions collected in the learning process are utilised to authenticate students in the examination process. Unlike biometrics and object-based methods, the PBAF, being a knowledge-based method, can be implemented to cover a large online population using standard input devices. The design, development, implementation and maintenance of the PBAF method can be cost effective. In our previous work, we:

- implemented the PBAF method in an online learning environment, to authenticate students, firstly at a course access level and secondly at examination access level [6].

- organised an empirical study to research the usability of the PBAF method in terms of memorability of questions, clarity of questions, syntactic variation and implementation of a traffic light system [7].

- performed an in-depth analysis of the design of questions and their impact on the usability attributes. The study reported an analysis of completion time of the profile questions and the results of a post study survey to present participants' feedback on layout and usability [16].

The challenge questions are a key to the PBAF approach and are designed to be reliable and unique as they pertain to information known to individual users. It is widely seen as a credential recovery technique [17]. Challenge questions are also employed for customer verification in online and telephone banking [18]. In a recent study, Just and Aspinall [19] reviewed the use of challenge questions as a second factor authentication in 10 UK banks, which indicated that the method was reliable and used for the security of monetary transactions in financial institutions.

Besides the anticipated benefits, challenge questions have some limitations. Some studies have reported usability and security issues related to the use of challenge questions in credential recovery [17,20]. In [17], it is also argued that the collection of sensitive information about users can raise privacy and ethical issues. The usability of any authentication approach is highly important for reliability and security. It is recognized that the memorability of challenge questions and lack of clarity may cause security and usability issues [7,21].

From the above discussion, it is evident that challenge questions can be useful as a second factor authentication. However, to achieve effective authentication using the PBAF method in online examinations, usability and security issues need to be investigated.

2.1 Profile based authentication

The PBAF is a multi-factor knowledge based authentication approach, which utilises login-identifier and password

and challenge questions. It integrates the learning and examination processes, whereby answers to profile questions collected during learning activities are utilised for authentication in the examination process.

Using the PBAF method, students are provided with a unique login-identifier and password for logging into the learning environment. After successful login, students are required to answer profile questions in order to gain access to learning resources. The profile questions are used to collect answers in order to build and update individuals' profiles. The profile is a student's description in the form of questions and answers. It is anticipated that learning is a recurrent activity and the students' profiles are consolidated in multiple visits. The secondary authentication process is triggered when students request to access an online examination. They are then required to provide matching answers to a set of challenge questions randomly selected from their profiles. The PBAF being a knowledge-based method can be implemented to cover a large online population and may provide adequate security against many authentication attacks. The PBAF was implemented on a Modular Object Oriented Dynamic Learning Environment (MOODLE) Learning Management System (LMS) for the purpose of this empirical study. MOODLE is a free source environment with a modular and extendable structure. A brief description of how the PBAF approach to student authentication works can be found below:

- *PBAF Setup:* The PBAF provides a configurable web interface. This is used to add pre-designed questions to the library for use as profile and challenge questions. The number of profile and challenge questions requested at learning and authentication phases are configurable items in this interface.

- *Profile Questions:* Profile questions are presented to students in order to build their profiles. Each profile question is presented to each individual student once. The profile questions are a subset of pre-designed questions added in the PBAF setup. Students are required to supply answers to these questions on each visit to obtain access to learning resources.

- *Challenge Questions:* The PBAF generates and presents random challenge questions when access to online examination is requested. The student registers n profile questions, and is presented with $t \leq n$ challenge questions upon authentication [7,22]. To an individual student, $r = t$ challenge questions must be answered correctly in order to access online examination. However, if an error tolerant traffic light system is implemented, it is sufficient to answer $r \leq t$ challenge questions correctly in order to access online examination. The challenge questions are randomized using a random floating-point value v in the range $0 < = v < 1.0$, which is generated by MySQL database [23]. The students' answers to challenge questions are authenticated and a *timestamp* is stored with individual questions in their respective profiles to exclude questions presented within the past 24 hours.

- *Traffic Light System:* To relax the authentication constraints for enhanced usability, a traffic light system is embedded in the PBAF. The traffic light system authenticates users based on the number of correct answers to challenge questions. A three scale classification is adopted to authenticate users, which are red, amber and green. Users in the red classification are locked out and denied access to examination. Users in the amber classification are presented more challenge questions to re-authenticate and users in the green classification are granted access to examination.

- *Authentication:* The authentication algorithm implements string-to-string comparisons to match the answers with the stored information. In earlier studies, researchers used a combination of algorithms for comparative analysis. In their work Schechter et al. [20] implemented an equality algorithm for string-to-string comparison, substring algorithms, and distance algorithms were also used. In another study, Just and Apsinall [24] proposed guidelines for designing usable and secure challenge questions which recommended removing white spaces, punctuation and capitalization for enhanced usability. The PBAF method implements the equality algorithm for exact match without the pre-processing of answers. The equality algorithm was chosen for better security and to use the results as a benchmark, which could be compared with those from revised algorithms to be investigated in future stages of this research. The nature of this algorithm means that students are allowed to access online examinations only if they provide exact answers to their challenge questions. The PBAF method implements randomization of questions during multiple attempts and poses questions which were not previously presented in the last 24 hours, in order to be effective against security threats including brute-force guessing attacks [25]. A specific number of incorrect answers to challenge questions locks out the user from further attempts and requires administrator intervention to unlock the account.

3. Study design and methodology

The aim of this study was to analyse the usability and security of the PBAF method in the context of online examinations. A set of 20 questions was compiled to cover the academic, personal, contact, favourite and date themes. The experiment was performed in an online environment and the empirical design and methodology was approved by the University of Hertfordshire's research ethics committee. The study was conducted to test the following hypotheses:

- The PBAF meets standard usability criteria of efficiency and effectiveness.
- The traffic light system enhances the usability of PBAF method by relaxing authentication constraints.
- The PBAF is secure against informed guessing attacks by friends and colleagues.

The above hypotheses were framed to analyse the usability attributes, which were informed by research work in the domain of usability and software quality [26,27]. Bevan [28] states that usability and quality complement each other and that usability is quality in use. As in [27], the quality factors include efficiency, effectiveness, satisfaction, accessibility, productivity, safety and international-ability. In a similar vein, Nielsen [29] defines usability as a property with multiple dimensions each consisting of different components. He also suggests that the different factors can conflict with each other. Nielsen defined a number of usability factors including learnability, efficiency, memorability, errors, and satisfaction. Learnability defines, how well a new user can use the system, while the efficient use of the system by an expert is expressed by efficiency. Effectiveness is the degree of accuracy and completeness with which the user achieves a specified task in a certain context [20]. If a system is used occasionally the factor memorability is used, which dictates effectiveness. Satisfaction is a qualitative attribute which largely depends upon users' feedback based on the effective and efficient use of the artefact. The authors evaluate applicable usability attributes in the context of online learning and examinations, which include efficiency, effectiveness, satisfaction and memorability of questions. In previous studies, the authors evaluated user satisfaction [16] and memorability [7] attributes, while this work analyses the efficiency and effectiveness of challenge questions used in the PBAF.

Previous research suggests that challenge questions can be vulnerable to guessing attacks by friends and colleagues [20,25]. Just and Aspinall [22] describe guessing in three categories, which are "Blind guessing", "Focused Guessing" and "Observation". In blind guessing, the attacker performs a brute-force attack without considering the question. In focused guessing, the attacker may still use a brute-force technique, however, the search space is cut down by considering the question type. In observation, the attacker performs an informed guess about both the user and question. Schechter [20] performed guessing attacks by acquaintances and statistical guessing in the context of credential recovery to evaluate security of challenge questions. We organised an informed guessing (observation) abuse case scenario in the context of online learning and examinations using the PBAF method. This study does not cover blind and focused guessing. The abuse case was performed to assess risks and mitigate any security threat using the method defined by ISO 31000 [30].

3.1 Participants recruitment

The participants were recruited from a pool of local and international undergraduate and postgraduate full time students from the UK and overseas universities. All the participants were informed and provided with study design and guidance notes explaining the aims and objectives of this research. Guidance notes were emailed to all participants to describe the registration procedure, access dates for learning, and the examination. Of the total 30 potential participants, 23 consented to participate in the experiment. In a follow-up abuse case scenario, we circulated a list of 10 participants requesting them to identify their colleagues and friends from the first cohort, who participated in the learning and examination phases of the study. A total of 6 participants consented to take part in the abuse case scenario. The participants recruited for the abuse case scenario were required to impersonate their friends and colleagues and attack the online examination for security analysis.

3.2 Questions design

The questions for this empirical study were compiled into five different themes i.e. academic, personal, favourite, contact, and date themes. The question design in the academic and contact themes was based on the University of Hertfordshire undergraduate admission form to minimize any privacy concerns. Questions in the personal and favourite themes were inspired from the corporate email service providers i.e. Google, Microsoft, AOL and Yahoo [20]. Usability, privacy and security were considered when designing the questions. The findings from PBAF adopting these questions will be used as a benchmark, which can be compared and optimised in the future stages of this research.

3.3 Empirical study phases

Our experiment was organised into five phases; setup phase, online registration phase, online learning phase, online examination phase and security test phase. The empirical activities shown in Figure 1 were performed remotely over the Internet in a simulated environment on MOODLE LMS. The PBAF was developed in PHP server side scripting language and integrated with the LMS deployed on a test server for the purpose of this empirical study. A simulation online learning course was created on a remote server and a mock-up online examination added to the course. The online course and examination were designed only to achieve the research objectives and was not an actual University course. Participants were required to answer the profile and challenge questions to authenticate their online examinations. The experiment was performed in the phases described below. Some initial configurations were performed in the initial setup phase before the study commenced.

Initial Setup Phase: An initial setup was required to set out values of the configurable variables. A set of 20 questions designed for the study was uploaded to the PBAF. The number of profile questions presented during the learning process is configurable and was set to 3. The number of challenge questions presented during the examination process is configurable and was set to 3. The following traffic light configuration was defined:

1. *Criteria 1-Red*: If the number of matched answers to the challenge questions is classified *red*, the participant is locked out and access to online examination is denied. The value of the red classification was set to 0.
2. *Criteria 2-Amber*: If the number of matched answers to the challenge questions is classified *amber*, the participant is presented with more challenge questions to authenticate iteratively. The value of the amber classification was set to 1.
3. *Criteria 3-Green*: If the number of matched answers to the challenge questions is classified *green*, the participant is authenticated and access to online examination is granted. The value of the green classification was set to 2.

Online Registration Phase: The experiment was started from the online registration phase as shown in Figure 1. The participants completed the registration and created their login-identifier and password. The login-identifier and password provides the primary authentication to access the simulation online course.

Online Learning Phase: The participants were required to access the LMS and visit the simulation online course accessed for a period of one month with a minimum of three days between each visit. As learning is a recurrent process, therefore, participants were required to visit the online course on multiple dates. The following steps were performed in the online learning phase.

- The Participants accessed the online course using their login-identifiers and passwords created in the registration phase.

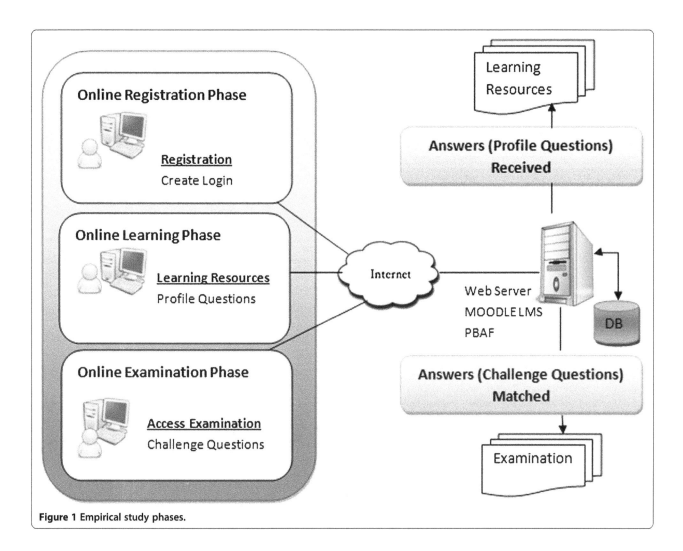

Figure 1 Empirical study phases.

- On each visit the participants were redirected to answer 3 profile questions in order to access the online course. For the purpose of the study reported here, the number of questions was set to 3 in the initial setup phase. This would allow the authors to collect sufficient data for the preliminary analysis, without causing fatigue to the participants.
- The profile questions and their answers were stored in the database to build and consolidate individual participant's profiles.

Online Examination Phase: On completion of the online learning phase, the participants were notified by email to access the online examination. There was an intervening period of 30 days between the participants' first access to learning and the online examination phases. The following steps were performed in the online examination phase.

- The participants accessed the online course using their login-identifier and password created in the registration phase.
- When the participants visited the online examination they were redirected to answer 3 challenge questions selected randomly from their profiles, in order to assess their access status. The challenge questions presented in the past 24 hours were excluded to mitigate brute-force, blind and focused guessing attacks.
- Authentication was performed using the *equality* algorithm for string-to-string comparison. The traffic light system was disabled in the participants' first visit to the online examination for comparative analysis of data with and without the traffic light system. The participants were granted access to the examination, when answers to all their 3 challenge questions matched the stored credentials. In the subsequent visits to online examinations, the traffic

light system was enabled as shown in Figure 2, and described below:

a) If the *number* of matched answers to the challenge questions is classified as *red,* deny access and block the participant's account.

b) If the *number* of matched answers to challenge questions is classified as *amber,* present more challenge questions and repeat the authentication. The amber classification is repeated until the status is changed or all the challenge questions in the individual's profile are exhausted. Those participants exhausting all their challenge questions are locked out.

c) If the *number* of matched answers to the challenge questions is classified as *green,* grant access to the examination.

Security Test Phase: We conducted a follow-up study for security assessment. An abuse case scenario was performed to risk assess the PBAF approach against guessing attacks. Research studies [20,25] suggest that challenge questions can be vulnerable to blind, focused and informed guessing attacks by adversaries, acquaintances, friends and colleagues. To evaluate the resilience of challenge questions to informed guessing attack by friends and colleagues, we performed an abuse case scenario involving pairs of friends and colleagues from the existing participants. As explained previously, this study does not cover statistical, blind and focused guessing. The use case presents a scenario, where an individual obtains the login-identifier and password of a friend or colleague, gains access to the online environment and performs *informed guessing* to answer challenge questions

during authentication. The following steps were taken to perform the abuse case scenario:

- We required the participants to identify their friends and colleagues from the first cohort participating in the previous phases of the study. Of the first cohort of 23 participants, a group of 6 volunteered to take part in the abuse case scenario and notified their friends.

- We paired the participants with their friends and colleagues so each individual can cross attack a friend's account.

- Fictitious passwords were created for participants in the abuse case scenario. The login-identifiers and passwords of friends and colleagues were amended for privacy reasons and shared with the designated participants to enable them to impersonate as their colleagues.

- The participants visited the course using their friends' login-identifier and password.

- The participants visited the online examination on behalf of their friends and were presented with 3 random challenge questions. Answers to the challenge questions were submitted using informed guesses. The authentication feedback was not revealed to the participants and stored in the database for security analysis.

- The traffic light system was enabled using the criteria outlined in the online examination phase. Using the traffic light system, the participants meeting the criteria in red classification were locked out. The participants meeting the amber classification criteria were recurrently presented with more questions until the status was changed or

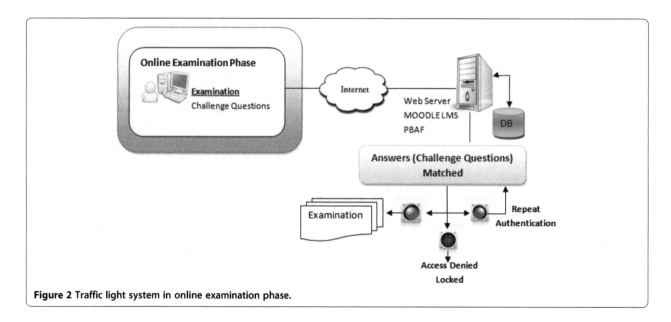

Figure 2 Traffic light system in online examination phase.

all the challenge questions in the respective profile were exhausted. The participants meeting the red classification criteria were locked out.

4. Results

Of all the invitees, 23 participated in the initial registration and 18 took part in the various phases of the empirical study by providing answers to 274 profile questions. A total of 13 participants answered 66 challenge questions in the online examination phase of the experiment and completed the authentication.

A group of 6 students participated in a follow-up security test phase and submitted answers to 24 challenge questions, guessing on behalf of their colleagues.

The usability and security analysis are discussed below.

4.1 Usability analysis

The usability results presented here are extracted from the data taken from the participants' interactions with the online learning and examination phases discussed in Study design and methodology. We have analysed the usability of questions in the online examination and traffic light authentication phases. In the online examination phase, participants managed to submit 38 (58%) matched answers, whereas, 28 (42%) unmatched due to various usability issues. The efficiency and effectiveness of questions in the context of online learning and examinations are evaluated in the discussion below.

4.1.1 Efficiency

Efficiency is a usability metric defined by ISO, which can be evaluated by measuring the completion time of each task and sub-tasks separately [27]. A system is considered efficient, if users are able to complete tasks in a reasonable time.

The efficiency was analysed from data collected during participants' answers to profile questions in the learning phase. To examine the efficiency of questions in the PBAF method, the "completion time" and "answer length" of answers to profile questions were measured. The mean score and standard deviation of completion time and answer length was computed and presented in Table 1. The correlation analysis of the two variables was measured to analyse the efficiency of profile questions used in this study. A Pearson Correlation was computed to examine the relationship between the "completion time" and the "answer length". Table 2 shows the Pearson r =0.152; p value 0.011 (p < 0.05) indicates a significant correlation between the two variables where n = 274. The small value of r = 0.152 suggests that there were other intervening variables affecting the completion time, however, these are not covered in this study. The potential factors that can impact the completion time include typing speed, question relevance to the individual, personal break, Internet connection

Table 1 Usability analysis: efficiency

Question themes	Completion time (seconds)		Answer length (characters)	
Academic questions	Mean	SD	Mean	SD
Find out about this course	14.14	7.98	7.0	6.11
Student number	14.55	8.52	3.0	2.9
Name of last school attended	14.60	6.67	14.86	9.38
Grades in highest qualification	15.14	6.29	2.0	2.47
Year of highest qualification	15.20	7.16	4.0	0
Month started the current course	15.61	8.06	5.0	2.03
Year started the current course	16.18	8.98	4.29	1.07
Highest qualification	16.93	6.80	9.40	8.47
Personal questions				
Father's surname	13.55	8.76	4.71	1.26
Country of birth	13.78	7.25	7.20	1.37
Best friend's surname	14.47	6.95	5.79	2.57
Dream job as a child	18.03	8.65	9.85	5.24
Favourite questions				
Hero of your childhood	14.70	5.94	11.71	5.31
Tutor	15.06	8.13	8	3.48
Module on this course	18.34	9.8	7.5	5
Contact questions				
Home Tel no with country code	15.73	8.78	10.60	3
Home address town	16.83	9.36	15	13.75
House name or number	17.18	7.8	19.58	18.55
Mobile number with country code	17.43	8.98	11.69	1.43
Date questions				
Date of birth	16.42	6.75	6.36	3.91

speed and any privacy concerns. The efficiency of questions in various themes is discussed below.

Academic Questions: The relevance of questions is important to inform the efficiency of the PBAF approach. The participants responded to pertinent academic questions, with an efficient completion time. As an example, the completion time of answers to profile questions *"Where did you find out about this course"*, *"student number"* and *"Last school attended"* was the

Table 2 Pearson correlation

		Answer length	Completion time
Answer length	Pearson correlation	1	.152*
	Sig. (2-tailed)		.011
	N	274	274
Completion time	Pearson correlation	.152*	1
	Sig. (2-tailed)	.011	
	N	274	274

*. Correlation is significant at the 0.05 level (2-tailed).

shortest in the academic theme with a mean completion time of 14.14, 14.55 and 14.60 seconds, which indicates that the relevance of questions is an important factor leading to increased efficiency.

Questions with answer hints can also contribute to enhanced efficiency. The findings indicate that embedded answer hints in questions were treated as an answer choice by participants, which enhanced efficiency. As an example, the profile question "*Where did you find out about this course*", shows a high degree of efficiency, because it was presented with an answer hint i.e. "Friend, Internet" to help participants understand the context of the question. Although the completion time of the question was efficient, 78% of the answers were identical and selected from the answer hint "Friend, Internet", which can be usable, but may lead to security risks.

The use of abbreviations in answers can affect the usability of challenge questions. It was noted that in spite of efficient completion time of 14.60 seconds, the length of answers to question "*Name of last school attended*", was the largest in the academic theme. To account for the length, further exploration of answers revealed that 44% of answers were abbreviations and 56% were full school names. Long school names resulted in increased answer length.

Question clarity is important for the efficient of responses. The completion time may increase for vague and unclear questions irrespective of their answer length. The completion time of answers to the profile question "*Grades in highest qualification*", was recorded in 15.14 seconds. The completion time was higher for an average answer length of 2 characters. The question does not explicitly specify grade type, which resulted in variations in answers. The detailed sorting of answers revealed that participant submitted different grade types (letters, percentage and description). The answers contained 64% letters "e.g. A, A*, A+", 22% percentage type and 14% descriptive texts.

Question context and relevance to individuals is highly important for the usability of the PBAF method. The profile question "*Month started current course*" was completed in 15.61 seconds. The detailed analysis of answers revealed that participants in the empirical study were originally enrolled on different courses at their respective institutions and questions in the context of the empirical simulation course needed further clarity. The participants were not particularly aware of "*current course*" in the context of a simulation course and the question vagueness contributed to delay in response time. Of the total answers to this question requesting "*month*" information, 50% were incorrect. A similar response was noted to profile question "*year started current course*" with a mean completion time of 16.18 seconds. The detailed exploration of answers revealed a

28% "*incorrect year*" or unrealistic answers. The increased completion time can be attributed to the relevance and clarity issues reported above with respect to "*current course*".

Questions with long anticipated answers can affect the usability. As an example, name of the institution or employers can be long and descriptive. The completion time of profile question "*highest qualification*" was 16.93 seconds, which is the largest in the academic theme with increased answer length.

Personal Questions: Personal questions are believed to be usable and widely used by the corporate email providers e.g. AOL, Yahoo, Google and Microsoft [20]. Our results indicate that the completion time of personal questions was efficient. The completion time of answers to profile questions "*Father's surname*", "*country of birth*" and "*Best friend's surname*" was 13.55, 13.78 and 14.47 seconds and the answer length was 4.71, 7.20 and 5.79 characters. The average completion time of the questions indicate slight variation with positive efficiency.

The personal questions requesting subjective information from the past resulted in a high completion time. As an example, the profile question "*Dream job as child*" resulted in higher completion time and answer length as 18.03 seconds and 9.85 characters.

In conclusion, the mean time incurred on all questions in the personal theme was 14.89 seconds, which is an efficient completion time in the online setting.

The results clearly indicate that better clarity and readability of questions in the personal theme was one of the factors resulting in enhanced efficiency.

Favourite Questions: Favourite questions have been widely used for credential recovery [20]. The favourite questions collect subjective information, which may change over time and circumstances, however, popular favourite questions can be usable. As an example, the completion time of profile questions "*Hero of childhood*" and "*Tutor*" was 14.70 and 15.06 seconds, which indicates positive efficiency.

As discussed earlier, the question's context and relevance is highly important for better usability. As an example, the completion time of the answer to profile question favourite "*Module on this course*" was 18.03 seconds. The "*module on this course*" in question was not relevant in the context of a simulation course and lacks clarity. The analysis of data revealed that 47% of answers contained unrealistic patterns like "NA, Nil, and Unknown".

A large number of questions requested subjective information; however, the overall efficiency of profile questions in the favourite theme was positive.

Contact Questions: The questions requesting contact information were created in a more generic way, to cover addresses for a wide range of participants in different geographic locations. However, this created clarity issues. The completion times of answers to profile questions *"Telephone number including country code"* and *"Address town"* was 15.73, 16.83 seconds respectively and answer length was 10.60, 15 characters. Detailed analysis of answers to *"Address town"* revealed that 33% of all answers contained full address and 67% were address town or city name, which indicates lack of clarity.

The completion time of answers to the profile question *"House name or number"* was 17.18 seconds with the largest answer length 19.58 characters. Analysis of the answers revealed that the generalization of question created ambiguity and answer lengths contained large variations. Participants' answers contained 42% full home address, 25% house number, 17% home phone number, 8% house name and 8% of city name, which shows rapid answers shift.

From the above discussion, a pattern can be noticed in answers to questions in the contact theme with increase in completion time and answer length, which may also affect the effectiveness during authentication process.

Date Questions: The date information is often presented and stored in varied formats. Without specifying a format, collection of date information can invite syntactic variation, which can affect the usability. The completion time of answers to profile question *"Date of birth"* was 16.42 seconds. The further analysis of participants' answers revealed that open and varied "date" format was used in answers with the use of special characters "/", "-" and descriptive "month name e.g. October". Using a standard date format can enhance the efficiency of date type questions.

Summary of Efficiency: In summary, the completion time reflects the efficiency and participants' understanding of questions and their ability to answer realistically. Questions with design flaws require extra thinking and time to respond and therefore it may result in distraction and have implications for the overall efficiency of the PBAF method. The shortcomings in question design may affect the efficiency of the PBAF and also reflect on usability during online examination, which is discussed below. Profile questions with an answer hint resulted in efficient completion time; however, this approach can create security risks.

The results reported here in terms of efficiency suggest that the question design should consider clarity, relevance and students' anticipation to conveniently answer the questions. Questions inviting long answers, as in the contact theme, may incur extra completion time and result in low efficiency.

For the reasons covered in this section, the efficiency hypothesis of the PBAF was supported for selective questions used in this study. However, it would be interesting to further investigate the efficiency of the PBAF method and revise questions with enhanced clarity in a real online course.

4.1.2 Effectiveness

Effectiveness may be considered to be the degree of accuracy of responses. Effectiveness, in the context of PBAF questions evaluation was taken to mean that participants were able to submit a maximum number of matched answers effectively with low error rate.

Effectiveness was analysed on data collected from participants' answers to challenge questions during the online examination. To examine effectiveness and accuracy, participants' answers to challenge questions were analysed into 5 common themes as academic, personal, contact, favourites and date. We used the equality algorithm in the empirical study. However, results were compiled to analyse the effectiveness if a more relaxed algorithm was implemented. The results of a relaxed algorithm were derived from the data collected in the online examination disregarding capitalisation, whitespaces and minor spelling errors using a combination of substring and distance algorithm as described in an earlier study [20]. Table 3 shows the crosstab analysis of data using the equality and relaxed algorithms under columns 3 to 6 headings. Data in columns 5 and 6 presented in bold-face show an increase in effectiveness when results were computed using a relaxed algorithm. The answers were submitted by all participants during authentication before access to the online examination was granted or denied. Since the challenge questions were posed randomly, therefore, the sample distribution was not uniform. The effectiveness of challenge questions using the equality and relaxed algorithms is discussed below.

Academic Questions: The relevance of questions can be important to recall answers and inform the effectiveness of the PBAF approach. It was hoped that questions with an answer hint would be easy to recall during authentication. However, the challenge question *"Find about this course"* received 2 (67%) matched answers during authentication. The analysis of answers revealed that one question failed to match as a result of syntactic variation.

Question context and relevance to individuals is important in reproducing the exact answers during authentication. The challenge question *"Month started current course"* received 2(100%) unmatched answers. As reported in the efficiency results, the text *"current course"* in the question is not relevant in the context of a simulation course, which led to usability issues.

Questions reported with clarity issues in the efficiency analysis, resulted in low effectiveness. One of the most obvious consequences of the question clarity can result

Table 3 Usability analysis: effectiveness

Question themes	N[2]	Equality algorithm		Relaxed algorithm[1]	
Academic questions		Matched	Unmatched	Matched	Unmatched
Student number	1	1(100%)	0(0%)	1(100%)	0(0%)
Year started the current course	3	3(100%)	0(0%)	3(100%)	0(0%)
Year of highest qualification	4	3(75%)	1(25%)	3(75%)	1(25%)
Highest qualification	4	3(75%)	1(25%)	**4(100%)**	**0(0%)**
Find out about this course	3	2(67%)	1(33%)	2(67%)	1(33%)
Name of last school attended	5	3(60%)	2(40%)	**4(80%)**	**1(20%)**
Grades in highest qualification	2	0(0%)	2(100%)	0(0%)	2(100%)
Month started the current course	1	0(0%)	1(100%)	**1(100%)**	**0(0%)**
Total		*15(65%)*	*8(35%)*	*18(78%)*	*5(22%)*
Personal questions					
Best friend's surname	6	6(100%)	0(0%)	6(100%)	0(0%)
Country of birth	4	4(100%)	0(0%)	4(100%)	0(0%)
Father's surname	3	2(67%)	1(33%)	**3(100%)**	**0(0%)**
Dream job as a child	2	1(50%)	1(50%)	**2(100%)**	**0(0%)**
Total		*13(87%)*	*2(13%)*	*15(100%)*	*0(0%)*
Favourite questions					
Tutor	6	1(17%)	5(83%)	**5(83%)**	**1(17%)**
Hero of your childhood?	3	3(100%)	0(0%)	3(100%)	0(0%)
Module on this course?	3	0(0%)	3(100%)	0(0%)	3(100%)
Total		*4(33%)*	*8(67%)*	*8(67%)*	*4(33%)*
Contact questions					
Home Tel no with country code	2	1(50%)	1(50%)	1(50%)	1(50%)
Home address town	4	1(25%)	3(75%)	**2(50%)**	**2(50%)**
House name or number	4	0(0%)	4(100%)	**1(25%)**	**3(75%)**
Mobile number including country code	1	0(0%)	1(100%)	0(0%)	1(100%)
Total		*2(18%)*	*9(82%)*	*4(36%)*	*7(64%)*
Date questions					
Date of birth?	5	4(80%)	1(20%)	**5(100%)**	**0(0%)**
Grand total	**66**	**38(58%)**	**28(42%)**	**50(76%)**	**16(24%)**

[1]Disregard capitalization, whitespace and minor spelling errors.
[2]Number of challenge questions.
Data in bold-face show an increase in effectiveness when results were computed using a relaxed algorithm.

in recall and syntactic variation in authentication during the online examination phase.

Using the equality algorithm, the challenge questions in the academic theme received 15(65%) matched answers and 8(35%) unmatched answers, which shows acceptable effectiveness. However, there is a potential to further improve the usability by addressing the issues reported.

A more relaxed algorithm would increase the effectiveness of questions in the academic theme by 13%. Manual sorting of the data revealed that 3 answers were penalized for capitalization, spelling mistakes and spacing, which would benefit from using the relaxed algorithm. The implementation of the relaxed algorithm would decrease the error rate and increase the effectiveness to 18(75%).

Personal Questions: Personal questions are believed to be more memorable and therefore, widely used for credential recovery [20]. The challenge questions in the personal theme are reported with enhanced effectiveness in the online examination phase. The challenge questions *"Best friend's surname"* and *"Country of birth"* received 6 (100%) and 4 (100%) matched answers during authentication, which shows a high degree of effectiveness.

Syntactic variation including capitalization, spacing, spellings, writing syntax, can affect the usability of open text answers to challenge questions. The answers were lexicographically correct, nevertheless, the string to string match failed using the equality algorithm.

Using the equality algorithm, the challenge questions in the personal theme received 13(87%) matched and 2 (13%) unmatched answers, which indicates a high degree of effectiveness with a large number of accurate answers during authentication.

A more relaxed algorithm would increase the effectiveness of questions in the personal theme by 13%. Manual sorting of the data revealed that 2 answers were penalized for capitalization and spacing, which would benefit from using the relaxed algorithm. The implementation of the relaxed algorithm would decrease the error rate and increase the effectiveness to 15(100%).

Favourite Questions: The challenge questions in the favourite theme are a subset of personal questions, which pertains to individual's favourites. Popular challenge questions can be easy to recall. As an example, the popular challenge question *"Hero of childhood"* received 3(100%) matched answers during authentication, which indicates a high degree of effectiveness. It was reported with positive efficiency and submitted in the shortest completion time in the favourite theme during online learning.

Syntactic variation can increase the usability challenges. The challenge question *"Tutor"* received 5(83%)

unmatched answers and resulted in low effectiveness. The analysis revealed that 80% of answers were lexicographically correct; however the equality algorithm did not produce an exact match.

The challenge question *"module on this course"* was also reported with 3(100%) unmatched answers. The analysis revealed a complete shift in the answer pattern largely because of relevance and clarity issues reported in the efficiency analysis. The results clearly indicate a knock-on effect of unclear questions.

Using the equality algorithm, the challenge questions in the favourite theme received 4(33%) matched and 8(67%) unmatched answers, which indicates low effectiveness.

A more relaxed algorithm would increase the effectiveness of questions in the favourite theme by 32%. Manual sorting of the data revealed that 2 answers were penalized for capitalization, which would benefit from using the relaxed algorithm. The implementation of the relaxed algorithm would decrease the error rate and increase the effectiveness to 8(66%).

Contact Questions: The challenge questions in the contact theme were generalized for wider implementation. However, the generalization of questions created ambiguity, which resulted in poor usability.

The ambiguous questions reported in the efficiency analysis, had a knock-on effect and resulted in low effectiveness. The challenge question *"Address town"* received 1 (25%) matched answers. In a similar vein, the challenge questions *"House name or number"* received 4 (100%) unmatched answers, which indicates very low effectiveness. The variation in answers reported in the efficiency analysis increased the degree of difficulty for participants to produce the exact answers during the authentication phase.

Using the equality algorithm, the challenge questions in the contact theme were reported with poor effectiveness and received 9 (83%) unmatched answers, which indicates a sharp decrease in effectiveness. Questions in the contact theme were also reported with poor efficiency in the preceding Section.

A more relaxed algorithm would increase the effectiveness of questions in the contact theme by 18%. Manual sorting of the data revealed that 2 answers were penalized for spelling mistakes, which would benefit from using the relaxed algorithm. The implementation of the relaxed algorithm would decrease the error rate and increase the effectiveness to 4 (36%).

Date Questions: The challenge question *"Date of birth"* received 4 (80%) matched results during authentication. Syntactic variation in the date format was reported in the efficiency analysis. The *"Date of birth"* question received a single unmatched answer as a result of syntactic variation in the date format. The date was submitted in different formats such as "dd/mm/yyyy", "dd-mm-yyyy" and "day, month, year".

Using the equality algorithm, the challenge questions in the date theme indicate a high degree of effectiveness and no change was observed in the findings, if a more relaxed algorithm was implemented.

Summary of Effectiveness: In summary, the results that emerged from data analysis indicate a high number of matched answers for academic, personal and date themes. The questions with better relevance and clarity were reported with a high degree of effectiveness. The questions reported with low clarity, ambiguity and format issues had a knock-on effect during authentication and resulted in poor effectiveness. The participants failed to submit matched answers to a large number of questions in the 'favourite' and 'contact' themes using the equality algorithm implemented in empirical trail. The effectiveness of questions in the context of this study would further increase by 18%, if a more relaxed algorithm was implemented to compensate for capitalisation, spacing and spelling mistakes. The overall effectiveness will increase from 38 (58%) to 50 (76%), which is a large increase.

It was observed that questions with objective information remained efficient and effective during the learning and (authentication) examination phases. Also, responses to subjective answers were frequently changing during the learning and examinations phases resulted in failed authentication.

Concluding this section, we can say that question design needs particular consideration to address clarity, ambiguity and relevance to target users.

4.2 Traffic light system analysis

To address the usability challenges posed by the question design, we developed and implemented a traffic light system shown in Figure 2 and based on the criteria outlined in Study design and methodology. The data presented in Table 3, was collected from the PBAF implementation, with and without the traffic light system. The findings revealed that, before using the traffic light system, 23% of the participants submitted exact answers to all their 3 challenge questions and authenticated successfully. Of the total answers submitted, 38% participants provided exact answers to 2 out of 3 and 31% to 1 out of 3 challenge questions. However, 8% of participants provided no matching answers to challenge questions in the online examination phase. The reasons for unmatched answers are discussed in the preceding section. Before the traffic light system, the PBAF locked out participants who failed to submit exact answers to all of their 3 challenge questions. The participants, who provided exact answers to 1 or 2 of their 3 challenge questions, formed 69% (i.e. 31% + 38%) of the total unsuccessful attempts largely because of usability issues reported earlier.

Given the results of the online examination phase and in order to minimize the usability issues, we set up the traffic light system as shown in Figure 2. The system employed a three scale criteria outlined in the study methodology. The classification is setup to analyse PBAF performance by relaxing the constraints for compensating the usability issues. This may create a usability and security trade off, which needs further experimentation.

The results revealed that implementation of a traffic light system improved authentication success rate and minimized the impact of usability issues. A summary of data 'before' and 'after' the traffic light implementation is presented in Table 4. Overall, authentication success rate for participants increased from 23% to 92% (61% + 31%).

The traffic light system can provide an enabling environment to reduce the usability challenges and enhance the performance of the PBAF method. However, we are aware that, with the implementation of such a traffic light system, *security analysis* of the PBAF is warranted on a larger sample size.

4.3 Security analysis

The security analysis presented here, is extracted from the data taken from the participants' interactions with the security test phase described in Study design and methodology. We have analysed the security of questions against informed guessing attacks. The security test phase does not cover blind and focused guessing. An abuse case scenario was performed to evaluate the security of questions used in this study.

4.3.1 Guessing by friends and colleagues

The analysis collected from the abuse case scenario is presented in Tables 5 and 6. A total of 6 participants made 9 attempts to guess the challenge questions on behalf of their friends and colleagues. The participants were allowed to perform multiple attempts if the traffic light system criteria were met.

Table 5 shows analysis of abuse case scenario in terms of participants' attempts and traffic light results using the equality algorithm. Of the 6 participants, 3 (50%)

Table 5 Security abuse case scenario and traffic light

Participants	Attempt	Matched	Unmatched	Authentication
P1	1st	0	3	Failed (Red)
P2	1st	0	3	Failed (Red)
P3	1st	0	3	Failed (Red)
P4	1st	1	2	Repeat (Amber)
P5	1st	1	2	Repeat (Amber)
P6	1st	1	2	Repeat (Amber)
P4	2nd	0	3	Failed (Red)
P5	2nd	0	3	Failed (Red)

failed to guess matched answers to any of their challenge questions on the 1st attempt and were classified *red*. The remaining 3 (50%) participants guessed matched answers to 1 out of 3 challenge questions and were classified *amber*. Of the 3 participants' classified *amber*, 1 dropped out of the process and the remaining 2 completed the abuse case scenario.

In the second attempt, 2 participants were presented with more challenge questions for authentication and failed to guess exact answers to any of these. They were classified *red* and locked out.

Table 6 shows the crosstab analysis of abuse case scenario using the equality and relaxed algorithms under columns 3, 4, 5 and 6 headings. Data presented in boldface in column 5 and 6 shows any changes to security level, when results were computed using the relaxed algorithm. The participants were presented 24 challenge questions randomly on behalf of their friends and colleagues. Using the equality algorithm, answers to 3 (13%) were successfully guessed by participants, whereas 21 (88%) of the answers failed to match their respective profile answers. A more relaxed algorithm would increase the number of matched answers to 5 (21%) at the cost of increasing security risk.

To conclude this section, informed guessing by friends and colleagues was not highly successful and participants could not authenticate. However, questions in the public, friends and colleague domain were vulnerable to guessing. The abuse case scenario is discussed below to examine challenge questions in the individual themes.

Academic Questions: The participants submitted a total of 13 answers to challenge questions in the academic theme. The participants successfully guessed one answer in the academic theme.

It was anticipated that academic information would be vulnerable to guessing by friends and colleagues. However, participants' answers to a large number of the challenge questions failed to match.

Although, it was likely that challenge questions "*Month started current course*" and "*Year started current course*" could be guessed by individuals on the same course,

Table 4 Traffic light system

Authentication before traffic light system				
Attempt	0/3 Matched	1/3 Matched	2/3 Matched	3/3 Matched
1	1(8%)	4(31%)	5(38%)	3(23%)

Authentication after traffic light system		
	Red	Amber	Green
	0/3 Matched	1/3 Matched	2-3/3 Matched
1	1(8%)	4(31%)	8(61%)
2	0(0%)	2(12%)	3(19%)
3	0(0%)	0(0%)	2(12%)

Table 6 Security analysis

Question themes	N	Security abuse case			
		Equality algorithm		Relaxed algorithm	
		Matched	Unmatched	Matched	Unmatched
Academic questions					
Student number	1	0(0%)	1(100%)	0(0%)	1(100%)
Year started the current course	3	0(0%)	3(100%)	0(0%)	3(100%)
Year of highest qualification	1	1(100%)	0(0%)	1(100%)	0(0%)
Highest qualification	2	0(0%)	2(100%)	0(0%)	2(100%)
Find out about this course	0	*NA	*NA	*NA	*NA
Name of last school attended	2	0(0%)	2(100%)	0(0%)	2(100%)
Grades in highest qualification	2	0(0%)	2(100%)	0(0%)	2(100%)
Month started the current course	2	0(0%)	2(100%)	0(0%)	2(100%)
Total		*1(8%)*	*12(92%)*	*1(8%)*	*12(92%)*
Personal questions					
Best friend's surname	1	0(0%)	1(100%)	0(0%)	1(100%)
Country of birth	2	1(50%)	1(50%)	**2(100%)**	**0(0%)**
Father's surname	1	0(0%)	1(100%)	**1(100%)**	**0(0%)**
Dream job as a child	0	*NA	*NA	*NA	*NA
Total		*1(25%)*	*3(75%)*	*3(75%)*	*1(25%)*
Favourite questions					
Tutor	1	0(0%)	1(100%)	0(0%)	1(100%)
Hero of your childhood?	0	*NA	*NA	*NA	*NA
Module on this course?	1	0(0%)	1(100%)	0(0%)	1(100%)
Total		*0(0%)*	*2(100%)*	*0(0%)*	*2(100%)*
Contact questions					
Home tel no with country code	1	0(0%)	1(100%)	0(0%)	1(100%)
Home address town	1	0(0%)	1(100%)	0(0%)	1(100%)
House name or number	1	0(0%)	1(100%)	0(0%)	1(100%)
Mobile number including country code	1	1(100%)	0(0%)	1(100%)	0(0%)
Total		*1(25%)*	*3(75%)*	*1(25%)*	*3(75%)*
Date questions					
Date of birth?	1	0(0%)	1(100%)	0(0%)	1(100%)
Grand total	**24**	**3(13%)**	**21(88%)**	**5(21%)**	**19(79%)**

*NA: Questions not presented due to randomization.
Data in bold-face show an increase in correct answers during abuse case when results were computed using a relaxed algorithm.

however, due to the clarity of questions reported earlier, participants failed to produce matching answers to these questions in all the 5 guesses.

The analysis of data using a more relaxed algorithm shows no change in the findings. However, the detailed exploration of the answers to challenge questions in the academic theme indicates security vulnerabilities and close guess possibilities by participants. A review of the academic questions is recommended to mitigate any risks.

Personal Questions: Participants submitted a total of 4 answers to challenge questions in the personal theme. It was anticipated that answers to personal questions would be by guessed by friends and colleagues. Schechter et al. [20] argue that the personal information can be found on the social media websites. Of all the personal challenge questions posed during the abuse case scenario, participants managed to guess matched answer to one question.

Personal information such as country of birth and place of birth can be vulnerable to informed guessing. The use of questions in the public domain can be vulnerable to guessing. It may not be true for all, but traditionally people use a common family and surname. Jobling [31] indicates that from five thousand years ago, fathers have passed their surname to children. The analysis of answers to profile question *"Father's surname"* in the learning phase revealed that, 64% of participants had a common surname as their fathers' and can be vulnerable to guessing attack.

A more relaxed algorithm would increase the security vulnerabilities of questions in the personal theme by 50% i.e. (75%-25%). Manual sorting of the data revealed that 2 answers failed to match during the security attack due to capitalization and spacing. The implementation of the relaxed algorithm shows decrease in security and increase in the number of matched answers from 1 (25%) to 3 (75%).

Favourite Questions: Participants submitted a total of 2 answers to challenge questions in the favourite theme. Questions in the favourite theme are widely used for credential recovery by email providers and banks. Although, an earlier empirical study [20] indicates that favourite questions are vulnerable to guessing, however, our findings indicate that questions in the favourite theme were resistant to an informed guessing attack.

The analysis of data in the favourite theme shows no change to the results, when a more relaxed algorithm was implemented.

Contact Questions: Participants submitted a total of 4 answers to challenge questions in the contact theme. Questions in the contact theme are likely to be known to friends and colleagues. Of all the challenge questions in the contact theme posed during the abuse case scenario, participants guessed matched answer to one question.

The challenge questions requesting phone or mobile numbers can be easily guessed by friends. It is likely that the contact numbers for friends and colleagues are stored in the phone or email address book and can be used for a guessing attack.

The analysis of data in contact theme shows no change to the results, when a more relaxed algorithm was implemented.

Date Questions: Participants submitted a single answer to challenge questions in the date theme. Although, "*date of birth*" is likely to be known by friends and colleagues, however, participants failed to guess a matched answer.

The analysis of data in date theme shows no change to the results, when a more relaxed algorithm was implemented.

Summary of Security Abuse Case: In summary, personal and academic questions are likely to be known to friends and colleagues. The challenge questions in the personal theme received one matched answer using an informed guessing attack. The questions in the personal theme were reported with positive efficiency, however, answer to personal questions can be guessed by friends and colleagues using the equality algorithm. Questions in the contact and academic themes can also be prone to guessing attacks by friends and family with one question each being successfully guessed by friends and colleagues. Although, the use of a relaxed algorithm may enhance the usability of challenge questions, however, it can also increase the security risks.

As a consequence of guessable and weak challenge questions and traffic light system, attackers may break security of the PBAF to reach their target.

5. Conclusion

The PBAF technique is a multi-factor knowledge based system, which uses challenge questions as repeat authentication in addition to login-identifier and password for student authentication in the online examination context.

In this study, the PBAF approach implemented text based academic, personal, favourite, contact and date questions for student authentication. The findings from the empirical study reported here suggest that challenge questions based authentication in online examinations can be an effective feature to resist adversaries' attacks, however, usability and security issues were reported in selective questions when used in the PBAF.

The usability metrics efficiency and effectiveness were evaluated. A large number of questions were reported with efficient completion time. The questions reported with clarity, ambiguity, relevance and format issues resulted in low efficiency and failed authentication, which also affected the effectiveness of the PBAF method. The results that emerged from data analysis using the

equality algorithm indicate a high number of matched answers during authentication for academic, personal and date themes. The participants failed to submit matched answers to a large number of questions in the favourite and contact themes. The majority of the questions reported with the clarity issues resulted in failed authentication. The implementation of a more relaxed algorithm to compensate for capitalisation, spelling mistakes and spacing, would further improve the usability attributes. Question design has a measurable effect on the overall usability and security of the PBAF approach, which needs particular consideration to address clarity, ambiguity, relevance, subjective, and objective information. The subjective answers were frequently changing with time and a shift in answers patterns was observed.

The findings of the study suggest that participants may not provide 100% exact answers to all their 3 challenge questions set out for this work, largely because of the usability challenges such as syntactic variation and memorability issues. The implementation of a traffic light system improved authentication outcome from 23% to 92%, by enabling multiple chances. However, during the abuse case scenario, the traffic light algorithm granted 2 out of 6 attackers a second chance to answer more challenge questions in order to re-authenticate. Nevertheless, the participants guessed correct answers on behalf of their friends and colleagues, largely because of poor question design.

The security abuse case analysis revealed that questions related to friends, colleagues and common public knowledge can be a security risk. Some questions such as "*year of starting current course*" or "*father's surname*" can be intelligently guessed which may pose security threats. The overall results show a potential of using the PBAF authentication for online examination. However, secure and usable implementation of the PBAF method largely depends upon the quality of question design.

While the initial results are promising, further research is necessary to analyse question design and privacy. Furthermore, the number of participants in this study was small and more analysis is warranted on a larger sample size. There is a need to re-visit the design of questions to balance the trade-off between usability and security keeping in view the study results. The multiple attempts in the traffic light system may encourage the attacker to repeat the attack pattern. To prevent the attacker from repeating the attack pattern, a password change could be enforced in the future, if the student is locked out due to attacker activities. Virzi's empirical study [32] on the number of subjects for usability identification indicates that as few as 5 users can identify 80% of the usability issues. However, a number of conclusions cannot be drawn reliably for challenge questions in this security analysis due to a small number of participants and therefore, it is imperative to verify the security results in a real educational context on a larger sample size.

Competing interests
The authors declare that they have no competing interests.

Authors' contributions
AU, HX and ML proposed the PBAF. AU designed, developed and implemented the PBAF in an online simulation course. AU also provided implementation guidance, put the layout of experimental validation and performance evaluation, and drafted the manuscript. HX, TB and ML carried out the structural and technical changes in the manuscript. TB helped and suggested statistical evaluation and recommended language modifications. All authors read and approved the final manuscript.

Acknowledgements
A special thank you goes to those who contributed to this paper: Bruce Christianson, Professor of Informatics, School of Computer Science University of Hertfordshire for his feedback on the research methodology and Paul Kirk Business Manager, IM & T, School of Postgraduate Medical and Dental Education Cardiff University for his help with the language review.

References

1. Strother JB (2002) An assessment of the effectiveness of e-learning in corporate training programs. Int Rev Res Open Dist Learn 3(1):2, Article 3.1
2. Ruiz JG, Mintzer MJ, Leipzig RM (2006) The impact of e-learning in medical education. Acad Med 81(3):207
3. Huiping J (2010) Strong Password Authentication Protocols. In: 4th International Conference on Distance Learning and Education (ICDLE). IEEE, San Juan, Puerto Rico
4. Deo V, Seidensticker RB, Simon DR (1998) U.S. Patent No. 5,721,781. U.S. Patent and Trademark Office, Washington, DC
5. Moini A, Madni AM (2009) Leveraging biometrics for user authentication in online learning: a systems perspective. IEEE Syst J 3(4):469–476
6. Ullah A, Xiao H, Lilley M (2012) Profile Based Student Authentication in Online Examination. In: International Conference on Information Society (i-Society 2012). IEEE, London, UK
7. Ullah A, Xiao H, Lilley M, Barker T (2012) Usability of Profile Based Student Authentication and Traffic Light System in Online Examination. In: The 7th International Conference for Internet Technology and Secured Transactions (ICITST-2012). IEEE, London
8. Karaman S (2011) Examining the effects of flexible online exams on students' engagement in e-learning. Educ Res Rev 6(3):259–264
9. Agulla EG, Rifón LA, Castro JLA, Mateo CG (2008) Is My Student at the Other Side? Applying Biometric Web Authentication to E-Learning Environments. In: Eighth IEEE International Conference on Advanced Learning Technologies. IEEE, Santander, Cantabria
10. Harmon OR, Lambrinos J, Buffolino J (2010) Assessment design and cheating risk in online instruction. Online J Dist Learn Admin 13(3), Retrieved on Feb. 03, 2013 from http://www.westga.edu/~distance/ojdla/Fall133/harmon_lambrinos_buffolino13.html
11. Colwell JL, Jenks CF (2005) Student Ethics in Online Courses. In: 35th Annual Conference Frontiers in Education (FIE '05). IEEE, IA, USA
12. Chen Y, Liginlal D (2008) A maximum entropy approach to feature selection in knowledge-based authentication. Decis Support Syst 46(1):388–398
13. Bruns R, Dunkel J, Von Helden J (2003) Secure Smart Card-Based Access To An eLearning Portal. Proceedings of the 5th International Conference on Enterprise Information Systems (ICEIS), Angers, France
14. Gil C, Castro M, Wyne M (2010) Identification in Web Evaluation in Learning Management System by Fingerprint Identification System. In: Frontiers in Education Conference (FIE). IEEE, WA, USA
15. Sahoo SK, Choubisa T (2012) Multimodal biometric person authentication: a review. IETE Tech Rev 29(1):54
16. Ullah A, Xiao H, Lilley M, Barker T (2012) Using challenge questions for student authentication in online examination. Int J Infonom (IJI) 5(3/4):9
17. Just M, Aspinall D (2009) Challenging Challenge Questions. In: Socio-Economic Strand. Oxford University, UK
18. Rabkin A (2008) Personal Knowledge Questions for Fallback Authentication: Security Questions in the Era of Facebook. In: In SOUPS 2008: Proceedings of the 4th Symposium on Usable Privacy and Security, vol 23. ACM, New York, NY, USA
19. Just M, Aspinall D (2012) On the Security and Usability of Dual Credential Authentication in UK Online Banking. In: Internet Technology And Secured Transactions, 2012 International Conferece. IEEE, London, UK
20. Schechter S, Brush AJB, Egelman S (2009) It's No Secret. Measuring the Security and Reliability of Authentication via. In: 30th IEEE Symposium on Security and Privacy. IEEE, CA, USA
21. Griffith V, Jakobsson M (2005) Messin'with Texas Deriving Mother's Maiden Names Using Public Records. In: Third International Conference, ACNS. Springer, NY, USA
22. Just M, Aspinall D (2009) Personal Choice and Challenge Questions: A Security and Usability Assessment. In: Proceedings of the 5th Symposium on Usable Privacy and Security. ACM, CA, USA
23. (2012) Mysql. MySQL Reference Manaual 12.6.2. Mathematical Functions. MySQL -The worlds most popular opensource database., [cited 2012 15/10/2012]; 5.0:[MySQL 5.0 Reference Manual]. Available from: https://dev.mysql.com/doc/refman/5.0/en/mathematical-functions.html#function_rand
24. Just M (2004) Designing and evaluating challenge-question systems Security & Privacy. IEEE 2(5):32–39
25. Just M, Aspinall D (2009) Choosing Better Challenge Questions. In: Symposium on Usable Privacy and Security (SOUPS). ACM, CA USA
26. Standardization I. O. F (1998) Ergonomic Requirements for Office Work with Visual Dispaly Terminals, Part 11: Guidance on Usability. ISO 9241-11, Geneva
27. Seffah A, Kececi N, Donyaee M (2001) QUIM: A Framework for Quantifying Usability Metrics in Software Quality Models. In: Quality Software, 2001 Proceedings Second Asia-Pacific Conference. IEEE, Hong, Kong
28. Bevan N (2001) International standards for HCI and usability. Int J Human-Comp Stud 55(4):533–552
29. Nielsen J, Hackos JT (1993) Usability Engineering. Academic press, San Diego
30. Purdy G (2010) ISO 31000: 2009—setting a new standard for risk management. Risk Anal 30(6):881–886
31. Jobling MA (2001) In the name of the father: surnames and genetics. TRENDS Genet 17(6):353–357
32. Virzi RA (1992) Refining the test phase of usability evaluation: how many subjects is enough? Hum Fact: J Hum Fact Ergonom Soc 34(4):457–468

Energy-aware resource allocation for multicores with per-core frequency scaling

Xinghui Zhao[1]* and Nadeem Jamali[2]

Abstract

With the growing ubiquity of computer systems, the energy consumption of these systems is of increasing concern. Multicore architectures offer a potential opportunity for energy conservation by allowing cores to operate at lower frequencies when the processor demand low. Until recently, this has meant operating all cores at the same frequency, and research on analyzing power consumption of multicores has assumed that all cores run at the same frequency. However, emerging technologies such as fast voltage scaling and Turbo Boost promise to allow cores on a chip to operate at different frequencies.

This paper presents an energy-aware resource management model, DREAM-MCP, which provides a flexible way to analyze energy consumption of multicores operating at non-uniform frequencies. This information can then be used to generate a fine-grained energy-efficient schedule for execution of the computations – as well as a schedule of frequency changes on a per-core basis – while satisfying performance requirements of computations. To evaluate our approach, we have carried out two case studies, one involving a problem with static workload (Gravitational N-Body Problem), and another involving a problem with dynamic workload (Adaptive Quadrature). Experimental results show that for both problems, the energy savings achieved using this approach far outweigh the energy consumed in the reasoning required for generating the schedules.

Keywords: Energy conservation; Resource management; Performance; Frequency scheduling

1 Introduction

With growing concerns about the carbon footprint of computers – computers currently produce 2–3% of greenhouse gas emissions related to human activities – there is ever greater interest in power conservation and efficient use of computational resources. The relationship between a processor's speed and its power requirement emerged as a significant concern: the dynamic power required by a CMOS-based processor is proportional to the product of its operating voltage and clock frequency; and for these processors, the operating voltage is also proportional to its clock frequency. Consequently, the dynamic power consumed by a CMOS processor is (typically) proportional to the cube of its frequency [1]. This motivated the general shift away from faster processors to multicore processors for delivering the more processor cycles to applications with ever increasing demands.

*Correspondence: x.zhao@wsu.edu
[1] School of Engineering and Computer Science, Washington State University, 14204 NE Salmon Creek Ave., 98686 Vancouver, WA, USA
Full list of author information is available at the end of the article

At the same time, another opportunity lay in the fact that not all computations always have to be carried out at the quickest possible speed. Dynamic voltage and frequency scaling (DVFS) can be used to deliver only the required amount of speed for such computations.

Existing analytical models for power consumption of multicores typically assume that all cores operate at the same frequency [2-4]. Although this is correct for current processors which use off-chip voltage regulators (i.e., a single regulator for all cores on the same chip), which set all sibling cores to the same voltage level [5], it does not fully capture the range of control opportunities available. For instance, in a multi-chip system, off-chip regulators can be used for per-chip frequency control [6] which enables a finer-grained control by allowing each chip's cores to operate at a different frequency. Even in the absence of the ability to control chip frequencies at a fine-grain, there is often a way to temporarily boost the frequency of cores. For example, Turbo Boost [7] provides flexibility of frequency control by boosting all cores to a higher frequency to achieve better performance when necessary and possible. Note that the frequency can be increased only when the processor is otherwise operating below rated power, temperature, and current specification limits.

Beyond these opportunities, the most recent advances in on-chip switching regulators [8] will enable cores on the same chip to operate at different frequencies, promising far greater flexibility for frequency scaling. Studies have shown that per-core voltage control can provide significant energy-saving opportunities compared to traditional off-chip regulators [9]. Furthermore, it has been shown recently [10] that an on-chip multicore voltage regulator (MCVR) can be implemented in hardware. Essentially a DC-DC converter, the MCVR can take a 2.4 V input and scale it down to voltages ranging from 0.4 to 1.4V. To support efficient scaling, MCVR uses *fast voltage scaling* to rapidly cut power according to CPU demands. Specifically, it can increase or decrease the output by 1 V in under 20 nanoseconds.

To fully exploit the potential of these technologies, a finer-grained model for power consumption and management is required. Because the frequency of a core represents the available CPU resources in time (cycles/second), it can naturally be treated as a computational resource, which makes it possible to address the problem of power consumption from the perspective of resource management. In this paper, we present a model for reasoning about energy consumed by concurrent computations executing on multicore processors, and mechanisms involved in creating schedules – of resource usage as well as frequencies at which processor cores should execute – for completing computation in an energy-efficient manner.

The rest of the paper is organized as follows. We review related work in Section 2; to better motivate our work, in Section 3, we take two frequency scaling technologies as examples to illustrate the effect of these technologies on energy consumption; Section 4 presents our DREAM-MCP model for multicore resource management and energy analysis; results from our experimental involving two problems with different characteristics are presented in Section 5; Section 6 concludes the paper.

2 Related work

Although *Moore's Law* has long predicted the advance in processing speeds, the exponential increase in corresponding power requirements (sometimes referred to as the *power wall*) presented significant challenges in delivering the processing power on a single processor. Multicore architectures emerged as a promising solution [11]. Since then, power management on multicore architectures has received increasing attention [12], and power consumption has become a major concern for both hardware and software design for multicore.

Li et al. were among the first to propose an analytical model [2] which brought together efficiency, granularity of parallelism, and voltage/frequency scaling, and to establish a formal relationship between the performance of parallel code running on multicore processors and the power they would consume. They established that by choosing granularity and voltage/frequency levels judiciously, parallel computing can bring significant power savings while meeting a given performance target.

Wang et al. have analyzed the performance-energy trade-off [3]. Specifically, they have proposed different ways to deploy the computations on the processors, in order to achieve various performance-energy objectives, such as energy or performance constraints. However, their analysis is based on a particular application (matrix multiplication) running on a specific hardware (FPGA based mixed-mode chip multiprocessors). A more general quantitative analysis has been proposed by Korthikanti et al. [4], which is not limited to any application or hardware. They propose a methodology for evaluating energy scalability of parallel algorithms while satisfying performance requirements. In particular, for a given problem instance and a fixed performance requirement, the optimal number of cores along with their frequencies can be calculated, which minimize energy consumption for the problem instance. This methodology has then been used to analyze the energy-performance trade-off [13] and reduce energy waste in executing applications [14].

These analytical studies make an assumption that all cores operate at the same frequency because of the hardware limitation of traditional off-chip regulators – a limitation that is about to be removed by recent advances.

There are a number of scenarios where finer grained control is possible. Even when off-chip regulators are used, if there are multiple chips, cores on different chips can be operating at different frequencies. For example, Zhang et al. have proposed a *per-chip adaptive frequency scaling*, which partitions applications among multiple multicore chips by grouping applications with similar frequency-to-performance effects, and sets a chip-wide desirable frequency level for each chip. It has been shown that for 12 SPECCPU2000 benchmarks and two server-style applications, per-chip frequency scaling can save approximately 20 watts of CPU power while maintaining performance within a specified bound of the original system.

However, two recent advances in hardware design promise even greater opportunities. The first of these is Turbo Boost [7], which can dynamically and quickly change the frequency at which the cores on a chip are operating during execution. Specifically, depending on the performance requirements of the applications, Turbo Boost automatically allows processor cores to run faster than the base operating frequency if they are operating below power, current, and temperature specification limits. Turbo Boost is already available on Intel's new processors (codename Nehalem). The second, and perhaps more important, is the emergence of on-chip switching regulators [8]. Using these regulators, the different cores on the same chip can operate at different frequencies. Studies [9] have shown that the energy savings made possible by using on-chip regulators far outweigh the overhead of having these regulators on the chip.

As for commercial hardware, the first generation of multicore processors which support per-core frequency selection are the AMD family 10h processors [15], but the energy savings on these processors are limited, because they still maintain the highest voltage level required for all cores. Most recently, it has been shown that the on-chip multicore voltage regulator together with the fast voltage scaling can be efficiently implemented in hardware [10], which can rapidly cut power supply according to CPU demand, and perform voltage transition within tens of nanoseconds.

These new technologies provide opportunities for energy savings on multicore architectures. However, a flexible analytical model is required to analyze power consumption on multicores with non-uniform frequency settings. Cho et al. addressed part of the problem in [16] by proposing an analysis which can be used to derive optimal frequencies allocated to the serial and parallel regions in an application, i.e., non-uniform frequency over time. Specifically, for a given computation which involves a sequential portion and a parallel portion, the optimal frequencies for the two portions can be derived, which can achieve minimum power consumption while maintaining the same performance as running the computation sequentially on a single core. However, this work is a coarse-grained analysis, and it does not consider non-uniform frequencies for different cores.

Besides theoretical model and analysis, significant work has been done to optimize power consumption at run-time through software-controlled mechanisms, or knobs. Approaches include dynamic concurrency throttling (DCT) [17], which adapts the level of concurrency at runtime based on execution properties, dynamic voltage and frequency scaling (DVFS) [18], or a combination of the two [19]. Among these [18] is particular interesting, because it considers per-core frequency. Specifically, a global multicore power manager is employed which incorporates per core frequency scaling. Several power management policies are proposed to monitor and control per-core power and performance state of the chip at periodic intervals, and set the operating power level of each core to enforce adherence to known chip level power budgets. However, the focus of this work is on passively monitoring power consumption,

rather than modelling power and resource consumption at fine-grain, and actively deploying computations power-efficiently.

In this paper, we address the problem from a different perspective: resource management point of view. First, we model resources and computations at fine-grain, and the evolution of the system as the process of resource consumption; second, we model energy consumption as the cost/consequence of a specific CPU resource allocation; third, the model is energy-aware, and can be used to generate an energy-efficient resource allocation plan for any given computations.

3 Effect of frequency scaling on energy consumption

Consider an application consisting of two parts: a sequential part s, followed by a parallel part p, so that the sequential part must be executed on a single core, and the parallel part can be (evenly or unevenly) distributed over multiple cores. Although we consider the case where all parallel computation happens in one stretch, this can be easily generalized to a case where sequential and parallel parts of the computation take turn, by having a sequence of sequential-parallel pairs. Let us also normalize the sum of the two parts to 1, i.e., $s + p = 1$. Analysis carried out in [16] shows how to optimize processor frequency for the case when the the parallel part can be evenly divided between a number of cores. To achieve minimum energy consumption while maintaining a performance identical to running the computation sequentially on a single core processor, the optimal frequencies for executing the sequential and parallel parts (f_s^* and f_p^*, respectively) are:

$$f_s^* = s + \frac{p}{N^{(\alpha-1)/\alpha}} \tag{1}$$

$$f_p^* = f_s^*/N^{\frac{1}{\alpha}} \tag{2}$$

where N is the number of cores, and α is the exponential factor of power consumption (we use the value of 3 for α, as is typical in the literature). In other words, the power consumption of a core running at frequency f is proportional to f^α.

In this section, we illustrate the effects of non-uniform frequency scaling on multicore energy consumption. Particularly, we extend the analysis in [16] to consider two specific technologies: per-core frequency, and Turbo Boost.

3.1 Per-core frequency

It turns out that when parallel workload cannot be evenly distributed among multiple cores, per-core frequency scaling can be used to achieve energy savings. This has been enabled by the latest technologies which support per-core frequency setting in multicore architectures [10].

We illustrate this for a simple case involving only 2 cores. Let us say that the ratio of the workloads on the 2 cores is q ($q > 1$). The performance requirement for the computation is 1, i.e., the computation must be completed in time $T = 1$. If the two cores must run at the same frequency, the optimal frequency is:

$$f_{uniform} = s + \frac{q}{1+q} \times p$$

If the cores can operate at different frequencies, i.e., using non-uniform frequency scaling, the optimal frequencies are:

$$f_1 = s + \frac{q}{1+q} \times p$$

$$f_2 = f_1/q$$

We use the formula from [16] for calculating the energy E consumed by a processor core operating at frequency f for time T:

$$E = T_{busy} \times f^3 + \lambda \times T \qquad (3)$$

where T_{busy} is the time during which the computation is carried out, λ is a hardware constant which represents the ratio of the static power consumption to the dynamic power consumption at the maximum processor speed. The first term in the formula corresponds to energy consumed for carrying out the computation (dynamic power), and the second term represents energy for the static power consumption during the entire period of execution. Processor temperature is not considered; therefore, energy for static power consumption is only related to λ and T.

Obviously, the frequency at which the core executing the sequential part of the computation executes, remains unchanged regardless of whether uniform or non-uniform frequencies are employed. We assume that the same core carries out the heavier of the two uneven workloads to be carried out in parallel. Any energy savings to be achieved from non-uniform frequency scaling are therefore on the other core operating at a lower frequency.

We first calculate the time period for the parallel part (let us call it T_p) of the computation, which is the focus of our attention:

$$T_p = \frac{p \times q/(1+q)}{s + p \times q/(1+q)}$$

Recall that p is the normalized size of the parallel part of the computation ($p = 1 - s$), and $q > 1$ is the ratio of the two uneven workloads. Next, we calculate the energy savings ΔE:

$$\Delta E = E_{uniform} - E_{non-uniform}$$
$$= \frac{T_p}{q} \times f_1^3 - T_p \times f_2^3$$
$$= T_p \times \left(\frac{1}{q} - \frac{1}{q^3}\right) \times f_1^3 \qquad (4)$$

For a given computation, the right hand side is a function of s and q. Figure 1 illustrates the energy savings which result from using per-core frequency scaling for the two cores.

This analysis can be generalized to n cores with uneven workload. Suppose the parallel portion of the computation is distributed to n cores, and the sequential portion of the computation is carried out by core 1. We assume that the ratio of the workload on the ith core and core 1 is q_i. If the performance requirement for the computation is $T = 1$, and all cores are running at the same frequency, the uniform frequency is:

$$f_{uniform} = s + \frac{1}{1 + \sum_{i=2}^n q_i} \times p$$

If the cores can operate at different frequencies, the optimal frequencies are:

$$f_1 = s + \frac{1}{1 + \sum_{i=2}^n q_i} \times p$$

$$f_i = q_i \times f_1, i \in [2, n]$$

Similar to the 2-core case, the saved energy comes from the cores which do not carry out the sequential portion of the computation. The time period for executing the parallel portion of the computation is:

$$T_p = \frac{p/\left(1 + \sum_{i=2}^n q_i\right)}{s + p/\left(1 + \sum_{i=2}^n q_i\right)}$$

Therefore, the saved energy resulting from using per-core frequency scaling is:

$$\Delta E = E_{uniform} - E_{non-uniform}$$
$$= \sum_{i=2}^n \left(q_i \times T_p \times f_1^3 - T_p \times f_i^3\right)$$
$$= T_p \times \sum_{i=2}^n \left(q_i - q_i^3\right) \times f_1^3 \qquad (5)$$

3.2 Turbo boost

When per-core frequency scaling is not available, turbo boost enables cores to vary their frequency during a computation; the boost is only for a short duration for now to avoid overheating. We now examine the opportunity for energy saving by using this facility. Consider N cores. If all cores must execute at the same frequency over the course of a computation, the frequency required for completing the computation within time $T (T = 1)$ can be computed as follows:

$$f_{uniform} = s + \frac{1-s}{N}$$

The time required for completion of the parallel part of the computation would be:

$$T_p = \frac{p/N}{s + p/N} = \frac{p}{s \times N + p}$$

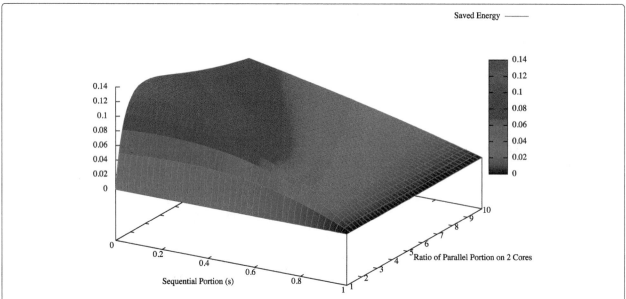

Figure 1 Saved energy on non-uniform per-core frequency technology. This figure shows the saved energy using per-core frequency scaling on two cores.

Because static power consumption does not change (by definition), we only consider the energy for dynamic power consumption of the two frequency scaling approaches. Energy required for the computation using uniform frequency is:

$$E_{uniform} = f_{uniform}^3 + (N-1) \times T_p \times f_{uniform}^3 \qquad (6)$$

We use the approach presented in [16] to calculate the optimal energy consumption when turbo boost technology is used, i.e., frequency can be changed over time. Suppose the frequency for the sequential portion of the computation is f_s, the frequency for the parallel portion is f_p, and the time it takes to carry out the sequential portion of the computation is t. Since the total execution time T is normalized to be 1, we have:

$$f_s = \frac{s}{t}$$

$$f_p = \frac{1-s}{(1-t) \times N}$$

The energy consumption can be expressed as a function of t, as follows:

$$
\begin{aligned}
E &= t \times f_s^3 + N \times (1-t) \times f_p^3 + N \times \lambda \\
&= t \times \left(\frac{s}{t}\right)^3 + N \times (1-t) \\
&\quad \times \left(\frac{1-s}{(1-t) \times N}\right)^3 + N \times \lambda \qquad (7)
\end{aligned}
$$

In order to calculate the value t which minimizes E, we then compute the derivative of E, with respect to t, and make it equal to 0, as follows:

$$\frac{dE}{dt} = \frac{-2 \times s^3}{t^3} + \frac{2 \times (1-s)^3}{(1-t)^3 \times N^2} = 0 \qquad (8)$$

Based on equation 8, we get the value t which minimizes E:

$$t^* = \frac{s}{s + \frac{p}{N^{2/3}}}$$

Therefore, the optimal frequencies for the sequential portion and parallel portion of the computation are:

$$f_s^* = \frac{s}{t^*} = s + \frac{p}{N^{2/3}} \qquad (9)$$

$$f_p^* = \frac{1-s}{(1-t^*) \times N} = \frac{s + \frac{p}{N^{2/3}}}{N^{1/3}} = \frac{f_s^*}{N^{\frac{1}{\alpha}}} \qquad (10)$$

Using the optimal frequencies f_s^*, f_p^*, and equation 7, we can compute the energy required for the computation when non-uniform frequency scaling, turbo boost, is used:

$$E_{non-uniform} = \left(s + \frac{1-s}{N^{2/3}}\right)^3 \qquad (11)$$

The energy saved by utilizing turbo boost technology is:

$$
\begin{aligned}
\Delta E &= E_{uniform} - E_{non-uniform} \\
&= \left(s + \frac{1-s}{N}\right)^3 \times \left(1 + (N-1) \times T_p\right) \\
&\quad - \left(s + \frac{1-s}{N^{2/3}}\right)^3 \qquad (12)
\end{aligned}
$$

The above formula is a function of s and N, as plotted in Figure 2. It shows that using Turbo Boost can save energy comparing to using uniform frequency for all cores.

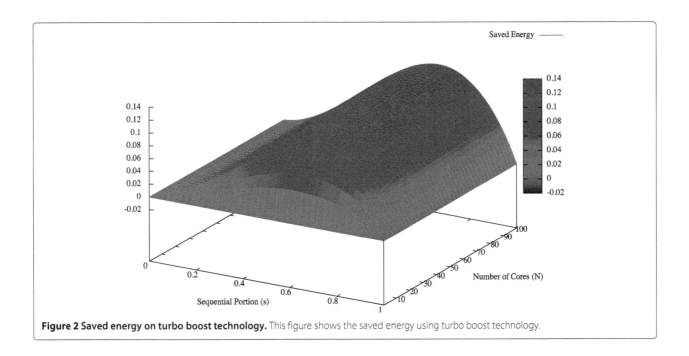

Figure 2 Saved energy on turbo boost technology. This figure shows the saved energy using turbo boost technology.

Our analysis thus far has shown that energy savings can be achieved by using non-uniform frequency technologies. However, the scenario in the analysis is simple: only one computation is considered, and workload and structure of the computation is well known. Next we address the problem of finding the optimal *frequency schedule* for a complex computation, with frequencies varying multiple times over the course of the computation's execution.

4 Reasoning about multicore energy consumption

In our previous work, we have constructed DREAM[a] (Distributed Resource Estimation and Allocation Model) [20] and related mechanisms [21] for reasoning about scheduling of deadline constrained concurrent computations over parallel and distributed execution environments. In the most recent work [22], this approach have been repurposed to achieve dynamic load balancing for computations which do not constrained by deadlines. Fundamental to this work is a fine grained accounting of available resources, as well as the resources required by computations. Here, we connect the use of resources by computations to the energy consumed in their use, leading to a specialized model, called DREAM-MCP (*DREAM* for *Multicore Power*). DREAM-MCP defines resources over time and space, and represents them using *resource terms*. A resource term specifies values for attributes defining a resource: specifically, the maximum available frequency, the time interval during which the resource is available, and the location of existence for the resource, *i.e.*, the core id. Computations are represented in terms of the resources they require. System state at

a specific instant of time is captured by the resources available at that instant and the computations which are being accommodated. We use labeled transition rules to represent progress in the system, and an energy cost function is associated with each transition rule to indicate the energy required for carrying out the transition.

4.1 Resource representation

Multicore processor resources are represented using *resource terms* of the form $[\![\mathfrak{r}]\!]_{\xi}^{\tau}$, where $\mathfrak{r}$ represents the maximum available frequency of the specific core (in *cycles/time*), τ is the time interval during which the resource is available ($\mathfrak{r} \times \tau$ is the number of CPU cycles over interval τ), and ξ specifies the *location* of the available resource, which is the *id* of the specific core.

Because each resource term is associated with a time interval τ, relationships between time intervals must be defined before we can discuss the operations on resource terms. Interval Algebra [23] is used for representing relations between time intervals. There are seven possible relations (thirteen counting inverse relations): before ($<$), equal ($=$), during (d), meets (m – first ends immediately before second), overlaps (o), starts (s – both start at the same time), and finishes (f – both finish at the same time). Table 1 shows all the possible relations between two time intervals.

Each time interval τ has a start time t_{start}, and an end time t_{end}. In this paper, we also use (t_{start}, t_{end}) as an alternative notation for time interval τ. Furthermore, binary operations on sets, such as union ($\cup$), intersection ($\cap$), relative complement ($\backslash$) are also available for time intervals.

Table 1 Possible relations between time intervals τ_1 and τ_2

Relation	Inverse relation	Interpretation	Illustration
$\tau_1 < \tau_2$	$\tau_2 > \tau_1$	τ_1 before τ_2	$\tau_1\tau_1\tau_1$ $\qquad\quad\tau_2\tau_2\tau_2$
$\tau_1\ m\ \tau_2$	$\tau_2\ mi\ \tau_1$	τ_1 meets τ_2	$\tau_1\tau_1\tau_1$ $\qquad\tau_2\tau_2\tau_2$
$\tau_1 = \tau_2$	$\tau_2 = \tau_1$	τ_1 equal τ_2	$\tau_1\tau_1\tau_1$ $\tau_2\tau_2\tau_2$
$\tau_1\ d\ \tau_2$	$\tau_2\ di\ \tau_1$	τ_1 during τ_2	$\tau_1\tau_1\tau_1$ $\tau_2\tau_2\tau_2\tau_2\tau_2\tau_2$
$\tau_1\ o\ \tau_2$	$\tau_2\ oi\ \tau_1$	τ_1 overlaps τ_2	$\tau_1\tau_1\tau_1$ $\quad\tau_2\tau_2\tau_2$
$\tau_1\ s\ \tau_2$	$\tau_2\ si\ \tau_1$	τ_1 starts τ_2	$\tau_1\tau_1\tau_1$ $\tau_2\tau_2\tau_2\tau_2\tau_2\tau_2$
$\tau_1\ f\ \tau_2$	$\tau_2\ fi\ \tau_1$	τ_1 finishes τ_2	$\tau_1\tau_1\tau_1$ $\tau_2\tau_2\tau_2\tau_2\tau_2\tau_2$

Resources in a multicore system can be represented by a set of resource terms. If two resource terms in a resource set have the same location and overlapping time intervals, they can be combined by a process of simplification, where for any interval for which they overlap, their frequencies are added, and for remaining intervals, they are represented separately in the set:

$$\left\{[\![\mathfrak{r}_1]\!]_\xi^{\tau_1}\right\} \cup \left\{[\![\mathfrak{r}_2]\!]_\xi^{\tau_2}\right\} = \left\{[\![\mathfrak{r}_1]\!]_\xi^{\tau_1\setminus\tau_2}, [\![\mathfrak{r}_2]\!]_\xi^{\tau_2\setminus\tau_1}, [\![\mathfrak{r}_1 + \mathfrak{r}_2]\!]_\xi^{\tau_1\cap\tau_2}\right\}$$

The simplification essentially aggregates resources available simultaneously at the same core, which can lead to a larger number of terms. Resource terms can reduce in number if two collocated resources with identical rates have time intervals that meet.

Note that if the time interval of a resource term is empty, the value of the resource term is 0, or null. In other words, resources are only defined during non-empty time intervals.

The notion of negative resource terms is not meaningful in this context; so, resource terms cannot be negative. We define an inequality operator to compare two resource terms, from the perspective of a computation's potential use of them. We say that a resource term is greater than another if a computation that requires the latter, can instead use the former, with some to spare. We specifically state it as follows:

$$[\![\mathfrak{r}_1]\!]_{\xi_1}^{\tau_1} > [\![\mathfrak{r}_2]\!]_{\xi_2}^{\tau_2}$$

if and only if $\xi_1 = \xi_2$, $\mathfrak{r}_1 > \mathfrak{r}_2$, and $\tau_2\ d\ \tau_1$. Note that it is not necessarily enough for the total amount of resource available over the course of an interval to be greater. Consider a computation that is able to utilize needed resources only during interval τ_2; if additional resources are available outside of τ_2, but not enough during τ_2, it does not help satisfy the computation.

The relative complement of two resource sets $\Theta_1 \setminus \Theta_2$ is defined only when for each resource term $[\![\mathfrak{r}_2]\!]_\xi^{\tau_2}$ in Θ_2, there exists a resource term $[\![\mathfrak{r}_1]\!]_\xi^{\tau_1} \in \Theta_1$, such that $[\![\mathfrak{r}_1]\!]_\xi^{\tau_1} > [\![\mathfrak{r}_2]\!]_\xi^{\tau_2}$. The relative complement of two resource sets is defined as follows:

$$\left\{\Theta_1, [\![\mathfrak{r}_1]\!]_\xi^{\tau_1}\right\} \setminus \left\{\Theta_2, [\![\mathfrak{r}_2]\!]_\xi^{\tau_2}\right\} = \left\{[\![\mathfrak{r}_1]\!]_\xi^{\tau_1} - [\![\mathfrak{r}_2]\!]_\xi^{\tau_2}\right\} \cup \Theta_1 \setminus \Theta_2$$

$$\text{where } \left\{[\![\mathfrak{r}_1]\!]_\xi^{\tau_1} - [\![\mathfrak{r}_2]\!]_\xi^{\tau_2}\right\} = \left\{[\![\mathfrak{r}_1]\!]_\xi^{\tau_1\setminus\tau_2}, [\![\mathfrak{r}_1 - \mathfrak{r}_2]\!]_\xi^{\tau_2}\right\}.$$

Union and relative complement operations on resource sets allow modeling of resources that join or leave the system dynamically, as typically happens in open distributed systems such as the Internet.

4.2 Computation representation

A computation consumes resources at every step of its execution. We abstract away *what* a distributed computation does and represent it by the *using what* sequence of its resource requirements for each step of execution. The idea is inspired by CyberOrgs [24,25], which is a model for resource acquisition and control in resource-bounded multi-agent systems.

In this paper, as the first step towards reasoning about resource/energy consumption of computations, we assume that computations only require CPU resources. We represent a computation using a triple (Γ, s, d), where Γ is a representation of the computation, s is the earliest start time of the computation, and d is the deadline by which the computation must complete. Particularly, the computation does not seek to begin before s and seeks to be completed before d. We assume the resource requirement of a computation Γ can be calculated by function ρ, as follows:

$$\rho(\Gamma, s, d) = [\mathfrak{q}]^{(s,d)}$$

where $\mathfrak{q}$ represents the CPU cycles the computation requires.

The function ρ represents the resource requirement of a computation Γ, and we say that this resource requirement is satisfied if there exists a core ξ, such that for all ξ-related resource terms which are during (s, d) $[\![\mathfrak{r}_i]\!]_\xi^{\tau_i}$:

$$\sum_i (\mathfrak{r}_i \times \tau_i) \geq \mathfrak{q}$$

The above formula states that the CPU cycles available during (s, d) are more than the resource requirement $\mathfrak{q}$, and serves as a test for whether computation (Γ, s, d) can be accommodated using resources available in the system.

Note that for a computation which is composed of sequential and parallel portions, its resource requirement can be represented by several simple resource requirements which would need to be simultaneously satisfied.

4.3 DREAM-MCP

For a computation that can be accommodated, different scheduling schemes result in different levels of energy consumption. To model all possible system evolution paths and the effects they have on overall energy consumption, we developed the DREAM-MCP model. DREAM-MCP models system evolution as a sequence of states connected by labeled transition rules specifying multicore resource allocation, and represents energy consumption as a cost function associated with each transition rule.

We define $\mathcal{S}$, the state of the system as $\mathcal{S} = (\Theta, \rho, t)$, where Θ is a set of resource terms, representing future available resources in the system, as of time t; ρ represents the resource requirements of the computations that are accommodated by the system at time t; and t is the point in time when the system's state is being captured.

The evolution of a multicore system is denoted by a sequence of states, and the progress of the system is regulated by a labeled transition rule:

$$\mathcal{S} \xrightarrow{u(\xi,f)_\Gamma} \mathcal{T}$$

where ξ is a core, f is the utilized frequency for core ξ, and Γ is a computation. The transition rule specifies that the utilization of CPU resource on core ξ – which is operating at frequency f – for computation Γ makes the system progress from state $\mathcal{S}$ to the next state $\mathcal{T}$. Here $u(\xi, f)_\Gamma$ denotes the resource utilization. If we replace the states in the above transition rule with the detailed (Θ, ρ, t) format, the transition rule would alternatively be written as:

$$\left(\left\{ [\![\mathfrak{r}]\!]_\xi^{(t,t')}, \Theta \right\}, \left\{ [\mathfrak{q}]^{(t,t'')}, \rho \right\}, t \right) \xrightarrow{u(\xi,f)_\Gamma}$$

$$\left(\left\{ [\![\mathfrak{r}]\!]_\xi^{(t+\Delta t,t')}, \Theta \right\}, \left\{ [\mathfrak{q} - f \times \Delta t]^{(t+\Delta t,t'')}, \rho \right\}, t + \Delta t \right)$$

where $[\![\mathfrak{r}]\!]_\xi^{(t,t')}$ is the available resource of core ξ, $[\mathfrak{q}]^{(t,t'')}$ is the resource requirement of Γ, and Δt is a small time slice determined by the granularity of control in the system. Here, the transition rule states that during the time interval $(t, t + \Delta t)$, the available resource ξ is used to fuel computation Γ. As a result, by time $t + \Delta t$, the computation Γ's resource requirement will be $f \times \Delta t$ less than it was at time t.

Note that f, the frequency at which core ξ is operating, may be different from the maximum available frequency $\mathfrak{r}$ ($f \leq \mathfrak{r}$). This enables cores to operate at lower frequencies for saving power.

Based on the analysis on power consumption of CMOS-based processors [1], the energy consumption associated

with the above transition rule can be represented by an energy cost function e:

$$e = \Delta t \times f^3 + \lambda \times \Delta t$$

where the first term on the right-hand side represents energy for dynamic power consumption and the second represents energy for static power consumption, where λ is a hardware constant.

Note that if certain resource becomes available, yet no computations require that type of resource, the resource expires. The resource expiration rule is defined as follows:

$$\left(\left\{ [\![\mathfrak{r}]\!]_\xi^{(t,t')}, \Theta \right\}, \rho, t \right) \xrightarrow{u(\xi)_\phi} \left(\left\{ [\![\mathfrak{r}]\!]_\xi^{(t+\Delta t,t')}, \Theta \right\}, \rho, t + \Delta t \right)$$

where $u(\xi)_\phi$ represents that core ξ is idle, i.e., it is not utilized by any computation.

The energy consumption for an expired resource only includes static power: $e = \lambda \times \Delta t$.

If there are multiple cores in the system, and during a time interval $(t, t + \Delta t)$, some resources are consumed, while others expire, we use a more general *concurrent* transition rule to represent this scenario:

$$\left(\left\{ \bigcup_{i=1}^{m} [\![\mathfrak{r}_i]\!]_{\xi_i}^{(t,t'_i)}, \Theta \right\}, \left\{ \bigcup_{i=1}^{n} [\mathfrak{q}_i]^{(t,t''_i)}, \rho \right\}, t \right)$$

$$\xrightarrow[u(\xi_{n+1})_\phi,\dots,u(\xi_m)_\phi]{u(\xi_1,f_1)_{\Gamma_1},\dots,u(\xi_n,f_n)_{\Gamma_n}} \left(\left\{ \bigcup_{i=1}^{m} [\![\mathfrak{r}_i]\!]_{\xi_i}^{(t+\Delta t,t'_i)}, \Theta \right\}, \right.$$

$$\left. \left\{ \bigcup_{i=1}^{n} [\mathfrak{q}_i - f_i \times \Delta t]^{(t+\Delta t,t''_i)}, \rho \right\}, t + \Delta t \right)$$

Note that in this scenario, there are m cores and n computations. To simplify the notation, we number the cores and corresponding resources by the numbers of the computations that are utilizing them. As a result, when there are n computations, the n cores serving them are named ξ_1 through ξ_n respectively, and the rest are named ξ_{n+1} and beyond.

The energy cost function for the above transition rule is:

$$e = \sum_{i=1}^{n} \left(\Delta t \times f_i^3 \right) + m \times \lambda \times \Delta t$$

where the first term on the right-hand side represents energy for dynamic power consumption, and the second represents energy for static power consumption. Note that non-uniform frequency scaling allows f_i to have different values for different cores, where uniform frequency requires them to be the same.

DREAM-MCP represents all possible evolutions of the system as sequences of system states connected by transition rules. Energy consumption of an evolution path can be calculated using the energy cost functions associated with the transition rules on that path; consumptions of these paths can then be compared to find the optimal schedule. In addition to exploring heuristic options, our ongoing work is also aimed at explicitly balancing the cost of reasoning against the quality of solution (See Section 6).

5 Experimental results

A prototype of DREAM-MCP has been implemented for multicore processor resource management and energy consumption analysis. The prototype is implemented by extending ActorFoundry [26], which is an efficient JVM-based framework for Actors [27], a model for concurrency. A key component of DREAM-MCP is the *Reasoner*, which takes as parameters the resource requirements of a computation and its deadline, and decides whether the computation can be accommodated using resources available in the system. For computations which can be accommodated, the *Reasoner* generates a fine-grained schedule, as well as a *frequency schedule* which instructs the system to perform corresponding frequency scaling.

To evaluate our prototype, we have implemented two applications, the Gravitational N-Body Problem (GNBP), and the Adaptive Quadrature, as two case studies. The way we evaluated our approach is as follows. We first carried out the computations on two systems, DREAM-MCP and an unextended version of ActorFoundry (AF). Note that in these experiments, we run the processors at the maximum frequency, because processors with per-core frequency scaling are not yet available. Specifically, we measured the execution times of a computation on DREAM-MCP, and the time taken for carrying the same computation AF. We treat the difference as the overhead of using DREAM-MCP mechanisms.

Although DREAM-MCP introduces overhead, it helps conserve energy by generating a per-core frequency schedule for the computation. We then calculated the energy consumption for the two systems, with the assumption that in DREAM-MCP the cores can be operated at non-uniform frequency as our frequency schedule specifies. We then compared the energy consumption of the two systems, and also calculated the portion of the energy cost due to the overhead introduced by DREAM-MCP.

For both case studies, the hardware we used to carry out the experiments is an Xserve with $2 \times$ Quad-Core Intel Xeon processors (8 cores) @ 2.8 GHz, 8 GB memory and 12 MB L2 cache. The experimental results are presented in the following sections.

5.1 Case study I: gravitational N-body problem

GNBP is a simulation problem which aims to predict the motion of a group of celestial objects which exert a gravitational pull on each other. The way we implement GNBP is as follows. A *manager* actor sends the information about all bodies to the *worker* actors (one for each body), which use the information to calculate the forces, velocities, and new positions for their bodies, and then send their updated information to the *manager*. This computation has a sequential portion in which the *manager* gathers all information about the bodies, and sends it to all *worker* actors, and a parallel portion is that each individual body calculates its new position, and sends a reply message to the *manager.*

We carried out our experiments in two stages. In the first stage, we used a computation which could be evenly divided over the 8 available cores; in the second stage, it could not. For the first stage, we carried out experiments for an 8-body problem in the two systems, DREAM-MCP and ActorFoundry (AF), for which the execution times are shown in Table 2 and Figure 3. Note that the processors run at maximum frequency in both cases.

As illustrated in Table 2, the extra overhead caused by the reasoning is 16 ms, which is approximately 11.5%. Because *Reasoner* is implemented as a single Java native thread which is scheduled to execute exclusively, the overhead it causes is in the form of sequential computation. We then normalize the GNBP execution time to 1, and we can calculate energy for dynamic power consumption of the two systems using Equations 6 and 7 from Section 3. We also calculated the extra energy consumption by reasoning itself. As shown in Figure 4, by consuming extra 2.178% of the energy requirement of the computation, DREAM-MCP can achieve approximately 20.7% of energy saving.

We next evaluated the case in which the computation can not be evenly distributed over 8 cores. We used a 12-body problem for illustration. The execution time in the two systems are shown in Table 3 and Figure 5. Note that the processors run at maximum frequency for both cases. The overhead caused by the reasoning is 21 ms, which is 9.3% of the execution time of AF.

Figure 6 shows the dynamic energy consumption of the two systems. By consuming 2% of the energy requirement of the computations, DREAM-MCP achieves 23.7% of energy saving.

Note that the experimental results on energy savings only indicate dynamic power consumption. Since the reasoning increases the total execution time of the computation, energy for static power consumption also increases. From Equation 3 in Section 3 (assuming we ignore processor temperature), it is only related to λ (hardware

Table 2 Execution time at maximum frequency (8-Body)

System	Sequential portion (ms)	Parallel portion (ms)	Overhead (%)
DREAM-MCP	70	85	11.5%
AF	54	85	0

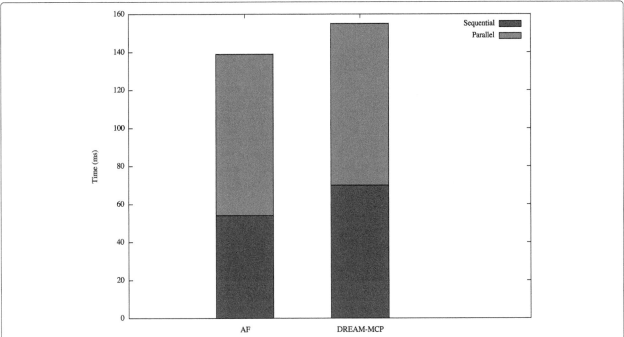

Figure 3 GNBP (8-Body): execution time at maximum frequency. This figure shows the execution time of the sequential and parallel portions of 8-Body problem on two systems, AF and DREAM-MCP.

constant) and T (execution time), i.e. $E_{static} = \lambda \times T$. Because the computational overhead of using DREAM-MCP is 11.5% for the case when computation can be evenly distributed, and 9.3% for the case when it cannot be evenly distributed, extra energy for static power

consumption is also 11.5% and 9.3% of the total static energy required by the computation respectively. Because different hardware chips have different λ values, given a λ, the total energy saving by using DREAM-MCP for a specific hardware chip, including both dynamic and static

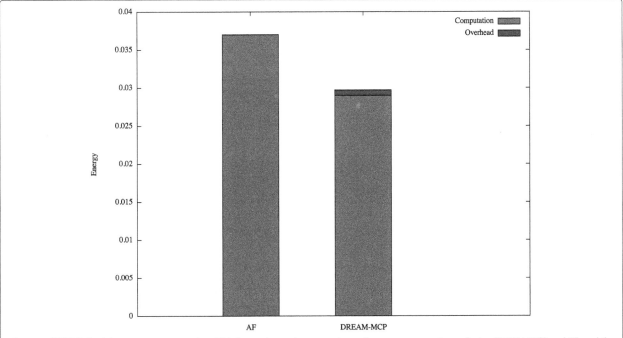

Figure 4 GNBP (8-Body): energy consumption. This figure shows the comparison of energy consumptions of using DREAM-MCP and AF, and the cost (overhead) resulting from the reasoning, for the 8-Body problem.

Table 3 Execution time at maximum frequency (12-Body)

System	Sequential portion (ms)	Parallel portion (ms)	Overhead (%)
DREAM-MCP	79	168	9.3%
AF	58	169	0

power consumption, can be calculated. Previous studies show that the static power for the current generation of CMOS technologies is in the order of magnitude 10% of the total chip power [28]. Therefore, the extra static power of our approach is approximately 1% of the total power, which is negligible.

5.2   Case study II: adaptive quadrature

Adaptive quadrature is a mathematical problem in which the value of the integral on a finite interval for a function $f(x)$ is calculated, *i.e.*,

$$\int_a^b f(x)dx$$

The algorithm for adaptive quadrature estimates the integral value based on the fundamental additive property of definite integral:

$$\int_a^b f(x)dx = \int_a^c f(x)dx + \int_c^b f(x)dx$$

where c is any point between a and b. To calculate the integral value, we assume that within a predefined fault tolerance, ε, the area of the trapezoid $(a, b, f(b), f(a))$ can be used as an estimation of the integral.

As should be obvious, the recursive nature of adaptive quadrature makes it an inherently different type of problem than GNBP. Particularly, the number of subproblems is not known in advance, making the workload dynamic.

We implement a concurrent version of adaptive quadrature as an actor system. Initially we create an actor to calculate the value of adaptive quadrature of $f(x)$ in the interval $[a, b]$. We then divide the interval $[a, b]$ into two subintervals: $[a, m]$ and $[m, b]$, where m is the mid point in $[a, b]$, and calculate the difference between the area of the trapezoid $(a, b, f(b), f(a))$ and the sum of the areas of two trapezoids in the two subintervals. if the difference is less than ε, the area of the trapezoid will be reported as the estimation of the integral for the interval. On the other hand, if the difference is greater than the predefined fault tolerance ε, the actor then creates two child actors, each of which is responsible for calculating the integral value on a subinterval. The original actor waits for the results from its child actors, and once they arrive, adds them.

For this case study, we used $f(x) = x\sin\left(\frac{1}{x}\right), x \in [0, 1]$ as the function to integrate, *i.e.*, the computation was to calculate $\int_0^1 x\sin\left(\frac{1}{x}\right) dx$ (we define f(0) = 0). We carried out experiments in the two systems, DREAM-MCP and ActorFoundry (AF), with the execution times shown in Table 4 and Figure 7. As shown in these results,

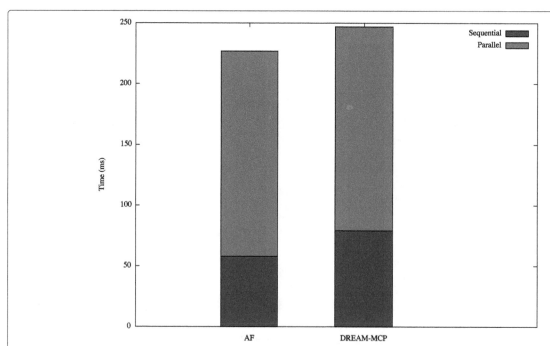

Figure 5 GNBP (12-Body): execution time at maximum frequency. This figure shows the execution time of the sequential and parallel portions of 12-Body problem on two systems, AF and DREAM-MCP.

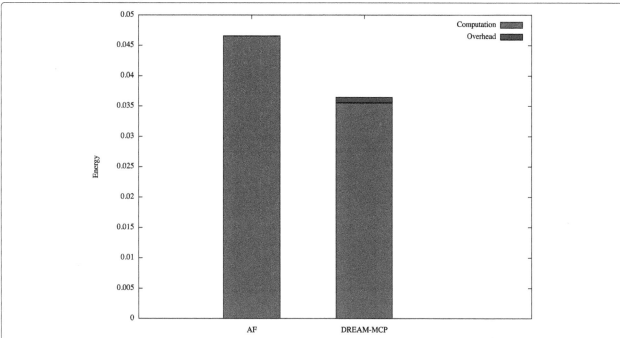

Figure 6 GNBP (12-Body): energy consumption. This figure shows the comparison of energy consumptions of using DREAM-MCP and AF, and the cost (overhead) resulting from the reasoning, for the 12-Body problem.

DREAM-MCP has a relatively high overhead of 20%, when compared with ActorFoundry. Majority of the overhead is caused by the reasoning, which is part of the sequential part of the computation in DREAM-MCP. Because of the dynamic workload, the reasoning must be invoked periodically in order to calculate the frequency schedules for the cores. In this particular experiment, the reasoning is invoked once per 500 ms, *i.e.*, 3 times in total. As shown in Figure 8, despite the high overhead, with DEREAM-MCP, we can achieve 13.6% of energy saving, and the energy cost by the reasoning is 3.5%.

5.2.1 Discussion

The Gravitational N-Body Problem and the Adaptive Quadrature represent two different types of computations. The workload of N-Body problem is static, that for Adaptive Quadrature is dynamically generated at runtime. As a result, more reasoning is required in Adaptive Quadrature, in order to calculate the frequency schedules for the cores. In the N-Body Problem, for both the cases where the workload is evenly and unevenly distributed among the cores, our approach can effectively save significant amount of energy. In Adaptive Quadrature, although the overhead caused by the reasoning is relatively high, at an extra 3.5% of the energy required by the actual computation, the savings achieved by DREAM-MCP are higher at 13.6%.

Note that our approach presented here is based on the assumption that per-core frequency scaling on a single chip is available. This is a finer-grained frequency scaling than the ones that are generally available, *e.g.*, per-chip frequency scaling. Our approach can be generalized to support per-chip frequency scaling in a multi-chip context, by restricting the frequencies for the cores on the same chip to be uniform. However, this analysis is beyond the scope of this paper.

6 Conclusion

Power consumption of multicore architectures is becoming important in both hardware and software design. Existing power analysis approaches have assumed that all cores on a chip must execute at the same frequency. However, emerging hardware technologies, such as fast voltage scaling and Turbo Boost, offer finer-grained opportunities for control and consequently energy conservation by allowing selection of different frequencies for individual cores on a chip. Deciding what these frequencies should be – the next challenge – is non-trivial.

Here, we first analyze the energy conservation opportunities presented by these two important hardware

Table 4 Adaptive quadrature: execution time at maximum frequency

System	Sequential portion (ms)	Parallel portion (ms)	Overhead (%)
DREAM-MCP	416	1404	27%
AF	20	1404	0

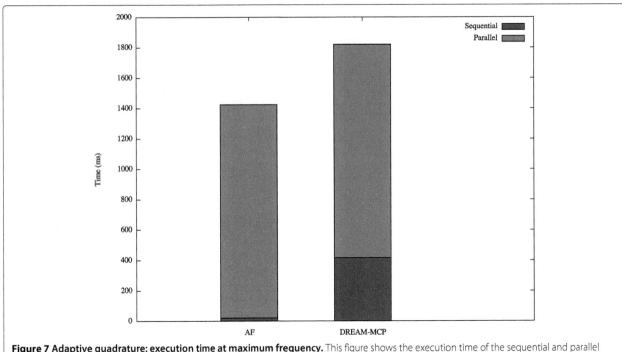

Figure 7 Adaptive quadrature: execution time at maximum frequency. This figure shows the execution time of the sequential and parallel portions of adaptive quadrature problem on two systems, AF and DREAM-MCP.

advances, and then build on our previous work on fine-grained resource scheduling in order to support reasoning about energy consumption. This reasoning enables creation of fine-grained schedules for the frequencies at which the cores should operate for energy-efficient execution of concurrent computations, without compromising on performance requirements. Our experimental evaluation shows that the cost of the reasoning is well worth it: it requires only a fraction of the energy it helps save.

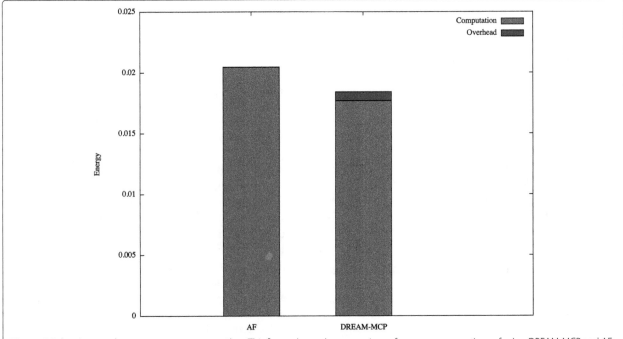

Figure 8 Adaptive quadrature: energy comsumption. This figure shows the comparison of energy consumptions of using DREAM-MCP and AF, and the cost (overhead) resulting from the reasoning, for the adaptive quadrature problem.

Work is ongoing in a number of directions. First, instead of first building a processor schedule based on computations' processor requirements and then translating it into a frequency schedule, we are working on an approach to build the schedules directly aiming for energy conservation; this would essentially pick the schedule with the best energy consumption profile from a number of schedules equally good from the processor scheduling perspective. Second, we hope to generalize our approach to make it applicable to distributed systems, mobile devices and systems involving them, each of which present different challenges. For instance, although our approach would apply to multicore mobile devices in principle, mobile applications can have very different characteristics from the types of problems we have evaluated our approach for in this paper. In that direction, the first author's group has made efforts toward profiling power consumption of different types of functionalities, and developing power-aware scheduling for mobile applications [29]. Finally, although the computational overhead of reasoning in the system is far below the benefit of doing it, we want to explore opportunities for explicitly balancing the overhead involved in reasoning against the quality of the schedule required. We hope to build on our previous work implementing a *tuner* facility for balancing the computational cost of creating fine-grained processor schedules against the cost of carrying out the actual computations [21]. The tuner carries out meta-level resource balancing between the reason and the computations being reasoned about; its parameters can be set manually or be set to self-tune at run-time in response to observations about the ongoing computation. We plan to adapt the approach to DREAM-MCP to enable a similar facility in terms of energy consumption.

Endnote
[a] Previously called ROTA (Resource Oriented Temporal logic for Agents) model [30].

Competing interests
The authors declare that they have no competing interests.

Authors' contributions
Dr. XZ developed the idea of viewing energy consumption from the perspective of resource control, and utilizing fine-grained resource control mechanisms to support energy-efficient executions of computations. The work presented in this paper is based on her Ph.D. thesis. Dr. NJ is Dr. XZ's former Ph.D. advisor, and the work was carried out under his guidance. Dr. NJ also helped with ideas of improving the model, designing experiments for evaluation, and possible future directions of the research. Both authors read and approved the final manuscript.

Author details
[1] School of Engineering and Computer Science, Washington State University, 14204 NE Salmon Creek Ave., 98686 Vancouver, WA, USA. [2] Department of Computer Science, University of Saskatchewan, 110 Science Place, S7N 5C9 Saskatoon, SK, Canada.

References
1. Burd TD, Brodersen RW (1995) Energy efficient CMOS microprocessor design. In: Proceedings of the 28th Hawaii international conference on system sciences, vol. 1. IEEE Computer Society, Washington DC, pp 288–2971
2. Li J, Martínez JF (2005) Power-performance considerations of parallel computing on chip multiprocessors. ACM Trans Archit Code Optim 2:397–422
3. Wang X, Ziavras SG (2007) Performance-energy tradeoffs for matrix multiplication on FPGA-based mixed-mode chip multiprocessors. In: Proceedings of the 8th international symposium on quality electronic design. IEEE Computer Society, Washington, DC, pp 386–391
4. Korthikanti VA, Agha G (2009) Analysis of parallel algorithms for energy conservation in scalable multicore architectures. In: Proceedings of the 38th international conference on parallel processing. IEEE Computer Society, Washington, DC, pp 212–219
5. Naveh A, Rotem E, Mendelson A, Gochman S, Chabukswar R, Krishnan K, Kumar A (2006) Power and thermal management in the Intel Core Duo processor. Intel Technol J 10(2):109–122
6. Zhang X, Shen K, Dwarkadas S, Zhong R (2010) An evaluation of per-chip nonuniform frequency scaling on multicores. In: Proceedings of the 2010 USENIX conference on USENIX annual technical conference. USENIX Association, Berkeley
7. (2008) Intel Turbo Boost Technology in Intel Core Microarchitecture (Nehalem) Based Processors. White paper, Intel. http://www.intel.com/technology/turboboost/. Accessed 16 Apr 2014
8. Kim W, Gupta MS, Wei G-Y, Brooks DM (2007) Enabling OnChip switching regulators for multi-core processors using current staggering. In: Proceedings of the workshop on architectural support for Gigascale integration. IEEE Computer Society, San Diego, CA, USA
9. Kim W, Gupta MS, Wei G-Y, Brooks D (2008) System level analysis of fast, per-core DVFS using on-chip switching regulators. In: Proceedings of the 14th IEEE international symposium on high performance computer architecture. IEEE Computer Society, Salt Lake City, UT, USA, pp 123–134
10. Kim W, Brooks D, Wei G-Y (2011) A fully-integrated 3-Level DC/DC converter for nanosecond-scale DVS with fast shunt regulation. In: Proceedings of the IEEE international solid-state circuits conference. IEEE Computer Society, San Francisco, CA, USA
11. Agerwala T, Chatterjee S (2005) Computer architecture: challenges and opportunities for the next decade. IEEE Micro 25:58–69
12. Kant K (2009) Toward a science of power management. Computer 42:99–101
13. Korthikanti VA, Agha G (2010) Energy-performance trade-off analysis of parallel algorithms. In: USENIX workshop on hot topics in parallelism USENIX Association, Berkeley, CA
14. Korthikanti V, Agha G (2010) Avoiding energy wastage in parallel applications. In: Proceedings of the international conference on green computing. IEEE Computer Society, Washington, DC, pp 149–163
15. (2009) AMD BIOS and kernel developers guide (BKDG) for AMD family 10h processors. http://developer.amd.com/wordpress/media/2012/10/31116.pdf. 16 Apr 2014
16. Cho S, Melhem RG (2008) Corollaries to Amdahl's law for energy. Comput Architect Lett 7(1):s25–s28
17. Chakraborty K (2007) A case for an over-provisioned multicore system: energy efficient processing of multithreaded programs. Technical report, Department of Computer Sciences, University of Wisconsin-Madiso
18. Isci C, Buyuktosunoglu A, Cher C-Y, Bose P, Martonosi M (2006) An analysis of efficient multi-core global power management policies: maximizing performance for a given power budget. In: Proceedings of the 39th annual IEEE/ACM international symposium on microarchitecture. IEEE Computer Society, Washington, DC, pp 347–358
19. Curtis-Maury M, Shah A, Blagojevic F, Nikolopoulos DS, de Supinski BR, Schulz M (2008) Prediction models for multi-dimensional power-performance optimization on many cores. In: Proceedings of the 17th international conference on parallel architectures and compilation techniques. ACM, New York
20. Zhao X (2012) Coordinating resource use in open distributed systems. PhD thesis, University of Saskatchewan
21. Zhao X, Jamali N (2011) Supporting deadline constrained distributed computations on grids. In: Proceedings of the 12th IEEE/ACM

international conference on grid computing. IEEE Computer Society, Washington DC, Lyon, France, pp 165–172

22. Zhao X, Jamali N (2013) Load balancing non-uniform parallel computations. In: ACM SIGPLAN notices: proceedings of the 3rd international ACM SIGPLAN workshop on programming based on actors, agents and decentralized control (AGERE! at SPLASH 2013). ACM, Indianapolis, pp 1–12

23. Allen JF (1983) Maintaining knowledge about temporal intervals. Commun ACM 26(11):832–843

24. Jamali N, Zhao X (2005) A scalable approach to multi-agent resource acquisition and control. In: Proceedings of the 4th international joint conference on Autonomous Agents and Multi-Agent Systems (AAMAS 2005). ACM Press, Utrecht, pp 868–875

25. Jamali N, Zhao X (2005) Hierarchical resource usage coordination for large-scale multi-agent systems. In: Ishida T, Gasser L, Nakashima H (eds) Lecture notes in artificial intelligence: massively multi-agent systems I vol. 3446. Springer, Berlin Heidelberg, pp 40–54

26. Karmani RK, Shali A, Agha G (2009) Actor frameworks for the jvm platform: a comparative analysis. In: In Proceedings of the 7th international conference on the principles and practice of programming in Java. ACM, New York, NY, Calgary, Alberta, Canada

27. Agha GA (1986) Actors: a model of concurrent computation in distributed systems. MIT Press, Cambridge

28. Su H, Liu F, Devgan A, Acar E, Nassif S (2003) Full chip leakage estimation considering power supply and temperature variations. In: Proceedings of the 2003 international symposium on low power electronics and design. ISLPED '03. ACM, New York, pp 78–83

29. Wang B, Zhao X, Chiu D (2014) Poster: a power-aware mobile app for field scientists. In: Proceedings of the 12th annual international conference on mobile systems, applications, and services. MobiSys '14. ACM, New York, pp 383–383

30. Zhao X, Jamali N (2010) Temporal reasoning about resources for deadline assurance in distributed systems. In: Proceedings of the 9th international Workshop on Assurance in Distributed Systems and Networks (ADSN 2010), at the 30th International Conference on Distributed Computing Systems (ICDCS 2010). IEEE Computer Society, Washington DC, Genoa, Italy

4

Middleware for efficient and confidentiality-aware federation of access control policies

Maarten Decat[*], Bert Lagaisse and Wouter Joosen

Abstract

Software-as-a-Service (SaaS) is a type of cloud computing in which a tenant rents access to a shared, typically web-based application hosted by a provider. Access control for SaaS should enable the tenant to control access to data that are located at the provider side, based on tenant-specific access control policies. Moreover, with the growing adoption of SaaS by large enterprises, access control for SaaS has to integrate with on-premise applications, inherently leading to a federated set-up. However, in the state of the art, the provider completely evaluates all policies, including the tenant policies. This (i) forces the tenant to disclose sensitive access control data and (ii) limits policy evaluation performance by having to fetch this policy-specific data. To address these challenges, we propose to decompose the tenant policies and evaluate the resulting parts near the data they require as much as possible while keeping sensitive tenant data local to the tenant environment. We call this concept *policy federation*. In this paper, we motivate the need for policy federation using an in-depth case study analysis in the domain of e-health and present a policy federation algorithm based on a widely-applicable attribute-based policy model. Furthermore, we show the impact of policy federation on policy evaluation time using the policies from the case study and a prototype implementation of supporting middleware. As shown, policy federation effectively succeeds in keeping the sensitive tenant data confidential and at the same time improves policy evaluation time in most cases.

Keywords: Software-as-a-Service; Security; Access control; Policy-based access control; Federation; Performance

1 Introduction

Software-as-a-Service or SaaS is a type of cloud computing in which a *tenant* rents access to a shared application hosted by a *provider* [1]. The tenant is an organization representing multiple end-users, who use the application through a thin client, typically a web browser. The provider protects the data in the application, for example by ensuring tenant isolation or preventing data leakage. However, for the tenant, SaaS is a form of outsourcing: while the SaaS application belongs to the provider, the application data, although hosted by the provider, still belongs to the tenant. Therefore, SaaS applications should also enable the tenants to control access to their data in the application, based on tenant-specific access control policies.

Traditional SaaS applications such as Google Apps (an office suite) and Salesforce (CRM) allow the tenant to control access to the application by offering the tenants a dashboard for configuring access control. These SaaS applications are mainly targeted at small and medium enterprises looking for a fully outsourced IT infrastructure and this approach fits them well.

Recently however, large enterprises have started to adopt SaaS as well, for example Cisco in the domain of CRM [2] or large hospitals in the domain of e-health [3,4]. While these enterprises employ SaaS to outsource specific, non core-business functionality, the organization-wide policies of the tenant still apply. These policies reason about data that remain stored in on-premise applications such as patient management or medical record systems (illustrated in Figure 1). A federated setup between tenant and provider is inherent to such a deployment context.

The federated set-up between tenant and provider poses important challenges. While techniques for federated authentication [5,6] allow user data to be securely shared between tenant and provider, the provider still completely evaluates the tenant policies. This approach causes two

*Correspondence: maarten.decat@cs.kuleuven.be
iMinds-DistriNet, KU Leuven, 3001 Leuven, Belgium

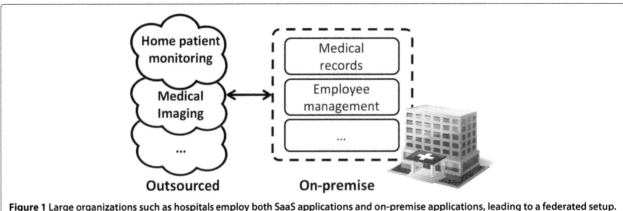

Figure 1 Large organizations such as hospitals employ both SaaS applications and on-premise applications, leading to a federated setup.

main problems: (i) it forces the tenant to disclose sensitive access control data, such as lists of patients being treated by a physician. Although the tenant may trust the provider with the data in the SaaS application, it does not necessarily trust the provider with this sensitive on-premise application data and wants to keep it confidential. Moreover, stringent regulatory requirements such as HIPAA [7] or the European DPD [8] even forbid the hospital to share this data. (ii) This approach limits policy evaluation performance by having to fetch the required data. Many of the access control policies require large amounts of access control data and fetching this data from the tenant takes a considerable amount of time.

To address these challenges, we introduce *policy federation*[a]. In this process, the tenant policies are decomposed and the resulting parts are evaluated near the data they require as much as possible while keeping sensitive tenant data local to the tenant premises. As shown, policy federation effectively succeeds in keeping the sensitive tenant data confidential and at the same time improves policy evaluation time in most cases.

This paper first presents an in-depth case study analysis in the domain of e-health motivating the need for policy federation. The paper then describes a confidentiality-aware policy federation algorithm for optimal policy evaluation time using a widely-applicable attribute-based policy model. Finally, the paper shows the impact of policy federation on policy evaluation time, using the policies from the case study and a prototype of supporting middleware.

In summary, the contributions of this paper are:

1. An in-depth case study analysis in the domain of e-health, showing the need for policy federation.
2. A full description of policy federation consisting of (i) an attribute-based policy model, (ii) a policy

federation algorithm and (iii) a description of supporting middleware.
3. A practical evaluation of the impact of policy federation on policy evaluation time, using the policies from the case study and a prototype of the supporting middleware for policy federation.

The rest of this paper is structured as follows. Section 2 discusses the context of this work: access control for SaaS applications. Section 3 describes the e-health case study that motivates this work. Section 4 defines the attribute-based policy model and Section 5 the policy federation algorithm. Section 6 evaluates policy federation in terms of performance and thereby elaborates on the design of supporting middleware. Section 7 provides a discussion of policy federation. Section 8 covers related work and Section 9 concludes this paper.

2 Context: access control and SaaS applications

This section first discusses access control in the domain of SaaS applications as background to this paper.

Access control is an important part of application-level security that limits the *actions* (e.g., read, write) which a *subject* (e.g., a physician) can take on an *object* in the system (e.g., a patient file). Access control rules are often externalized from the application they constrain and expressed in modular, declarative *access control policies* for reasons of separation of concerns and modifiability. Policy-based access control fits SaaS applications well, because it allows tenant-specific security logic to be externalized from the shared application and be bound at run-time.

Multiple models have been proposed for expressing access control policies, such as Mandatory Access Control (MAC, [9]), Discretionary Access Control (DAC, [9]) and Role-Based Access Control (RBAC, [10]). The more recent Attribute-Based Access Control (ABAC, [11]) generalizes previous models and expresses access control policies in terms of key-value properties called *attributes* of the subject (e.g., the subject id, username or roles), the object (e.g., the object id, location or content) and the environment (e.g., the time, physical location or usage context). Attributes provide increased expressivity with regard to previous models and offer a unit of data transport between the different components or parties involved in access control. For both reasons, this work builds upon ABAC.

The reference architecture for policy-based access control infrastructures was defined by IETF and DMTF and refined by the XACML standard [12]. In the reference architecture (see Figure 2), the policy decision point (PDP) makes the actual access control decision. The policy enforcement point (PEP, e.g., an API or a reference monitor) requests an access control decision from the PDP through the context handler. An access control request generally consists of information about the subject, the object, the action and the environment. The context handler gathers initially known attributes from one or more policy information points (PIPs, e.g., a database), which the PDP uses to evaluate the applicable policies loaded from the policy administration point (PAP). Since the required attributes for evaluating a policy depend on the values of former attributes, it is generally impossible to determine the set of required attributes up-front and the PDP can request additional attributes from the context handler if needed. Eventually, the PDP returns its decision (permit or deny), which the PEP enforces.

3 Case study analysis: home patient monitoring

To show the need for policy federation, this section describes the SaaS application that inspired this work: a home monitoring system for patients of cardiovascular diseases, provided to hospitals as a service. As stated in the introduction, large enterprises and non-profit organizations have started to adopt SaaS, amongst others in the domain of e-health. Health care organizations employ on-premise applications for core-business functionality such as patient data management, but outsource functionality which is not core-business to SaaS applications, such as the patient monitoring system. This section firsts

gives an overview of the system, then illustrates the hospital's access control policies for the SaaS application and finally describes the problem statement of this paper in detail.

3.1 Overview of the system

The home patient monitoring system (HPMS, see Figure 3) allows patients of cardiovascular diseases to be monitored continuously after leaving the hospital by wearing sensors such as a chest band or a wrist band. These sensors collect measurements such as the electric activity of the heart, the blood pressure or the temperature. The measurements are sent from the patients to the application back-end using a smart-phone as an intermediary device and are then stored and processed by the provider. In the first place, the provider employs telemedicine operators which continuously check upon their patients. For this, the system offers an overview of the patient's status, showing recent measurements, health charts and an estimated risk level. If medical assistance is required, the patient's physician at the hospital is notified. These physicians can also check upon the status of the patient proactively using a status overview similar to that of the telemedicine operators. A patient's status can also be viewed by the patients themselves or by other physicians and nurses at the hospital, for example when the patient is admitted there. Finally, the system provides functionality such as patient questionnaires and shared notes on a patient overview.

The HPMS is a good example of a state-of-the-art SaaS application. In this system, the hospital is the tenant of the application and in itself manages multiple end-users, i.e., the patients, physicians and nurses. Next to the HPMS, the hospital also employs other SaaS applications, e.g., for medical imaging, and on-premise applications, e.g., for patient records or employee management.

As for all e-health applications, security is paramount for the HPMS. For example, it handles personal data and is subject to stringent regulatory requirements (e.g., HIPAA [7] or the European DPD [8]). Of these security requirements, this paper focuses on the sub-domain of access control.

3.2 Access control policies from the case study

The hospital's access control policies that apply to the HPMS provide a good example of policies that apply to current SaaS applications. This section first discusses the general structure of the hospital policies and then provides a part of these policies in detail.

3.2.1 Structure of the hospital's policies

As mentioned in Section 2, this work builds upon attribute-based access control, which structures policies

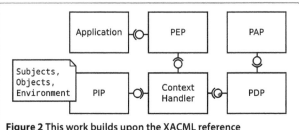

Figure 2 This work builds upon the XACML reference architecture for policy-based access control infrastructures [12].

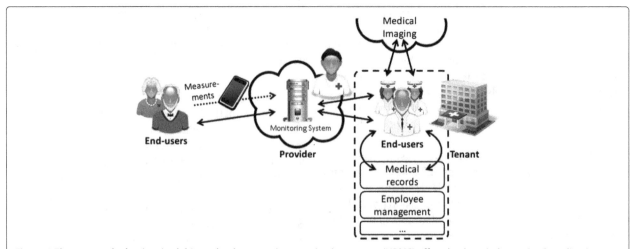

Figure 3 The case study that inspired this work: a home patient monitoring system (HPMS) offered to hospitals as a SaaS application. Next to the HPMS, the hospital also employs several on-premise applications (e.g., for employee management) and several other off-premise SaaS applications (e.g., for medical imaging).

by making the distinction between the subject, the object, the action and the environment. We apply the same structure in this discussion.

Objects and actions. The objects of the hospital policies and the possible actions on them are determined by the structure of the data in the HPMS. The previous section mentioned five types of application data: (1) the raw measurements, (2) the overview of the patient's status, (3) the notifications sent to physicians, (4) the notes added to a patient's status overview and (5) the patient questionnaires. The actions on these objects are as follows: The raw measurements, the patient's status overview and the notifications are all created by the system and cannot be altered; end-users can only view them. Notes on the other hand can be created, viewed, updated and deleted. Patient questionnaires can be created and assigned to patients by physicians. Patients can view and fill in open patient questionnaires and both patients and physicians can view completed patient questionnaires. Next to the five types of application data, the hospital can also constrain access to the HPMS as a whole.

Subjects. The subjects of the hospital policies are determined by the structure of the hospital. The hospital consists of multiple medical departments, such as cardiology, oncology, elder care, general medicine and the emergency department. Each department employs nurses and specialist physicians, such as cardiologists, oncologists, surgeons and anesthetists. The general medicine department also employs a number of general practitioners. Inside a department, the personnel is structured in teams, for example, consisting of multiple cardiologists, a

head cardiologist and assisting nurses. Finally, the hospital also provides a number of supporting services, such as general administration and finances.

Environment. The environment of the hospital policies provides the current time and date.

3.2.2 Detailed policies

Following the general policy structure, this section illustrates a hospital policy from the case study in detail by zooming in to the policies for viewing the status overview of a patient. Of all the actions, this action can be executed by the most types of subjects, leading to the most extensive policies in the case study. Other actions are constrained by similar rules. We start from broad organization-wide policies and end with specific policies for specific kinds of subjects. Notice that while we try to be as specific as possible, the textual format is still informal and a translation step towards a more formal policy language is necessary to remove all ambiguities. We provide the XACML encoding and an extensive overview of the required attributes on-line [13].

The following organization-wide policies of the hospital also apply to the HPMS:

P_1. A member of the medical personnel can not access any data about a patient who has explicitly withdrawn consent for him or her, except in case of emergency.

The following hospital policies apply to the HPMS as a whole:

P_2. Only physicians, nurses and patients can access the HPMS.

P_3. Of the physicians, only general practitioners, physicians of the cardiology department, physicians of the elder care department and physicians of the emergency department can access the HPMS.

P_4. Of the nurses, only nurses of the cardiology and the elder care department can access the HPMS.

P_5. Nurses can only access the HPMS during their shifts.

P_6. Nurses can only access the HPMS from the hospital.

P_7. Of the nurses of the cardiology department, all nurses can access the HPMS.

P_8. Of the nurses of the elder care department, only nurses who have been allowed to use the HPMS can access the HPMS.

The following hospital policies apply to viewing the status of a patient:

P_9. Physicians of the cardiology department, physicians of the elder care department and physicians of the emergency department can always view a patient's status in case of emergency (triggered by the physician, triggered by a telemedicine operator or as indicated by the monitoring data).

P_{10}. General practitioners can only view the status of a patient who is currently on consultation or whom they treated in the last two months or for whom they are assigned the primary general practitioner at the hospital or for whom they are assigned responsible in the HPMS.

P_{11}. Head physicians of the cardiology department can view the patient status of any patient in the HPMS.

P_{12}. Physicians of the cardiology department can view the patient status of any patient treated by themselves or by a physician in their team.

P_{13}. Physicians of the elder care department can only view the patient status of a patient who is currently admitted to their care unit or whom they have treated in the last six months.

P_{14}. Physicians of the emergency department can only view the status of a patient in case the status of that patient is bad.

P_{15}. Nurses can only view a patient's status of the last 5 days.

P_{16}. Nurses of the cardiology department can only view the patient status of a patient admitted to their nurse unit for whom they are assigned responsible, up to three days after they were discharged.

P_{17}. Nurses of the elder care department can only view the patient status of a patient currently admitted to their nurse unit for whom they are assigned responsible.

P_{18}. A patient can only access the HPMS if (still) allowed by the hospital.

P_{19}. A patient can only view his own status.

3.2.3 Analysis

In terms of attribute-based access control, the 19 policies given above require 30 different attributes in total, such as the subject id, the department of the subject, the list of patients treated by a physician, the owner of an object, the current date etc (see [13]). Of these attributes, 19 are hosted by the hospital (e.g., the list of patients treated by a physician), 7 are hosted by the provider (e.g., the owner of an object) and 4 are shared in the policy evaluation process (e.g., the id of the subject making the request). Of the 19 tenant attributes, 8 are sensitive, such as the lists of patients. The number of policies required to reach a decision for a single request ranges from 3 to 7 (with a mean of 4.79) and the number of attributes ranges from 4 to 13 (with a mean of 7.65). The case study illustrates that the policies of a tenant of a SaaS application require attributes from both the tenant and the provider. This leads to a federated set-up, which is the focus of this work.

3.3 Problem statement and solution

As discussed in the introduction, the hospital's access control policies would be evaluated by the provider in traditional SaaS applications. This causes two main problems:

1. The hospital would be forced to share all required attributes with the provider, including sensitive attributes which the hospital does not want to share for reasons of limited trust or even cannot share by law. More precisely, we assume the provider to be honest, but curious: the provider correctly communicates with the tenant, but can analyze the communication for the tenant's sensitive data and has an interest in this from a business point of view, because of a malicious employee or because of an external attacker. We do not directly take into account third party attacks such as eavesdropping on the channel between tenant and provider since other solutions exist for those.

2. All required attributes would have to be fetched by the provider during policy evaluation. While the presented policies are only a subset of all hospital policies and will also be much more detailed in practice, the policies already require 30 different attributes of which 19 are hosted by the hospital. Given that a single attribute request can have a large latency because of the complex data flows in federated applications and the geographical distance between tenant and provider, this approach would limit the performance of policy evaluation.

Both issues can be addressed if the hospital evaluates parts of its policies itself. For example, if the hospital evaluates whether a user has treated the owner of the status overview in the last two months (P_{10}), this data remains confidential. Similarly, if the hospital evaluates whether a user is a general practitioner (P_3), this data does not have to be fetched by the provider. In this approach, tenant and provider will cooperate to achieve an access control decision, a concept we call *federated authorization* [14]. In this paper, we describe how to decompose and distribute the hospital policies over the provider and the hospital based on the location and sensitivity of the attributes, a process we call *policy federation*.

The complete solution presented in this paper consists of three parts: (i) an attribute-based policy model which allows us to reason about policy federation, (ii) the actual policy federation algorithm and (iii) a description, prototype and evaluation of supporting middleware. In the next sections, we discuss each of these.

4　Policy model

In order to reason about policy federation, this section first defines an attribute-based policy model based on the core features of current policy languages such as XACML [12]. This minimal subset supports all the policies of the case study, but remains generic in order to guarantee its wide applicability. Several other authors have taken similar approaches, e.g., Crampton and Huth [15]. With respect to these, our model focuses on the aspects related to policy federation, i.e., the general structure of a policy and how a policy is evaluated.

4.1　Structure of a policy

The policy model used in this work represents policies using the concept of a policy tree, similar to [15,16]. Each policy in the tree states for which requests it is applicable by means of a target. The leafs of the policy tree are called *atomic policies*, the others are called *composed policies*.

4.1.1　Atomic policies

Atomic policies state in which conditions a certain request is permitted and in which it is not. They therefore consist of a target, an effect and a condition. The target determines whether the policy applies to the request or not. The effect of a policy is either Permit or Deny, respectively permitting or denying the request. The condition determines whether the effect holds or not. Thus, the result of evaluating a policy is either Permit, Deny or NotApplicable.

As mentioned before, this work builds upon ABAC and as a consequence, targets and conditions are expressions on the attributes of the subject (s), the object (o), the action (a) and the environment (e). Such expressions can contain three kinds of elements: (i) functions, e.g., "and", "in" or "==", (ii) attribute references, e.g., "s.roles" referring to the roles of the subject and (iii) literal values, e.g.,

"physician". Possible attribute types are primitive types such as integers, strings, booleans and dates, or lists of these.

Using the notation $P_{Atom}=$ < *Target, Effect, Condition*>, policy P_1 as defined in Section 3.2 can be represented as follows:

P_1 = <*a.id == "access" & "medical_personnel" in s.roles, Deny, s.id in o.owner_withdrawn_consents & ...* >

4.1.2　Composed policies

Composed policies combine the results of several other policies, either atomic policies or other composed policies. They therefore consist of a target, a policy combination algorithm and an ordered list of sub-policies. The target is defined the same as for atomic policies. The policy combination algorithm combines the effects of the sub-policies into the effect of the composed policy. In order to remain compatible to XACML, we limit ourselves to three policy combination algorithms, which suffice to express the policies from the case study: PermitOverrides, DenyOverrides and FirstApplicable [12]. Notice that policy evaluation requires a single result, i.e., the access control decision. Since every set of policies can be combined to a single combined policy using the policy combination algorithms, we assume the policy tree to have a single root, which applies to all requests.

Using the notation P_{Comp} = <*Target, PolicyCombinationAlgorithm, Sub-policies*>, the example policies of Section 3.2 can be combined into a single composed policy as follows (illustrated in Figure 4):

P_0 = <*true, FirstApplicable, [P_1, P_2, <"physician" in s.roles, DenyOverrides, [P_3, P_9, ..., P_{14}]>, <"nurse" in s.roles, DenyOverrides, [P_4, ...]>, ...* >

4.1.3　Sensitive elements

In the model, two elements of a policy can be declared sensitive: (i) the attributes used in a policy and (ii) the policies themselves. For composed policies, confidentiality applies to the whole policy tree below it. In practice, these confidentiality constraints can be expressed by providing a separate meta-policy or by annotating the access control policies themselves. Since attributes can be referenced multiple times throughout a policy, using a separate meta-policy provides the advantage of central management. Policy elements on the other hand are best annotated in the access control policies themselves. The result for the policies of the case study is available on-line [13].

4.2　Policy evaluation

The evaluation of a policy structured as described above also impacts policy federation. We here define two

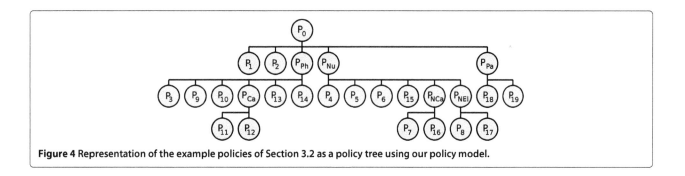

Figure 4 Representation of the example policies of Section 3.2 as a policy tree using our policy model.

aspects: (i) the order in which the elements of the policy tree are evaluated and (ii) how attributes are fetched.

4.2.1 Evaluation order

A policy is evaluated by first evaluating its target. If the policy does not apply to the request, NotApplicable is returned. If the policy does apply, its condition is evaluated (in case of an atomic policy) or its sub-policies are evaluated (in case of a composed policy) and the result is returned. For composed policies, the sub-policies are evaluated in the given order; as a consequence, the policy tree is evaluated depth-first. For now, we assume all sub-policies and expressions to be evaluated sequentially.

4.2.2 Fetching attributes

As mentioned in Section 2, the required attributes are fetched from their respective policy information points during policy evaluation. Because the required attributes for evaluating a policy depend on the values of former attributes, it is generally impossible to determine the set of required attributes up-front and we generally assume that an attribute is only fetched when it is required. To enable this, the identifiers of the subject, the object and the action are given by the policy enforcement point for initiating the policy evaluation. We also make the realistic assumption that attribute values are cached during the evaluation of a policy for a single request in order to avoid unnecessary attribute fetches and to guarantee correct evaluation of policies that require the same attribute multiple times in the presence of out-of-band attribute updates. We do not take into account attribute caching across multiple requests in order to avoid freshness issues.

5 Policy federation algorithm

Based on the policy model described in the previous section, this section defines the policy federation algorithm, i.e., the algorithm that will decompose and deploy the tenant policies across tenant and provider. We first give an overview of the algorithm and then go into each of

the major steps. Finally, we discuss the correctness of the algorithm in terms of policy equivalence.

5.1 Overview

The goal of the policy federation algorithm is to decompose and distribute the tenant policies so that sensitive attributes and policies remain confidential and the evaluation performance is optimized, i.e., the evaluation duration is minimized. For attribute-based policies, this evaluation duration is mainly determined by the latency of fetching the required attributes [17]. The latency of a remote attribute fetch between tenant and provider will be an order of magnitude larger than a local database call, taking into account the complex data flows in federated applications and the geographical distance between tenant and provider. Therefore, the goal of the algorithm is to minimize the number of requests between tenant and provider.

An important design decision is the granularity of the policy distribution. In theory, even internal parts of an atomic policy could be distributed. However, we deliberately limit the granularity to sub-policies in the policy tree. As such, the decomposed policy remains compatible with existing policy infrastructures and the existing policy combination algorithms can be used for handling the results. However, this approach also limits the granularity of policy decomposition. Therefore, the first step in the algorithm is to normalize larger policies into an equivalent set of smaller policies, which can then be separately deployed. Afterward, the algorithm tries to combine multiple remote policy references into a single reference again, in order to minimize the number of remote policy evaluation requests.

An overview of the resulting policy federation algorithm is given in Algorithm 1. The algorithm requires two inputs: (i) the policy P to be federated, annotated with sensitivity labels in the policy tree and (ii) the list of attributes, each having a location and sensitivity label. The location of an attribute is either tenant-side or provider-side, the sensitivity label of an attribute or policy is a boolean that determines whether the attribute or policy can be shared with the provider or not. The algorithm provides three outputs: (i) *root*: the policy at the root of the new policy tree which can reference remote policies, (ii) S_P: the set of referenced policies to be deployed provider-side and (iii) S_T: the set of referenced policies to be deployed tenant-side. Throughout the algorithm, several policy transformations are applied to the policy tree (see Equations (T1–T9)). Of these transformations, T1, T2, T3 and T4 allow policies to be split in an equivalent set of smaller policies; T5, T6 and T7 allow sub-policies of combined policies to be combined; T8 and T9 show the commutativity of PermitOverrides and DenyOverrides. The correctness of these rules can be proven using their respective decision tables. The algorithm itself consists of three major steps: normalization, decomposition and combination. In the next sections, we go into detail about each of these steps.

Algorithm 1 Overview of the policy federation algorithm. The methods normalize(), decompose() and combine() are defined in Algorithms 2, 3 and 4.

Inputs: *P*: a policy, annotated with sensitivity labels (true or false), *A*: a list of attributes, each having a location (tenant-side or provider-side) and sensitivity label (true or false).

Outputs: *root*: the policy at the root of the new policy tree which can reference remote policies, S_P: the set of referenced policies to be deployed provider-side, S_T: the set of referenced policies to be deployed tenant-side.

$S_P, S_T = [\,]$
// Step 1: Normalization
$P = normalize(P)$
// Step 2: Decomposition
$root = decompose(P, "providerSide")$
// Step 3: Combination
$root = combine(root)$
for Policy p **in** S_T: S_T.replace(p, combine(p))
for Policy p **in** S_P: S_P.replace(p, combine(p))

5.2 Step 1: normalization

As said, the goal of the normalization step is to convert larger policies into an equivalent set of smaller policies, which can then be separately deployed. Therefore, the first step of the federation algorithm iteratively applies transformations T1, T2, T3 and T4 as defined in Equations (T1–T4) to the given policy *P* until no more sub-policies can be transformed, as shown in Algorithm 2.

Algorithm 2 Definition of the `normalize()` method.

---

def normalize(Policy p):
  Policy p' = p.applyTransformations([T1, T2, T3, T4])
  if p' != p:
    // a transformation was applied
    return normalize(p')
  else:
    if p **is** AtomicPolicy: **return** p
    else: // composed policy
      for Policy sub **in** p.subpolicies:
        p.subpolicies.replace(sub, normalize(sub))
    return p

Notice that transformations T1 to T4 only utilize `or` statements. The reason for this is that we want to remain compatible to XACML and only employ FirstApplicable, PermitOverrides and DenyOverrides, but converting an `and` statement would require other policy combination algorithms. For example, the equivalents of T1 and T2 would require the policy combination algorithm BothApplicable.

5.2.1 Results from the case study

When applying the federation algorithm to the policies from the case study, P_9 will be split into three times three parts because both its target and condition consist of a ternary term that can be split using T1 or T3. Similarly,

$$< T_1 | T_2, E, C > \Leftrightarrow < true, FirstApplicable, [< T_1, E, C >, < T_2, E, C >] > \quad (T1)$$

$$< T_1 | T_2, PCA, [P_1...P_n] > \Leftrightarrow < true, FirstApplicable, [< T_1, PCA, [P_1...P_n] >, < T_2, PCA, [P_1...P_n] >] > (T2)$$

$$< T, Permit, C_1 | C_2 > \Leftrightarrow < T, PermitOverrides, [< true, Permit, C_1 >, < true, Permit, C_2 >] > \quad (T3)$$

$$< T, Deny, C_1 | C_2 > \Leftrightarrow < T, DenyOverrides, [< true, Deny, C_1 >, < true, Deny, C_2 >] > \quad (T4)$$

$$< T, PermitOverrides, [P_1, P_2, P_3] > \Leftrightarrow < T, PermitOverrides, [< true, PermitOverrides, [P_1, P_2] >, P_3 >] > \quad (T5)$$

$$< T, DenyOverrides, [P_1, P_2, P_3] > \Leftrightarrow < T, DenyOverrides, [< true, DenyOverrides, [P_1, P_2] >, P_3 >] > \quad (T6)$$

$$< T, FirstApplicable, [P_1, P_2, P_3] > \Leftrightarrow < T, FirstApplicable, [< true, FirstApplicable, [P_1, P_2] >, P_3 >] > \quad (T7)$$

$$< T, PermitOverrides, [P_1, P_2] > \Leftrightarrow < T, PermitOverrides, [P_2, P_1] > \quad (T8)$$

$$< T, DenyOverrides, [P_1, P_2] > \Leftrightarrow < T, DenyOverrides, [P_2, P_1] > \quad (T9)$$

P_{10} will be split in four parts using T3, P_{12} in two parts using T3 and P_{13} in two parts using T3.

5.3 Step 2: decomposition

After the policy tree has been normalized, step 2 of the algorithm decomposes it so that every sub-tree is deployed on its optimal location (see Algorithm 3). The algorithm estimates the cost of evaluating a certain sub-tree either provider-side or tenant-side in terms of evaluation time and minimizes the total evaluation cost as follows: If the cost of evaluating a sub-policy of a composed policy on the same side as the composed policy is larger than the cost of evaluating it on the other side plus the cost of making a policy evaluation request, the sub-policy is deployed on the other side and it is replaced by a remote policy reference to it. The algorithm applies this reasoning recursively starting from the top policy, which should always be deployed provider-side. For a policy that handles sensitive attributes or is labeled sensitive itself, the cost of evaluating it provider-side is infinite (i.e., it has to be evaluated tenant-side). For the other cases, we here define several cost functions, which focus on the number of required attributes.

Algorithm 3 Definition of the decompose() method. $C_{i,P}$, $C_{i,T}$ and C_{PR} are as defined in Section 5, S_T and S_P are as defined in Algorithm 1.

---

def decompose(Policy p, Side parentSide):
  if p **is** ComposedPolicy:
    for Policy sub **in** p.subpolicies:
      p.subpolicies.replace(sub, decompose(sub))
  $(C_{i,P}, C_{i,T})$ = evaluationCost(p)
  if parentSide == "tenantSide":
    if $C_{i,P} + C_{PR} < C_{i,T}$:
      S_P.add(p)
      return new RemotePolicyReference(p)
    else: return p
  else:
    if $C_{i,T} + C_{PR} < C_{i,P}$:
      S_T.add(p)
      return new RemotePolicyReference(p)
    else: return p

5.3.1 Cost functions for atomic policies

For atomic policies, the cost functions are as follows:

$$C_{Atom,P} = N_{A,P} * C_L + N_{A,T} * C_R \qquad \text{(CF1)}$$

$$C_{Atom,T} = N_{A,T} * C_L + N_{A,P} * C_R \qquad \text{(CF2)}$$

The cost functions determine the cost of the provider ($C_{Atom,P}$) and the tenant ($C_{Atom,T}$) evaluating a certain atomic policy based on the total number of required

provider attributes ($N_{A,P}$) and tenant attributes ($N_{A,T}$) and the cost for fetching an attribute locally (C_L) or remotely (C_R). The location of every attribute determines the cost of fetching the attribute: C_L will be much smaller than C_R.

An important detail is the handling of cached attributes (see Section 4.2). The cost of fetching an attribute from the cache is assumed to be zero and the cost functions should only take into account newly required attributes. However, it is impossible to fully statically determine the set of cached attributes, for example because previous policies in the policy tree can be fully evaluated, but still return NotApplicable. In order to come to a static estimation, we assume the worst case and calculate the minimal set of cached attributes by only taking into account the attributes required by the targets of previously evaluated policies, i.e., super-policies, previous policies on the same level and previous policies on the same level as super-policies. In case an atomic policy has a target that matches all requests, the attributes in the condition are taken into account as well. In case a composed policy has a target that matches all requests, the required attributes of the first policy are taken into account. For simplicity, we assume that non-sensitive cached attributes are shared between tenant and provider by adding them to the policy evaluation requests. Notice that the cost functions above also assume the worst case by taking into account all attributes of the policy, while some attributes may not be needed every time, e.g., the attributes required by the condition if the policy is not applicable (see Section 3.2.3).

5.3.2 Cost functions for composite policies

For composite policies, the cost functions are as follows:

$$C_{Comp,P} = N_{A,P} * C_L + N_{A,T} * C_R + \sum K_{i,P} \qquad \text{(CF3)}$$

$$C_{Comp,T} = N_{A,T} * C_L + N_{A,P} * C_R + \sum K_{i,T} \qquad \text{(CF4)}$$

$N_{A,P}$, $N_{A,T}$, C_L and C_R are defined similarly as for atomic policies. Notice that composite policies only directly require attributes because of their targets and that again, cached attributes are not taken into account. $K_{i,P}$ and $K_{i,T}$ represent the cost of evaluating the i'th sub-policy P_i of composite policy P_{Comp} in case P_{Comp} is evaluated provider-side or tenant-side respectively. In case P_i is evaluated on the other side than P_{Comp}, a policy evaluation request is needed, which has a cost $C_{PR} \simeq C_R$. To take this into account, we define $K_{i,P}$ as the minimum of the cost of evaluating P_i when evaluating P_{Comp} provider-side, thereby actually deciding on the optimal evaluation location of P_i:

$$K_{i,P} = min(C_{i,P}, C_{i,T} + C_{PR}) \qquad \text{(CF5)}$$

$K_{i,T}$ is defined similarly:

$$K_{i,T} = min(C_{i,P} + C_{PR}, C_{i,T}) \qquad \text{(CF6)}$$

For atomic policies, $C_{i,P}$ and $C_{i,T}$ are defined as CF1 and CF2; for composed policies, $C_{i,P}$ and $C_{i,T}$ are defined recursively as CF3 or CF4.

5.3.3   Results from the case study

The policies from the case study all require more tenant attributes than provider attributes, except for P_9. As a result, most of the policy tree will be deployed tenant-side, starting from the root and only P_9 (or more precisely, the policy tree resulting from normalizing P_9) is still deployed provider-side. Because the root policy P_0 is deployed tenant-side, a provider-side policy reference is inserted as new root.

5.4   Step 3: combination

Finally, the third step of the algorithm tries to combine remote policy references in order to minimize the number of policy evaluation requests between tenant and provider (see Algorithm 4). More precisely, the algorithm combines multiple policies referenced in a single composed policy into a larger equivalent composed policy and combines their remote policy references into a reference to the new combined policy. For this, the algorithm employs transformations T5, T6 and T7 as defined in Equations (T5–T7). In case of FirstApplicable, only consecutive remote policy references in the sub-policies can be combined; in case of PermitOverrides or DenyOverrides, all remote policy references can be combined since these algorithms are commutative as shown by transformations T8 and T9 of Equations (T8–T9).

Algorithm 4 Definition of the `combine()` method. S_T and S_P are as defined in Algorithm 1.

```
def combine(Policy p):
  if p is AtomicPolicy: return p
  else:
    Policy[ ][ ] groups = p.getCombinableSubpolicies()
    for Policy[ ] group in groups:
      ComposedPolicy cp =
          new ComposedPolicy(p.target, p.pca, group)
      S_P.replace(group, cp) // no effect if group not in S_P
      S_T.replace(group, cp) // no effect if group not in S_T
      p.subpolicies.replace(group,
          new RemotePolicyReference(cp)
    return p
```

5.4.1   Results from the case study

The policy tree resulting from normalizing and decomposing the policies from the case study does not allow

to combine multiple remote policy references. The final policy tree is shown in Figure 5.

5.5   Discussion: policy equivalence

An important property of the policy federation algorithm is that the federated policy gives the same results as the original policy. To make this more concrete, we here introduce the notion of policy equivalence.

Definition: Policy equivalence   Two policies P_1 and P_2 are equivalent iff for every request R and context Ctx, evaluating P_1 leads to the same decision as evaluating P_2. The context Ctx is a collection of attribute values of the subject, the object, the action and the environment: $Ctx = (A_S, A_O, A_A, A_E)$. The request R is a subset of the context: $R \subset Ctx$.

Our policy federation algorithm maintains policy equivalence because (1) only step 1 and step 3 transform the policy tree and every applied transformation (see Equations (T1–T9)) maintains policy equivalence and (2) both the original policy and the federated policy share the same context since the policies deployed provider-side will only require provider attributes and non-sensitive tenant attributes and all non-sensitive attributes are available to both tenant and provider. An equivalent decomposition also leads to an equivalent distribution, except for the fact that distributed policy evaluation can introduce network exceptions.

6   Performance evaluation

In this section, we evaluate policy federation in terms of performance. For the performance evaluation, we can evaluate the impact of policy federation on policy evaluation time and the performance of the algorithm itself. The policy federation algorithm is meant to be run at policy deployment time, i.e., independently of the policy evaluation flow, and therefore does not introduce run-time overhead. For the policies presented in the case study, the algorithm takes about 11 ms; for policies of one order of magnitude larger[b], the algorithm still takes less than 2 seconds. Because these durations fit the asynchronous execution of the federation algorithm, we do not provide details about the algorithm and focus on the impact of policy federation on policy evaluation time.

6.1   Prototype

To measure the performance impact of policy federation, we implemented a prototype of both the federation algorithm (2KLOC) and a middleware system supporting policy federation (6KLOC). Both build upon the SunXACML policy evaluation engine. The source code is publicly available at [13].

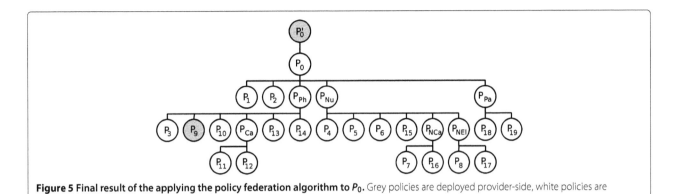

Figure 5 Final result of the applying the policy federation algorithm to P_0. Grey policies are deployed provider-side, white policies are deployed tenant-side. For readability reasons, the normalizations of P_9, P_{10}, P_{12} and P_{13} are not shown.

Figure 6 shows the architecture of the supporting middleware in terms of the XACML reference architecture for policy-based access control infrastructures (see Section 2). As shown, both the provider and the tenant have a PAP, a PDP, a context handler and one or more PIPs since both will evaluate policies. The provider hosts the SaaS application and therefore also the PEP. The provider hosts the attributes concerning the objects in the application (A_O) and the provider part of the environment ($A_{E,P}$) and the tenant hosts the attributes concerning the subjects of the application (A_S) and the tenant part of the environment ($A_{E,T}$). Non-sensitive attributes are made available to the other party by means of an attribute service, the PDPs by means of a Remote Policy Decision Point (RPDP). The RPDPs and attribute services are published as SOAP web-services implemented on top of Apache Tomcat 7 using the Apache CXF services framework. The Policy Federation Layer shown in Figure 6 is the

focus of this work. This layer cooperates with the tenant and provider PAP in order to deploy the tenant policies after the initial decomposition step. For more information about the supporting middleware, we refer to [14].

6.2 Test set-up

The performance impact of policy federation can be expected to depend on the characteristics of the policy, e.g., its size, the number of required attributes, the location of these attributes etc. Thus, in order to give a realistic view of the performance impact of policy federation, we employ the policies from the case study and measure (i) the number of remote requests (i.e., attribute requests or policy evaluation requests) between tenant and provider needed for evaluating the policies and (ii) the total policy evaluation time. In the first place, we compare two cases: (i) provider-side evaluation: in this case the policies are completely evaluated provider-side and

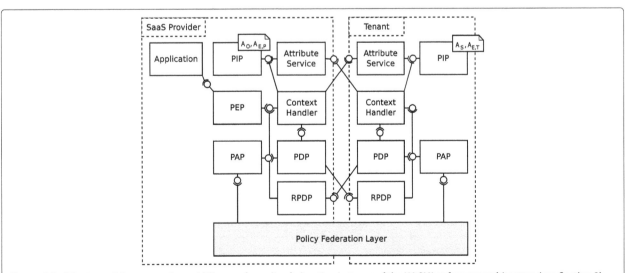

Figure 6 Architecture of the supporting middleware for policy federation in terms of the XACML reference architecture (see Section 2). The Policy Federation Layer is the focus of this work.

(ii) federated evaluation: in this case, the policies are deployed across tenant and provider as resulting from the federation algorithm. For completeness, we also compare the results to (iii) tenant-side evaluation: in this case the policies are completely evaluated tenant-side. We employ 26 different access requests that together cover every branch of the original policy tree. Notice that in the provider-side case, sensitive attributes are fetched from the tenant.

Each of the main components of the prototype runs on a separate machine with 1GiB RAM and a single core of 2.40GHz running Ubuntu 12.04. Attributes are stored locally on the machine that requires them. Using fixed network delays, the round-trip time of a request between tenant and provider is set to 10 ms. Tests are run sequentially and PDP evaluation is done in a single thread. Each test starts with 500 warm-up requests and is repeated until the confidence interval lies within 2% of the sampled mean for a confidence level of 95%.

6.3   Results

Figure 7 shows the results of the performance tests. Because the federation algorithm does not take into account the frequency of each request, we do not state means over all requests, but list the results for each access request separately.

We can make several observations from the figure. First, provider-side evaluation requires the same or larger number of remote requests than tenant-side and federated evaluation in all cases, leading to longer evaluation times in most cases. This is caused by the fact that the policies from the case study require more tenant attributes than provider attributes. Request 13 is the most extreme case, where all required attributes are stored tenant-side

and 7 attribute requests are replaced by a single policy evaluation request.

Second, in most cases, federated evaluation leads to the same or smaller number of remote requests than tenant-side evaluation. The same number is achieved if P_9 (i.e., the part of the policy tree that is deployed provider-side) is not required to reach an access control decision, e.g., for requests 13 to 16. Smaller numbers are achieved in the other cases, e.g., requests 4 to 7. In these cases, multiple attribute fetches from tenant to provider are replaced by a single policy evaluation request. This shows the intended results of the federation algorithm. However, the smaller number of remote requests does not lead to proportionally shorter evaluation times, e.g., for requests 4, 5 and 6. This is caused by the larger overhead of a policy evaluation versus an attribute fetch, while the federation algorithm assumed both to be equal. In requests 24 and 25, tenant-side and federated evaluation even perform worse than provider-side evaluation because of this.

Finally, for requests 8 and 22 to 26, federated evaluation leads to larger numbers of remote request and longer evaluation times than tenant-side evaluation. This is caused by the fact that P_9 is evaluated, but all attributes required to come to a decision are already cached. Thus, federated evaluation requires a policy evaluation request, while tenant-side evaluation does not require any attribute fetches.

7   Discussion

In the previous sections, we presented the technique of policy federation, which aims to decompose access control policies over multiple parties for confidentiality and improved performance. In this section, we discuss the

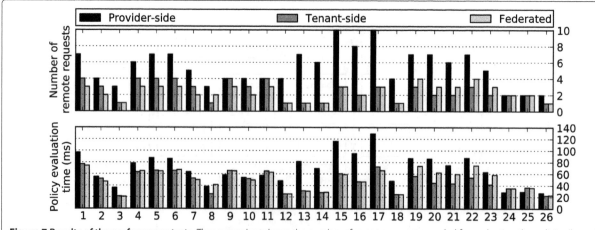

Figure 7 Results of the performance tests. The upper chart shows the number of remote requests needed for evaluating the policies (lower is better), the lower chart shows the resulting policy evaluation time in milliseconds (lower is better). For each access request, we show the results for provider-side evaluation, tenant-side evaluation and federated evaluation. As shown, the federated policy provide the best results for most access requests.

results of this work and in which ways it can be refined and extended.

7.1 Confidentiality

Policy federation effectively succeeds in keeping the sensitive tenant attributes and policies confidential. However, two potential threats to this work are (i) the increased attack surface of the tenant by the introduction of the RPDP service and (ii) possible inference of policies or attributes by the provider using the complete set of access requests and decisions. For the former, we argue that the risk of the increased attack surface is low since only the provider should be given access to the RPDP service. For the latter, we argue that the possibly inferred knowledge is limited since both the tenant policies and the required attributes remain confidential and the provider can only request the tenant to evaluate the policies resulting from the federation algorithm. However, future work is required to answer this question more quantitatively, for example using techniques such as logical abduction.

Towards the future, the employed confidentiality model can be refined. The algorithm now assumes that an attribute or policy is labeled sensitive or non-sensitive. In a more extensive case, a sensitivity policy could express more complex rules, for example, limiting attribute release to some parties based on their identity or defining a certain combination of multiple attributes as confidential.

7.2 Performance

The performance evaluation showed that policy federation has the ability to improve policy evaluation performance. With the maturation of policy-based and attribute-based access control, access control policies will only grow in both size and complexity and the performance gain of policy federation can be expected to increase as well.

In order to achieve further improved results, the algorithm can be refined in several ways. First, remote policy references can be extended with local targets in order to avoid the unnecessary policy requests mentioned in Section 6.3. Second, the algorithm achieves sub-optimal results because of the overhead of a policy evaluation versus an attribute fetch. While policy evaluation engines are expected to provide improved performance towards the future (e.g., [18]), the cost functions in the algorithm can be refined to take into account this overhead. As a further extension, performance properties of the provider and tenant infrastructures can be taken into account as well. Finally, the algorithm now only statically reasons about policies. In order to further optimize towards common access requests, the algorithm can be applied at run-time, thereby incorporating run-time statistics.

7.3 Obligations and attribute updates

Another part of future work is to incorporate obligations, i.e., actions which should be performed in conjunction with enforcing the access control decision [12]. For example, obligations can be used to specify that the user should agree to a license agreement or that the policy infrastructure should write out a log, send an e-mail to an administrator or update an attribute value. In [14], the impact of incorporating obligations in federated authorization is described. However, similar to attributes and policies in the policy tree, the tenant can regard certain obligations as sensitive and thus, obligations should be incorporated in the process of policy federation as well.

An interesting subset of obligations are attribute updates. Attribute updates can be used to model history-based policies [19], e.g., a separation-of-duty policy that states that a member of the help desk cannot view both insurance and financial documents of a single organization or a policy that limits the number of views of a document. Both attribute updates and history-based policies introduce extra complexity in policy federation because (1) attribute updates require concurrency control in case of distributed policy evaluation [17] and (2) history-based policies are known to have a large impact on performance [19]. Both are therefore interesting tracks for future research.

7.4 Generalization to N > 2 parties

A final possible extension of this work is a generalization to more than two parties. This paper focused on a tenant renting access to a SaaS application and that tenant wanting to enforce tenant-specific access control policies on that application. This situation can be extended to more than two parties, e.g., a patient monitoring system provided to multiple hospitals which collaboratively provide care to the same patient. In our experience, this situation reduces to each hospital applying its specific policies to the shared application, in which case the algorithm can separately be applied to each hospital policy without change. Should a situation arise that does not show this pattern (i.e., a federation in which a single policy reasons about data of more than two parties), the algorithm should be extended. However, we do expect the techniques in this paper to apply to this situation as well.

8 Related work

This work describes rewriting and optimizing access control policies. In general, it has been inspired by the work on query optimization in database systems, which similarly discusses transformation rules, heuristic-based optimization and cost-based optimization for distributed execution. In essence, this work applies these techniques to the domain-specific tree-structured policy model described in Section 4. For an overview of this large body of work, we refer to [20]. Specifically in the domain of policy-based access control, several other authors have also focused on the problem of policy decomposition and distribution. Bauer et al. [21] describe a distributed system for constructing formal proofs, aimed at access control. Amongst others, they also briefly discuss tactics to take into account confidentiality of input data and to improve performance based on the location of the input data. This work extends and applies the general principles discussed in their work on practical policy trees to achieve an algorithm for policy federation. Ardagna et al. [16] focus on controlled disclosure of sensitive access control policies and also discuss policy decomposition and transformation rules. However, their goal is to provide a limited view on sensitive policies. Therefore, their approach does not maintain policy equivalence and does not directly apply to our goal. Finally, the work of Lin et al. [22] sketches a theoretical framework for policy decomposition and distribution based on performance and confidentiality requirements. Their goal is similar to ours and their work has been an important influence. However, they describe a theoretical approach based on a simplified policy model, limiting applicability. Thus, this work extends theirs with a more widely-applicable policy model, a description of supporting middleware and a real-life evaluation.

Several other authors have also investigated the problem of confidentiality-aware access control for outsourced applications and other solutions exist. For example, Asghar et al. [23] employ attribute and policy encryption, extending the work of di Vimercati et al., e.g., [24]. This approach is dual to policy federation and should allow all tenant data to be securely shared with the provider, but also introduces performance overhead and is still limited in policy expressivity, for example only being able to compare attributes with literal values.

Finally, this work fits in a growing collection of performance-enhancing tactics for policy-based and attribute-based access control. This work builds upon the idea of improving policy evaluation performance by focusing on attribute fetching, as first introduced by Brucker and Petritsch [25]. Policy federation can be complemented with the work of several other authors, e.g., Wei et al. [26], who focus on decision caching and Gheorghe et al. [27], who focus on infrastructure reconfiguration for optimal attribute retrieval and cross-request attribute caching.

9   Conclusions

In this paper we described access control for SaaS applications and focused on the challenges of confidentiality-aware and efficient policy evaluation, as motivated by an e-health case study. We proposed to address these challenges by decomposing and distributing the tenant-specific policies across tenant and provider in order to keep sensitive tenant data local while evaluating parts of the policies near the data they require as much as possible. This process, we call *policy federation*. We defined a widely-applicable attribute-based policy model, described an algorithm for policy federation in detail and elaborated on the design of supporting technology. Our approach succeeds in keeping the sensitive tenant data confidential and has the ability to improve policy evaluation time as well. This work fits in a growing collection of performance techniques for policy-based and attribute-based access control. With the maturation of these technologies and the growing ecosystem of service-oriented business coalitions, we believe that the need for federated access control and for policy federation in particular will only grow.

Endnotes

[a] We first discussed this concept in [28].

[b] For this, we randomly constructed an artificial policy tree of five levels, each composed policy having a branching factor of three and each policy requiring five random attributes.

Abbreviations

ABAC: Attribute-based access control; HPMS: Home patient monitoring system; PAP: Policy administration point; PDP: policy decision point; PEP: Policy enforcement point; PIP: Policy information point; RPDP: Remote policy decision point.

Competing interests

The authors declare that they have no competing interests.

Authors' contributions

MD carried out the definition of the policy model and the implementation of the prototype. MD and BL collaboratively carried out the design of the policy federation algorithm and the performance evaluation. MD, BL and WJ collaboratively carried out the case study analysis and the the the conceptual and architectural design of our solution. All authors read and approved the final manuscript.

Acknowledgements

This research is partially funded by the Research Fund KU Leuven, by the EU FP7 project NESSoS and by the Agency for Innovation by Science and Technology in Flanders (IWT). With the financial support from the Prevention of and Fight against Crime Programme of the European Union (B-CCENTRE).

References

1.   Mell P, Grance T (2009) The NIST definition of cloud computing. Natl Ins Standards Tech 53(6): 50
2.   Centralizing Information on a Global Scale: Cisco Deploys Salesforce to 15,000 Users with Siebel Integration and PRM Capabilities. http://www.salesforce.com/uk/customers/hi-tech-hardware/cisco.jsp (2009)
3.   E-Health Information Platforms (E-HIP). http://distrinet.cs.kuleuven.be/research/projects/E-HIP (December 2013)
4.   Healthcare professional's collaboration Space (Share4Health). http://distrinet.cs.kuleuven.be/research/projects/Share4Health (December 2013)

5. Security Assertion Markup Language (SAML) v2.0. http://www.oasis-open.org/standards#samlv2.0 (March 2005)

6. OpenID Authentication 2.0 - Final. http://openid.net/specs/openid-authentication-2_0.html (December 2013)

7. U. S. Department of Health and Human Services (1996) Health insurance portability and accountability act (HIPAA). Retrieved from http://www.hhs.gov/ocr/privacy/hipaa/understanding/index.html

8. European Commision (1995) Directive 95/46/EC of the European Parliament and of the Council of 24 October 1995 on the protection of individuals with regard to the processing of personal data and on the free movement of such data. Retrieved from http://old.cdt.org/privacy/eudirective/EU_Directive_.html

9. Latham D (1985) Department of Defense Trusted Computer System Evaluation Criteria. Tech. rep., US Department of Defense

10. Ferraiolo DF, Sandhu R, Gavrila S, Kuhn DR, Chandramouli R (2001) Proposed NIST standard for role-based access control. ACM Trans Inf Syst Secur 4(3): 224–274. http://doi.acm.org/10.1145/501978.501980

11. Jin X, Krishnan R, Sandhu R (2012) A unified attribute-based access controls model covering DAC, MAC and RBAC. In: Data and applications security and privacy XXVI. Springer, Berlin, Heidelberg, pp 41–55. http://dx.doi.org/10.1007/978-3-642-31540-4_4

12. Moses T (2005) eXtensible Access Control Markup Language (XACML) Version 2.0. OASIS Standard. https://www.oasis-open.org/committees/tc_home.php?wg_abbrev=xacml

13. Maarten Decat - Policy Federation. https://distrinet.cs.kuleuven.be/software/policy-federation/

14. Decat M, Lagaisse B, Van Landuyt D, Crispo B, Joosen W (2013) Federated authorization for software-as-a-service applications. In: On the move to meaningful internet systems: OTM 2013 Conferences. Springer, Berlin, Heidelberg, pp 342–359

15. Crampton J, Huth M (2010) An authorization framework resilient to policy evaluation failures. In: Proceedings of the 15th European Conference on Research in Computer Security. Springer-Verlag, Berlin, Heidelberg, pp 472–487. http://dx.doi.org/10.1007/978-3-642-15497-3_29

16. Ardagna C, Capitani di Vimercati S, Foresti S, Neven G, Paraboschi S, Preiss FS, Samarati P, Verdicchio M (2010) Fine-grained disclosure of access policies. In: Soriano M, Qing S, Lopez J (eds) Information and communications security. lecture notes in computer science, vol. 6476. Springer, Berlin, Heidelberg, pp 16–30. http://dx.doi.org/10.1007/978-3-642-17650-0_3

17. Decat M, Lagaisse B, Crispo B, Joosen W (2013) Introducing concurrency in policy-based access control. In: Proceedings of the 8th workshop on middleware for next generation internet computing. ACM, New York, pp 3:1–3:6

18. Liu AX, Chen F, Hwang J, Xie T (2008) Xengine: a fast and scalable xacml policy evaluation engine In: Proceedings of the 2008 ACM SIGMETRICS. SIGMETRICS '08. ACM, Annapolis, MD, USA, pp 265–276. http://doi.acm.org/10.1145/1375457.1375488

19. Gama P, Ribeiro C, Ferreira P (2006) A scalable history-based policy engine. In: Policies for Distributed Systems and Networks, 2006. Policy 2006. Seventh IEEE International Workshop on. IEEE, pp 100–112. http://doi.ieeecomputersociety.org/10.1109/POLICY.2006.8

20. Elmasri RA, Navathe SB (1999) Fundamentals of database systems, 3rd edn. Addison-Wesley Longman Publishing Co., Inc., Boston

21. Bauer L, Garriss S, Reiter M (2005) Distributed proving in access-control systems. In: Security and Privacy, 2005 IEEE Symposium on. IEEE Computer Society, Los Alamitos, pp 81–95

22. Lin D, Rao P, Bertino E, Li N, Lobo J (2008) Policy decomposition for collaborative access control. In: Proceedings of the 13th ACM SACMAT. ACM, New York, pp 103–112

23. Asghar M, Ion M, Russello G, Crispo B (2011) Espoon: Enforcing encrypted security policies in outsourced environments. In: Availability, Reliability and Security (ARES), 2011 Sixth International Conference on. IEEE Computer Society, Los Alamitos, pp 99–108

24. di Vimercati SDC, Foresti S, Jajodia S, Paraboschi S, Samarati P (2007) A data outsourcing architecture combining cryptography and access control. In: Proceedings of the 2007 ACM workshop on computer security architecture, CSAW '07. ACM, Fairfax, Virginia, USA, pp 63–69. http://doi.acm.org/10.1145/1314466.1314477

25. Brucker A, Petritsch H (2010) Idea: efficient evaluation of access control constraints. In: Engineering Secure Software and Systems. Springer, pp 157–165. http://dx.doi.org/10.1007/978-3-642-11747-3_12

26. Wei Q (2009) Towards improving the availability and performance of enterprise authorization systems. Ph.D. thesis, University of British Columbia

27. Gheorghe G, Crispo B, Carbone R, Desmet L, Joosen W (2011) Deploy, adjust and readjust: Supporting dynamic reconfiguration of policy enforcement 7049: 350–369. http://dx.doi.org/10.1007/978-3-642-25821-3_18

28. Decat M, Lagaisse B, Joosen W (2012) Toward efficient and confidentiality-aware federation of access control policies. In: Proceedings of the 7th Workshop on Middleware for Next Generation Internet Computing. ACM, Montreal, Quebec, Canada, pp 4:1–4:6. http://doi.acm.org/10.1145/2405178.2405182

eContractual choreography-language properties towards cross-organizational business collaboration

Alex Norta[1*], Lixin Ma[1,3], Yucong Duan[2], Addi Rull[1], Merit Kõlvart[1] and Kuldar Taveter[1]

Abstract

Meaningfully automating sociotechnical business collaboration promises efficiency-, effectiveness-, and quality increases for realizing next-generation decentralized autonomous organizations. For automating business-process aware cross-organizational operations, the development of existing choreography languages is technology driven and focuses less on sociotechnical suitability and expressiveness concepts and properties that recognize the interaction between people in organizations and technology in workplaces. This gap our suitability- and expressiveness exploration fills by means of a cross-organizational collaboration ontology that we map as a proof-of-concept evaluation to the eSourcing Markup Language (eSML). The latter we test in a feasibility case study to meaningfully support the automation of business collaboration. The developed eSourcing ontology and eSML is replicable for exploring strengths and weaknesses of other choreography languages.

Keywords: Smart contracting; Choreography; eSourcing; Suitability; Expressiveness; Cross-organizational; B2B; Business process; Sociotechnical; Decentralized autonomous organizations

1 Introduction

With the emergence of new automation paradigms such as service-oriented computing (SOC) and cloud computing (CC), the way companies collaborate with each other experiences significant changes. SOC [1] comprises the creation of automation logic in the form of web services. In CC [2], access to web-based applications, web services, and IT infrastructure as a service happens through the Internet. Web services [3] are an important vehicle for enabling organizations to cooperate with each other by cross-organizationally linking business processes [4-7] with choreography languages for the purpose of electronic outsourcing. More recently, a trend-reinforcement occurs with so-called decentralized autonomous organizations and -corporations that are powered by smart contracts [8,9] to form agreements with people via the block chain [10]. The ontological concepts and properties for the design of smart-contracting systems [11] we derive from legal principles, economic theory, and theories of reliable and secure protocols. The smart contract itself is a computerized transaction protocol [12] that executes the terms of a contract. The blockchain is a distributed database for independently verifying the chain of ownership of artefacts in hash values that result from cryptographic digests [13].

With respect to existing choreography languages, the most notable are versions of the Business Process Execution Language such as AbstractBPEL [14] and BPEL4Chor [15], Web Services Choreography Description Language (WS-CDL) [16], Business Process Modeling Notation (BPMN) [17,18] Let's Dance [19], ebXML BPSS [20] and more recently, the Business Choreography Language (BCL) [21]. However, not only existing choreography languages but also other XML-based languages for SOC lack adoption by industry. A reason is the approach for language development that does not take into account sociotechnical suitability and expressiveness deficiencies that recognizes the interaction between people in organizations and technology in workplaces. Sociotechnical systems comprise theory about the social aspects of people and society and technical aspects of organizational

---
*Correspondence: alex.norta.phd@ieee.org
[1]Tallinn University of Technology, Akadeemia Tee 15A, 12618 Tallinn, Estonia
Full list of author information is available at the end of the article

structure and processes. Suitability means that choreography languages comprise concepts and properties to allow the formulation of real-world business-collaboration scenarios in many perspectives. Expressiveness means the constructs of a choreography language have semantic clarity for ensuring uniform enactment behaviour by different business process engines. Additionally, contractual agreements are the foundation of business collaboration. This paper fills the gap by answering the research question how to systematically develop a language for cross-organizational and contract-based collaboration specifications. From there we deduce several sub-questions. What is the collaboration context and model the specification language must cater for? What are the main suitability- and expressiveness concepts and -properties? The means to answer the research questions are first, a so-called eSourcing ontology [22] that comprises the concepts and properties we generate from the suitability and expressiveness study. The eSourcing ontology development with the tool Protégé [23] allows for an application of the HermiT OWL reasoner [24] to check for the ontology consistency, identify subsumption relationships between classes, and so on. Secondly, as a means of feasibility evaluation, the eSourcing ontology we translate into the eSourcing Markup Language eSML for which we give the schema definition [25] and additional documentation online. The core difference in the approach to developing eSML is the existence of process views [4] for respective collaborating organizations for establishing a contractual consensus during the collaboration-setup phase. These process views are subsets of larger in-house processes of which extensions remain opaque to the counterparty to protect privacy, business secrets, and so on.

The objective is to enable contractual flexibility as significant changes in integral business processes must be enabled by a high degree of automation. Traditionally, if something will happen in the future, then a contract must include rules that regulate these particular instances. Usually, most of regulation is unnecessary since presupposed events never occur. Therefore, automation requires taking a deductive approach towards contracting by exploring relevant concepts with a focus on the basic contractual elements only. It is sufficient to determine only the concepts and properties without which a transaction cannot be executed [26]. In general, basic contractual elements comprise of parties, offer, acceptance, rights and obligations. Furthermore, the reduction of contractual elements helps to overcome difficult legal issues such as what law to apply, the legal context, how to determine rights and obligations. The common source of reference to the basic contractual elements is not any national law, but lex mercatoria [27] and supranational model rules, e.g., PECL[a], PICC[b], DCFR[c], CISG[d], Incoterms[e].

The structure of the paper follows the design-science method [28,29] for the development of eSML and is as follows. Section 2 presents a business-collaboration model that evolves from case studies in the research project called CrossWork [30,31], namely eSourcing [4,7,32,33]. In Section 3, we further explore the collaboration model in a pattern-based way [32] with the objective of generating the essential concepts for eSML to gain business-collaboration suitability. Next, assuming the control-flow perspective is dominant for enacting business collaborations, we present in Section 4 the expressiveness-assurance in eSML. Section 5 presents in a feasibility evaluation the resulting structure of eSML and shows examples, followed by discussing a "proof-of-construction" application system. Section 6 gives related work and finally, Section 7 concludes this paper and discusses future work.

2 Business collaboration model

In the EU research project CrossWork [30,31], observing business collaborations of industry partners reveals characteristic features. An original equipment manufacturer (OEM) develops value chains in an in-house business process according to different perspectives, e.g., control flow of tasks, information flow, personnel management, allocation of production resources, and so on. The CrossWork case studies [31] reveal that the basis for business collaboration between organizations are contracts. The basis has implications for the suitability exploration in the sequel. Next, Section 2.1 explains the orthogonal collaboration dimensions of client/server versus peer-to-peer (P2P). Section 2.2 discusses the structural properties of the client/server collaboration model. Finally, Section 2.3 shows how the collaboration model with the same structural properties also enables P2P-collaboration when the roles of the collaboration-elements change.

2.1 Collaboration dimensions

Figure 1 conceptually depicts conceptually a complex collaboration scenario of an OEM with suppliers. The reasons for acquiring services externally are manifold, e.g., the OEM can not produce with the same quality, or an equally low price per piece, the production capacity is not available, required special know-how is lacking, and so on.

The horizontal ellipses in Figure 1 denote the client/server-integration of outsourced in-house process parts to lower-level clients who provide services to the vertically adjacent higher tier of a supply chain [32]. The outsourced business processes are refined with additional process steps by the respective suppliers. The refinements remain opaque to the service consumer and the supplier only has awareness of the OEM's outsourced respective process but the remaining in-house process remains

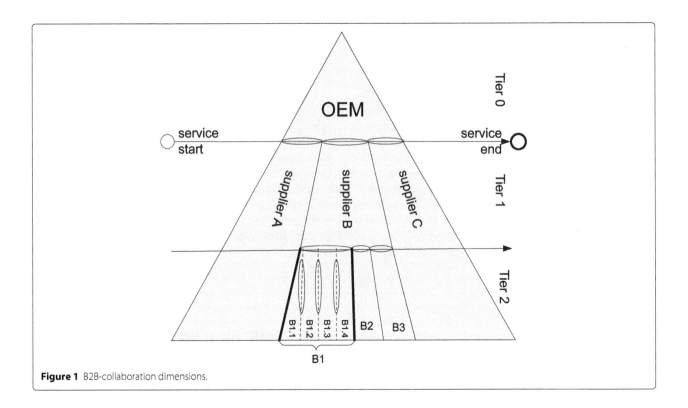

Figure 1 B2B-collaboration dimensions.

opaque. For client/server-integration, several projects investigate enterprise interoperability [34-36].

Vertical ellipses in Figure 1, depict a P2P-collaboration within a cluster of small and medium sized enterprises (SME). If several SMEs form a composed service in a P2P way [37], they together turn into a supplier for a higher-level service consumer. In this paper, we consider the vertical collaboration between organizations by the means of service choreography for the subsequent suitability and expressiveness exploration.

2.2 Client/server-collaboration model

As an explanation of vertical business collaboration, Figure 2 depicts a three-level model as part of an eSourcing example [4,7,32]. The three-level model is instrumental for not forcing collaborating parties into connecting their information infrastructures directly. The processes in Figure 2 depict the control-flow perspective of the eSourcing concept that focuses on structurally harmonizing on an external level the intra-organizational business processes of a service consuming and one or many service providing organizations into a business collaboration. Important elements of eSourcing are the support of different visibility levels of corporate process details for the collaborating counterparts and flexible mechanisms for service monitoring and information exchange. Recently, leading IT-enterprises launched eSourcing [38] application systems [39,40] to enable business collaboration and

in [33] we evaluate these systems against the eSourcing Reference Architecture eSRA.

The very top and bottom of Figure 2, show the internal levels of the service consumer and -provider respectively where processes are directly enactable by legacy systems, which caters towards a heterogeneous system environment, e.g., by workflow management systems. Furthermore, processes of the OEM and service providers on a conceptual level are independent from infrastructure and collaboration specifics. In the center of Figure 2, the external level stretches across the respective domains of eSourcing parties where structural process matching takes place and for which eSML is applicable. Either collaborating counterparties project only interfaces, or parts, or all of the respective conceptual-level processes to the external level for performing business-process matching [4,7]. A contractual consensus between collaborating parties comes into existence when the projected processes are matched externally, i.e., when they are equal. Not projected process parts remain opaque to the collaborating counterparts.

More recently, research in [4] demonstrates with BPMN and BPEL the feasibility of this approach with industry standards. The eSourcing model in Figure 2 shows we use Petri-net formalism for exploring structural properties [7]. The dashed monitoring arcs [32] in Figure 2 connect the conceptual business processes via the external level into a configuration. In Section 4, we expand on the structural properties of eSourcing configurations.

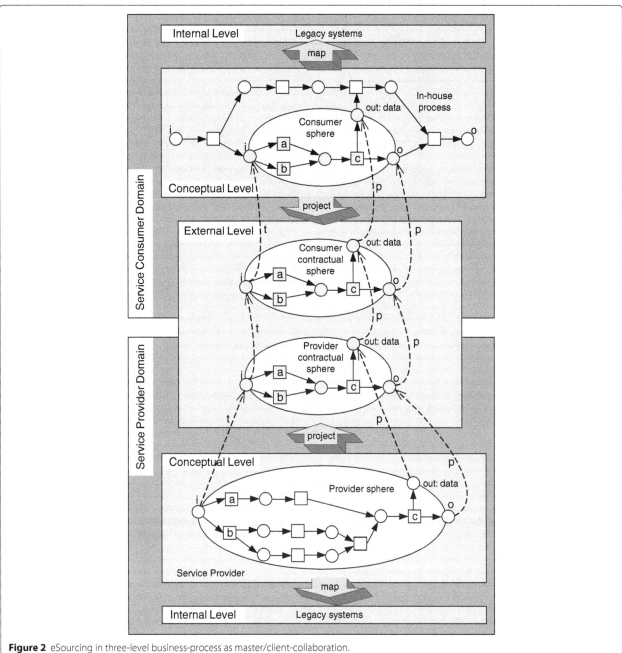

Figure 2 eSourcing in three-level business-process as master/client-collaboration.

2.3 P2P-collaboration model

With the same structural properties as explained above related to Figure 2, also P2P-collaboration are possible when the roles of the collaboration-model elements change. Figure 3 depicts these changed roles conceptually.

In comparison to the master/client-collaboration of Figure 2, the in-house process of a service consumer is a so-called business-network model (BNM) [41] in the P2P-case. A BNM captures choreographies that are relevant for a business scenario. A BNM contains legally valid template contracts that are service types with assigned roles. Together with the BNM, the service types with their roles are available in a collaboration hub that houses business processes as a service (BPaaS-HUB) [42] in the form of subset process views [4]. The latter addresses the need to semi-automatically find collaboration parties and learn about their identity, services, and reputation. A BPaaS-HUB enables speedy business-partner discovery and support for on-the-fly background checking with a matching of services.

On the external layer of Figure 2, now service offers match with service types from the BNM identically to

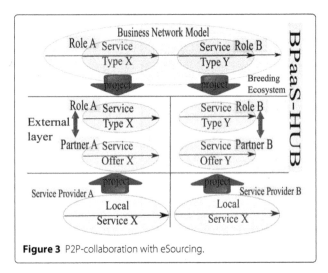

Figure 3 P2P-collaboration with eSourcing.

the contractual sphere of collaborating parties in Figure 2. Additionally, a collaborating partner must match into the role specifics associated with a respective service type. The matching must follow the same structural rules as expressed in Section 2. Likewise, the local services of the service providers in Figure 2 are behavioural sub-classes to their corresponding service offers the same way as the provider's contractual sphere relates to the provider sphere. In the sequel, we discuss the structural properties such collaboration configurations must adhere to.

Next, we explore the required set of concepts and properties for specifying a contractual electronic choreography-specification language.

3 Ontological suitability exploration

There are two angles for approaching the suitability exploration. First, in Section 3.1 we explore cross-organizational collaboration from the paradigm that contracts are the foundation. This is the differentiating approach to choreography development that we ontologically explore by generating the HermiT-OWL reasoner [43] checked eSourcing ontology first that we translate as a means of feasibility evaluation into eSML secondarily. For downloading, we provide links in Section 1. In Section 3.2, a pattern-based exploration further details the contractual collaboration paradigm that are again input for the eSourcing ontology- and eSML development.

3.1 eContract-based exploration

For ensuring that the eSourcing ontology and the subsequently deduced eSML comprises sociotechnial concepts to allow the formulation of real-world business-collaboration in relevant perspectives like control-flow, data-flow, resources and so on, the case-study findings culminating in the eSourcing model of Figure 2, require more exploration. Taking pre-existing work about

contract automation [44] into account, we extend the set of concepts and properties for the eSourcing ontology and eSML to achieve suitability in accordance with Section 2 where we deduce features from the business collaboration model.

The eSourcing ontology we base on a smart contracting foundation [9] namely the XML-based language ECML (*Electronic Contracting Markup Language*) [44]. Thereby, the latter is also incorporated into eSML that we use for the feasibility evaluation in the sequel. A smart contract is a legally enforceable agreement in which two or more parties commit to certain obligations in return for certain rights [45,46]. Contracts are instruments for organizing business collaborations. Smart contracting aims at using information technologies to significantly improve the efficiency and effectiveness of paper contracting, allowing companies to support newly emerging business paradigms, while still being legally protected.

Although ECML permits business-process definitions, it lacks a clear collaboration-model support as proposed by eSourcing. Inheriting concepts from ECML, at the highest abstraction level, a contract in the eSourcing ontology and eSML answers three conceptual questions i.e., the Who, Where, and What question for which we refer the reader to [44] for further details.

3.1.1 The Who concept

This concept that we depict in Figure 4, legally clearly identifies the contracting parties by including the class party. Parties are actors that have rights and obligations that are listed in the eSourcing configuration. Concerning the relationship cardinalities, it is defined that at least two party specifications must be part of a contract. It is also possible to have more than two parties defined. For example, an original manufacturer can agree with several suppliers to be part of one contract.

In a contract, several third parties termed mediators may optionally be part of an electronic contract. Mediators represented by class mediator participate in the enactment of an eSourcing configuration without statements about rights/obligations. Consequently, mediators do not have to sign the eContract. If their relations definition with the parties is legally binding, the mediators become a party in the same, or in a separate contract that states their rights and obligations. For example, a mediator verifies whether an eSourcing configuration that is part of a contract terminates successfully from a control-flow point of view. In order to safeguard business details from each other, the contracting parties are not allowed to check such correct termination themselves without disclosing their business secrets to each other.

Contracting parties and optional numbers of mediators are in a relationship with several other classes.

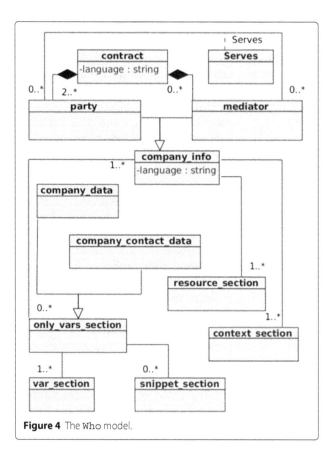

Figure 4 The Who model.

3.1.2 The Where concept

In Figure 5, we distinguish two basic aspects of the electronic contracting context, i.e., the business context and the legal context. Thus, the Where-section comprises two separate parts. In addition, a third subsection optionally references other electronic contracting provisions that are not part of the core legal and business context.

All three classes named `business_context_provisions`, `legal_context_provisions`, and `other_context_provisions` are subclasses of the grouping class named `all_section`. It references the classes `process_section`, `var_section`, `rule_section`, and `snippet_section`.

3.1.3 The What concept

As depicted in Figure 6, the What-model contains concepts related to the exchanged values and their related conditions. Two main subsections of the What-concept are the `exchanged_value` and the corresponding `exchange_provisions` for the value exchange. These classes are defined separately for every respective contractual party involved in contracting.

In a case of product exchange, the product description employs data constructs. In a case of service exchange, the service description combines data-flows and process constructs. The corresponding financial reward for the received value (in non-barter exchanges) uses the same constructs as a service description subsection. The value-exchange provisions subsection requires the use of rule and process-specification constructs. Examples for exchange provisions are rules for determining how late payment needs to be handled, how cancellations are dealt with, or definitions for calculating interest adjustments in payments.

The `company_data` comprises, e.g., the name of a contracting party or mediator, the type of legal organization, and so on. The `company_contact_data` refers to the geographic location of an eSourcing party to uniquely identify according to legal requirements a contracting party, or a mediator.

The class `resource_section` is the root of the resource perspective comprising a contracting `party`, or a `mediator` with optionally attached resource definitions. However, the latter is superfluous unless a mediator is part of commercial exchanges. Resources are actors and non-actors of which the latter is either consumable, or non-consumable.

The classes `company_data` and `company_contact_data` are subclasses of class `only_vars_section` that contains variables and so-called process snippets. The class `var_section` is a connection to the data-flow perspective that includes company description, trade registration number, VAT registration number, address of registration, etc. The class `snippet_section` references so-called contract snippets that are attachable to particular contract definitions, e.g., to attach general terms and conditions. We refer to [25] for details about the resource perspective that is part of the *Who*-concept.

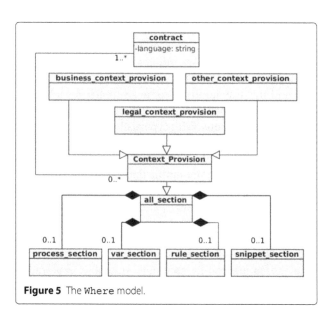

Figure 5 The Where model.

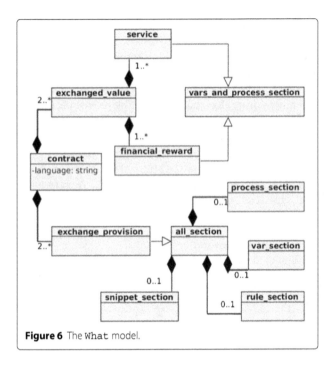

Figure 6 The What model.

The Who-, What-, and Where concepts respectively correspond to the concepts of agents, the knowledge by agents, and the agents' environment respectively. We understand agents as autonomous entities situated in an environment that perceive events occurring in the environment, reason based on knowledge, and act on the basis of perceived events. The concept of agents and related concepts are crucial in negotiating and achieving contracts within sociotechnical systems as contracts can only occur between autonomous entities that should be conceptually understood as agents. We refer to [47] for a detailed discussion.

The concept of agents and related concepts are particularly relevant for the P2P-collaboration model within a cluster of SMEs overviewed in Section 2.3 as SMEs are autonomous entities. According to the P2P-collaboration model, several SMEs form a composed service in a P2P way and this way jointly become a supplier for a higher-level service consumer. The P2P-collaboration model between autonomous SMEs is partially, or fully automated [47] by software agents that negotiate and conclude contracts on behalf of the enterprises. The software agents need the eSML for representing the contracts.

Next, we further explore the suitability features of electronic contracting in using patterns that are conceptual and on the outset technology-agnostic.

3.2 Pattern-based exploration

The chosen method for continued suitability exploration of additional business-collaboration concepts is as follows. To translate the eSourcing model of Figure 2 into a suitable ontology and subsequently, a choreography language, we deduce several feature dimensions in the form of axes that create a multi-dimensional, logical space. On every axis, dimension values detail the eSourcing feature an axis represents. By taking a subset of axes, we create a logical space that represents a particular eSourcing perspective. Consequently, the axes and their contained values serve as a taxonomy for ordering and relating to each other a set of perspective-relevant patterns. Note, we present a high-level overview of the pattern space and refer to [32] for the actual pattern specifications.

The three axes in Figure 7 represent different eSourcing dimensions with values. The created multi-dimensional space is instrumental for deducing eSourcing-construction elements for protecting internal business details, ensuring data exchange that adheres to correct control-flow, and for permitting the service consumer a controlled observation of the service provider's enactment progress. Correspondingly, the axes of the multi-dimensional space of Figure 7, represent the conceptual dimensions called contractual visibility, conjoinment, and monitorability [32]. The first conceptual dimension permits deducing interaction patterns [25] that occur during the setup phase of an electronic business collaboration. The interaction patterns are input for the proof-of-construction prototype we give in Section 5.4. The latter two conceptual dimensions of Figure 7 turn into eSML language constructs in the sequel.

The cube dimensions and values of Figure 7, are as follows. Contractual visibility focuses on the amount of business-process nodes a collaborating party projects to an external level to be visible for the counterparty. First, a *white-box* value means all nodes of a process part to be sourced are externalized. In case of a *black-box* value, only the interfaces of that process part are projected. Finally, the *gray-box* value means, the interfaces and a subset of the nodes and arcs of the externally sourced process part are projected.

Conjoinment focuses on the exchange of business information between the domains of the collaborating parties. Consequently, the business processes within the domains contain equal conjoinment constructs. *One-directional* conjoining implies that there is one *out-*, or *in*-directed information exchange between the domains of a service consumer and provider. *Bi-directional* conjoining is initiated by an *out*-directed information exchange to the domain of the collaborating counterpart who returns the communication exchange immediately to the initiating party.

Monitorability covers the way how nodes in the consumer's and provider's conceptual-level business processes link to each other via constructs with the properties termed *messaging* and *polling*. The nodes of the externalized process part connect to nodes in the corresponding

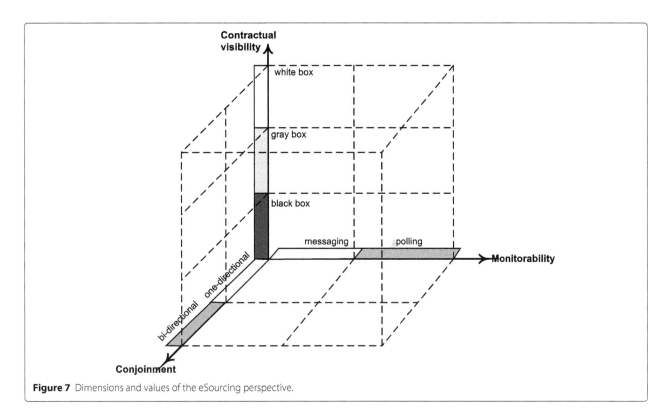

Figure 7 Dimensions and values of the eSourcing perspective.

service-provider process. The degree of monitorability of service provisioning for a service consumer increases by the amount of node linkages. At a minimum, all interface nodes of both domain processes need to be linked with each other. Additional nodes may be linked that belong to the respective business processes of service consumers and service providers. We refer to [32] for detailed pattern specifications and to [25] for collaborating counterparty-interaction patterns during setup.

The remainder of this section shows concepts in models that are instrumental for supporting the logical pattern space.

3.2.1 Data-package model
In an eSourcing configuration, a contract defines variables and documents that are relevant for enactment. Figure 8 shows entities for integrating such data into an eSourcing configuration. A `contract` references a `data_definition_section` that in return references one or several `data_package` instances. These data packages optionally contain a set of variables and documents.

It must be possible to reference data by other electronic contracting elements. It is essential for safeguarding that data have specific types to allow for assured contract processing. Data types set basic constraints on the allowed values for a data element. Two classes of required data types we identify, namely standard- and special data types.

The identified data types we adopt from ECML and in [44] further details and examples can be found.

3.2.2 Process model
In Figure 9, the process model contains classes that belong to the control-flow perspective. A `process_section` may contain no or multiple process definitions. A process is a type of route, which is the root class for a process definition. All remaining classes of the `process_section` in [25] are part of the eSourcing perspective. The majority of those classes are for defining and mapping the life-cycles of service consumer- and provider processes that are involved in an eSourcing configuration.

The class `life_cycle_definition` is optionally multiple times part of `process_section` and

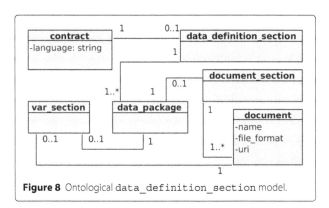

Figure 8 Ontological `data_definition_section` model.

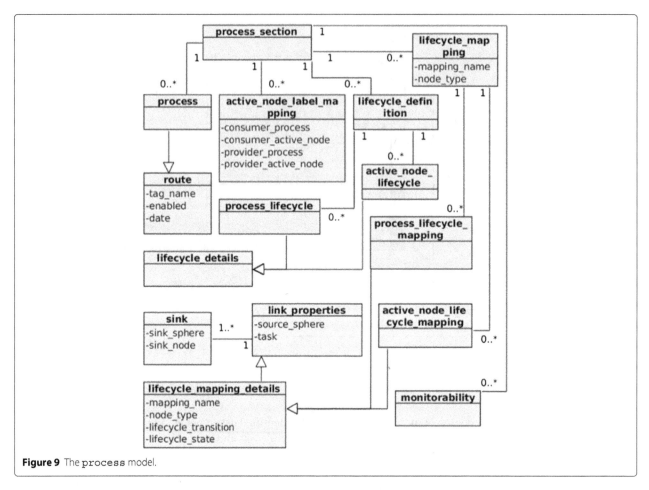

Figure 9 The process model.

instrumental for defining life-cycle stages of entire processes, or merely active nodes that are part of respective processes. Such definitions are part of consumer- and provider processes. The classes `process_lifecycle` and `active_node_lifecycle` are subclasses of `lifecycle_details`. The latter class is part of the eSourcing perspective that we explain in the sequel.

After specifying the lifecycles of respective processes and their contained active nodes, labels that express equal tasks have different expressions. Thus, class `active_node_label_mapping` is instrumental to define such semantic equivalence that is important for verifying projection inheritance of a consumer sphere and the refinement sphere of a service provider. Class `lifecycle_mapping` allows to map life-cycle stages of different processes and active nodes belonging to the domains of a service consumer and -provider. The mapping expresses such labels with different names are semantically equal.

3.2.3 Lifecycle-definition model
The model about different types of life-cycle elements in Figure 10 is an adjacent sub-model to `route` [25] with an associated class `lifecycle_details`.

The classes of Figure 10 define the lifecycles of processes and active nodes that are part of an eSourcing configuration. Accordingly, Figure 10 depicts that `lifecycle_details` is a subclass of `lifecycle_elements`.

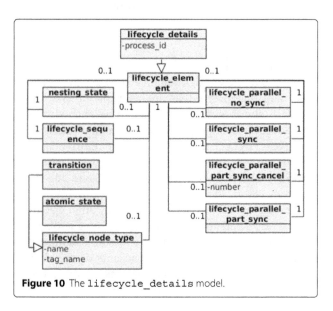

Figure 10 The `lifecycle_details` model.

There exists a mutual reference between class `lifecycle_elements` and the extracted lifecycle control-flow classes. Concretely, states are either of the type `nesting_state`, or `atomic_state`. For the first class, on a lower level of a nesting state, further lifecycle elements exist, including another instance of `nesting_state`. On the other hand, class `atomic_state` is not further refinable on a lower level. Finally, transitions propel the lifecycle of a process, or active node from one state to the next.

3.2.4 Monitorability model

The classes in Figure 11 are part of the monitorability dimension of the eSourcing perspective to link active- and passive nodes that belong to the respective contractual spheres of a service consumer and -provider. On a process level, nodes are only active, i.e., task, transition, send task, receive task, send transition, receive transition, bi-directional task, and bi-directional transition. The only

two cases of passive nodes exist on a life-cycle level of tasks where nested states and atomic states exist.

By defining monitoring links between nodes of respective eSourcing domains, it is possible for one contracting party to observe the progress of process enactment of the eSourcing counterpart. Usually the monitoring direction is from service consumer to provider. However, it is also possible that monitorability constructs of different directions are used in a P2P-collaboration.

The monitorability classes of Figure 11 fall into the categories polling-, or messaging constructs. In polling, the consumer frequently requests the status of the linked node in the domain of the service provider. Upon perceived enactment change, the linked node in the domain of the service consumer follows the change. Polling an active node with a life-cycle follows a mirroring of state changes, or transition firings. Polling a transition on a process level returns information about the firing of a linked node. The class `enactment_propagation` is for signalling the enactment of an eSourcing sphere starts in the domain

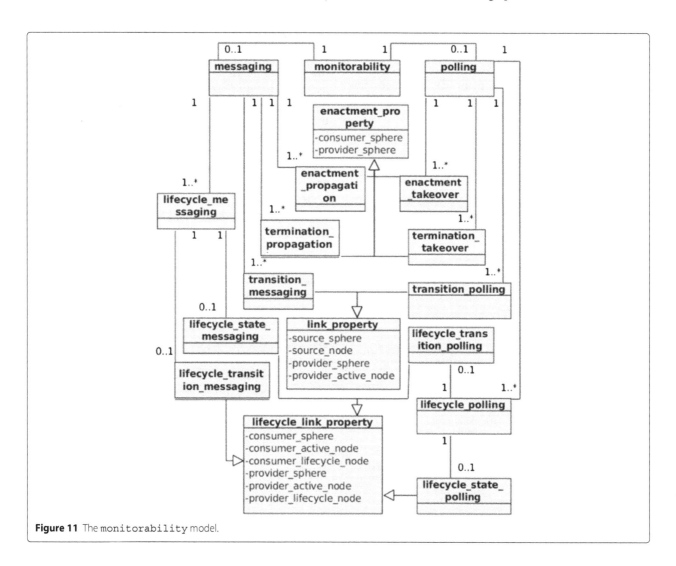

Figure 11 The monitorability model.

of the service consumer. This enactment commencement propagates to the service provider. Messaging classes link nodes from the process enacting domain to the observing counterparty. Thus, for linking two transitions in opposing eSourcing domains, the firing message triggers behaviour mirroring by the linked node. For linked tasks, lifecycle-state and -transition changes are events the task in the counterparty domain follows. Finally, class `enactment_termination` is for polling the completion of a service provision, which the service consumer mirrors so that the remainder of the consumer's in-house process commences with enactment.

3.2.5 Transition-type model

In Figure 12, class `transition_type` is central for all active nodes belonging to the control-flow perspective and the conjoinment dimension of the eSourcing perspective. We refer to [25] for full details. As Figure 12 shows, class `transition_type` is also a central connection to the workflow-data perspective. The class `lock_type` is initially set for a data package, which the `lock_change` tag changes. The `common_var_attributes` contains properties for all simple and complex variables.

The class named `data` in Figure 12 is central for the workflow-data perspective. An instance of `data` optionally references one or many data-packages that contain different variables and/or document definitions.

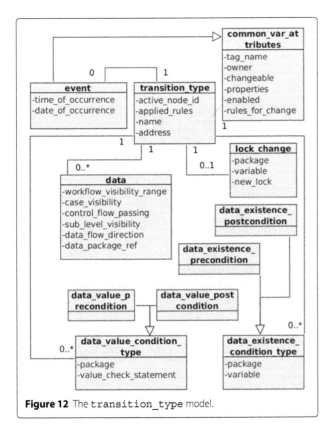

Figure 12 The `transition_type` model.

If `workflow_visibility_range` in `data` is true, a package is visible in all cases of a process template for all active nodes contained. If `case_visibility` is true, a data package is visible for all cases.

The `data_flow_direction` specifies the passing of data elements from a block-task instance to the corresponding sub-workflow that defines its implementation. When no further explicit assignment definition exists, no data passing happens since data has a global status. Thus, all lower-level elements are automatically aware of the data package. If additional assignment tags exist then edata passing uses either a dedicated data channel, or an integrated control- and data channel, i.e., in the latter case data flows along control flow.

The property `control_flow_passing` is instrumental for supporting `data_flow_direction`. Upon defining `data_types` on a block level, setting `control_flow_passing` to true implies the use of an integrated control- and data channel. As a result, data flows from one node to the next along control flow.

By using `sub_level_visibility` in combination with a `data_package_ref` definition for a control-flow block element, we specify to which lower-level degree the `data_package_ref` is visible. For example, if a block has 5 lower levels of routing elements and level 4 we define in a `sub_level_visibility` tag then elements located on the lowest level do not have visibility of the data package, i.e., the 5th level below the definition level of the specific data package.

In Figure 12, `transition_type` references other classes that are part of the workflow-data perspective. The reference `data_existence_precondition` is to check the presence of a variable as a prerequisite for the enactment of an active node and `data_existence_postcondition` defines the presence of a variable as a postcondition that must hold after the completed enactment of an active node. The superclass `data_existence_condition_type` comprises properties for defining which variable in a package must exist.

Finally, the classes `data_value_precondition` and `data_value_postcondition` define pre- and postconditions for the enactment of active nodes. However, differently to the case above where variable existence is the criteria, here the variables must have a particular value. Therefore, the superclass `data_value_condition_type` contains a property for checking the value of a variable.

3.2.6 Data model

The classes in Figure 13 support further data-flow models and belong exclusively to the data-flow perspective. The central class is `data` that is replicated in the routing

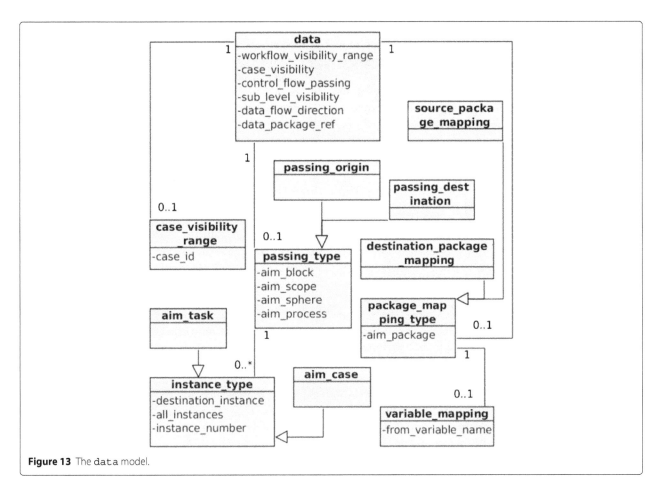

Figure 13 The data model.

models of [25] and Figure 12 to denote a connection between the respective models.

With `case_visibility_range`, we specify the set of cases where a data package is equally visible. Class `passing_destination` supports passing data packages between tasks. Class `passing_destination` is instrumental for two different scenarios. When `data_type` definition is on a block level, then explicit data passing from a block level to a contained lower-level element happens with specification `passing_destination`. Furthermore, a `passing_destination` specification assigns task-level data packages explicitly to the higher level, e.g., a block. Instead of passing a data package per se, `destination_package_mapping` and `source_package_mapping` map parts of a data package in one process node onto properties of another data package at some other location.

In Figure 13, `passing_type` is a superclass of `passing_origin` and `passing_destination`. Thus, depending on the visibility level for destination passing, the properties in `passing_type` are for setting detailed definitions in the subclasses `passing_origin` and `passing_destination`. Identifying the

referenced classes `aim_task` and `aim_case` gives several options. For example, several instances of a task exist within a case, or an eSourcing configuration is equally instantiated several times. Thus, the superclass `instance_type` identifies data visibility for either all instances, or a subset of either tasks, or cases.

Finally, class `package_mapping_type` in Figure 13 serves as a superclass of `destination_package_mapping` and `source_package_mapping`. The superclass contains a property for targeting a data package for mapping variables onto another package. During that mapping, a transformation function is available that employs `package_mapping_type` references class `variable_mapping`. Next, we address semantic expressiveness assurance of electronic contracting.

4 Expressiveness exploration

The eSourcing example in Figure 2 uses labelled Petri nets [48,49]. The special type of Petri nets used for the conceptual levels of resourced, namely workflow nets (WF-nets) [50], has one unique passive input node and one unique passive output node. Furthermore, all other active and passive nodes in a WF-net contribute to its processing. WF-nets carry the property of *soundness* [51,52], which informally states after the completion of a net, only one token must remain in the unique passive output node and all other passive nodes must be empty. WF-nets present an opportunity to verify the soundness before enactment of an overall process for ensuring a smooth enactment, e.g. with the powerful tool Woflan [53].

Starting with the domain of the service consumer in Figure 2, an in-house process shows on the conceptual level a WF-net. The in-house process contains a subnet termed a consumer sphere that is visualized with a grey ellipse. On the border of the consumer sphere, labelled passive nodes are interface places. Only one interface place is *i*-labelled and only one is *o*-labelled. The other interface places are either *in* or *out*-labelled to denote an exchange direction of business-critical information between the in-house process and its contained consumer sphere. Furthermore, the labelling implies whether an interface place has an input arc or an output arc in the sphere. If an interface place is *i*-, or *in*-labelled, it has one output arc to an active node in the sphere. If an interface place is *o*-, or *out*-labelled, it has one input arc from an active node in the sphere.

The in-house process is mapped to the internal level of Figure 2 onto legacy systems. A service provider enacts the consumer sphere and therefore projected to the external level to become the consumer contractual sphere. From the opposite eSourcing domain a, complementary provider contractual sphere is projected to the external level. Since the respective contractual spheres in Figure 2 are isomorph, a consensus is given between the eSourcing parties, which is the prerequisite for a contract [54].

The provider contractual sphere is complemented by a provider sphere on the conceptual level. Compared to the provider contractual sphere, additional nodes refine the provider sphere. In Figure 2, such refinement we depict by unlabelled active nodes in the provider sphere that do not exist in the provider contractual sphere. Hence, the refinement remains opaque for the collaborating counterpart. If the isomorph external-level processes are connected graphs, the refinement must be in accordance with *projection inheritance* [55] that is informally defined as follows. If it is not possible to distinguish the behaviours of processes x and y when executing arbitrary active nodes of x, but when only the effects of active nodes that are also present in y are considered, then x is a subclass of y. Thus, process x inherits the projection of the process definition y while process x conforms to the dynamic behaviour of its superclass by *hiding* active nodes new in x. Furthermore, such processes in an inheritance relation always have the same termination options. Note that Woflan [53] is also instrumental for verifying projection inheritance.

For relating the consumer sphere, the respective contractual spheres, and the provider sphere, the obligatory requirement of *well-directedness* of an eSourcing configuration must be fulfilled. This requirement focusses on the interface places of the spheres, which are part of exchange channels between spheres and the remaining in-house process. An eSourcing configuration is well-directed when the interface places of the consumer sphere, the respective contractual spheres of the service consumer and provider, and the provider sphere are equal in number and labelling.

An eSourcing configuration is formally mapped to so called bilateral workflow nets [7] so that a *collapsing* procedure is applicable for checking the correct termination on an interorganizational level. On the top right side of Figure 2, the in-house process and the provider sphere fulfill the well-directedness requirement. The bottom of Figure 2 shows the collapsed net with a removed consumer sphere replaced with the provider sphere in the in-house process. As a result, the collapsed net must be a sound WF-net. If the projections to the external level result in isomorph contractual spheres that are connected graphs, the collapsed net must be a subclass net of the consumer in-house process according to projection inheritance. In any case, the overall process resulting from the collapsing procedure of an eSourcing configuration must always terminate correctly, i.e., be a sound WF-net.

Next, we discuss the practical application of the eContracting approach.

5 Feasibility evaluation

For the feasibility study, we translate the concepts and properties of the HermiT-reasoner [43] verified eSourcing ontology into a machine-readable language eSML for which Section 1 comprises footnote hyperlinks to the ontology and the website with the schema definition.

For evaluating eSML, we consider a business case from the automobile industry. Briefly and related to Figure 1, in the automobile industry, OEMs have several tiers of suppliers that agree to deliver systems collaboratively. For example, the OEM assembles cars with systems like a cockpit, or an engine, etc. These systems are manufactured by Tier 1 that gets the components for those systems from a Tier 2 supplier. By applying eSourcing with specifying the inter-organizational collaboration with eSML, we facilitate the complex coordination effort between collaborating parties. In [31], the reader finds further details about the background of the industrial case study for this feasibility evaluation.

For the remainder, Section 5.1 shows the structure of eSML and also gives code examples that stem from a case study with industry. In Section 5.2, we explain an existing system architecture that enables the collaboration of decentralized autonomous organizations in a smart-contracting way that utilizes process views. Next,

Section 5.3 explains the lifecycle for setting up smart contracts based collaborations, including how to let them evolve. Finally, Section 5.4 show the lifecycle of eSML instantiations and enactment.

5.1 eSourcing markup language

We show the high-level structure of the business-collaboration language. As explained earlier, eSML uses parts of the ECML [44] schema as a foundation. Figure 14 reflects this fact by considering an entire eSML instance as a contract between collaborating parties and by structuring the eSML content into the blocks Who, Where, and What, as explained in Section 3. We refer to [25] for more information about ECML the definition of company data and company-contact data and the Where block.

The bold typed eSML-definitions in Figure 14 are extensions and modifications that are not part of the ECML foundation. In the Who block, extensions for eSML are the resource definition and the data definition. In the

What block, the XRL adoption permits the use of control-flow patterns for business-process definitions that have semantic clarity. However, extensions exist for adopting the conjoinment nodes described in Section 3.2 and for linking to the resource- and data-definition sections of eSML that are both based on respective pattern collections [56,57]. The life-cycle definitions [25] are for the business processes and contained tasks.

The life-cycle-mapping block addresses establishing semantic equivalence between, firstly, the life-cycles of the inter-organizationally harmonized business processes, and secondly, for the life-cycles of tasks from the opposing domains. Different labels of tasks belonging to processes of opposing domains may be semantically equal. To establish a semantic equality, the second part of the mapping block focuses on the mapping of task labels in the `active_node_label_mapping` tag. Such mapping is relevant for establishing a contractual consensus between collaborating parties. The monitorability (see Section 3.2) block of Figure 14 specifies how much of the enactment phase the service consumer perceives. Next, we show eSML examples that result from a CrossWork case study [31] and refer to [25] for the full eSML schema, models and more code examples.

5.1.1 Resource-perspective definition

The code extract in Listing 1 is part of the resource definition where an organizational unit is defined as a permanently existing organization. Thus, it is not a unit that dissolves at a certain point in time, e.g., an organization set up for the purpose of managing a project that has a deadline. In Line 11 the name of the organizational unit is defined, followed by the definition of the start date. Organizational units may have a business objective assigned. In the code example of Listing 1 this definition is omitted.

Listing 1 Resource-definition specification example in eSML.

```
10 <permanent_organizational_unit>
11   <name>Procurement_Department</name>
12   <start_date>2005-01-01</start_date>
13   <description/>
14   <business_objectives/>
15   <resource_nref>
16     <resource_type_ref>
17       Department_Head
18     </resource_type_ref>
19     <number>1</number>
20   </resource_nref>
21   <resource_nref>
22     <resource_type_ref>
23       Department_Clerk
24     </resource_type_ref>
25     <number>33</number>
26   </resource_nref>
27   <individual_resource>
28     Actor2
29   </individual_resource>
30 </permanent_organizational_unit>
```

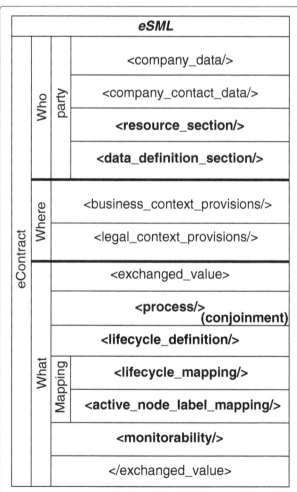

Figure 14 An overview of an eSML instantiation.

The organizational unit has department members that are defined as roles. These roles are separately specified in the resource section of the eSML file. According to Line 19 the procurement department has one head of department. In Line 17, the `Department_Head` is a unique identifier for an separate extensive role definition. Similarly, Lines 22-24 specify that the procurement department has a resource assigned with the role name `Department_Clerk`. In the line below the number of individuals is given that slip into the mentioned role of a clerk. Finally, in Line 28 an individual is directly specified as a procurement-department member with the identifier `Actor2`.

5.1.2 Data-flow definition

The central part of the data-flow definition in an eSML file is a data package. Such data packages flow through a business process and are exchangeable to the opposing organizational domain. Following the data-flow pattern specifications [57], in an eSML instantiation, data has a particular visibility ranging from only a task to all instances of a business process and even its environment; a certain interaction type that focuses on the way data is communicated with, e.g, a data package is communicated from a task to another task; or from a block to a different process instance, and so on. Data has different transfer type specifications, e.g., by a copy, a reference, by value, etc. Finally, a data-flow element interacts with the control-flow perspective, e.g., a pre- or postcondition of data existence for a task, data-value based condition evaluation, etc.

Listing 2 Data-definition specification example in eSML.

```
10 <data_definition_section>
11  <data_package>
12   <package_id>cd</package_id>
13   <var_section>
14    <string_var
15     tag_name="Bill of Material"
16     var_id="BOM"
17     changeable="false"
18     enabled="enabled">
19      Surrounding Box; Gearing
20    </string_var>
21   </var_section>
22   <document_section>
23    <document>
24     <document_id>
25      cadDrawing
26    </document_id>
27     <name>
28      Cad Drawing of complete GearBox
29     </name>
30     <uri>
31      http://www.ve.com/gearBox.3ds
32     </uri>
33    </document>
34   </document_section>
35  </data_package>
36 </data_definition_section>
```

The code extract of Listing 2 specifies a data package with a contained variable and a document section. In Line 14, a variable is specified with its attributes. The bill of material is changeable, i.e., the value may be modified, and it is enabled for use. Additionally, Lines 24-32 define a document that is a CAD drawing and is available at a particular `uri`.

Listing 3 Data-package transfer example in eSML.

```
10 <receive_transition
11  active_node_id="CO"
12  name="Receive_Order">
13  <data>
14   <data_flow_direction>
15    input
16   </data_flow_direction>
17   <data_package_ref>
18    cd
19   </data_package_ref>
20  </data>
21  <data>
22   <data_flow_direction>
23    input
24   </data_flow_direction>
25   <data_package_ref>
26    do
27   </data_package_ref>
28  </data>
29 </receive_transition>
```

Listing 3 is an example of data packages are used with elements in the control-flow of an eSML instantiation. A receive node is specified that receives two data packages from the domain of a collaborating counterpart. In Line 13 the data package with the identifier *cd* is specified as an input. Additionally, in Line 17 the data package with the identifier *id* is equally input to the receiving node.

5.1.3 Structure of process-harmonization definition

The code extract in Listing 4 shows how to harmonize the structure of processes. For every collaborating party an `exchanged_value` section specifies if a service is either provided or consumed, which depends on the role a collaborating party slips into.

Listing 4 Business-process harmonization example comprising several collaborating parties in eSML.

```
10 <exchanged_value>
11   <service>
12   <process_section>
13    <process
14    tag_name="Gearbox_Production"
15    process_id="GB_production">
16     <parallel_sync>
17      <sourcing_sphere>
18       omitted control-flow routing elements
19      </sourcing_sphere>
20      <sourcing_sphere/>
21      <sourcing_sphere/>
22     <parallel_sync/>
23    </process>
24    <lifecycle_definitions/>
25    <lifecycle_mappings/>
26     <active_node_label_mapping/>
```

```
27    <monitorability/>
28    </process_section>
29   </service>
30  </exchanged_value>
```

Several `sourcing_spheres` may be part of a process specification. Lines 17-21 of Listing 4 specify that three sourcing spheres are embedded in a `parallel_sync` construct. Thus, the sourcing spheres are contained in parallel branches of control. The sourcing spheres are matched by spheres in `exchanged_value` sections of the same eSML instantiation that belong to opposing collaborating parties. For the matching, we specify grey-box contractual visibility pattern (see Section 3.2). In its final state where a consensus is specified in an eSML instantiation, the content of opposing sourcing spheres must match in content. In Lines 17-21, we omit control flow code for space limitation. In Lines 24-26, further eSML constructs specify further inter-organizational business process harmonization. The constructs for mapping life-cycles and for monitorability specifications are in the `exchanged_value` section of the service consumer.

5.1.4 Life-cycle definition

In an eSourcing configuration, the heterogeneous system environment of the internal level needs to be inter-organizationally harmonized. The business processes of collaborating parties may have deviating life-cycles on a process and task level. For the enactment phase, it is relevant to specify a synchronization of the life-cycles.

Listing 5 Lifecycle-definition example in eSML.

```
10 <lifecycle_definitions>
11   <process_lifecycle>
12   <lifecycle_sequence>
13     <atomic_state
14     name="VE_process_ready"
15     tag_name="ready"/>
16   <transition
17     name="VE_process_start_enactment"
18     tag_name="start_enactment"/>
19     ....more
20     tag_name="ended"/>
21     </lifecycle_sequence>
22   </process_lifecycle>
23   <active_node_lifecycle/>
24 </lifecycle_definitions>
```

In Listing 5, we shown that life-cycles for a process are specified with control-flow constructs. In Line 13, a not further decomposable atomic state is defined. However in a life-cycle, states are possible that contain further nested states. Accordingly, eSML contains a `nesting_state` construct that comprises lower-level states. The life-cycle of a process or a task is propelled by transitions of which Line 16 shows an example. In Line 23, the `active_node_life-cycle` of a task is defined with the same control-flow constructs for the specification of process life-cycles. We refer the reader to [25] for code

examples about mapping lifecycle definitions between different tasks and processes belonging to separate counterparties.

5.1.5 Mapping definitions

If a heterogeneous system environment with different life-cycles is harmonized in one eSourcing configuration, it may be important for the enactment infrastructure to specify in an eSML instantiation how the respective life-cycles fit together. As the previous case study shows, in an eSourcing configuration several service providers are included with one service consumer. Thus, for life-cycle harmonization it is relevant to include all service providers. The respective life-cycle steps that are specified as equal may have diverting names but are still semantically equivalent. The same holds for the mapping of task labels from the domains of opposing parties.

The code extract below shows how life-cycles are mapped. In Line 11 the mapping of process life-cycles starts with first specifying the life-cycle label of the service consumer. From Line 17 onwards the semantically equivalent labels of two service providers are specified. For every life-cycle step this specification needs to be repeated.

Listing 6 Lifecycle-definition mapping example in eSML.

```
10 <lifecycle_mappings>
11   <process_lifecycle_mapping
12   mapping_name="process_ready"
13   node_type="lifecycle_state">
14   <consumer_sphere>
15    OEM_Sphere1
16   </consumer_sphere>
17   <consumer_active_node>
18    OEM_process_ready
19   </consumer_active_node>
20   <provider>
21   <provider_sphere>
22   Provider_SP1_1
23   </provider_sphere>
24   <provider_active_node>
25   SP1_process_idle
26   </provider_active_node>
27   <provider_sphere>
28   Provider_SP2
29   </provider_sphere>
30   <provider_active_node>
31   SP1_process_idle
32   </provider_active_node>
33   </provider>
34   </process_lifecycle_mapping>
35   <active_node_lifecycle_mapping
36   mapping_name="node_complete"
37   node_type="lifecycle_transition">
38   <consumer_sphere>
39   OEM_Sphere1
40   </consumer_sphere>
41   <consumer_active_node>
42   OEM_active_node_complete
43   </consumer_active_node>
44   <provider>
45   <provider_sphere>
46   Provider_SP1_1
47   </provider_sphere>
```

```
48  <provider_active_node>S
49  P1_active_node_complete
50    </provider_active_node>
51    <provider_sphere>
52  Provider_SP2
53    </provider_sphere>
54    <provider_active_node>
55  SP2_active_node_complete
56      </provider_active_node>
57    </provider>
58  </active_node_lifecycle_mapping>
59  </lifecycle_mappings>
```

For the mapping of task labels, a code extract is given in Listing 7. In Line 11 the specification of a service-consumer task label starts by first naming the process a task is contained in followed by the label of a task. In Line 17 similar specifications are given for the domain of the service provider. Differently to life-cycle mappings, there is always one label of the service consumer that is mapped to a label of one service provider because the concept of eSourcing assumes a task is always serviced by one provider.

Listing 7 Mapping active node labels in eSML.

```
10  <active_node_label_mapping>
11    <consumer_process>
12  GB_production
13    </consumer_process>
14    <consumer_active_node>
15  CO
16    </consumer_active_node>
17    <provider_process>
18  PP_SP1_1
19    </provider_process>
20    <provider_active_node>
21  Local_CO
22    </provider_active_node>
23  </active_node_label_mapping>
```

5.1.6 *Monitorability definition*

The code in Listing 8 is for specifying monitorability links with between the business processes of collaborating parties. The more monitorability patterns are specified, the more enactment progress the service consumer is able to follow. Many monitorability patterns are specified in [32] to cater for differing linking functionalities in a heterogeneous system environment of eSourcing configurations.

Listing 8 Monitorability specification in eSML.

```
10  <monitorability>
11    <polling/>
12    <messaging>
13    <transition_messaging>
14    <consumer_sphere>
15  SP1_Sphere1
16    </consumer_sphere>
17    <consumer_active_node>
18  CO
19    </consumer_active_node>
20    <provider>
21    <provider_sphere>
22  PP_SP1_1
23    </provider_sphere>
```

```
24    <provider_active_node>
25  Local_CO
26    </provider_active_node>
27    </provider>
28    </transition_messaging>
29    <messaging>
30  </monitorability>
```

An example for a monitorability specification is given in Listing 8 with two parts, namely one for the specification of polling constructs and one for specifying messaging constructs. In Lines 13-19, a transition-messaging monitorability construct is defined. First, the transition identifier in the domain of the service consumer represents the target node. In Lines 20-27, the source node for the messaging construct is specified located in the domain of the service provider.

5.2 eContracting architecture

To enable the setup and enactment of process-view based collaboration evolution, a system must meet a set of requirements. First, there must exist a service that facilitates the matching of service offers from collaborating parties and service requests from consuming organizations. Second, the collaborating parties house internally a component for the distributed binding and enactment of emergency cases. Third, with tool support, the parties must rapidly develop service offers and concrete services. Fourth, each collaborating party is capable of orchestrating its own internal legacy system for automating the collaboration. Finally, due to the heterogeneity of the collaboration, a translation service must exist for bridging the differences (technical, syntactic, semantic, pragmatic) between collaborating parties.

The eSourcing Reference Architecture [33] supports these requirements. Figure 15 depicts the resulting architecture in UML-component diagram notation that takes into account the above listed requirements. The *Service-HUB* [42] as a trusted third party service in the middle that satisfies the first requirement and is suitable for the rapid setup phase in an emergency scenario. Each party has on an external layer an *eSourcing_Middleware* for the technical binding after a successful setup that satisfies the second requirement. During the distributed collaboration-enactment, the *eSourcing_Middleware* exchanges data via a security-ensuring gateway with the other parties. Thus, the *eSourcing_Middleware* also comprises external workflow- and rules-enactment services that coordinate each other not only internally but also via the gateway with other parties. We assume there exists in each party a conceptual layer with a service for *Setup_Support* that satisfies the third requirement and comprises tools for not only rapidly internally designing services and rules with the help of pattern libraries [58], but also includes a local verification- and simulation service. Next, each party has an internal layer with a service for *Legacy_Management*

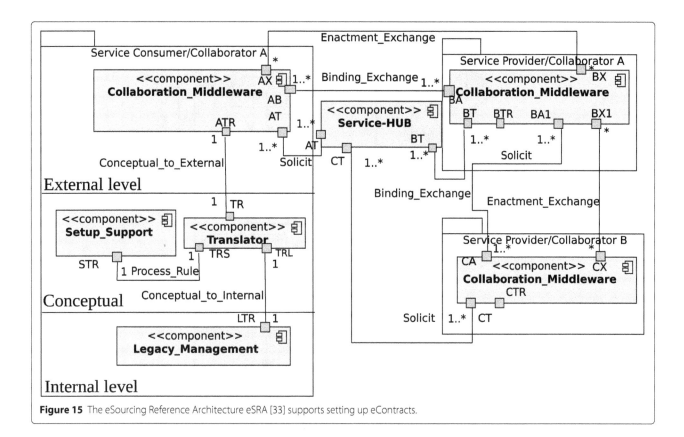

Figure 15 The eSourcing Reference Architecture eSRA [33] supports setting up eContracts.

that satisfies the fourth requirement and comprises local workflow- and rules enactment services that coordinate each other for the orchestration of Web-service wrapped internal legacy systems. Finally, the external- and internal enactment services exchange via a *Translator* service on the conceptual layer of each party to bridge the heterogeneous collaboration aspects. The *Translator* satisfies the final requirement and also connects on the conceptual layer with the *Setup_Support* service. Note that we omit in Figure 15 the conceptual- and internal layer with the exception of the *Hiring company* due to space limitations.

5.3 eContracting lifecycle

The generalized lifecycle in Figure 16 depicts conceptually and clockwise on the one hand the initial steps for setting up a cross-organizational collaboration configuration with the components of the system architecture in Figure 15. On the other hand, a subset of the lifecycle steps allows for a process-view based evolution of a collaboration configuration.

We first explain below the elementary steps of the lifecycle in Figure 16 relate to the architecture in Figure 15. Alphabetic letters relate the explanations to the respective lifecycle steps. Support for the conceptual formulation (a) of business processes and their accompanying rules involves the *eSourcing_Setup_Support* component. The latter comprises functionality for re-using business rules

and process patterns for rapid conceptual-layer business process formulation.

Mapping details from the conceptual layer business-process to the internal layer (b) pertains to binding the tasks of a conceptual-layer process involving the *eSourcing_Setup_Support* to the Web-service ports that wrap legacy systems in the *Legacy_Management* so that an enactment-time orchestration of the latter is possible. The mapping also involves the *Translator* component from a conceptual- to an internal layer. Projecting from the conceptual layer business-process details to the external layer (c) involves the *Translator* component that creates different notation-formats to cater for business-process heterogeneity, e.g, from BPEL on the conceptual layer to BPMN on the external layer.

Brokering capability of projected business processes (d) for both the service consumer and the service provider must be able to place their projected process views into a broker environment of a *Service-HUB* component. This functionality is important for collaborations in an anonymous environment. The process views must be searchable for potential business partners. Bidding capability for projected processes views (e) is part of the *Service-HUB* component. The collaborating counter-party evaluates and chooses the subjectively best bid.

Negotiation support for setting up a collaboration configuration with known collaborating parties (f) is relevant

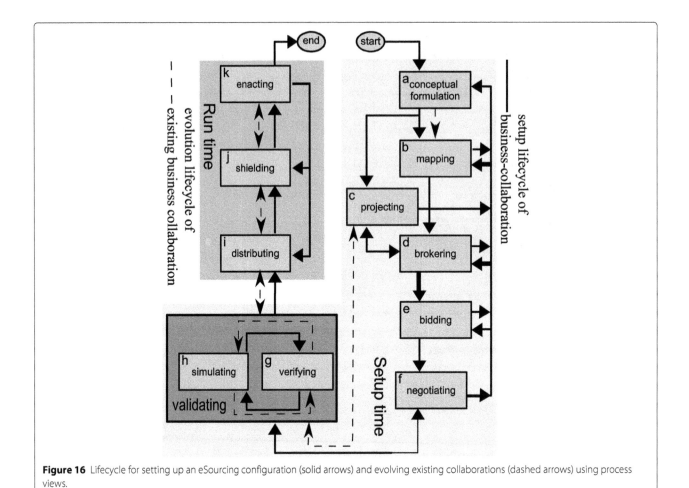

Figure 16 Lifecycle for setting up an eSourcing configuration (solid arrows) and evolving existing collaborations (dashed arrows) using process views.

after collaborating parties have found each other, they need a *Service-HUB* component for starting the contracting negotiations on the external layer of a collaboration configuration. This negotiation involves the projection of process views onto the external layer until achieving a matching that establishes a consensus between the service provisioning and service consumption.

Verifying perspectives of a collaboration configuration (g) from a control-flow point of view is important to verify a collaboration configuration for correct termination [7]. A verification must ensure that a service provisioning internally adheres to the externally promised collaboration behaviour. Simulation of a collaboration configuration (h) addresses that despite verification, errors may still occur during service enactment. Hence, a simulation component for business processes must be available for a-priori enactment simulation.

Distribution of business processes (i) to the external- and internal layer we cater for in the *Translator* component on the conceptual-layer. Shielding of business processes and legacy systems on concern-separating layers (j) must ensure the legacy systems that are Web-service wrapped and part of the internal layer, are

safeguarded by data-monitoring functionality. Finally, the Enactment of a ready collaboration configuration (k) takes place with distributed rules- and process engines that are on the one hand part of the external layer's *eSourcing_Middleware* component and on the other hand, the *Legacy_Management* component of the internal layer.

After a completed setup phase, the enactment of a collaboration configuration commences. The actual enactment components must be present on an internal layer for orchestrating legacy systems. Additional enactment components on the external layer need to choreograph the internal components of the respective collaborating parties.

Finally, besides the full collaboration-setup lifecycle in Figure 16 that culminates in the enactment stage, there is a subset-lifecycle embedded denoted by dashed arrows for process-view based collaboration evolution. The start is from (k) to (a) for first performing changes to the existing internal business process. Next, the internal-process projection (c) to the external-layer process view that culminates in a verification (g) and also optional simulation (h). Changes to the process view must be propagated into the domains of collaborating counterparties. In the latter case, a verification (g) and simulation (h) assures the re-established soundness of the overall business collaboration. Distribution (i) and shielding (j) precede a continued enactment (k) of the changed business collaboration. A dashed, bi-directional arrow in Figure 16 denotes that a faulty exception occurring at a specific lifecycle stage leads to a rollback into a previous lifecycle stage.

5.4 *eSML* enactment

As part of eSML we adopt for control-flow specifications the e*X*changable *R*outing *L*anguage XRL as an instance-based workflow language that uses XML for the representation of process definitions and Petri nets [48,49] for its semantics. The definition of XRL [59] contains as routing elements a catalog of control-flow patterns [60-63] that result in strong control-flow expressiveness. These routing elements are equipped with Petri-net semantics [64], namely, every routing element stands for an equivalent *workflow net* (WF-net) [50,51,65] that can be connected with other routing elements into a bigger WF-net.

An XRL route is a consistent XML document, that is, a well-formed and valid XML file with top element route [25]. The structure of any XML document forms a tree. In case of XRL, the root element of that tree is the route that contains exactly one so-called routing element. A routing element is an important building block and can either be simple (no child routing elements) or complex (one or more child routing elements). A complex routing element specifies whether, when and in which order the child routing elements are carried out.

To evaluate the expressiveness of eSML, the control-flow specification realizes the WF-net semantics of XRL by mapping to PNML [66-68], an XML-based interchange format that permits the definition of Petri-net types. A style-sheet translator contains mapping rules [64] to PNML for every XRL control-flow construct.

Due to page limitation, in Figure 17, we can only explain the lifecycle of a business process as it is carried out by the enactment application XRL/flower [69] that is adoptable for an eSRA-based implementation. Woflan [51,70] for checking control-flow soundness, is part of XRL/flower. Note that new control-flow elements adopted in XRL merely require an additional mapping rule in the stylesheet translator while the enactment engine remains unchanged. We refer to [25] for further details.

6 Related work

Contracting is part of Web-service choreography in some research work that only takes a technical position. In [71], contracts are descriptions of the observable behaviour of multiple services to tackle the problem of composition as sets of inout- and output actions. The authors show that a compliant group of contracts is still compliant after replacement by one of its subcontract. In [72], the same authors relate the theory of contracts with the notion of choreography conformance, used to check whether an aggregation of services correctly behaves according to a high level specification of their possible conversations based on input- and output actions. Projection and contract refinement achieve composition of choreography.

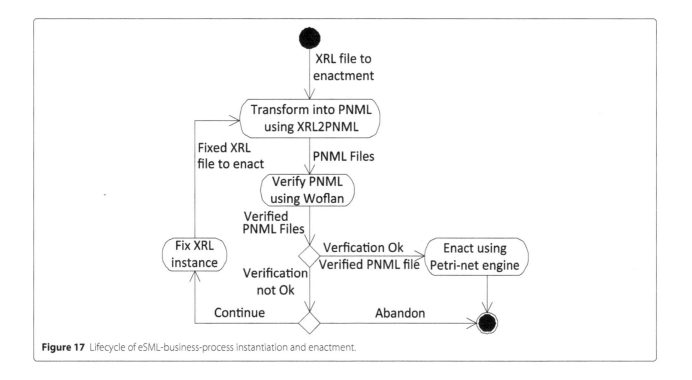

Figure 17 Lifecycle of eSML-business-process instantiation and enactment.

The authors in [73] state support for automated service contracting and enactment is crucial for any large scale service environment, where large numbers of clients and service providers interact. Concurrent Transaction Logic is instrumental to model and reason about service contracts to allow iterative processes in the specification of service contracts and enable reasoning about such contracts. Thereby, the authors limit themselves in their notion of contracts to technical service choreographies, service policies and contract requirements.

In [74], the authors consider contracts as labelled transition systems over located action names, representing operations at a certain location over a network. In this technicality focussed approach, the authors study the foundational aspects of contract compliance in a language independent way. The language independent representation of contracts allows for choreography projection in structured operational semantics. The evaluation applies the theory of contract compliance with industry-standard choreography specifications such as WS-CDL.

The related work has in common that no sociotechnical approach for the concept of contracting in service choreography recognizes the interaction between people and technology in cross-organizational collaborations. We address this gap by choosing a reality-based notion of a legal contract that states a consensus between collaborating parties must be present. This consensus in eSML represents the matching of process views by a service consumer and service provider, which is fundamentally different to the listed related work of purely technical focus.

Various aspects of negotiating and agreeing contracts between software agents acting on behalf of enterprises or individuals are described in [75].

7   Conclusions

This paper presents the ontological concepts and properties of smart contracting that is an essential ingredient for the management of decentralized autonomous organizations. The resulting eSourcing ontology that we define in the ontology language OWL and check with the HermiT reasoner, is input for developing the eSourcing Markup Language eSML. The latter is a choreography language for cross-organizational business collaboration. eSML results from a sociotechnical methodical, case study-based suitability and expressiveness exploration that ensures the language comprises essential collaboration concepts with a foundation for semantic clarity.

As eSML adopts a real-life contracting foundation, collaborating parties use process views they project externally for cross-organizational matching. Once a matching occurs, a consensus exists that is the essential criteria for establishing a contract. The process views are subsets of larger business processes inside the domains of collaborating parties. We use a subset of ECML as a base language for eSML that we enhance with additional schemas for process-view matching, and cross-organizational conjoinment and monitorability for achieving suitability. Furthermore, assuming that the control-flow perspective in a business collaboration is best explored, the expressiveness in eSML we address by adopting WF-net based semantics that is verifiable with tool support. Employing setup-interaction patterns of collaborating parties, we evaluate eSML in a proof-of-construction prototype for the setup and enactment of business collaborations in the CrossWork research project.

For future work, we plan to further enhance the eSourcing ontology with law researchers towards providing a mature ontology for advancing smart contracting. Furthermore, we plan to carry out more case studies with eSML in research projects about designing cyber-physical systems with smart-object orchestration. In those studies, we want to address expressiveness extensions into more Internet of Things perspectives. Additionally, an important extension for the eSourcing ontology and eSML is an adoption of concepts and properties to cater for adopting advanced security assurance measures that are relevant for open cyber-physical systems collaborations. Another open research issue is the safeguarding of business collaborations with transactionality concepts that need to go further than traditional transactions from the database- and workflow domains, i.e., pertaining to blockchain-related variants such as sidechains, treechains, minichains, and so on. Thus, future work will explore such electronic business transactions with the objective of understanding how to extend eSML for ensuring a safeguarding of cyber-physical system collaborations, preferably by using blockchain technology.

Endnotes

[a] Principles of European Contract Law developed by the Lando-Comission in Europe http://www.jus.uio.no/lm/eu.contract.principles.parts.1.to.3.2002/

[b] UNIDROIT Principles of International Commercial Contracts 2010 http://www.unidroit.org/english/principles/contracts/principles2010/integralversionprinciples2010-e.pdf

[c] Principles, Definitions and Model Rules of European Private Law known as Draft Common Frame of Reference http://ec.europa.eu/justice/contract/files/european-private-law_en.pdf

[d] United Nations Convention on Contracts for the International Sale of Goods, adopted 11 April 1980.

[e] International Chamber of Commerce rules http://www.iccwbo.org/products-and-services/trade-facilitation/incoterms-2010/the-incoterms-rules/.

Competing interests

The authors declare that they have no competing interests.

Authors' contributions

AN is the leading author who invented the eSourcing collaboration framework based on which we deduce the eContracting concept of this paper together with the evaluation that cilminates in eSML. This claim is backed by the listed literature references where Alex Norta is an author. LM was involved in the earlier OrChor'14 workshop-paper version that lead to the invitation for the special edition of the Journal of Internet Services and Applications. LM performed extensive proof reading and editing the submitted version. YD was also involved in the earlier OrChor'14 workshop-paper version that lead to the invitation for the special edition of the Journal of Internet Services and Applications. He additionally redesigned the conceptual-property depictions of Section 3 that are input for the eSML schema definitions. AR and MK are law-scientists and checked the approach from a professional legal perspective. The findings entered the introduction of this paper for justifying the sound legal foundation of the work in this paper. KT checked the paper from an artificial agent perspective at the end of Section 3.1. All authors read and approved the final manuscript.

Acknowledgement

This paper was supported in part by CNSF grant 61363007 and by HNU grant KYQD1242 and HDSF201310; the Dawn Program of Shanghai Education Commission (11SG44); the Research Fund for the Doctoral Program of Higher Education of China (20123120130001).
The work is supported by the National Natural Science Foundation of China(NSFC) under Grant No. 61202376, Shanghai Leading Academic Discipline Project under Grant No. XTKX2012, and Shanghai Engineering Research Center Project under Grant No. GCZX14014 and C14001.

Author details

[1]Tallinn University of Technology, Akadeemia Tee 15A, 12618 Tallinn, Estonia. [2]Hainan University, Haikou, China. [3]University of Shanghai for Science and Technology, Shanghai, China.

References

1. Allen P, Higgins S, McRae P, Schlamann, H (eds.): (2006) Service Orientation: Winning Strategies and Best Practices. Cambridge University Press
2. Antonopoulos N, Gillam L (2010) Cloud Computing: Principles, Systems and Applications. Springer
3. Alonso G, Casati F, Kuno H, Machiraju V (2004) Web Services: Concepts, Architectures and Applications. Springer-Verlag, Berlin Heidelberg
4. Eshuis R, Norta A, Kopp O, Pitkanen E (2013) Service outsourcing with process views. IEEE Trans Serv Comput 99(PrePrints):1. doi:10.1109/TSC.2013.51
5. Jung JY, Kim H, Kang SH (2006) Standards-based approaches to b2b workflow integration. Comput Ind Eng 51(2):321–334. doi:10.1016/j.cie.2006.02.011
6. Khalaf R (2007) From rosettanet pips to bpel processes: A three level approach for business protocols. Data Knowl Eng 61(1):23–38. doi:10.1016/j.datak.2006.04.006
7. Norta A, Eshuis R (2010) Specification and verification of harmonized business-process collaborations. Inform Syst Front 12:457–479. doi:10.1007/s10796-009-9164-1
8. Butterin V (2014) A next-generation smart contract and decentralized application platform. White Paper
9. Szabo N (1997) Formalizing and securing relationships on public networks. First Monday 2(9). http://firstmonday.org/ojs/index.php/fm/article/view/548/469
10. Nakamoto S (2008) Bitcoin: A peer-to-peer electronic cash system. Consulted 1(2012):28
11. Patron T The Bitcoin Revolution: An Internet of Money. Travis Patron
12. Swan M (2015) Blockchain Thinking: The Brain as a DAC (Decentralized Autonomous Organization). Texas Bitcoin Conference
13. Panikkar BS, Nair S, Brody P, Pureswaran V (2014) ADEPT: An IoT Practitioner Perspective. IBM
14. Lohmann N, Kleine J (2008) Fully-automatic Translation of Open Workflow Net Models into Simple Abstract BPEL Processes. In: Modellierung, vol. 12. Gesellschaft für Informatik E.V., Berlin, Germany. p 14
15. Decker G, Kopp O, Leymann F, Weske M (2007) Bpel4chor: Extending bpel for modeling choreographies. In: Web Services, 2007. ICWS 2007. IEEE International Conference On. IEEE. pp 296–303
16. Jordan D, Evdemon J, Alves A, Arkin A (2014) Web Services Choreography Description Language 1.0. http://www.w3.org/TR/ws-cdl-10/
17. Decker G, Barros A (2008) Interaction modeling using bpmn. In: BPM'07: Proceedings of the 2007 International Conference on Business Process Management. Springer, Berlin, Heidelberg. pp 208–219
18. Model BP (2011) Notation (bpmn) version 2.0. Object Management Group specification. http://www.bpmn.org
19. Zaha JM, Barros A, Dumas M, ter Hofstede AHM (2006) Let's dance: A language for service behavior modeling. In: Meersman R, Tari Z (eds). On the Move to Meaningful Internet Systems 2006: CoopIS, DOA, and ODBASE. Lecture Notes in Computer Science, vol. 4276. LNCS Springer, Montpellier, France. pp 145–162
20. Eisenberg B, Nickull D (2001) ebXML Technical Architecture Specification, Technical report, Organization for the Advancement of Structured Information Standards (OASIS)
21. Motal T, Zapletal M, Werthner H (2009) The Business Choreography Language (BCL) - A Domain-Specific Language for Global Choreographies. In: SERVICES-2 '09: Proceedings of the 2009 World Conference on Services - II. IEEE Computer Society, Washington, DC, USA. pp 150–159. doi:10.1109/SERVICES-2.2009.25
22. Norta A (2015) eSourcing.owl ontology. Tallinn University of Technology. http://tinyurl.com/nogogon
23. Knublauch H, Fergerson RW, Noy NF, Musen MA (2004) The protégé owl plugin: An open development environment for semantic web applications. In: The Semantic Web–ISWC 2004. Springer. pp 229–243
24. Horrocks I, Motik B, Wang Z (2012) The hermit owl reasoner. In: OWL Reasoner Evaluation Workshop (ORE 2012). CEUR Workshop Proceedings, CEUR-WS.org
25. Norta A (2007) Exploring Dynamic Inter-Organizational Business Process Collaboration. PhD thesis, Technology University Eindhoven, Department of Information Systems
26. Nimmer RT (2007) The legal landscape of e-commerce: Redefining contract law in an information era. J Contract Law 23(1):10–31
27. Gaillard E (1995) Thirty years of lex mercatoria: Towards the selective application of transnational rules. ICSID Rev 10(2):208–231
28. Hevner AR, Ram S, March ST, Park J (2004) Design science in information system research. MIS Q 28(1):75–105
29. March ST, Storey VC (2008) Design science in the information systems discipline: an introduction to the special issue on design science research. Manag Inform Syst Q 32(4):6
30. Grefen P, Eshuis R, Mehandjiev N, Kouvas G, Weichhart G (2009) Internet-based support for process-oriented instant virtual enterprises. IEEE Internet Comput 13(6):65–73
31. Mehandjiev N, Grefen P (2010) Dynamic Business Process Formation for Instant Virtual Enterprises. Springer
32. Norta A, Grefen P (2007) Discovering Patterns for Inter-Organizational Business Collaboration. Int J Cooperative Inform Syst (IJCIS) 16:507–544. doi:10.1142/S0218843007001664
33. Norta A, Grefen P, Narendra NC (2014) A reference architecture for managing dynamic inter-organizational business processes. Data Knowl Eng 91(0):52–89
34. Alonso G, Fiedler S, Hagen C, Lazcano A, Schuldt H, Weiler N (1999) WISE: business to business e-commerce. In: Proc. of the 9th International Workshop on Research Issues on Data Engineering, Sydney, Australia. pp 132–139
35. Hoffner Y, Ludwig H, Gülcü C, Grefen P (2005) Architecture for Cross-Organizational Business Processes. In: Procs. 2nd Int. Workshop on Advanced Issues of E-Commerce and Web-Based Information Systems, Milpitas, CA, USA. pp 2–11
36. Lazcano A, Schuldt H, Alonso G, Schek HJ (2001) Wise: Process based e-commerce. IEEE Data Eng Bull 24(1):46–51
37. Kutvonen L, Ruokolainen T, Metso J (2007) Interoperability middleware for federated business services in web-Pilarcos. Int J Enterprise Inform Syst Spec Issue Interoperability Enterprise Syst Appl 3(1):1–21

38. Kutvonen L, Norta A, Ruohomaa S (2012) Inter-enterprise business transaction management in open service ecosystems. In: Enterprise Distributed Object Computing Conference (EDOC), 2012 IEEE 16th International. IEEE. pp 31–40

39. SAP (2015) Sourcing & Procurement Solutions. SAP.com. http://www.sap.com/solution/lob/procurement/software/sourcing/index.html

40. ORACLE (2015) ORACLE Sourcing. ORACLE.com. http://www.oracle.com/us/products/applications/ebusiness/procurement/053985.html

41. Ruokolainen T, Ruohomaa S, Kutvonen L (2011) Solving service ecosystem governance. In: Enterprise Distributed Object Computing Conference Workshops (EDOCW), 2011 15th IEEE International. IEEE. pp 18–25

42. Norta A, Kutvonen L (2012) A cloud hub for brokering business processes as a service: A "rendezvous" platform that supports semi-automated background checked partner discovery for cross-enterprise collaboration. In: SRII Global Conference (SRII), 2012 Annual. pp 293–302

43. Shearer R, Motik B, Horrocks I (2008) Hermit: A highly-efficient owl reasoner. In: CEUR Workshop Proceedings, Proceedings of the Fifth OWLED Workshop on OWL: Experiences and Directions, collocated with the 7th International Semantic Web Conference (ISWC-2008), Karlsruhe, Germany, vol. 432

44. Angelov S (2006) Foundations of B2B Electronic Contracting. Dissertation, Technology University Eindhoven, Faculty of Technology Management, Information Systems Department

45. Reinecke JA (1984) Introduction to Business: A Contemporary View. Allyn & Bacon

46. Duan Y (2012) A survey on service contract. In: Software Engineering, Artificial Intelligence, Networking and Parallel & Distributed Computing (SNPD), 2012 13th ACIS International Conference On. IEEE. pp 805–810

47. Sterling L, Taveter K (2009) The Art of Agent-oriented Modeling. MIT Press

48. (1998) Lectures on Petri Nets I: Basic Models(Reisig W, Rozenberg G, eds.), Vol. 1491. Springer, Heidelberg, Germany

49. Lectures on Petri Nets II: Applications (1998)(Reisig W, Rozenberg G, eds.), Vol. 1492. Springer, Heidelberg, Germany

50. Ellis C, Nutt G (1993) Modelling and Enactment of Workflow Systems. In: Marsan M. A. (ed). Application and Theory of Petri Nets 1993, vol. 691. Springer, Heidelberg, Germany. pp 1–16

51. Aalst W (1998) The Application of Petri Nets to Workflow Management. J Circuits Syst Comput 8(1):21–66

52. Kindler E, Aalst W (1999) Liveness, Fairness, and Recurrence. Inform Process Lett 70(6):269–274

53. Verbeek H, Basten T, Aalst W (2001) Diagnosing Workflow Processes using Woflan. Comput J 44(4):246–279

54. Angelov S, Grefen P (2003) The 4W framework for B2B e-contracting. Int J Netw Virtual Organizations 2(1):78–97

55. Aalst W (2000) Inheritance of Interorganizational Workflows: How to Agree to Disagree Without Loosing Control?. BETA Working Paper Series, WP 46, Eindhoven University of Technology, Eindhoven

56. Russell N, van der Aalst WM, ter Hofstede AH, Edmond D (2005) Workflow resource patterns: Identification, representation and tool support. In: Advanced Information Systems Engineering. Springer. pp 216–232

57. Russell N, Ter Hofstede AH, Edmond D, van der Aalst WM (2005) Workflow data patterns: Identification, representation and tool support. In: Conceptual Modeling–ER 2005. Springer. pp 353–368

58. Norta A, Hendrix M, Grefen P (2006) On the Move to Meaningful Internet Systems 2006: CoopIS, DOA, and ODBASE. In: Meersman R, Tari Z. (eds). Lecture Notes in Computer Science, vol. 4277. LNCS Springer, Montpellier, France. pp 834–843

59. Aalst W, Kumar A (2003) XML Based Schema Definition for Support of Inter-organizational Workflow. Inform Syst Res 14(1):23–47

60. Workflow Patterns Home Page. http://workflowpatterns.com/

61. Aalst W, Hofstede A, Kiepuszewski B, Barros AP (2000) Advanced Workflow Patterns. In: Etzion O, Scheuermann P (eds). 7th International Conference on Cooperative Information Systems (CoopIS 2000) Vol. 1901. pp 18–29

62. Kiepuszewski B (2002) Expressiveness and Suitability of Languages for Control Flow Modelling in Workflows PhD thesis, Queensland University of Technology, Queensland University of Technology, Brisbane, Australia. citeseer.nj.nec.com/kiepuszewski02expressiveness.html

63. Kiepuszewski B, Hofstede A, Aalst W (2003) Fundamentals of Control Flow in Workflows. Acta Informatica 39(3):143–209

64. Aalst W, Verbeek HMW, Kumar A (2001) XRL/Woflan: Verification of an XML/Petri-net based language for inter-organizational workflows (Best paper award). In: Altinkemer K, Chari K. (eds). Proceedings of the 6th Informs Conference on Information Systems and Technology (CIST-2001). Informs, Linthicum, MD. pp 30–45

65. Aalst W (1997) Verification of Workflow Nets. In: Azéma P, Balbo G (eds). Application and Theory of Petri Nets 1997. Springer, Heidelberg, Germany Vol. 1248. pp 407–426

66. Billington J, Christense S, Van Hee K, Kindler E, Kummer O, Petrucci L, Post R (2003) The Petri Net Markup Language: Concepts, Technology, and Tools. In: Aalst W, Best E (eds). Proc. of the 24th International Conference, ICATPN 2003, Lecture Notes in Computer Science. Springer, Eindhoven, The Netherlands. pp 483–505

67. LIP6 (2015) Welcome to PNML.org. http://www.pnml.org/

68. Weber M, Kindler E (2003) The petri net markup language. In: Ehrig H, Reisig W, Rozenberg G, Weber H (eds). Petri Net Technology for Communication-Based Systems Advances in Petri Nets. Lecture Notes in Computer Science. Springer. p 455

69. Norta A (2004) Web supported enactment of petri-net based workflows with XRL/Flower. In: Cortadella J, Reisig W (eds). Proc. of the 25th International Conference on the Application and Theory of Petri Nets 2004. Lecture Notes in Computer Science. Springer, Bologna, Italy. pp 494–503

70. Verbeek H, Basten T, Aalst W (2001) Diagnosing Workflow Processes Using Woflan. Comput J Br Comput Soc 44(4):246–279

71. Bravetti M, Zavattaro G (2007) Contract based multi-party service composition. In: Arbab F, Sirjani M (eds). International Symposium on Fundamentals of Software Engineering. Lecture Notes in Computer Science, vol. 4767. Springer. pp 207–222. doi:10.1007/978-3-540-75698-9_14. http://dx.doi.org/10.1007/978-3-540-75698-9_14

72. Bravetti M, Zavattaro G (2007) Towards a unifying theory for choreography conformance and contract compliance. In: Lumpe M, Vanderperren W (eds). Software Composition. Lecture Notes in Computer Science, vol. 4829. Springer. pp 34–50. doi:10.1007/978-3-540-77351-1_4. http://dx.doi.org/10.1007/978-3-540-77351-1_4

73. Roman D, Kifer M (2008) Semantic web service choreography: Contracting and enactment. In: The Semantic Web-ISWC 2008. Springer. pp 550–566

74. Bravetti M, Zavattaro G (2009) Contract compliance and choreography conformance in the presence of message queues. In: Bruni R, Wolf K. n. (eds). Web Services and Formal Methods, Lecture Notes in Computer Science, vol. 5387. Springer. pp 37–54. doi:10.1007/978-3-642-01364-5_3. http://dx.doi.org/10.1007/978-3-642-01364-5_3

75. Ossowski S (2013) Agreement Technologies:Law, Governance and Technology. Springer

6

An open virtual multi-services networking architecture for the future internet

May El Barachi[1]*, Nadjia Kara[2], Sleiman Rabah[3] and Mathieu Forgues[4]

Abstract

Network virtualization is considered as a promising way to overcome the limitations and fight the gradual ossification of the current Internet infrastructure. The network virtualization concept consists in the dynamic creation of several co-existing logical network instances (or virtual networks) over a shared physical network infrastructure. We have previously proposed a service-oriented hierarchical business model for virtual networking environments. This model promotes the idea of network as a service, by considering the functionalities offered by different types of network resources as services of different levels – services that can be dynamically discovered, used, and composed. In this paper, we propose an open, virtual, multi-services networking architecture enabling the realization of our business model. We also demonstrate the operation of our architecture using a virtualized QoS-enabled VoIP scenario. Moreover, virtual routing and control level performance was evaluated using proof-of-concept prototyping. Several important findings were made in the course of this work; one is that service-oriented concepts can be used to build open, flexible, and collaborative virtual networking environments. Another finding is that some of the existing open source virtual routing solutions such as Vyatta are only suitable for building small to medium size virtual networking infrastructures.

Keywords: Network virtualization; Future Internet; Service-oriented architecture; Virtual routing; Vyatta

1 Introduction

The concept of virtualization consists in the decoupling of physical resources from the service-level view, by adding an abstract layer (software), in between. The implementation of this concept gives the end-user the illusion of direct interaction with the physical resources, while allowing efficient utilization of resources/infrastructures and enhanced flexibility. Different forms of virtualization have been proposed, such as storage virtualization, server virtualization, application virtualization and more recently network virtualization. Storage virtualization refers to the separation of physical disk space from the logical assignment of that space, using various techniques (e.g. RAID and SAN). Server virtualization consists in the partitioning of the resources of a single physical machine into multiple execution environments (or virtual machines), each running its own operating system and server applications. Application virtualization refers to the isolation of a certain application from the operating system on which it runs, in order to achieve OS-independence and limit the effect of applications incompatibilities.

Network virtualization is an emerging concept that applies virtualization to entire networks. The basic idea behind network virtualization consists in the dynamic creation of several co-existing logical network instances (or virtual networks) over a shared physical network infrastructure [1]. Unlike Virtual Private Networks (VPNs) [2] that are limited to traffic isolation capabilities and do not allow customization nor administrative control, virtual networks (VNets) can potentially be built according to different design criteria and operated as service tailored networks.

In the Internet domain, network virtualization is considered as a promising solution for the "Internet ossification" problem – A condition by which the sheer size and scope of the Internet architecture renders the introduction and deployment of new technologies very difficult due to the high cost of migration and the difficulty of achieving wide consensus among the many involved stakeholders [3]. By enabling a logical segmentation of the physical Internet infrastructure and the co-existence of heterogeneous virtual networking architectures on

* Correspondence: may.elbarachi@zu.ac.ae
[1]College of Technological Innovation, Zayed University, Khalifa City B, P.O. Box 144534, Abu Dhabi, United Arab Emirates
Full list of author information is available at the end of the article

top of it, network virtualization is often seen as a corner-stone of the future Internet architecture [4].

Beyond the Internet's context, there are several important motivations behind the network virtualization concept. One of these motivations is the cost effective sharing of physical networking resources, by partitioning the resources of an existing infrastructure into slices and the allocation of these slices to different VNets (operated by different service providers). Another motivation is the potential for having customizable and service tailored networking solutions via the addition of new technologies or customized versions of existing technologies, in the virtualization layer.

Aiming to contribute to a future service-tailored Internet architecture, the main goal of this work is to propose and validate an open, service-oriented network virtualization platform for the future Internet. Our platform (dubbed the Open Virtual Playground) promotes the idea of "network as a service" by defining different levels of services to which networking resources are mapped, and which can be dynamically discovered, used, and composed. It relies on a novel service-oriented hierarchical business model [5,6] that introduces new business roles, and proposes the concept of vertical hierarchy between virtual network providers, as well as the concept of service building block and service reuse and composition.

The contributions of our work are of three folds: 1) It proposed a fine-grained, service oriented network virtualization architecture which encompasses the control functions needed for the instantiation, control, and management of virtual networks; 2) It details a concrete QoS-enabled VoIP scenario showcasing the architecture's operations, which include the REST-based interactions for the virtual networks' instantiation phase, and the SIP/COPS/MEGACO based interactions for the service invocation and usage phase; and 3) It discusses the implementation and performance evaluation of two prototypes related to the virtual data plane and the virtual control plane operation.

The rest of this paper is organized as follows: In section (The network virtualization concept: principles, goals, and motivating scenarios), we start with some background information about network virtualization and present two concrete use cases that could be enabled by this technology. In section (The open virtual playground architecture), we present an overview of our previously proposed business model, discuss the different components of our proposed Open Virtual Playground architecture, and illustrate its operation using a virtualized QoS-enabled VoIP scenario. This is followed by prototype-based performance evaluations, in section (Solution validation). We end the paper with a discussion of related work, before drawing our conclusions.

2 The network virtualization concept: principles, goals, and motivating scenarios

A virtual networking environment can be seen as a dynamic and collaborative environment, in which a large pool of virtualized networking resources can be offered and leased on demand. In such an environment, a number of logical network instances (virtual networks) co-exist over a shared physical network infrastructure. A virtual network essentially consists of a set of virtual nodes connected by virtual links, and forming a virtual topology. This topology is a subset of the underlying physical topology, in which each virtual node (guest) is hosted on a certain physical node (host) and each virtual link is established over a physical path. In this environment, each virtual network is operated by a single entity, and virtual networks are logically isolated from each other. Several primitive forms of virtual networks have been proposed in the past, including virtual private networks (VPNs), overlay networks, and active/programmable networks. All these forms limit virtualization to a certain layer (e.g. application layer for overlay networks) and do not offer full administrative control and customization capabilities.

From an architectural perspective, network virtualization promotes several design goals [1], the most prominent ones being: the *coexistence* of multiple VNets (operated by different providers) within the same environment; *recursion and inheritance* between VNets allowing the nesting/creation of a VNet on top of another VNet (thus forming a hierarchy); *flexibility* by allowing a provider to implement an arbitrary network topology, routing and forwarding functionalities and customized control protocols in a VNet; *manageability* allowing a provider to have full administrative control over a VNet; *isolation* between co-existing VNets to improve fault-tolerance, security and privacy; and *heterogeneity* of VNets as well as the physical infrastructures on which they rely.

There are several important motivations behind the network virtualization concept, including: *cost-effective sharing of physical networking resources*; *customizable networking solutions*; and the *convergence of existing network infrastructures*. Furthermore, several challenges must be addressed to enable the realization of this concept. Examples of these challenges include: the definition of *standard interfaces* between the different levels of the virtual networking hierarchy; the definition of *control functions related to the instantiation and configuration of virtual nodes/links*; ensuring *scalability* at the level of virtual nodes/links; enabling the *dynamic discovery of available physical/virtual resources*; the definition of *efficient global resource management strategies*; and the definition of suitable *business models and charging schemes* for virtual environments.

To illustrate the potential of the network virtualization concept, we now present two concrete use cases that could be enabled in virtual networking environments.

In order to define these use cases, we first analyzed the trends and proposed scenarios for future communication networks, such as the ones presented in the 4Ward project documents [7]. Afterwards, we focused on examining the limitations of the current Internet and on defining scenarios that would offer appealing services while addressing those limitations via virtualization.

Among the known areas of weakness of the current Internet architecture requiring innovation, we mention: stronger security; better mobility; more flexible routing; enhanced reliability; and better quality of service guarantees [8]. As for the categories of services studied, we chose the following categories: 1) VoIP as it represents one of the most important categories of applications offered in the current Internet; and 2) Context-aware smart applications (i.e. applications that are aware of the context surrounding them and capable of dynamically adapting to changing situations) as they are seen as one of the "killer" applications of the future.

2.1 VoIP service with two-dimensional QoS scheme

IP telephony is one of the important and popular application areas supported by the Internet. However, one of the main challenges faced by IP telephony is the inability to offer adequate quality of service guarantees to users, due to the inherent best effort nature of the current Internet architecture and the high cost of migration to new QoS technologies in a network as large as the Internet.

Our first use case illustrates how new QoS schemes could be introduced in existing networking infrastructures using the network virtualization concept. In this use case, a virtualized VoIP service with a two-dimensional QoS scheme is realized as follows: At the lowest level, we find the physical networking infrastructure (owned and managed by a Physical Infrastructure Provider), on top of which a first VNet (VN1) is instantiated and operated by a Virtual Infrastructure Provider. The latter deploys in VN1 a new QoS scheme enabling the differentiation between different classes of traffic (e.g. conversational, streaming, interactive, and background traffic classes), based on their resources requirements. Building on VN1 capabilities, a second VNet (VN2) is instantiated and deployed by a service provider offering sophisticated VoIP services and a session prioritization scheme enabling the distinction between sessions based on their level of importance from the user's perspective. This scheme, which constitutes a second QoS dimension, would enable the user to choose the appropriate class for each call (e.g. silver, gold, and platinum) based on its level of importance. We note that the value added in this scenario consists in the support of a two-dimensional QoS scheme and the support of sophisticated VoIP services. This value was added via the instantiated virtualization layers, without affecting the physical infrastructure, thus providing a smooth path for migration.

2.2 Context-aware value added services

Context-awareness is defined as the ability to use contextual (or situational) information to provide relevant information and/or services to the user [9]. Contextual information is usually collected using wireless sensor networks (WSNs).

Context-aware applications are an emerging category of intelligent applications that offer personalized services by adapting their behavior according to the users' needs and changing situation (e.g. personalized healthcare applications and smart shopping applications). These applications are seen as one of the "killer" applications of the future. The following scenario illustrates how such applications could be supported in a virtualized networking environment.

In this scenario, we find at the lowest level the PIPs, some of which are managing regular communication infrastructures, while others manage various types of WSNs used for the collection of different types of contextual information (e.g. spatial, physiological, and environmental data). On the top of these WSNs, we find VN1 that acts as a specialized network dedicated for the management of sensory information. Then, at the third level, we find a second VNet (VN2) leveraging the information management capabilities of VN1 as well as the communication capabilities of physical communication network to offer context-aware value added services to end users.

3 The open virtual playground architecture

In this section, we give an overview of our previously proposed network virtualization business model, and then present the Open Virtual Playground architecture.

3.1 Overview of proposed business model

Our previously proposed business model [6] is a service-oriented hierarchical model in which different levels of services (offered by various players) can be dynamically discovered, used, and composed. Figure 1 depicts our proposed model, in which four levels of services are defined, namely: 1) *Essential services* constituting mandatory services needed for the basic operation of the network (i.e. routing/transport services); 2) *Service enablers* consisting of the common functions needed to support the operation of end-user services (e.g. session/subscription management, charging, security, and QoS management); 3) *Service building blocks* acting as elementary services that can be used/combined to form more complex services (e.g. presence and call control); and 4) *End user services* constituting the value-added services offered to users.

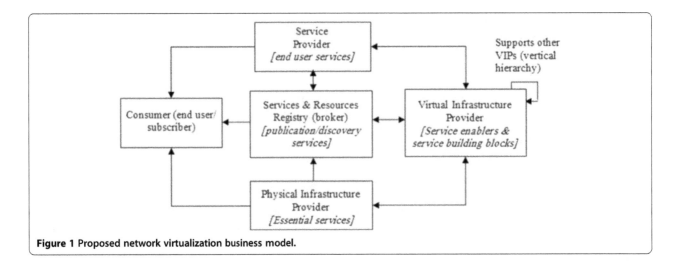

Figure 1 Proposed network virtualization business model.

Our business model defines five business roles, namely: 1) *The Physical Infrastructure Provider* (*PIP*) that owns and manages a physical network infrastructure and can partition its resources using some virtualization technology. The services offered by the PIP are essential bearer services. 2) *The Service Provider* (*SP*) that has a business agreement with the subscriber and offers value added services, which could be simple or composite (i.e. formed by combining service building blocks); 3) *The Virtual Infrastructure Provider* (*VIP*) that finds and aggregates virtual resources (offered by one or more PIPs), deploys any protocols/technologies in the instantiated VNet, and operates it as a native network. The VIP supports SPs or other VIPs with service enablers and service building blocks and has no direct business agreement with consumers; We envision three potential variations of the VIP role: a) A VIP that adds value in the virtualization layer by introducing a new technology or customizing existing protocols – the resulting VNet can be used by a SP to offer VAS running on it or resold to another VIP that leverages its capabilities to form another VNet on top of it (i.e. forming a vertical hierarchy); b) A VIP that uses virtualization to achieve interworking between heterogeneous physical infrastructures – the result being a unified network for others to use; and c) A VIP that implements more advanced services in the virtual layer to offer application building blocks that can be used by service providers to compose new value added services; 4) *The Consumer* who acts as the subscriber and the end user of value added services; and 5) *The Services and Resources Registry* (*SRR*) acting as broker by providing information to find other parties and the services/resources they offer. This functional separation of roles enables the creation of an open and collaborative networking environment in which a rich set of resources and services are offered.

3.2 The proposed architecture

In this section, we present our proposed open virtual multi-services networking architecture, named the *Open Virtual Playground*. This architecture was designed to be *open* to different entities/roles/players and also open to change (i.e. dynamic and flexible), in addition to relying on *virtual*ization technology as a central concept in its operation, and offering a *playground* area for multi-players to interact, collaborate, and offer different services.

We start by presenting the overall architecture and its related functional entities and interfaces, and then present an illustrative session management scenario detailing its operation. The architecture was designed based on the defined business roles and the proposed functional split between them.

3.2.1 Functional entities and interfaces

As shown in Figure 2, the Open Virtual Playground architecture we are proposing is a layered architecture that introduces data and control planes at each of the three levels of the hierarchy. While the data plane provides essential data transportation functionality, the control plane encompasses all the control and management functions needed for the provisioning of different levels of services.

In order to realize the three main roles defined in our business model (i.e. PIP, VIP, and SP) and achieve the proposed functional split between them, three hierarchical levels are defined in our architecture, namely: 1) The physical network level (managed by the PIP); 2) the first virtual network level (managed by a VIP); and 3) the second virtual network level (managed by a SP). The consumer role accesses the services offered by the SP by interacting with the lowest level of the hierarchy (i.e. the physical network), while the SRR (i.e. the broker role) is

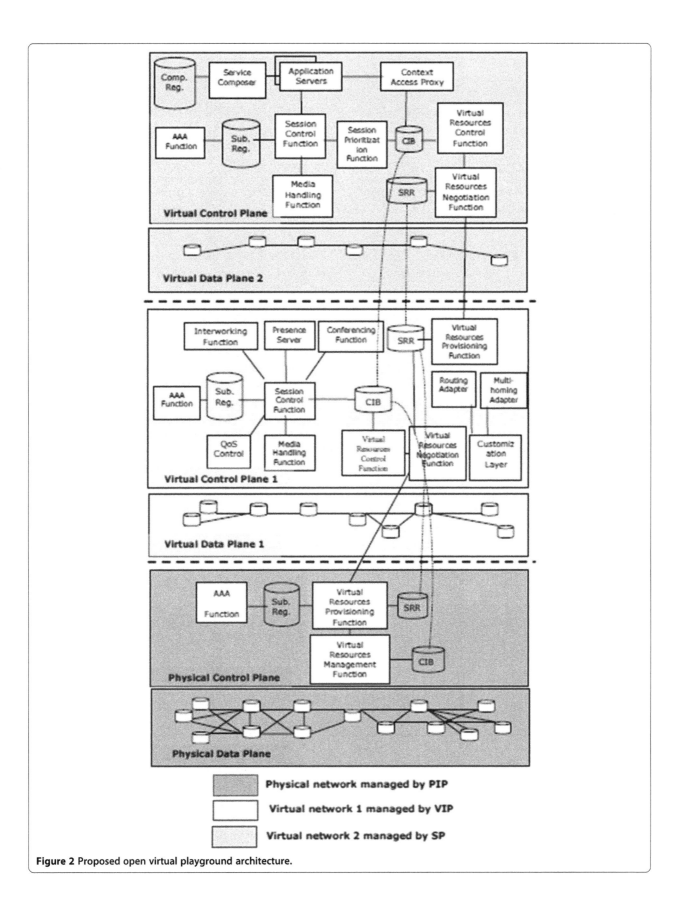

Figure 2 Proposed open virtual playground architecture.

a vertical role that interacts with all three levels of the hierarchy.

Similar to all business models, one entity could play several business roles at the same time. For instance a VIP could also play the role of a SP (i.e. offering both virtual topologies and value added services to end users). This situation would result in a two-tier architecture, encompassing two hierarchical levels (i.e. the physical network level and one virtual network level). While such model involves less interactions, it lacks the flexibility, openness, and role specialization achieved by the three-tier architectural model. In fact, maintaining the VIP as a separate entity offers the level of abstraction and separation between PIPs and SPs required to build virtual networks that are customized for particular service and user requirements. Furthermore, using a VIP as intermediary role simplifies the negotiation and virtual resource allocation process, in cases involving multiple SPs and multiple PIPs [10]. This process becomes much more complex when those SPs are directly interacting with multiple PIPs, in a fully distributed fashion (i.e. forming a full mesh topology). For the rest of this paper, we assume that each role is played by a separate entity, and focus on the three-tier hierarchical model which is described below.

At the *Physical Network Level*, we find the physical data plane containing regular and virtual routers connected to form the physical network infrastructure, as well as the physical control plane responsible for the following functions: Resource publication, resource negotiation, resource allocation and provisioning, and resource management. These functions are achieved using the following entities: The Services and resources registry (SRR) used for the publication/discovery of information about available resources; the Context information base (CIB) used for the management of contextual information related to the physical network (e.g. resources status and security level); the Subscription Registry containing all clients' subscription/authorization/authentication information; the AAA function using this information to authenticate, authorize, and charge VIPs for network resources utilization; the virtual resources provisioning function responsible for the negotiation of resources with VIPs, the allocation of virtual resources and the instantiation of virtual topologies; and the virtual resources management function responsible for the dynamic resource (re)allocation to VNets taking into consideration the resources status and the needs of VNets.

At the *First Virtual Network Level*, we find a virtual data plane encompassing a set of virtual nodes connected by virtual links (essentially a subset of the underlying physical topology), as well as virtual control plane 1. This latter encompasses the following functions: a set of service enablers and service building blocks, service

publication, resource negotiation, resource discovery/selection, and service deployment/management. These functions are carried by the following entities: a SRR, a CIB, and a Sub. Reg. (playing similar roles to their peer entities in the lower layer, but in relation to VNet1 operation); a number of entities offering common support functions (e.g. session control, media handling, and interworking); a number of service building blocks (e.g. presence and conferencing); modules offering a customization of existing protocols (e.g. a content-based routing adapter and a multi-homing adapter); a virtual resources negotiation function used for the discovery and negotiation of resources (with PIP(s)) and the composition/instantiation of the VNet topology; a virtual resources control function responsible for the deployment of protocols and the operation of the VNet; and a virtual resources provisioning function used for the negotiation of virtual resources with other VIPs or SPs wishing to add another level in the hierarchy.

Similarly, the *Second Virtual Network Level* consists of a virtual data plane and a virtual control plane. The latter is responsible for the following: a set of end user services, end user service publication, resource negotiation, resource discovery/selection, service deployment/management, and service composition. We should mention that the SRR and the CIB repositories are distributed across all the levels of the hierarchy and a *cross-layered communication* between them enables the formation/maintenance of a global view of the physical/virtual networks contexts and available services/resources.

3.2.2 Illustrative session management scenario

To illustrate our architecture's operation, we now describe how the QoS-enabled VoIP scenario presented in section (VoIP service with two-dimensional QoS scheme) could be realized using it.

In this scenario, we find the following roles: a PIP managing the infrastructure offering communication capabilities; a VIP instantiating VN1 to offer QoS control, session control, and media handling as service enablers; and a SP instantiating VN2 to offer the VoIP value-added service, implementing a second QoS dimension (silver, gold, platinum), to consumers. Figure 3 illustrates the QoS-enabled VoIP service composition diagram, in terms of lower level sub-services, and how those sub-services are mapped onto physical networking resources.

As shown in Figures 3 and 4, the QoS-enabled VoIP scenario is divided into two phases: 1) the virtual networks' instantiation phase; and 2) the end-user service invocation and usage phase. Figure 4 depicts the virtual networks' instantiation phase that was realized using REST-based interactions between the different entities. REST is a network architectural style for distributed

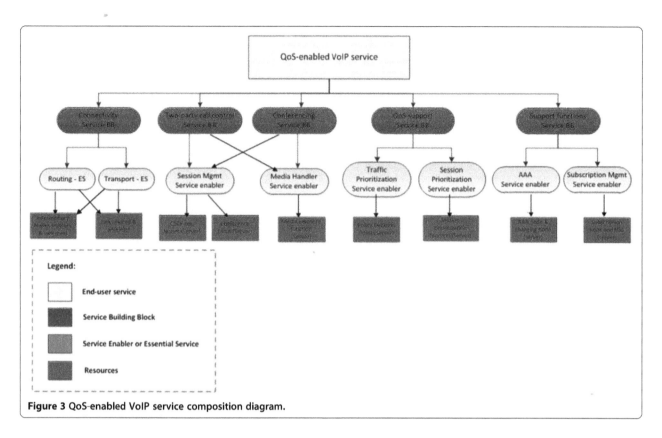

Figure 3 QoS-enabled VoIP service composition diagram.

hypermedia systems. There are several motivations behind our choice of REST-based interfaces, namely: its reliance on existing well known Web standards opens the door for various players to adopt such unified interfaces, for which the necessary infrastructure has already become pervasive; the fact that REST is simple, lightweight, and easy to develop; and the fact that it is resource-oriented and supports a wide range of resource description mechanisms.

Figure 5 illustrates the end-user service invocation and usage phase of the scenario. This phase was realized using three main protocols: SIP used for session control; COPS used for the exchange of policy-based resource allocation decisions; and MEGACO/H.248 used for the control of media handling nodes. We chose these protocols because of their extensibility and the fact that they provided the needed functionalities and are among the protocols supported in next generation networks.

As shown in Figure 4, the scenario starts when a PIP publishes (through its VRPF1) a description of the resources (step 1) it offers as well as their related constraints in a document that is used to populate the broker, using a POST request. In this request, the broker's resource creation service URI is specified. Once the resources' descriptions are created, a 200 OK message (step 2) is sent back to the PIP. In turn, the VIP (wishing to create VN1) sends a PIP discovery request (step 3) containing a document describing the resources to be

leased, their desired availability, cost, and constraints. This request is sent using a GET message to the broker, which replies back (step 4) with a list of available providers that can satisfy the specified requirements. Upon receiving the PIPs list, the best PIP is selected by the VIP, using a selection/matching algorithm (step 5). Similarity-based matching algorithms such as the ones proposed in [11,12] can be used in this step. The VIP then sends a resource negotiation request (step 6), specifying the requested essential services and their constraints, to the selected PIP. After checking resources availability (step 7), the PIP replies with a resource negotiation response (step 8), specifying the offered resources and accepted constraints to the VIP, which concludes the negotiation process with a resource negotiation acknowledgement (step 9) confirming the negotiated resources and constraints. At this stage, the PIP carries a resource allocation and virtual topology instantiation process for VN1 (step 10), and sends an acknowledgement (step 11) of the topology instantiation to the VIP's VRNF, which is propagated to the VIP's VRCF (step 12). Afterwards, the VIP asks the PIP to deploy and test the specified service enablers (step 13), and gets a 200 OK message as reply (steps 15, 16). Once the service enablers are deployed and tested, the VIP's VRPF asks the broker to publish a description of the service enablers and their constraints (step 17), which in case of success results in a 200 OK message (step 18).

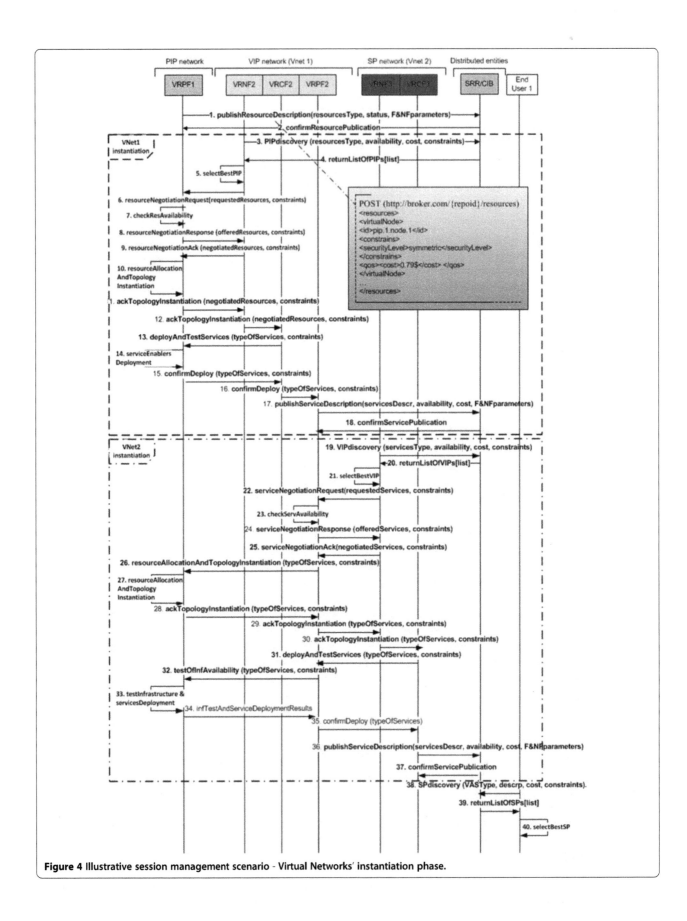

Figure 4 Illustrative session management scenario – Virtual Networks' instantiation phase.

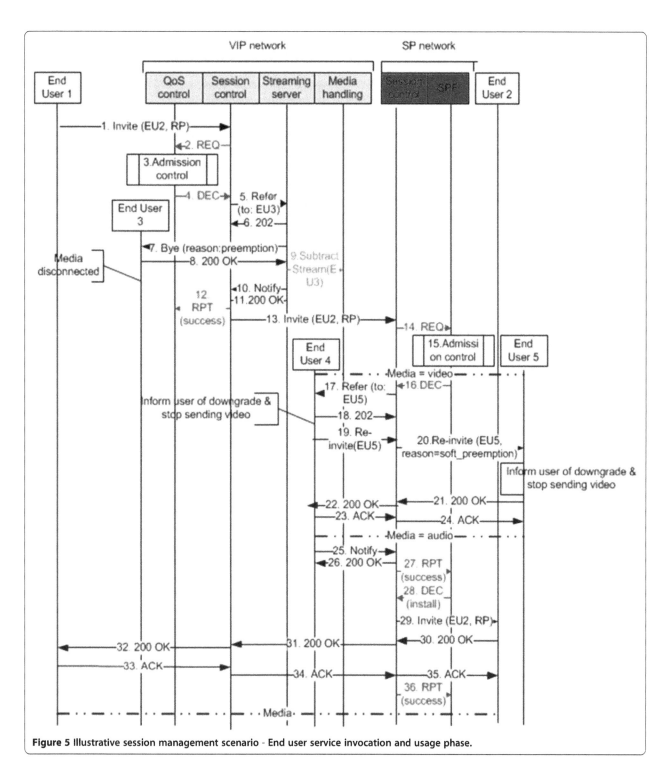

Figure 5 Illustrative session management scenario - End user service invocation and usage phase.

Meanwhile, a SP (wishing to create VN2) sends (using its VRNF) the broker a VIP discovery request (step 19) containing a document describing the service enablers to be used, their desired availability, cost, and constraints. The broker replies with a list of VIPs offering service enablers that comply with the request (step 20). Later, in step 21, the SP selects the best VIP to which he submits a service negotiation request (step 22). In steps 23 to 35, interactions related to service enablers' usage negotiation, VN2 topology instantiation, and the deployment of the QoS-enabled VoIP end user service offered by the SP are carried, similarly to the VIP::VN1 case. The main difference lays in the message parameters that refer to a different type of service in this case. When the end user service is successfully deployed and tested, the SP sends its description to the broker (steps 36, 37). This description is then discovered (steps 38, 39) by the consumer that uses it to select the best SP (step 40).

Afterwards, the consumer (end-user 1) binds to the selected SP and invokes the QoS-enabled VoIP service, as depicted in Figure 5. In that case, end user 1 attempts to initiate a VoIP session of a certain category (e.g. platinum) with end user 2 by sending a SIP INVITE message, carrying a resource priority (RP) header (set according to the session category) to the session control function in the VIP network. In order to allocate resources to the call, the session control function sends the QoS control function (in the same network) a call admission request using a COPS REQ message (including the session information). After running a admission control algorithm (enabling the distinction between different classes of traffic), the QoS control function determines that an ongoing media streaming session must be terminated in order to free resources for the new VoIP session to be established. Therefore, the QoS control function sends a "trigger_termination" decision (using a COPS DEC message) to the session control function in relation to the (previously admitted) media streaming session between end user 3 and the streaming server. The session control function then sends a SIP REFER message instructing the media streaming server to terminate the session it has with end user 3. The server carries this instruction by sending a SIP BYE message, containing a reason header with the value "preemption", to end user 3, as well as a MEGACO subtractStream instruction to the media handling function. After the streaming session is terminated successfully, the streaming server sends a notification to the session control function (using a SIP NOTIFY message). This last returns a COPS RPT message indicating that it has enforced the QoS control function decision, then forwards the initial INVITE message to the session control function in the SP network.

In VNet2, similar interactions occur to enforce the second QoS dimension, in which differentiation between different classes of VoIP sessions (e.g. silver, gold, and platinum) is achieved. For instance, the session control function in the SP network interacts with the Session prioritization function (SPF) to admit the call in this VNet. In this case, a decision is made to downgrade an ongoing call (from video to audio) before admitting the new call. Therefore, a downgrade instruction is sent to end user 4, which carries it by sending a SIP re-INVITE to end user 5 (containing "audio" as new media type), thus renegotiating the session parameters. After the session is successfully downgraded, a COPS RPT (report state) message is returned to the SPF, which then authorizes the establishment of the VoIP session between end users 1 and 2.

It should be noted that the two proposed QoS schemes could potentially be supported using one virtual networking layer. In that case, both the QoS control function (needed for traffic prioritization) and the SPF (needed for session prioritization) must be implemented within this virtual network layer, which could add additional cost and complexity. On the other hand, implementing the two QoS schemes in two different virtual layers showcases the ability of a virtual network to build on the capability of another virtual network, in order to offer more advanced services to end users. This recursion and nesting capability could lead to a vertical hierarchy of virtual networks and advanced multi-tier architectures.

4 Solution validation

Two prototypes were built in order to validate our solution. The first prototype focused on the implementation and testing of the virtual data plane, while the second prototype focused on the realization and performance evaluation of the virtual control plane. For simplicity, we combined the roles of VIP and SP, and used a scenario with two layers: Layer 1 (consisting of the physical network level), and Layer 2 (consisting of the first virtual network level).

4.1 Virtual routing platform prototype

In order to validate and test the operation of the virtual data plane, we implemented a virtual routing platform using the open source Vyatta router. This router can be used to build physical or virtual routing platforms for small to large size enterprises. It provides almost all of the routing functionalities offered by others routing products (e.g., Cisco, Juniper, Extreme Networks). The main advantage of the Vyatta routing solution is its ability to be executed as a virtual machine using different virtualization technologies such as Xen and VMWare. Furthermore, it offers APIs that ease the integration of the virtual routing platform on a top of physical infrastructures. In this project, it has been used to build a virtual routing platform in order to validate the operation of the virtual data plane in our architecture, and evaluate its performance. The virtual routing platform built is illustrated in Figure 6.

As shown in the figure, the network was split in two separated areas. Area 1 included routers of cities A, B and C while area 2 included routers of cities D, E and F. Each router of a city was connected to its corresponding host. These areas were connected via routers G and H. Two hosts were connected to routers of cities G and H (e.g., Hosts G1 and G2 were connected to Node G). For cities A to F, we used two routers: master and backup. Four servers, each with 36 GB of disk space capacity were used to support this platform. Two HP servers were used to implement servers 1 and 2, each with

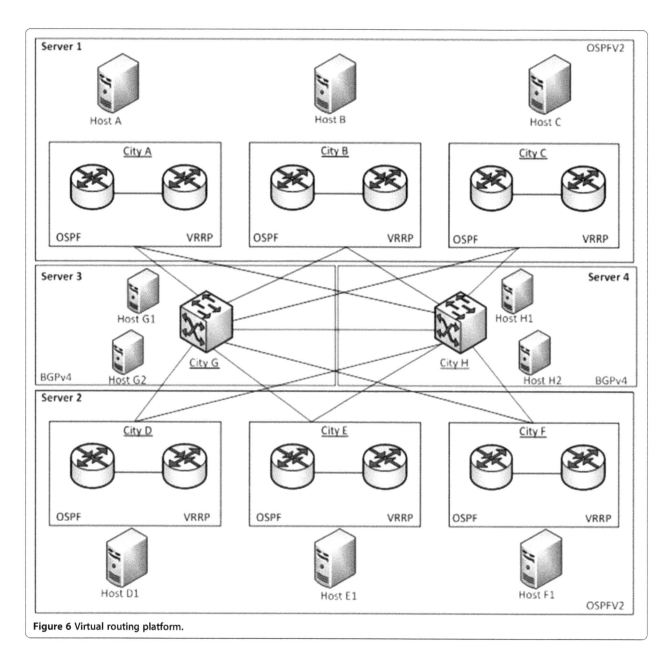

Figure 6 Virtual routing platform.

2x3.183GHz CPU and 3 Network interface Cards (NICs). Two Compaq servers hosted servers 3 and 4, each with 5 NICs. Server 3 had a 2x1.396 GHz CPU, while server 4 had a 1x1.396 GHz CPU. Each router was implemented using Vyatta version 6.3 as a virtual machine, with 1 CPU, 512 MB of memory, 4 GB of disk space and 3 NICs for cities A to F and 4 NICs for cities G and H. The main functionalities supported on each router were:1) OSPFv2 (servers 1 and 2) and BGPv4 (servers 3 and 4); 2) static routing, route redistribution between BGP and OSPF; 3) Static and dynamic (DHCP) IP address allocation; 4) Ethernet and VLAN (802.1Q) encapsulation; 5) Virtual Routing Redundancy Protocol (VRRP), CLI and SSHv2 administration and authentication; 6) Netflow Syslog and SNMPv2c diagnostics protocols. The hosts of cities A to H were implemented on virtual machines, each with 1 CPU, 256 MB of memory, 20GB disk space and 2 NICs. They were used to install a set of test tools to generate traffic across this network and to measure a set of performance metrics, namely: *JPerf* used to measure the data rate between two hosts using four TCP connections; *PingInfoView* used to measure delay in milliseconds taken by a router to answer a network request; *Ping* used to measure packet loss; *traceroute/pathping* used to determine the route taken by a packet from source to destination; *ping and timer* to determine the time taken for routing load balancing; and *Ostinato traffic generator* used to measure the load in packets/sec on processors, memories, disks of the servers hosting the virtual routers. The technical specifications of the different platform components are summarized in Table 1 below.

Among the experiments conducted, we generated 4 TCP connections, each of 20 Mbps, using the JPerf tool, on each host. Each generated traffic was sent from one host to the other hosts in this network (e.g., from host A to host B, C, D, E, F, G and H). Then, using JPerf, we measured the data rate between the Hosts. Table 2 shows the data rate in Mbps between hosts A to H.

This performance shows that data rates in a virtual environment are comparable to those obtained in a traditional physical routing platform.

We also measured the delay taken by a router to answer to a network request and the packet loss. Therefore, we performed stress test using the traffic generator Ostinato which was installed on the hosts A to H as well as on hosts G1, G2, H1 and H2. Ostinato was configured to generate 10 data streams, each of 1000 packets/second, that are sent one after the other and looping back from the first stream. These streams were sent from each host to the other hosts (e.g., from host H to host A, B, C, D, E, F and G). The generated traffic yields to 6293 MHz, 6279 MHz, 2548 MHz and 1393 MHz of CPU usage as well as 2.02 GB, 2.04 GB, 1.29 GB and 951 MB of memory usage for server 1, 2, 3 and 4 respectively. This corresponds to almost 99%, 99%, 91% and 100% of total CPU capacity usage and almost 35%, 35%, 43% and 32% of total memory capacity usage for server 1 and 2, 3 and 4 respectively. Using the PingInfoView tool, we measured the delay and the packet loss. These performances are summarized in Table 3.

A significant packet loss and almost 200 ms of delay were noticed on Host H1 and H2. These behaviors were due to the fact that server 4 has a smaller CPU capacity than server 3 and the traffic loads that yielded to 100% of CPU capacity usage. Therefore, it is important to provide enough CPU capacity in the network environment under heavy traffic load.

Moreover, using PathPing, we analyzed the route taken by packets from source (e.g., Host B) to destination (e.g., host D). We noticed that packets took the appropriate routes. For instance, for PathPing from Host B to Host D, packets went through router G with a delay of almost 1 ms and no packet loss. The number of hops between routers was varying from 1 to 3. This allowed us to validate that the routing protocols (BGP and OSPF) were well configured. Moreover, using Ping and a timer, we measured the fault tolerance recovery time. For instance, we sent Ping message from Host D to router D. We turned off master router D and backup router D replaced it. We computed the difference between the timestamp of the last packet send by the master router and the timestamp of the first packet send by the backup router. We noticed that the recovery time was almost of 6 seconds and only one packet was lost.

As a conclusion, the BGP and OSPF routing protocols, the Ethernet and VLAN encapsulation as well as fault tolerance functionality are well supported by virtual routing platform using existing virtualization technologies. Moreover, the performance of a routing infrastructure built in a virtual environment using virtual machines is almost comparable to the routing performance in a physical network.

4.2 Virtual control plane prototype

As a second validation phase for our proposed solution, we focused on the implementation and testing of the control functions needed for the instantiation, control, and management of virtual networks. In this prototype, only a subset of the components proposed in section (The proposed architecture) was implemented. Furthermore, for

Table 2 Bandwidth measurements (Mbps)

	A	B	C	D	E	F	G	H
A	X	55.3	55.3	77	83.2	76.2	84.8	59.6
B	55.1	X	55.8	81	79.3	82.9	84.7	62
C	56.3	55.8	X	81.1	81.4	79.5	85.2	59.2
D	77.2	77.7	82.1	X	54.1	53.4	77.2	65.1
E	82.2	79.4	76.4	55.8	X	52.7	75.8	63.7
F	76.6	80.1	78.1	51.8	52.5	x	78	64.7
G	82.3	82.8	83.6	83.6	85.4	83.6	x	67
H	58.3	53.2	55.7	54.6	58.6	58.3	56.2	x

Table 1 Virtual routing platform specifications

Prototype component	Technical specification
Server 1	HP server with 2x3.183GHz CPU, 3 NICs, and 36 GB of disk space
Server 2	HP server with 2x3.183GHz CPU, 3 NICs, and 36 GB of disk space
Server 3	Compaq server with 2x1.396 GHz CPU, 5 NICs, and 36 GB of disk space
Server 4	Compaq server with 1x1.396 GHz CPU, 5 NICs, and 36 GB of disk space
Virtual Routers - for cities A to F	Vyatta version 6.3 as a virtual machine, with 1 CPU, 512 MB of memory, 4 GB of disk space and 3 NICs
Virtual Routers - for cities G and H	Vyatta version 6.3 as a virtual machine, with 1 CPU, 512 MB of memory, 4 GB of disk space and 4 NICs
Hosts of cities A to H	Running on virtual machines, each with 1 CPU, 256 MB of memory, 20GB disk space and 2 NICs

Table 3 Delay and packet loss measurements

Host A	Average ping time (ms)	Succeed count	Packet lost (%)
Host A	0	10	0
Router A	7	10	0
Router G	9	10	0
Router E	10	10	0
Router F	10	10	0
Host G1	10	10	0
Router D	11	10	0
Host G2	11	10	0
Router B	13	10	0
Host E	16	10	0
Host B	17	10	0
Host F	21	10	0
Router C	22	10	0
Host C	26	10	0
Host D	34	10	0
Router D	80	10	0
Router E	80	10	0
Router F	80	10	0
Router B	86	10	0
Router C	93	10	0
Host H1	190	4	60
Router H	217	10	0
Host H2	217	3	70

the brokerage node (the SRR/CIB), we opted for a centralized design in this first stage of implementation. Figure 7 depicts the software architecture of the implemented prototype and the technologies used.

Our implementation consists of three management nodes, namely: the *PIP Management Node* (*PMN*); the *VIP Management Node* (*VMN*); and the *Broker Node* (*BN*). Each node encompasses a repository that contains resource related information and hosts the application logic realizing the functionalities of the corresponding roles (e.g. PIP, VIP, and Broker). This application logic is a set of software modules written in the Java programming language and providing JFC/Swing-based user interfaces for the administrators.

We use XML to describe the resources and formulate the various requests (e.g. discover and negotiation requests), and XSD (XML-Schema Definitions) to define the structure of the data models and specify constraints on the data contained in the XML documents. Each document exchanged between two roles is a data model (an instance of our proposed information model). Reference [13] can be consulted for a detailed description of our proposed information model.

We selected Jersey [14], an open source JAX-RS (JSR 311) reference implementation, to implement the REST interfaces, and Grizzly web server [15] to deploy the web services. Moreover, we used JAXB 2 [16] for marshaling and un-marshaling of the XML data contained in REST messages' body.

In this implementation, the BN is the key node encompassing a resource naming/identification module, as well as ranking and clustering engines, which are involved in the resource publication and discovery processes. In our approach, we store resource properties such as node type (e.g. VM, vRouter) and operating system type, virtualization environment in separate columns, whereas the XML document containing the resource description is stored as is in the same table. When received, resource publication and discovery requests are first stored in the Request Queue and later forwarded by the Request Dispatcher to the appropriate module. We use a 32 digits-based identification scheme to identify each advertised resource.

The discovery request contains two parts: the selection parameters (e.g. OS type, node type, virtualization environment); and the set of selection constraints that could be applied on functional attributes such as CPU and memory. To select the optimal resources, the Resource Discovery and Selection Engine (RDS) queries the repository to get a set of resources having similarities in their description. In such a query, the selection parameters described in the discover request are taken into consideration, which helps in filtering the resources that do not match part of the request. Afterwards, the RDS processes the returned set of resources to evaluate their functional attributes if they correspond to the selection constraints specified in the discovery request.

The PMN sends resource publication requests to the BN, and processes virtual network instantiation and resource negotiation requests for the PIP. It uses a local database to store and manage resource information and description templates as well as monitors allocated resources and updates their registered information in the broker. In addition to other components, the PMN architecture includes a Resource Instantiation and Configuration engine that handles virtual resource instantiation, configuration, and testing. This engine allows the management and control of the substrate resources.

Finally, in addition to discovering the resources needed to deploy end-user services, the VMN interacts with the PMN to negotiate resources. To build the locals and the broker databases, we used the open source RDBMS PostgreSQL [17] that offers native XML support for storing XML documents, SQL/XML publishing/querying functions, full-text search, as well as full-text indexing and XPath support. Furthermore, PostgreSQL stores an XML document in its text representation, which results

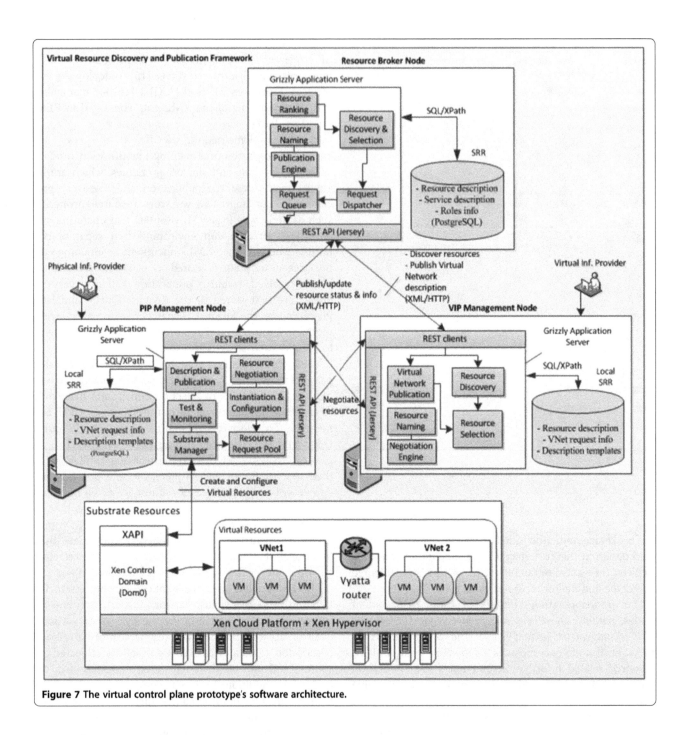

Figure 7 The virtual control plane prototype's software architecture.

in fast information retrieval and adds flexibility in terms of resources' description by eliminating the need to change tables' schema whenever additional information is added to the document. Upon receiving a resource publication request, the publication engine validates and parses the resource description, and stores the received documents as is in the database. Resources are indexed based on their identifier that is stored in a separate column. This enhances the selection process by eliminating

unnecessary parsing of an XML document since the resource identifier contains already the type of resource.

For the virtualization of substrate nodes, we used the Xen Cloud Platform (XCP) [18] that includes the Xen Hypervisor as well as Xen API (Xen Management API or XAPI). Based on Para-virtualization principles, Xen has proven to be the virtualization platform of choice due to its capabilities in terms of performance, features, and isolation level among virtual machines. XAPI provides programmatic access to, and remote administration of, Xen-enabled virtual resources through XML-RPC services.

We implemented the Substrate Manager (SM) using Xen Server's SDK that is provided by Citrix. The SM is responsible for automatically instantiating a virtual topology as described in the VNet request. We automated the resource provisioning process by eliminating the human intervention needed to create the requested virtual resources and configure their network settings. For this matter, we prepared a set of virtual machine templates on which we deployed Shell scripts that enable the addition or removal of Ethernet interface(s), the modification of a VM's IP address, as well as setting/removing a static route between two nodes (in case of a virtual router). In order to execute such scripts, the SM uses an SSH connection to the targeted virtual machine. In addition to creating and configuring virtual resources, the SM monitors the status of the running resources and displays their dynamic attributes on the PIP's interface. In this implementation, we selected Vyatta [19] used in our first prototype to connect two or more virtual networks.

4.2.1 Prototype setup and test scenarios

As shown in Figure 8, the experimental setup consisted of two management nodes (one PMN and one VMN), one broker node, and four nodes that represent substrate resources. The PMN and VMN and the substrate

nodes are DELL Precision 390 machines equally equipped with Intel Core™ Duo E6550, 2.33GHz processor and 4GB of RAM, 10000 RPM HDD, and 100MBPS link. Since the Broker node is expected to process all the incoming publication and discovery requests, we used an HP Z210 Workstation machine. It is equipped with Quad Core™ i5 processor, 4GB of RAM (1333 MHz DDR3), 7200 RPM HDD, and 100MBPS link. All the nodes are interconnected with Ethernet links through a Cisco Catalyst 2950 series Switch forming a LAN.

We installed Linux operating system (Ubuntu 12.04 LTS) and the required tools and frameworks on the management and the broker nodes. On the remaining four machines, we installed XCP and prepared a set of virtual machines templates configured with 1CPU, 512 MB of RAM, 20GB of disk space, and 5Mbps links. In this setup, we run two to four VMs on the same node.

Prior to run the experiments, we have generated a set of resource description XML documents containing all the possible resources description to be used during the evaluation process. Such documents were published into the broker using a PUT REST message in order to populate its repository with the required data.

We successfully tested the interactions related to the virtual network instantiation scenario as depicted in Figure 4. First, the PMN published the description of the virtual machines and Vyatta routers that we installed on the substrate resources to the broker. Then, the VMN

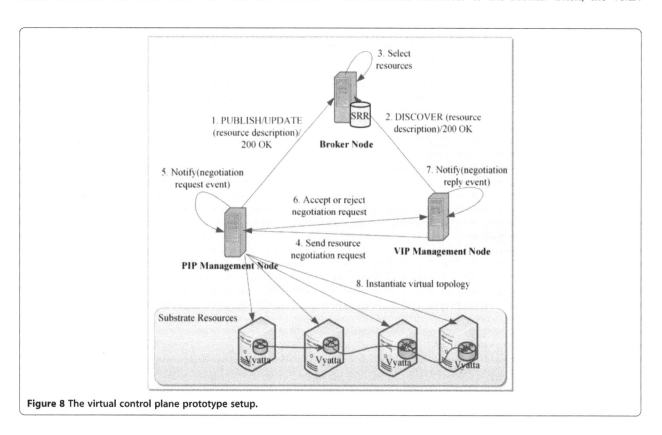

Figure 8 The virtual control plane prototype setup.

sent a discovery request to the broker. Afterwards, the broker node retrieved the information needed as described in the request from its resource repository and selected the resource candidates. After receiving the list of selected resources that best match the discovery request parameters, the VMN starts the resources' negotiation process by sending a negotiation request (containing a list of requested resources and related constraints) to the PMN. Upon receipt of the negotiation request by the PMN, a notification message is displayed on the PIP console. The negotiation process goes through two phases. First, the PMN rejected the offer and sent back the request to the VMN. Then the VMN sent another request which was accepted by the PMN. Upon reaching an agreement, the PMN instantiated the virtual topology and started the virtual resources (using XAPI client). When the requested resources started successfully, the PMN updated their published information in the broker. Figures 9, 10, and 11 illustrate three of the screen shots of our prototype operation – namely the VIP resource discovery view, the PIP resource publication view, and the PIP virtual topology management view.

4.2.2 Basic performance evaluation

To assess the basic performance of the prototype, we used the setup described in the previous section and evaluated the interactions related to resource publication (between the PMN and the BN), resource discovery (between the VMN and the BN), resource negotiation (between the VMN and PMN), and resource instantiation (between the PMN and the machines representing substrate resources). We used JMeter [20] to evaluate the REST APIs' performance, and we modified the application logic that is deployed on the management nodes to add support for measuring internal operations' processing times.

Table 4 shows the evaluation results. Each result represents the mean value calculated over 20 trials.

In the table, the response time for resource publication is calculated at the PMN as the difference between the time when the PMN's publication module sends a publication request and the time it receives a response from the BN. The time for publishing a resource includes the time taken to extract description of resources from the REST message's body and the time to store it in the broker's

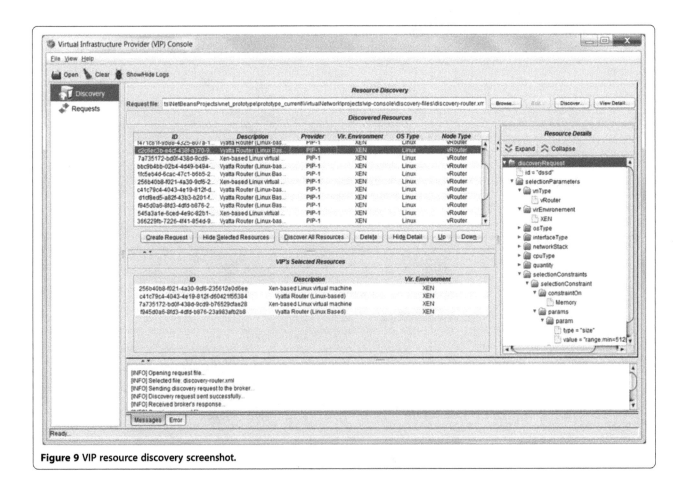

Figure 9 VIP resource discovery screenshot.

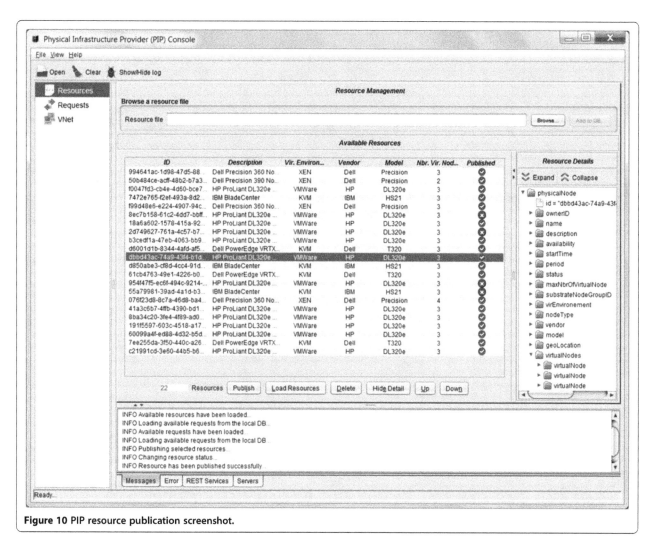

Figure 10 PIP resource publication screenshot.

repository. The results shown in the table are the average measurements over 20 trials. For each trial, we sent one resource publication request containing a document describing 2 virtual resources. On average, it took 245 ms to process this publication request, which generated 31.3 Kbytes of network load – values that we consider as reasonable. However, as we increased the number of publication requests, the response time and network load measurements increased. This is due to the request processing overhead and the concurrent access to the resources' database.

The resource discovery response time, which gives an indication about the performance of the selection algorithm, is calculated from the moment the VMN's discovery module sends a discovery request until it receives a response with the selected resources. This includes the time used for the execution of the selection algorithm and the database query time to get the list of potential resources. To perform the resource discovery experiments, we populated the resources' repository with the descriptions of 5000 different resources. The results

shown in the table are related to the tests done with one resource discovery request of two virtual resources and 50 processed resources during the selection process. On average, it took 183 ms and 23.2 KB of generated network load to process such a request. Additional tests show that as the number of discovered resources increases, the response time and the network load increase as well, due to the increased number of resources that are taken into account by the selection algorithm and the increase in size of the list of matched resources that is sent back.

The resource negotiation response time, measured at the VMN level, is calculated from the moment the VMN's negotiation module sends a negotiation request until the response is received from the PIP. On average, it took 187 ms and 34.9 KB of generated load to process a resource negotiation request related to two virtual resources.

Finally, for virtual topology instantiation, the response time is measured at the PMN level from the moment a VNet instantiation request is received until the booting

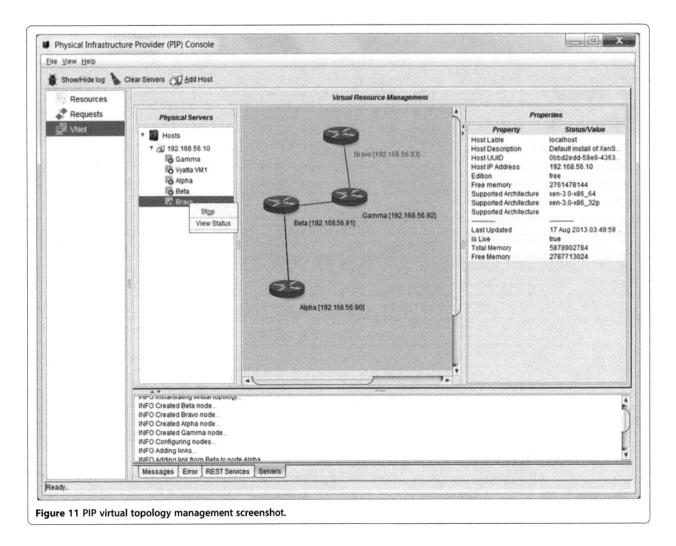

Figure 11 PIP virtual topology management screenshot.

of the virtual machines and the configuration of their virtual interfaces (through the XAPI client) is completed. In our test scenario, the virtual topology consisted of four Vyatta virtual routers connected by three links, as shown in Figure 11. On average, it takes one minute and 10 seconds to create and configure a Vyatta virtual machine, while it takes 5 minutes 55 seconds to create and configure a virtual topology consisting of four Vyatta virtual routers and three virtual links.

Analyzing those results, we conclude that the system yields an acceptable performance for the recurring operations (i.e. resource publication, discovery, and negotiation). As for the virtual topology instantiation operation, it does result in a significant response time due to its nature that requires the creation and configuration of virtual machines and their connection to form the requested topology. However, this operation is only required once, when the VNet is created. Furthermore, the automation of virtual resources configuration using SSH and shell scripts eases and speeds up the virtual topology instantiation process. It should be noted that the virtual topology instantiation time occurs during the first phase

Table 4 Network load and response time measurements

Operations	Interactions	Response time (ms)	Network load (KB)
Resource Publication [1 request/2 virtual resources published]	PMN – BN	245	31.3
Resource Discovery/selection [1 request/2 virtual resources discovered/50 resources processed during selection]	VMN – BN	183	23.2
Resource negotiation [1 request/2 virtual resources negotiated]	VMN – PMN	187	34.9
Virtual Topology instantiation [4 virtual routers, 3 virtual links]	PMN – substrate nodes	355000	142.2

(i.e. the virtual networks instantiation phase shown in Figure 4) and does not affect the performance of real-time end user services (e.g. VoIP) during their usage and operation (which constitutes the second phase shown in Figure 5). In fact, virtual networks are typically instantiated, the end user services are deployed on them at a later stage, when needed.

4.2.3 Scalability testing

In order to evaluate the behavior of the system under heavy load conditions, we conducted some stress tests, focusing on the publication and discovery related interactions. As test setup, we built a LAN consisting of 5 machines connected by a Cisco Catalyst 2950 series switch. One of those machines (HP Z210 workstation) acted as the Broker, while the other four machines (DELL 390) acted as either a PMN or a VMN (depending on the test scenario). Different test scenarios in which the nodes' roles and the number of generated requests were varied were conducted. Figures 12 and 13 show the stress testing results for the resource publication and discovery operations.

Analyzing the stress testing results, we notice that Grizzly is a suitable application server for the hosting of the broker node, due to its robustness and ability to handle a very large number of simultaneous requests (up to 2000 requests/sec can be supported). Due to those capability, our broker was able to handle very high traffic loads, without crashing. In fact, the system was tested for up to 15,000 publication requests (describing up to 120,000 resources) without failure. As the number of publication request increased, the response time to

process the requests increased in an exponential fashion, while the network load increased in a linear fashion. This exponential increase in response time is due to several factors such as: Database overhead caused by reading/writing records; description documents marshaling and un-marshaling; and HTTP requests' processing overhead.

As for the discovery operation, the broker was successfully tested for up to 12,000 discovered resources, and the response time and network load both showed exponential growth patterns with respect to the number of discovered resources. For 12,000 resources, the response time reached 23.7 minutes, and the generated network load reached 44.2 MB, due to the resource property information that is embedded in the response message.

5 Related work

Several management and control architectures have been proposed for virtualized networks. However, to the best of our knowledge, these proposals have not yet fully investigated a service-oriented hierarchical architecture, in which different types of functionalities that could be offered by a network resource (e.g., low level routing/transport functionalities, high level application logics) can be dynamically discovered, used and composed.

In [21], authors propose a layered network architecture based on four planes: data, management, control, and knowledge. These planes are implemented using different isolated virtual networks sharing the same physical infrastructure. This architecture enables the reuse of the current Internet's data plane and the deployment of concurrent next generation Internet that provides new

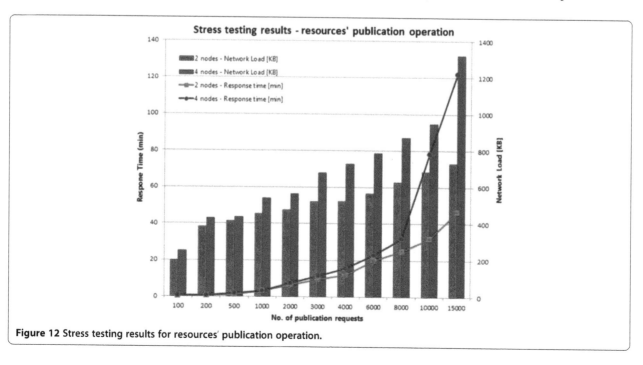

Figure 12 Stress testing results for resources' publication operation.

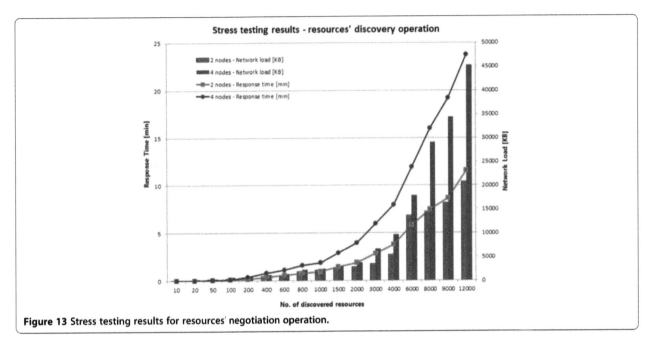

Figure 13 Stress testing results for resources' negotiation operation.

network functionalities. However, network resource discovery, usage and composition are not considered and the network partitioning proposed in [21] is far from what could be done by the architecture proposed in this paper.

A few architectures have been proposed for virtualized networks that support resources publication, discovery and access. One example is the service-oriented framework for composing network and cloud services [22]. That proposed framework is based on SOA architecture and virtualization in cloud computing [23] as well as the network virtualization business model described in [1]. The key drawback of this proposal is that a very coarse-grained service-oriented architecture is proposed with no detail on the service publication, composition, and discovery.

The Service-oriented MGON (MultiGranular Optical Network) [24] is fine-grained service-oriented network architecture that has been proposed for cloud environment. This solution provides a mapping strategy of application requests expressed in terms of QoS parameters (e.g., delay, bandwidth) to technology-specific attributes (e.g., burst size, wavelength, path) in order to offer different levels of service granularity to clouds. However, it proposes resource discovery strategy based on proprietary control and management interface with new packet format specifically tied to optical networks. Moreover, unlike the network virtualization environment where multiple heterogeneous networks can be shared by different service providers, MGON relies on a flat virtualized network architecture with a traditional ISP business model.

A hierarchical architecture for virtualized network has been proposed in [25]. It targets the virtual resource management issue and proposes a framework to discover, select and use network resources in order to build virtual networks. However, no detailed information is given on how resources are discovered and selected.

In reference [26], the authors discuss how SOA (Service Oriented Architecture) can be leveraged to realize the concept of Network as a Service (NaaS), thus enabling the convergence of virtual networking and cloud computing. Different technologies related to the realization of the NaaS concept are discussed in the paper, including network service description, discovery, and composition solutions. None of these solutions present an end-to-end architecture for network virtualization.

6 Conclusions and lessons learned

Network virtualization is an emerging concept that enables the dynamic creation of virtual networks over a shared physical network infrastructure. There are several motivations behind this concept, including increased flexibility, diversity, and manageability in networking environments. We have previously proposed a service-oriented hierarchical business model for virtual networking environments. This model aims at creating a dynamic and collaborative environment, in which a large pool of virtualized networking resources, which are seen as services (of different levels), can be dynamically discovered, used, and composed. In this paper, we proposed an open virtual multi-services networking architecture enabling the realization of our business model. Furthermore, we illustrated our architecture's operation using a virtualized QoS-enabled VoIP scenario. This paper also presented performance analysis of a virtual routing platform that was implemented using open source Vyatta router.

Furthermore, a proof-of-concept prototype of the virtual control plane was implemented using a variety of technologies and tools, such as: Jersey, Grizzly Web server, JAXB, PostgreSQL, Vyatta virtual router, and the Xen Cloud Platform (XCP). Basic performance measurements and stress testing results of the main operations were also collected and analyzed.

During the course of this project, we learned several important lessons. The first is that service-oriented concepts can be very useful for building open, flexible, and collaborative virtual networking environments, in which various network functionalities are considered as services that can be reused and composed, and roles are considered to be distributed and loosely coupled entities interacting via programmable interfaces. Another lesson we learned is that the Vyatta routing solution is suitable for small-size to mid-size network infrastructures with performance behaviors almost comparable to those of a physical network. A third lesson learned is that Vyatta routing solution is not adapted to large-size networks (e.g., backbone network). Indeed, we noticed that due to overwhelming data traffic sent through the platform, the Vyatta processor load increases very fast and therefore the processor of the hypervisor (in our case VMWare) quickly becomes saturated. Moreover, it may be difficult to run a virtual machine that provides a network interface with high data rates to ensure the transfer of higher traffic load. However, servers with greater capacities than those chosen in this paper should be considered to identify what would be the maximum traffic load supported by such platform.

Abbreviations
VPNs: Virtual Private Networks; VNets: Virtual Networks; WSNs: Wireless Sensor Networks; PIP: Physical Infrastructure Provider; VIP: Virtual Infrastructure Provider; SRR: Services and Resources Registry; CIB: Context Information Base; PMN: PIP Management Node; VMN: VIP Management Node; BN: Broker Node; RDS: Resource Discovery and Selection Engine; XCP: Xen Cloud Platform; SM: Substrate Manager; MGON: MultiGranular Optical Network; SOA: Service Oriented Architecture; NaaS: Network as a Service.

Competing interests
The authors declare that they have no competing interests.

Authors' contributions
MEB is the lead of the research team, proposing the research topic and managing/coordinating research activities. NK is an expert in virtualization and had contributions related to the business modeling and the architecture. SR carried the design and implementation work related to the virtual control plane prototype, and performed the related performance evaluation. MF Worked on the virtual routing platform prototype implementation and testing. All authors read and approved the final manuscript.

Acknowledgement
This paper is an extended version of the article presented at IEEE CCNC 2012, under the title of "Open Virtual Playground: Initial Architecture and Results".

Author details
[1]College of Technological Innovation, Zayed University, Khalifa City B, P.O. Box 144534, Abu Dhabi, United Arab Emirates. [2]Department of Software and IT Engineering, University of Quebec, 1100 Notre-Dame, West, Montréal, Quebec, H3C 1 K3, Canada. [3]Faculty of Engineering and Computer Science, Concordia University, 1515 St. Catherine W, Montreal, Quebec, H4G 2 W1, Canada. [4]Ericsson Canada, 8400 Blvd, Décarie Montréal, Québec, H4P 2 N2, Canada.

References

1. Chowdhury N, Boutaba R (2009) Network virtualization: state of the art and research challenges. IEEE Commun Mag 47(7):20–26
2. Rosen E and Rekhter Y (2006) "BGP/MPLS IP Virtual Private Networks (VPNs)," RFC 4364, Internet Engineering Task Force
3. Turner JS and Taylor "Diversifying the Internet". In: Proceedings of IEEE Global Telecommunications Conference (GLOBECOM'05), IEEE Press, St. Louis, MO, USA, pp. 1-6.
4. Anderson T, Perterson L, Shenker S, Turner J (2004) Overcoming the internet impasse through virtualization. In Proceedings of ACM HOTNETS, San Diego, CA, USA
5. El Barachi M, Kara N and Dssouli R (2010) "Towards a Service-Oriented Network Virtualization Architecture". In: Proceedings of the 3rd ITU-T Kaleidoscope Event 2010 (K-2010), pp 1–7.
6. El Barachi M, Kara N and Dssouli R (2012) "Open Virtual Playground: Initial Architecture and Results". In: Proceedings of the 9th IEEE Consumer Communications and Networking Conference 2012 (CCNC 2012), pp 576–581.
7. "4WARD – Architecture and Design for the Future Internet: Project-wide Evaluation of Business Use Cases". Public deliverable No. FP7-ICT-2007-1-216041-4WARD/D-1.2, European Union's 7th Framework, Sweden, December 2009.
8. Feldmann A (2007) Internet clean-slate design: What and why?". SIGCOMM CCR 37(3):59–64
9. Abowd G, Dey A, Brown P, Davies N, Smith M and Steggles P "Towards a Better Understanding of Context and Context-Awareness". In: Hans-Werner Gellersen (Ed) Proceedings of the 1st international symposium on Handheld and Ubiquitous Computing (HUC '99), Springer-Verlag, London, UK, UK, pp 304-307
10. Hasam M, Amarasinghe H and Karmouch A "Network Virtualization: Dealing with multiple infrastructure providers". In: Proceedings of the IEEE International Conference on Communications (ICC 2012), IEEE Press, Ottawa, ON, Canada, pp 5890–5895
11. Medhioub H, Houidi I, Louati W and Zeghlache D (2011) "Design, implementation and evaluation of virtual resource description and clustering framework". 25th IEEE International Conference on Advanced Information Networking and Applications 2011, IEEE Press, Biopolis, pp 83–89.
12. Houidi I, Louati W, Zeghlache D, Papadimitriou P and Mathy L (2010) "Adaptive virtual network provisioning". In: Proceedings of the ACM SIGCOMM Workshop on Virtualized Infrastructure Systems and Architectures, ACM Press, New York, NY, USA, pp 41-48.
13. El Barachi M, Rabah S, Kara N, Dssouli R and Paquet J (2013) "A Multi-Service Multi-role Integrated Information Model for Dynamic Resource Discovery in Virtual Networks". In: Proceedings of the IEEE Wireless Communications and Networking Conference 2013 (WCNC 2013), IEEE Press, Shanghai, China, pp 4777–4782.
14. "Jersey," [Online]. Available: http://jersey.java.net/.
15. "Project Grizzly" [Online]. Available: http://grizzly.java.net/.
16. "JAXB Project" [Online]. Available: https://jaxb.java.net/.
17. "PostgreSQL Global Development Group" [Online]. Available: http://www.postgresql.org/.
18. "Xen Cloud Platform" Xen Porject, [Online]. Available: http://www.xen.org/products/cloudxen.html.
19. "Vyatta," Brocade, [Online]. Available: http://www.vyatta.com/.
20. "JMeter™" Apache Software Foundation, [Online]. Available: http://jmeter.apache.org/.
21. Jin D, Li Y, Zhou Y, Su L and Zeng L (2009) "A virtualized-based network architecture for next generation internet". In: Proceedings of the Third International Conference on Anti-counterfeiting, Security, and Identification in Communication, IEEE Press, Hong Kong, pp 58–62.
22. Qiang D (2011) "Modeling and performance analysis on network virtualization for composite network-cloud service provisioning". In: Proceedings of the 11th IEEE World Congress on Services, pp 548–555.

23. Zhang L-J and Zhou Q (2009) "CCOA: Cloud Computing Open Architecture", In: the Proceedings of the 1st Symposium on Network System Design and Implementation (NSDI '09), IEEE Press, Los Angeles, CA, USA, pp 607-616.

24. Zervas G, Martini V, Qin Y, Escalona E, Nejabati R, Simeonidou D, Baroncelli F, Martini B, Torkmen K, Castoldi P (2010) Service-oriented multigranular optical network architecture for clouds. IEEE/OSA J Opt Commun Netw 2 (10):883–891

25. Lv B, Wang Z, Huang T, Chen J and Liu Y "Hierarchical Virtual Resource Management Architecture for Network Virtualization". In: Proceedings of the 6th International Conference on Wireless Communications Networking and Mobile Computing (WiCOM 2010), IEEE Press, Chengdu, pp 1–4

26. Duan Q, Yan Y, Vasilakos AV (2012) A survey on service-oriented network virtualization toward convergence of networking and cloud computing. IEEE Trans Netw Serv Manag 9(4):373–392

7

Virtual network security: threats, countermeasures, and challenges

Leonardo Richter Bays[1], Rodrigo Ruas Oliveira[1], Marinho Pilla Barcellos[1], Luciano Paschoal Gaspary[1*] and Edmundo Roberto Mauro Madeira[2]

Abstract

Network virtualization has become increasingly prominent in recent years. It enables the creation of network infrastructures that are specifically tailored to the needs of distinct network applications and supports the instantiation of favorable environments for the development and evaluation of new architectures and protocols. Despite the wide applicability of network virtualization, the shared use of routing devices and communication channels leads to a series of security-related concerns. It is necessary to provide protection to virtual network infrastructures in order to enable their use in real, large scale environments. In this paper, we present an overview of the state of the art concerning virtual network security. We discuss the main challenges related to this kind of environment, some of the major threats, as well as solutions proposed in the literature that aim to deal with different security aspects.

Keywords: Network virtualization; Security; Threats; Countermeasures

1 Introduction

Virtualization is a well established concept, with applications spanning several areas of computing. This technique enables the creation of multiple virtual platforms over a single physical infrastructure, allowing heterogeneous architectures to run on the same hardware. Additionally, it may be used to optimize the usage of physical resources, as an administrator is able to dynamically instantiate and remove virtual nodes in order to satisfy varying levels of demand.

In recent years, there has been a growing demand for adaptive network services with increasingly distinct requirements. Driven by such demands, and stimulated by the successful employment of virtualization for hosting custom-built servers, researchers have started to explore the use of this technique in network infrastructures. Network virtualization allows the creation of multiple independent virtual network instances on top of a single physical substrate [1]. This is made possible by instantiating one or more virtual routers on physical devices and establishing virtual links between these routers, forming topologies that are not limited by the structure of the physical network.

In addition to the ability to create different topological structures, virtual networks are also not bound by other characteristics of the physical network, such as its protocol stack. Thus, it is possible to instantiate virtual network infrastructures that are specifically tailored to the needs of different network applications [2]. These features also enable the creation of virtual testbeds that are similar to real infrastructures, a valuable asset for evaluating newly developed architectures and protocols without interfering with production traffic. [3] For these reasons, network virtualization has attracted the interest of a number of researchers worldwide, especially in the context of Future Internet research. Network virtualization has been embraced by the Industry as well. Major Industry players – such as Cisco and Juniper – nowadays offer devices that support virtualization, and this new functionality allowed infrastructure providers to offer new services.

In contrast to the benefits brought by network virtualization, the shared use of routing devices and communication channels introduces a series of security-related concerns. Without adequate protection, users from a virtual network might be able to access or even interfere with traffic that belongs to other virtual networks, violating

*Correspondence: paschoal@inf.ufrgs.br
[1] Institute of Informatics, Federal University of Rio Grande do Sul, Porto Alegre, Brazil
Full list of author information is available at the end of the article

security properties such as confidentiality and integrity [4,5]. Additionally, the infrastructure could be a target for denial of service attacks, causing availability issues for virtual networks instantiated on top of it [6,7]. Therefore, it is of great importance that network virtualization architectures offer protection against these and other types of threats that might compromise security.

Recently, attention has been drawn to security concerns in network infrastructures due to the discovery of pervasive electronic surveillance around the globe. Although all kinds of networks are potentially affected, the shared use of physical resources in virtual network environments exacerbates these concerns. As such, these recent circumstances highlight the need for a comprehensive analysis of current developments in the area of virtual network security.

In this paper, we characterize the current state of the art regarding security in network virtualization. We identify the main threats to network virtualization environments, as well as efforts aiming to secure such environments. For this study, an extensive literature search has been conducted. Major publications from the literature have been studied and grouped according to well known classifications in the area of network security, as well as subcategories proposed by the authors of this paper. This organization allows the analysis and discussion of multiple aspects of virtual network security.

The remainder of this paper is organized as follows. Section 2 presents a brief background on the area of network virtualization as well as a review of related literature. Section 3 introduces the taxonomy used to classify the selected publications. Section 4 exposes the security vulnerabilities and threats found in the literature, while Section 5 presents the security countermeasures provided by solutions found in previous proposals. In Section 6, we discuss the results of this study, and in Section 7 we summarize the main current research challenges in the area of virtual network security. Last, in Section 8 we present our conclusions.

2 Background and literature review

In this section, we first provide a brief background on the area of network virtualization, highlighting its most relevant concepts. Next, we present a review of literature closely related to virtual network security.

2.1 Background

Network virtualization consists of sharing resources from physical network devices (routers, switches, etc.) among different virtual networks. It allows the coexistence of multiple, possibly heterogeneous networks, on top of a single physical infrastructure. The basic elements of a network virtualization environment are shown in Figure 1. At the physical network level, a number of autonomous

systems are represented by interconnected network substrates (e.g., substrates A, B, and C). Physical network devices are represented by nodes supporting virtualization technologies. Virtual network topologies (e.g., virtual networks 1 and 2), in turn, are mapped to a subset of nodes from one or more substrates. These topologies are composed of virtual routers, which use a portion of the resources available in physical ones, and virtual links, which are mapped to physical paths composed of one or more physical links and their respective intermediate routers.

From the point of view of a virtual network, virtual routers and links are seen as dedicated physical devices. However, in practice, they share physical resources with routers and links from other virtual networks. For this reason, the virtualization technology used to create this environment must provide an adequate level of isolation in order to enable the use of network virtualization in real, large scale environments.

Over the years, different methods for instantiating virtual networks have been used. Typical approaches include VLANs (Virtual Local Area Networks) and VPNs (Virtual Private Networks). Recently, Virtual Machine Monitors and programmable networks have been employed to create virtual routers and links over physical devices and communication channels. These approaches are briefly revisited next.

2.1.1 Protocol-based approaches

Protocol-based approaches consist of implementing a network protocol that enables the distinction of virtual networks through techniques such as tagging or tunneling. The only requirement of this kind of approach is that physical devices (or a subset of them) support the selected protocol.

One example of protocol-based network virtualization are VLANs. VLANs consist of logical partitions of a single underlying network. Devices in a VLAN communicate with each other as if they were on the same Local Area Network, regardless of physical location or connectivity. All frames sent through a network are tagged with their corresponding VLAN ID, processed by VLAN-enabled routers and forwarded as necessary [8]. Since isolation is typically based only on packet tagging, this approach is susceptible to eavesdropping attacks.

Another commonly used approach is the creation of Virtual Private Networks. VPNs are typically used to provide a secure communication channel between geographically distributed nodes. Cryptographic tunneling protocols enable data confidentiality and user authentication, providing a higher level of security in comparison with VLANs. VPNs can be provided in the physical, data link, or network layers according to the protocols being employed [9].

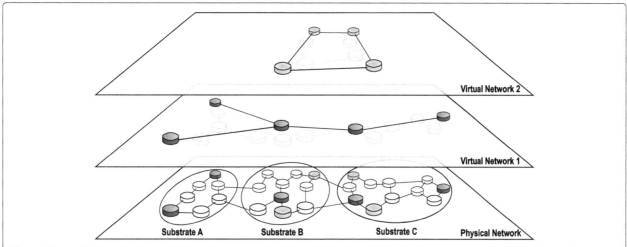

Figure 1 Network virtualization model, denoting a scenario with multiple physical substrates (Substrate A, B, and C) and virtual networks (Virtual Network 1 and 2).

2.1.2 Machine virtualization-based approaches

Machine virtualization-based approaches consist of creating virtual networks by means of groups of interconnected virtual machines. Virtual Machine Monitors are used to instantiate virtual routers, and virtual links are established between them, regardless of physical network topology. Table 1 shows different machine virtualization-based techniques that can be used to create virtual networks, as well as a brief explanation and an example of each.

This alternative is remarkably flexible and relatively cheap, as it allows the use of customized software and does not require the use of specific hardware[1]. However, it is more demanding in terms of resource usage in comparison to previously described protocol-based approaches. Additionally, it may introduce security concerns associated with server virtualization, some of which are mentioned in Sections 4 and 5. A general study on the security issues that arise from the use of machine virtualization was performed by van Cleeff et al. [10].

2.1.3 Programmable networks

Programmable routers have been used to enable the creation of virtual networks. Although this is not a new concept, research in this area has been recently stimulated by the inception of Software-Defined Networking (SDN). This paradigm consists of decoupling the data plane and the control plane in network devices. More specifically, devices such as routers and links retain only the data plane, and a separated control plane manages such devices based on an overview of the entire network.

OpenFlow [11], one of the most promising techniques for implementing this paradigm, defines a protocol that allows a centralized controller to act as the control plane, managing the behavior of network devices in a dynamic manner. The controller communicates with network devices through a secure connection, creating and managing flow rules. Flow rules instruct network devices on how to properly process and route network traffics with distinct characteristics. Through the establishment of specific flow rules, it is possible to logically partition physical networks and achieve data plane isolation. This isolation enables the creation of virtual networks on top of an SDN environment. OpenFlow gave rise to the Open Networking Foundation, an organization ran by major companies within the area of computer networks that aims to disseminate this type of technology.

Table 1 Virtualization techniques

Technique	Description	Examples
Full virtualization	The Virtual Machine Monitor emulates a complete machine, based on the underlying hardware architecture. The guest Operating System runs without any modification.	VMware Workstation, VirtualBox
Paravirtualization	The Virtual Machine monitor emulates a machine which is similar to the underlying hardware, with the addition of a hypervisor. The hypervisor allows the guest Operating System to run complex tasks directly on non-virtualized hardware. The guest OS must be modified in order to take advantage of this feature.	VMware ESX, Xen
Container-based virtualization	Instead of running a full Virtual Machine, this technique provides Operating System-level containers, based on separate userspaces. In each container, the hardware, as well as the Operating System and its kernel, are identical to the underlying ones.	OpenVZ, Linux VServer

2.2 Literature review

To the best of our knowledge, there have been no previous attempts at characterizing the state of the art regarding security in network virtualization. However, there have been a number of similar studies in other, closely related fields of research. We now proceed to a review of some of the main such studies.

Chowdhury *et al.* [1] provide a general survey in the area of network virtualization. The authors analyze the main projects in this area (both past projects and, at the time of publication, current ones) and discuss a number of key directions for future research. The authors touch upon the issues of security and privacy both while reviewing projects and discussing open challenges; however, as this is not the main focus of this survey, there is no in-depth analysis of security issues found in the literature.

Bari *et al.* [12] present a survey that focuses on data center network virtualization. Similarly to the aforementioned study, the authors survey a number of key projects and discuss potential directions for future work. When analyzing such projects, the authors provide insights on the fault-tolerance capabilities of each one, in addition to a brief discussion on security issues as one of the potential opportunities for future research.

In addition to the general studies on network virtualization presented so far, a number of surveys on cloud computing security have also been carried out. Cloud computing environments tend to make use of both machine and network virtualization, making this a highly relevant related topic for our study. However, while there is some overlap between cloud computing security and virtual network security, we emphasize that cloud computing represents a very specific use case of network virtualization and, therefore, poses a significantly distinct set of security challenges. Zhou *et al.* [13] provide an investigation on security and privacy issues of cloud computing system providers. Additionally, the authors highlight a number of government acts that originally intended to uphold privacy rights but fail to do so in light of advances in technology. Hashizume *et al.* [14], in turn, focus on security vulnerabilities, threats, and countermeasures found in the literature and the relationships among them.

Last, Scott-Hayward *et al.* [15] conducted a study on SDN security. As explained in Section 2.1.3, this is one of the technologies on top of which network virtualization environments can be instantiated. The authors first analyze security issues associated with the SDN paradigm and, afterwards, investigate approaches aiming at enhancing SDN security. Last, the authors discuss security challenges associated with the SDN model.

3 Taxonomy

The first step towards a comprehensive analysis of the literature was the selection of a number of publications from quality conferences and journals. To this end, we performed extensive searches in the ACM and IEEE digital libraries using a number of keywords related to network virtualization and security. We then ranked the literature found through this process according to the average ratio of citations per publication of the conferences or journals in which these papers were published. All publications from top tier conferences or journals with a consistent number of citations per publication were considered relevant and, therefore, selected. The remaining papers were analyzed and generally discarded.

Following the aforementioned process, a taxonomy was created in order to aid the organization and discussion of the selected publications. For this purpose, two well known classifications in the area of network security were chosen. Papers are organized according to the *security threats* they aim to mitigate, and afterwards, according to the *security countermeasures* they provide. As different authors have different definitions for each of these concepts, these classifications are briefly explained in the following subsections. The direct connection between them and the area of virtual network security is explained in sections 4 and 5, respectively.

In addition to these broad classifications, subcategories were created in order better organize this body of work. Figure 2 presents the full hierarchical organization that will be used in sections 4 and 5. Dark gray boxes represent broad categories used in the literature [16,17], while white boxes denote subdivisions proposed and created by the authors of this paper.

3.1 Security vulnerabilities and threats

There are a number of potential malicious actions, or threats, that may violate security constraints of computational systems. Shirey [16] describes and divides the consequences of these threats into four categories, namely *disclosure*, *deception*, *disruption*, and *usurpation*.

Unauthorized *disclosure* is defined as gaining unauthorized access to protected information. Sensitive data may be erroneously exposed to unauthorized entities, or acquired by an attacker that circumvents the system's security provisions.

Deception is characterized by intentionally attempting to mislead other entities. For example, a malicious entity may send false or incorrect information to others, leading them to believe that this information is correct. Fake identities may be used in order to incriminate others or gain illegitimate access.

Disruption means causing failure or degradation of systems, negatively affecting the services they provide.

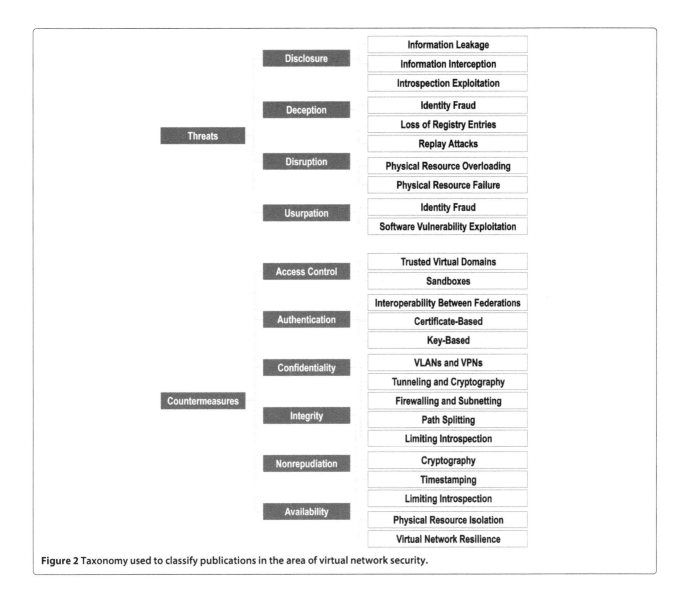

Figure 2 Taxonomy used to classify publications in the area of virtual network security.

This may be done by directly incapacitating a system component or the channel through which information is delivered, or by inducing the system to deliver corrupted information.

Last, through *usurpation*, an attacker may gain unauthorized control over a system. This unauthorized control may allow the attacker to illegitimately access protected data or services, or tamper with the system itself in order to cause incorrect or malicious behavior.

These threat categories, as well as the previously mentioned subcategories we have created, also cover vulnerabilities and attacks. For ease of comprehension, vulnerabilities and threats are discussed collectively in Section 4. Table 2 presents the relationships between vulnerabilities and threats in network virtualization environments. This table is organized according to the previously described taxonomy and lists all vulnerabilities found in the literature and the threats associated with each one.

Additionally, the terms threat and attack are used interchangeably throughout the paper, as a threat may be understood as a potential attack (while an attack is the proper action that takes advantage of a vulnerability to violate a security policy).

3.2 Security countermeasures

Due to the existence of the previously described threats, computational systems must provide a series of countermeasures in order to maintain a desirable level of security. Stallings [17] categorizes these essential countermeasures into six subdivisions (referred to by Stallings as "security services"), namely *access control, authentication, data confidentiality, data integrity, nonrepudiation,* and *availability.*

Access control allows a system to administer which entities will be able to access its functions, and what permissions each of these entities will have. In order to grant

Table 2 Relationships between vulnerabilities and threats in network virtualization environments

Threat categories		Vulnerabilities	Threats
Disclosure	Information Leakage	Lack of ARP table protection	ARP table poisoning
		Placement of firewall rules inside virtual nodes	Subversion of firewall rules
	Information Interception	Lack of ARP table protection	ARP table poisoning
		Transmission of data in predictable patterns	Traffic Analysis attacks
		Uncontrolled handling of multiple, sequential virtual network requests from a single entity	Inference and disclosure of sensitive topological information
		Unprotected exchange of routing information among virtual routers	Disclosure of sensitive routing information
	Introspection Exploitation	Uncontrolled Introspection	Data theft
Deception	Identity Fraud	Improper handling of identities: - within individual networks;	Injection of malicious messages with forged sources
		- among federated networks;	Privilege escalation
		- during migration procedures.	Abuse of node removal and re-addition in order to obtain new (clean) identities
	Loss of registry entries	Uncontrolled rollback operations	Loss of registry entries
	Replay attacks	Lack of unique message identifiers	Replay attacks
Disruption	Physical Resource Overloading	Uncontrolled resource allocation	Performance degradation
			Abusive resource consumption
		Uncontrolled handling of virtual network requests	Exhaustion of resources in specific parts of the infrastructure
		Lack of proactive or reactive recovery strategies	Denial of Service attacks
	Physical Resource Failure	Lack of proactive or reactive recovery strategies	Failure of virtual routers/networks
		Uncontrolled resource reallocation after failures	Overloading of remaining virtual routers after failures
Usurpation	Identity Fraud	Improper handling of identities and associated privileges	Privilege escalation
	Software Vulnerability Exploitation	Privilege escalation in Virtual Machine Monitors	Unauthorized control of physical routers

individual access rights and permissions, entities must be properly authenticated in the system.

The purpose of *authentication* is to ensure that entities communicating with each other are, in fact, the entities they claim to be. The receiver of a message must be able to correctly identify its sender, and an entity must not be able to impersonate another.

Providing adequate *data confidentiality* means ensuring that third parties do not have access to confidential information being transmitted between two entities. Additionally, the system should inhibit attackers from deriving information by analyzing traffic flow characteristics.

Data integrity has the purpose of assuring that data stored by entities or transmitted through a network are not corrupted, adulterated or destroyed. Attacks such as duplication, modification, reordering, and replay of messages must be prevented. Furthermore, mechanisms for recovering from data corruption may also be provided.

In communications between peers, *nonrepudiation* provides a way to settle disputes when an entity denies having performed a certain action. The goal of this service is to prevent entities from falsely denying participation in any (possibly malicious) network-related activity.

The last security countermeasure is *availability*. System resources must be available upon request by an authorized entity, and the system must also conform to its performance specifications. In order to maintain availability, countermeasures against attacks such as *denial of service* must be provided.

4 Security vulnerabilities and threats

In this section, we present a comprehensive list of vulnerabilities and threats found in network virtualization environments. The interested reader should refer to Table 2 for a systematic review of such vulnerabilities and threats.

While some of the threats listed in this section are a result of accidental actions, we emphasize that all threats – intentional or accidental – have an effect on security. As an example of an accidental attack, it is common for virtual routers to attempt to use all available resources (as virtualization tends to be transparent and virtual routers are typically not aware that they are not running on dedicated physical hardware). If the network virtualization environment does not adequately limit the resource usage of each virtual router, even this unintentional abuse may cause disruption on other networks hosted on the same substrate or cause the degradation or failure of critical services provided by the virtualization environment.

4.1 Disclosure

In an environment where physical resources are shared between a number of virtual networks, there is a series of behaviors that may result in undesired disclosure of information. Threats related to disclosure of private or sensitive information are explained next.

4.1.1 Information leakage

Cavalcanti et al. [18] mention the possibility of messages being leaked from one virtual network to another. In this type of attack, an entity may disclose private or sensitive information to members of other virtual networks, who should not have access to such information. The authors state that this may be achieved through ARP table poisoning. For example, a malicious user may spoof the IP address of a node that is able to send messages to the virtual network with which it intends to communicate. Wolinsky et al. [19] describe a similar attack, in which virtual nodes send messages to outside the boundaries of a network virtualization environment. This would make it possible for messages to reach physical nodes that not only do not belong to any virtual network, but are hosted outside of the virtualized network infrastructure. According to the authors, if data isolation is achieved by means of firewall rules, malicious users may be able to subvert such rules by escalating privileges and gaining root access on a virtual node.

4.1.2 Information interception

Attackers in a virtual network environment may capture messages being exchanged between two entities in order to access their content. This type of attack, often referred to as "eavesdropping" or "sniffing", may lead to theft of confidential information [4,5,20]. Wu et al. [20], specifically, mention ARP table poisoning as a means of achieving this. In contrast to the ARP poisoning attack described by Cavalcanti et al. [18] (explained in Section 4.1.1), in this case the attack would be used in order to mislead physical routers into forwarding packets meant to one entity to another one, allowing a malicious entity to sniff such packets. This is a common threat in any networking

environment, but the use of shared physical resources by multiple virtual networks further exacerbates this problem. According to these and other authors, such as Cui et al. [21], networking solutions provided by virtual machine monitors may not properly isolate data belonging to different virtual networks. This means that members of one virtual network may be able to access data being transferred by other virtual networks sharing the same substrate.

Even if data inside network packets is protected (e.g. through the use of cryptography), entities may be able to derive sensitive information by analyzing them. In traffic analysis attacks, described by Huang et al. [22], entities acquire such information by analyzing characteristics of traffic flows between communicating entities in virtual networks. These characteristics include which entities communicate with which other entities, frequency of communication, and packet sizes, among others. For example, an entity that is involved in frequent, short communications with a high number of other entities may be a central point of control in the network. Knowing this, a malicious user could launch an attack directed at that entity, aiming to cause a considerable amount of disruption with limited effort. As previously mentioned, this attack is effective even if traffic is encrypted, making any type of virtual networking environment a potential target.

In addition to the previously detailed forms of information interception, which may also affect traditional network environments, other forms are specific to network virtualization. One such form is the use of multiple virtual network requests to disclose the topology of the physical infrastructure, explored by Pignolet et al. [23]. This constitutes a security threat, as infrastructure providers typically do not wish to disclose this information. The authors demonstrate that by sequentially requesting a number of virtual networks with varying topological characteristics and analyzing the response given by the infrastructure provider (i.e., whether the request can be embedded or not), they are able to gradually obtain information about the physical topology. Moreover, the authors determine the number of requests needed to fully disclose the physical topology on networks with different topological structures (tree, cactus, and arbitrary graphs). Conversely, Fukushima et al. [24] state that the entity controlling a physical network may obtain confidential routing information from virtual networks hosted on top of it. As current routing algorithms require routing information to be sent and received through virtual routers, sensitive information may be disclosed to the underlying network.

4.1.3 Introspection exploitation

Introspection is a feature present in virtual machine monitors that allows system administrators to verify the current state of virtual machines in real time. It enables external observers to inspect data stored in different parts of the virtual machine (including processor registers, disk, and memory) without interfering with it. While this feature has valuable, legitimate uses (*e.g.*, enabling administrators to verify that a virtual machine is operating correctly), it may be misused or exploited by attackers in order to access (and potentially disclose) sensitive data inside virtual machines [10]. This problem is aggravated by the fact that virtual nodes may be moved or copied between multiple virtual machine monitors, as sensitive data may be compromised through the exploitation of this feature on any virtual machine monitor permanently or temporarily hosting such virtual nodes.

4.2 Deception

We have identified three subcategories of threats that may lead to deception in virtual network environments. These subdivisions – namely identity fraud, loss of registry entries and replay attacks – are explained next.

4.2.1 Identity fraud

In addition to dealing with unauthorized disclosure, Cabuk *et al.* [5] and Wu *et al.* [20] also describe threats related to deception in virtual network environments. Specifically, virtual entities may inject malicious messages into a virtual network, and deceive others into believing that such messages came from another entity.

Certain characteristics of virtualized network environments increase the difficulty of handling identity fraud. The aggregation of different virtual networks into one compound network, known as federation, is indicated by Chowdhury *et al.* [25] as one of such characteristics. Federation raises issues such as the presence of separate roles and possible incompatibility between security provisions or policies from aggregated networks. Another complicating factor mentioned by the authors is the dynamic addition and removal of entities. An attacker may force a malicious node to be removed and re-added in order to obtain a new identity.

Other characteristics that complicate the handling of identity fraud involve operations such as migration and duplication of virtual nodes, as mentioned by van Cleeff *et al.* [10]. The study presented by the authors refers to virtualization environments in general. Therefore, in the context of this study, a virtual node may refer to either a virtual router or a virtual workstation. If a virtual node is migrated from one physical point to another, the identity of the machine that contains this virtual node may change. Moreover, virtual nodes may be copied to one or more physical points in order to provide redundancy, which may lead to multiple entities sharing a single identity. Both of these issues may cause inconsistencies in the process of properly identifying the origin of network messages, which may be exploited in identity fraud attacks.

4.2.2 Loss of registry entries

Van Cleeff *et al.* [10] also mention issues related to logging of operations in virtualization environments. If information regarding which entity was responsible for each operation in the network is stored in logs inside virtual machines, entries may be lost during rollback procedures. Likewise, logs of malicious activities performed by attackers may also be lost.

4.2.3 Replay attacks

Fernandes and Duarte [26] mention replay attacks as another form of deception in virtual networks. In this type of attack, a malicious entity captures legitimate packets being transfered through the network and retransmits them, leading other entities to believe that a message was sent multiple times. The authors explain that virtual routers may launch attacks in which they repeat old control messages with the intention of corrupting the data plane of the attacked domain.

4.3 Disruption

In a network virtualization environment, proper management of resources is crucial to avoid disruption. The main sources of disruption in such environments are related to the abuse of physical resources (either intentional or unintentional) and the failure of physical devices.

4.3.1 Physical resource overloading

Physical resource overloading may lead to failure of virtual nodes, or cause the network performance to degrade below its minimum requirements. This degradation may cause congestion and packet loss in virtual networks, as stated by Zhang *et al.* [27]. In addition to causing disruption in already established networks, overloading may also hinder the deployment of new ones.

Resource requirements themselves can be a point of conflict in virtual network environments. As explained by Marquezan *et al.* [28], multiple virtual networks may require an excessive amount of resources in the same area of the substrate network. While such prohibitive demands may be unintentional, they may also be due to a coordinated attack. This may not only happen during deployment operations, but also during the lifetime of virtual networks.

It is also possible for one virtual network to disrupt another by using more than its fair share of resources. This concern is explored by a number of authors in their respective publications [26,29-31]. Isolation and fair distribution of physical resources among virtual networks are essential to maintain the network virtualization environment operating properly. This includes assuring that the minimum requirements of each network will be fulfilled, as well as prohibiting networks from consuming more resources than they are allowed to.

Overloading may also be caused by attacks aimed at the physical network infrastructure. Attacks may originate from within a virtual network hosted in the same environment, or from outside sources. The most common threats are Denial of Service (DoS) attacks, as presented by Yu *et al.* [6] and Oliveira *et al.* [7]. A single physical router or link compromised by a DoS attack may cause disruption on several virtual networks currently using its resources.

4.3.2 Physical resource failure

As previously stated, the failure of physical devices is one of the sources of disruption in virtual infrastructures [32-34]. Possible causes range from the failure of single devices (a physical router, for example, may become inoperative if one of its components malfunctions) to natural disasters that damage several routers or links in one or more locations [35]. Additionally, further complications may arise as the remainder of the network may be overloaded during attempts to relocate lost virtual resources. In addition to being valuable from the point of view of fault tolerance, countermeasures for mitigating the effect of failures may also be applied in the event of attacks such as DoS, as in both cases there is a need for redirecting network resources away from compromised routers or links.

4.4 Usurpation

In virtual network environments, usurpation attacks may allow an attacker to gain access to privileged information on virtual routers, or to sensitive data stored in them. Such attacks may be a consequence of identity fraud or exploited vulnerabilities, which are explained next.

4.4.1 Identity fraud

As previously mentioned in Section 4.2, identity fraud attacks can be used to impersonate other entities within a virtual network. By impersonating entities with high levels of privilege in the network, attackers may be able to perform usurpation attacks. As an example, the injection of messages with fake sources mentioned by Cabuk *et al.* [5] is used for this purpose. By sending a message that appears to have been originated from a privileged entity, attackers may perform actions restricted to such entities, including elevating their own privilege level.

4.4.2 Software vulnerability exploitation

Roschke *et al.* [36] mention that virtual machine monitors are susceptible to the exploit of vulnerabilities in their implementation. According to the authors, by gaining control over a virtual machine monitor, attackers can break out of the virtual machine, obtaining access to the hardware layer. In an environment that uses full virtualization or paravirtualization to instantiate virtual routers, exploiting such vulnerabilities may enable an attacker to have full control over physical routers. By gaining access

to physical devices, attackers could easily compromise any virtual networks provided by the infrastructure. As examples of such threats in practice, the Common Vulnerabilities and Exposures system lists a number of vulnerabilities in different versions of VMware products that allow guest Operating System users to potentially execute arbitrary code on the host Operating System [37-40].

5   Security countermeasures

In this section, we explore solutions published in the literature that aim to provide security and protect the environment from the aforementioned security threats.

5.1   Access control

Access control makes use of authentication and authorization mechanisms in order to verify the identity of network entities and enforce distinct privilege levels for each. This countermeasure is approached in two different manners in the literature, namely Trusted Virtual Domains and sandboxes. While these approaches are closely related to the notion of controlled execution domains, note that access control is performed in order to ensure that entities are granted the appropriate privilege levels.

5.1.1   Trusted virtual domains

Cabuk *et al.* [5] devised a framework to provide secure networking between groups of virtual machines. Their security goals include providing isolation, confidentiality, integrity, and information flow control in these networks. The framework provides the aforementioned security countermeasures through the use of Trusted Virtual Domains (TVDs). Each TVD represents an isolated domain, composed of "virtualization elements" and communication channels between such elements. In Cabuk's proposal, the virtualization elements are virtual workstations. However, the concept of TVDs may be applied to any device supporting virtualization.

Figure 3 depicts a virtual network infrastructure with three TVDs (A, B, and C). Gray routers represent gateways between these domains. While the gateway between TVDs B and C is simultaneously within both domains, the gateways between A and B are isolated – making use of an auxiliary TVD (AB) in order to communicate.

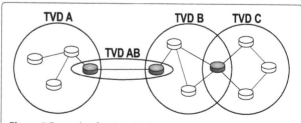

Figure 3 Example of a virtual infrastructure with three Trusted Virtual Domains, as described by Cabuk *et al.* [5].

Access control is performed when virtual machines join a TVD, ensuring that only machines that satisfy a given set of conditions are able to join. This admission control may be applied continuously in case prerequisites to join a TVD are changed. Additionally, TVDs leverage access policies to prevent unauthorized access.

5.1.2 Sandboxes

Wolinsky et al. [19] use virtual machine sandboxes in order to provide security in large scale collaborative environments. Although this work focuses on networked virtual machines hosting virtual workstations, this concept can be extended to virtual networks. Sandboxes are used to limit virtual machine access to physical resources, preventing malicious virtual machines from accessing data within other virtual machines. Moreover, each virtual machine supports IPSec, enabling the creation of secure communication channels, and X.509, providing virtual machine authentication. The authentication process is detailed in Section 5.2.

5.2 Authentication

Authentication aims to ensure that entities in a network environment are who they claim to be. In virtual network environments, providing proper authentication is complicated by factors such as the federation of virtual networks or mobility of virtual routers and links. Approaches that aim to deal with such difficulties are explained next.

5.2.1 Interoperability between federated virtual networks

Although isolation is one of the main security requirements in virtual networking, there are cases in which distinct virtual networks must be able to cooperate. The federation of virtual networks can, for example, enable end-to-end connectivity – through virtual devices of distinct virtual networks – or allow access to distinct services. However, it may not be possible to provide interoperability due to the heterogeneous nature of virtual networks (which may implement different, incompatible protocols). Chowdhury et al. [25] partially tackle this issue with a framework that manages identities in this kind of environment. The main objective of the work is to provide a global identification system. To this end, the authors employ a decentralized approach in which controllers and adapters are placed in each virtual network. Controllers provide functionalities such as address allocation and name resolution, while adapters act as gateways between virtual networks, performing address and protocol translations. The proposed global identification system does not restrict the internal identification mechanisms used locally by virtual networks, allowing each virtual network to keep its own internal naming scheme. Additionally, global identifiers used by this framework are unique, immutable, and not associated with physical location, in order to not hinder the security or mobility of virtual devices.

5.2.2 Certificate-based

As previously mentioned, the framework presented by Cabuk et al. [5] makes use of Trusted Virtual Domains (TVDs) to provide access control and network isolation. The authentication necessary to support access control is provided by means of digital certificates. These certificates ensure the identity of entities joining the network. Additionally, the system makes use of Virtual Private Networks (VPNs) to authenticate entities in network communications.

Analogously, Wolinsky et al. [19] use IPSec with X.509-based authentication for the purpose of access control in their system. In order to access the system, joining machines must request a certificate to the Certification Authority (CA). The CA responds by sending back a signed certificate to the node. The IP address of the requesting node is embedded into the certificate in order to prevent other nodes from reusing it.

5.2.3 Key-based

Fernandes and Duarte [26,31] present an architecture that aims to provide efficient routing, proper resource isolation and a secure communication channel between routers and the Virtual Machine Monitor (VMM) in a physical router. In order to ensure efficiency, virtual routers copy routing-related information to the VMM – in this case, the hypervisor. This process is performed by a plane separation module, which separates the data plane (which contains routing rules) and the control plane (responsible for creating routing rules). As a result, packets matching rules in the hypervisor routing table do not need to be redirected to virtual routers, resulting in a significant performance speedup. However, the process of copying routing information needs to be authenticated such that a malicious router is not able to compromise the data plane of another router.

In order to prevent identity fraud, the system requires mutual authentication between virtual routers and the VMM. Figure 4 depicts a simplified representation of the proposed architecture. The authors consider a Xen (paravirtualization)-based environment, in which virtual routers reside in unprivileged domains (DomUs) while the hypervisor resides within the privileged domain (Dom0). Each virtual router, upon instantiation, connects to the hypervisor following the client–server paradigm and performs an initial exchange of session keys using asymmetrical cryptography. The use of unique keys allows the hypervisor to verify the identity of distinct virtual routers in different unprivileged domains (in this example, $DomU_1$, $DomU_2$, and $DomU_3$) and to isolate traffic between them. After this initial key exchange, the secure

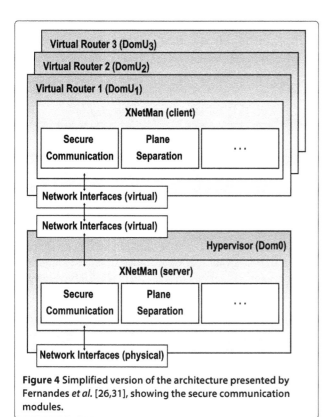

Figure 4 Simplified version of the architecture presented by Fernandes *et al.* [26,31], showing the secure communication modules.

communication module is used by other system modules in order to securely exchange messages with the hypervisor.

5.3 Data confidentiality

As network virtualization promotes the sharing of network devices and links among multiple entities, data confidentiality is a major security-related concern. Next, we explore approaches that leverage different protocols and techniques in order to provide secure communication within virtual networks.

5.3.1 VLANs and VPNs

The security goals approached by Cabuk *et al.* [5] include integrity, data isolation, confidentiality, and information flow control. Other than integrity, the remaining three goals, are directly related, and are tackled by a data confidentiality mechanism. The framework uses TVDs to control data access. However, virtual machines that belong to different TVDs may be hosted in the same physical machine. Therefore, it is necessary to ensure proper isolation, preventing a TVD from accessing data that belongs to another TVD.

The proposed solution for this challenge employs a combination of VLANs and VPNs. VLANs are used to identify packets belonging to different networks, allowing VLAN-enabled devices to route packets to the appropriate

network interfaces, thus providing adequate isolation. Untrusted physical channels, however, may require a higher level of security. Therefore, if necessary, VPNs are used to provide data confidentiality by means of end-to-end cryptography.

5.3.2 Tunneling and cryptography

Wolinsky *et al.* [19] make use of tunneling in order to isolate network traffic between virtual machines (in this case, virtual workstations). Two tunneling approaches are employed. In the first approach, the host system runs a tunneling software that captures packets incoming from physical interfaces and forwards them to virtual machines. In the second approach, the tunneling software runs inside virtual machines, and traffic is restricted within virtual networks through the use of firewall rules. According to the authors, while the second approach is easier to deploy, malicious users may be able to subvert this firewall, compromising the system. Although the focus of Wolinsky *et al.* is isolation between virtual workstations, we believe that the techniques used to achieve such isolation could be extended to virtual routers in network virtualization environments.

Fernandes and Duarte [26,31] deal with data confidentiality in communications between a virtual router and the Virtual Machine Monitor (VMM) hosting it. After the authentication process, described in Section 5.2, virtual routers use symmetrical cryptography in order to securely communicate with the VMM.

Huang *et al.* [22] present a framework that provides secure routing. In the environment presented by the authors, routing information that is propagated through a virtual network is confidential and needs to be kept secret from unauthorized network entities. Routing information is categorized in groups, and group keys are assigned to virtual routers. Therefore, routing information can be encrypted, ensuring that only routers with the correct key are able to decrypt this information. Thus, routing information relative to a given group is protected against unauthorized access from other groups, other virtual networks or the physical network itself.

Similarly to the previously described approach, Fukushima *et al.* [24] aim to protect sensitive routing information in virtual networks from being disclosed to entities controlling the physical network. To achieve this goal, the authors make use of a strategy based on Secure Multi-party Computation (SMC). SMC allows multiple entities to perform joint computations on sensitive data they hold without disclosing such data. Each entity has access to the result of the global computation, but not to any data held by other entities. This is achieved through the use of one-way functions, which are easy to evaluate but hard to invert. In the context of virtual network routing, SMC allows a virtual router to compute optimal routes without needing to share the information that it holds. As SMC requires full-mesh connectivity between computing nodes, the authors decompose the virtual network into locally connected subsets of routers, called *cliques*. The SMC-based distributed routing algorithm is run locally in each *clique*, and the results of local computations are then shared between *cliques*.

As the employment of cryptographic techniques requires physical devices that are capable of supporting protocols that enable them and generates processing and bandwidth overheads, Bays *et al.* [4] devise an optimization model and a heuristic algorithm for online, privacy-oriented virtual network embedding. Clients may require end-to-end or point-to-point cryptography for their networks, as well as requiring that none of their resources overlap with other specific virtual networks. Both the optimal and heuristic approaches take into account whether physical routers are capable of supporting cryptographic algorithms in order to ensure the desired level of confidentiality and guarantee the non-overlapping of resources (if requested). Additionally, both methods feature precise modeling of overhead costs of security mechanisms in order to not underestimate the capacity requirements of virtual network requests. This proposal is in line with research performed in the area of virtual network embedding, such as the work of Alkmim *et al.* [41].

5.3.3 Firewalling and subnetting

As previously mentioned in Section 5.3.2, Wolinsky *et al.* [19] make use of firewall rules (in addition to tunneling techniques) in order to prevent communications between different virtual networks. In addition to using firewalls for this purpose, Wu *et al.* [20] also employ subnetting (*i.e.*, each virtual network is bound to a unique subnet) in order to provide an additional layer of security against unauthorized information disclosure.

5.3.4 Path splitting

In addition to encryption of routing information, Huang *et al.* [22] use variable paths in virtual networks to propagate data flows. Figure 5 illustrates the employment of path splitting in order to hinder an information interception attack. Communication between a virtual router hosted on Physical Router (PR) 1 and another one hosted on PR 7 is split among two different paths – one passing through PR 3 and 6, and the other, through PR 2 and 4 (represented by dashed lines). Even if traffic between these two virtual routers is not encrypted, the threat is partially mitigated as the attacker only has access to part of the information being exchanged (packets passing through the link between PR 3 and 6). Moreover, when used in combination with encryption (as in the work of Huang *et al.*), this approach helps mitigate traffic analysis attacks.

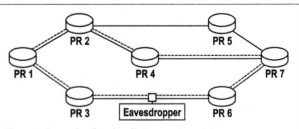

Figure 5 Example of path splitting used to mitigate an information interception attack.

It is worth noting that while in this example the attacker is only eavesdropping on one physical path, in reality, multiple devices may be compromised. In this case, splitting traffic among an increasing number of paths would lead to progressively higher levels of security (or, conversely, to increasingly higher costs for an attacker to capture the full traffic).

5.3.5 Limiting introspection

Finally, van Cleeff *et al.* [10] present recommendations for safer use of virtualization. One of these recommendations is to limit, or even disable, the introspection feature, which allows virtual machine monitors to access data inside virtual machines. While useful, this functionality may be exploited by attackers, as previously explained on Subsection 4.1.3.

5.4 Data integrity

Similarly to confidentiality, data integrity is a major concern as a result of shared network devices and communication channels. Next, we describe approaches that aim to establish a desired level of integrity in virtual network environments.

5.4.1 Cryptography

In addition to authentication (*i.e.*, source integrity) and confidentiality, the framework developed by Cabuk *et al.* [5] makes use of VPNs to provide data integrity to virtual networks. The use of cryptographic tunneling protocols prevents malicious entities from manipulating messages going through the network. As previously discussed, the authors use IPSec as the tunneling protocol.

5.4.2 Timestamping

As previously discussed, replay attacks are one of the threats to data integrity that may be present in network virtualization environments. The addition of unique identifiers inside encrypted messages makes it possible to detect duplicated messages, and therefore, replay attacks. For this purpose, the architecture proposed by Fernandes and Duarte [26,31] inserts timestamps inside encrypted messages in order to ensure that messages are non-reproducible.

5.4.3 Limiting introspection

Besides mitigating information theft, disabling or limiting introspection also prevents data tampering. According to van Cleeff *et al.* [10], this functionality allows the VMM to modify applications running inside it, which may cause inconsistencies. Another recommendation consists of specifically designing applications that facilitate batch processing and checkpointing. According to the authors, this minimizes security issues associated with rollback and restore operations that may otherwise threaten integrity.

5.5 Nonrepudiation

Nonrepudiation provides evidences regarding which (potentially malicious) actions have been performed by which entities. This security countermeasure is highly valuable in the context of network virtualization environments, in which a number of physical devices are shared by different users. Nevertheless, we are not aware of any publication that targets this countermeasure specifically.

5.6 Availability

Last, we present proposals that aim to maintain the availability of network virtualization environments. The key concerns in this area of security are providing proper resource isolation and mitigating attacks that target physical or virtual devices. Approaches aiming to deal with such concerns are explained in the following subsections.

5.6.1 Physical resource isolation

One of the main concerns regarding availability is the abuse of physical resources by virtual networks. Virtual networks may attempt to use as much resources as possible in order to maximize their performance. If the environment is not adequately protected, this behavior may lead to the exhaustion of physical resources, compromising the availability of other virtual networks hosted on the same substrate. Therefore, physical resources must be shared in a fair manner, and actions performed by a virtual network must not negatively impact others.

According to Wu *et al.* [29], the sharing of physical resources by packet processors is usually only performed at a granularity of entire processor cores. The authors claim that finer-grained processor sharing is required in order to provide scalability for network virtualization environments. Thus, the authors propose a system that allows multiple threads to share processor cores concurrently while maintaining isolation and fair resource sharing. However, typical multithreading approaches consider a cooperative environment, which is not the case in network virtualization. The authors devise a fair multithreading mechanism that allows the assignment of different priorities to each thread. Additionally, this mechanism takes into account the history of how much processing has

been performed by each thread. Inactivity times are also considered in order to guarantee that threads will not stay idle for too long. The evaluation performed by the authors shows that the proposed mechanism is able to properly distribute processing resources according to the defined priorities. Furthermore, while it requires more processing power, it is able to provide better resource utilization in comparison to coarse-grained approaches.

Kokku *et al.* [30] propose a network virtualization scheme that provides resource isolation while aiming to maximize substrate utilization. It allows virtual networks to have either resource-based reservations (*i.e.*, reservations calculated as a percentage of available resources in the substrate) or bandwidth-based reservations (*i.e.*, reservations based on the aggregate throughput of the virtual network). Virtual networks are divided in two groups according to the type of reservation required, and treated independently by a scheduler. This scheduler treats flows that belong to different virtual networks with distinct priorities, based on the reservations and average resource usage rate of each network. The authors present an evaluation performed on an implemented prototype, showing that the proposed scheme was capable of ensuring that each virtual network met its reservations.

Fernandes and Duarte [26] present a network monitor that employs plane separation in order to provide resource isolation in network virtualization environments. The system is able to allocate resources based on fixed reservations, as well as to redistribute idle resources between virtual networks that have a higher demand. Additionally, an administrator is able to control the amount of resources to be used by each virtual network, as well as set priorities for using idle resources. The system continuously monitors the consumption of physical resources by each virtual router. If any virtual router exceeds its allowed use of bandwidth, processing power, or memory, it is adequately punished by having packets dropped, or a percentage of its stored routes erased. Harsher punishments are instituted if there are no idle resources available. Conversely, given punishments are gradually reduced if the router stops using more than its allocated resources. This system is capable of adequately preventing physical resources from being overloaded, and packet drops employed by the punishment mechanism do not cause a major impact on network traffic.

In another publication [31], the same authors extend the previously described network monitor. This new system introduces the idea of short term and long term requirements, based on the time frame in which they must be met. Short term requirements may be allocated in an exclusive or non-exclusive manner, while long term requirements are always non-exclusive. In this context, exclusive requirements are always allocated (even if part of the allocated resources is idle), while non-exclusive requirements are only allocated when necessary. The system prioritizes virtual networks that have used the lowest portion of their requirements, and an adaptive control scheme is used in order to improve the probability that long term requirements, if needed, will be met. The presented evaluation shows the improvement of this system over the original [26] in terms of guaranteeing that the demands of each virtual network will be met, as well as reducing resource load on the physical substrate.

5.6.2 *Virtual network resilience*
Even with proper physical resource isolation, maintaining availability remains a challenge in virtualized networks. The virtualization layer must be resilient, maintaining its performance and mitigating attacks in order to sustain its availability. Some of the publications described next approach the issue of virtual network resilience from the point of view of fault tolerance. Nonetheless, we emphasize that the solutions described in these publications may also be used as a response to attacks that cause the failure or degradation of physical devices or links.

The solution presented by Yeow *et al.* [32] aims to provide network infrastructures that are resilient to physical router failures. This objective is achieved through the use of backups (*i.e.*, redundant routers and links). However, redundant resources remain idle, reducing the utilization of the physical substrate. To minimize this problem, the authors propose a scheme that dynamically creates and manages shared backup resources. This mechanism minimizes the number of necessary backup instances needed to achieve a certain level of reliability. While backup resources are shared, each physical router is restricted to hosting a maximum number of backup instances in order not to sacrifice reliability. The connectivity between each virtual router and its neighbors is preserved in all of its backups, both in terms of number of links and bandwidth reservations.

The illustration on the left side of Figure 6 shows a simple representation of how backup nodes (represented as circles) may be shared among different virtual networks. For example, the two backup nodes at the right side of this figure are shared between Virtual Network 1 and Virtual Network 3, regardless of whether they belong to one or the other. The right side of Figure 6, in turn, depicts in greater detail how backups are allocated to virtual routers. A virtual router C_1 has virtual routers B_1 and B_2 as its backups. Since C_1 has a virtual link connecting it to another router, N_1, a virtual link with the same bandwidth reservation (depicted as 1 in the figure) is also established between each backup node and N_1 in order to preserve the connectivity of the original router.

Meixner *et al.* [35] devise a probabilistic model for providing virtual networks that are resilient to physical disasters. Disasters are characterized by the occurrence of multiple failures in the physical network, as well as the possibility of correlated cascading failures during attempts to recover network resources. The virtual link mapping strategy guarantees that the failure of a single physical link will not disconnect any virtual network, and aims at minimizing virtual network disconnection in the event of a disaster (*i.e.*, simultaneous failure of multiple links). Additionally, excess processing capacity in the physical network is used to create a backup router for each virtual network, which reduces disconnection in the event of disasters and provides additional processing capacity for the recovery phase. When attempting to recover virtual network resources, the model analyzes all possible virtual router replacements in an effort to replace affected virtual routers in a way that ensures the virtual network will not be disconnected by any post-disaster failures.

The system presented by Zhang *et al.* [27] uses redundant virtual networks in order to provide reliable live streaming services. It is able to detect path failures and traffic congestion, dynamically redirecting data flows.

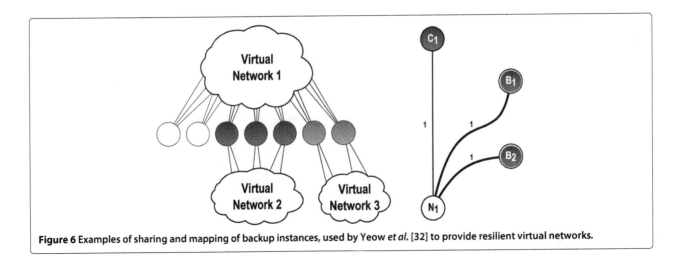

Figure 6 Examples of sharing and mapping of backup instances, used by Yeow *et al.* [32] to provide resilient virtual networks.

Initially, the data flow is distributed equally through available virtual networks. Figure 7 depicts the distribution of a data flow through virtual networks, using multiple paths between a server and a client. Gradually, the number of packets routed through each virtual network is adapted according to its relative bandwidth capacity. Additionally, an active probing mechanism is used to detect failures in the physical network or routing problems (changes in routing tables, for example, may have a significant impact in live streaming applications). If an issue is detected, the system is able to redirect data flows away from problematic networks and redistribute it among the remaining ones. Experiments performed by the authors demonstrate advantages in using multiple networks instead of a single one, with increasing gains when using up to four virtual networks. Additionally, the authors claim that the bandwidth cost of the probing mechanism is negligible.

Chen et al. [33] propose a virtual network embedding strategy that aims at ensuring survivability. Load balancing is employed in the embedding process in order to balance the bandwidth consumption of substrate links. Moreover, backup links are reserved for each accepted virtual network, but not activated until a failure occurs. Backup links are allocated in physical paths that do not overlap with the path hosting the original link, guaranteeing that a single physical link failure will not simultaneously affect the original virtual link and one or more of its backups. These backup resources may be shared by multiple virtual networks or reconfigured over time in order to improve efficiency.

Zhang et al. [34] devise a strategy for computing the availability of Virtual Data Centers (VDCs), as well as an algorithm for reliable VDC embedding. In order to determine VDC availability, the authors consider the availability of individual, heterogeneous components, as well as

dependencies among them. The embedding mechanism aims at meeting minimum availability criteria while optimizing resource usage. Virtual devices are divided into replication groups (groups in which any virtual device may serve as a backup if another fails). In order to minimize resource consumption, VDCs are embedded on physical devices with the lowest level of availability that still meets the desired level. In a similar way, a minimum number of backups is assigned to each replication group in order to meet availability requirements.

Unlike the previously described approaches in the area of virtual network resilience, Oliveira et al. [7] present a strategy based on "opportunistic resilience", which does not employ backup resources. The bandwidth demand of each virtual link is split over multiple physical paths. As a consequence, physical link failures are less likely to cause a virtual link disconnection (an affected virtual link will remain operational, albeit with less capacity). Additionally, when link failures occur, a reactive strategy is used in order to reallocate the lost capacity over unaffected paths, attempting to fully restore the bandwidth of degraded virtual links.

Distributed Denial of Service (DDoS) attacks are a common threat to the availability of network services. The system proposed by Yu and Zhou [6] aims to detect such attacks on community networks (federated virtual networks that belong to cooperating entities). The devised solution leverages communication between virtual routers that belong to different entities in this collaborative environment to detect possible attacks at an early stage. Virtual routers located on the edges of the community network monitor traffic passing through them and calculate the entropy of its flows. Traffic surges in any of these flows will cause the entropy to drop, indicating a possible attack. If this occurs, other routers are notified

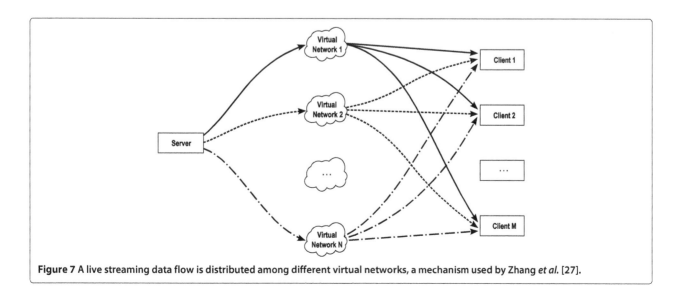

Figure 7 A live streaming data flow is distributed among different virtual networks, a mechanism used by Zhang et al. [27].

and instructed to calculate the entropy rate of this suspected flow. Calculated values are compared, and if they are similar, a DDoS attack is confirmed.

6 Discussion

A number of insights can be obtained from the extensive investigation of the state of the art reported in this paper. First, it is possible to observe that the publications in the area are not equally distributed between the main security categories. Tables 3 and 4 show, respectively, the security threats and security countermeasures approached in these publications. In both tables, publications have been grouped together according to the security elements they approach, whenever possible. It is noticeable that disruption and availability – a security threat and a countermeasure that are directly correlated – are approached in the majority of these publications. This is likely due to the high prevalence of attacks aiming at causing disruption. These attacks are relatively simple but can be highly

Table 3 Security threats mentioned in publications in the area of virtual network security

Publication	Threats			
	DI	DE	DR	US
[4]	×			
[19]	×			
[21]	×			
[22]	×			
[23]	×			
[24]	×			
[10]	×	×		
[20]	×	×		
[5]	×	×		×
[25]		×		
[26]		×	×	
[36]				×
[6]			×	
[7]			×	
[27]			×	
[28]			×	
[29]			×	
[30]			×	
[31]			×	
[32]			×	
[33]			×	
[34]			×	
[35]			×	

From left to right: Disclosure, Deception, Disruption, Usurpation.

Table 4 Security countermeasures provided by publications in the area of virtual network security

Publication	Countermeasures					
	AC	AU	CO	IN	NR	AV
[4]			×			
[20]			×			
[22]			×			
[24]			×			
[19]	×	×	×			
[5]	×	×	×	×		
[26]		×	×	×		×
[31]		×	×	×		×
[10]		×	×			
[25]		×				
[6]						×
[7]						×
[27]						×
[29]						×
[30]						×
[32]						×
[33]						×
[34]						×
[35]						×

From left to right: Access Control, Authentication, Confidentiality, Integrity, Nonrepudiation, Availability.

devastating, especially in an environment that makes heavy use of shared resources (as a single physical failure may disrupt several virtual networks). Disclosure and confidentiality follow closely behind, being present in a similar number of publications as disruption/availability. Once again, this is linked to physical resource sharing. Similarly to disruption attacks, such sharing means that a single well-placed sniffer may be able to acquire sensitive information from multiple virtual networks at once. Moreover, there are also privacy concerns between infrastructure providers and virtual network requesters (as the former may have access to data that the latter considers confidential).

Second, only a small number of publications approach more than one threat or countermeasure simultaneously. No single publication has dealt with threats in more than two of the four categories, or presented solutions that provide more than four security countermeasures, out of a total of six. Additionally, one security countermeasure in particular – nonrepudiation – was not approached by any of the publications. The combination of authentication and integrity, which exists in some publications, can be considered as the basis for the provision of nonrepudiation, but this specific countermeasure is not targeted. Nonrepudiation is a highly valuable (albeit challenging) security countermeasure for network virtualization environments, and will be further discussed in Section 7.

Third, we were able to conclude that many of the threats that affect network virtualization environments also affect traditional networks. However, we emphasize that these threats affect traditional and virtual network environments in different ways. In most cases, the effects of these threats are greatly exacerbated by certain characteristics of virtual network environments. Information interception, physical resource overloading, physical resource failure, and software vulnerability exploitation are aggravated by the fact that a number of virtual routers may share a physical router. Therefore, as previously explained, an attack of any of these types targeting a single physical router may affect several virtual networks. Further, it is more difficult to recognize (and, therefore, to perform countermeasures against) identity fraud and replay attacks due to the dynamicity of network virtualization environments, as virtual routers may be freely moved among physical routers and assume different identities. Loss of registry entries and information leakage, as described in the studied literature, are limited to virtual network environments. Moreover, threats related to introspection are also inherent to these types of environments, as this is a (potentially exploitable) feature of virtual machine monitors.

Last, we can observe the employment of different virtualization techniques in some publications. For example, Cabuk et al. [5] implemented a prototype of their framework based on a paravirtualization platform, while Huang et al. [22] consider an underlying network based on programmable routers. Further, Fernandes and Duarte [26,31] build a hybrid solution that combines paravirtualization with plane separation, a core idea of programmable networks. Although the majority of publications do not target specific network virtualization techniques, we emphasize that different types of platforms have their own sets of benefits, as well as security concerns, which need to be taken into account.

7 Challenges

Despite the existence of a sizable body of work in virtual network security, some challenges remain open. In this section, we summarize some of the main research challenges in this area. We emphasize, however, that these challenges should not be considered exhaustive, but rather as a starting point for further discussions in the area.

One clear opportunity for research in virtual network security is the provisioning of nonrepudiation – which, to the best of our knowledge, has not yet been approached. Nonrepudiation requires providing proof of actions performed by entities on a network, which can be used for holding entities accountable for malicious activity. We deem nonrepudiation an essential security countermeasure for virtual networking environments in order to accurately backtrace attacks – not only to ensure that punitive actions will be taken against the attackers but also to properly contain the attacks themselves. In the event of a DDoS attack, for example, this countermeasure could enable administrators to pinpoint the origins of the attack with a high level of precision – which otherwise tends to be a very difficult task. Moreover, nonrepudiation may even prevent attacks, in the sense that malicious users who are aware that such a mechanism is in use may refrain from carrying out attacks in order to avoid exposing themselves. Provisioning nonrepudiation can be challenging for a number of reasons, such as the complexity of securely storing and handling digital certificates – used for proving that an action was, indeed, performed by a given entity – and the negative impact this has on network performance. Moreover, it is necessary to maintain a desired level of privacy for virtual network requesters as well as end users. Nevertheless, we envision that the importance of this countermeasure will grow steadily as network virtualization becomes increasingly prominent in production environments.

In addition to privacy issues related to nonrepudiation, there are also concerns regarding the privacy of general data stored in virtual routers or sent through virtual networks. Although such data may be protected from being intercepted by other entities, infrastructure providers have physical access to all data stored in virtual networks they are hosting. Although this issue has been approached by some authors, their proposed strategies are often based on strong assumptions, such as the ability to choose which physical entity (out of a number of entities controlling the physical substrate) will host each of its routers – a feature that may not commonly be available in practice.

Another opportunity stems from the multiple levels of heterogeneity present in network infrastructures. As previously mentioned, in addition to the use of heterogeneous hardware devices, it is common for network substrates to be composed of a number of physical networks that belong to different entities. As such, there is a need for uniform methods for requesting, negotiating, and enforcing security requirements across devices that may have incompatible interfaces and entities with potentially conflicting policies.

Last, software platforms used to instantiate virtual networks may not always offer adequate protection against security threats. Moreover, although virtualization technologies are gradually evolving and becoming more mature, both hardware and software are susceptible to vulnerabilities that may be exploited by attackers.

Consequently, research efforts that build on top of network virtualization need to consider these security issues and, most importantly, overhead costs of additional security mechanisms that may be necessary, in order to ensure that they will be suitable for real world environments.

We emphasize, once again, that this is not an exhaustive list of challenges in the area. The essence of network virtualization is based on layers upon layers with increasing levels of abstraction (*e.g.*, the physical substrate, the virtualization layer, virtual networks, and services running on top of them). Consequently, we envision that a number of other challenges may be present in all of these layers – much like the ones listed in this section.

8   Conclusions

Network virtualization enables the subdivision of a single network infrastructure into multiple virtual architectures. The benefits of this technique apply to a wide range of applications, including the creation of virtual testbeds, community networks, and cloud computing infrastructures. Furthermore, network virtualization has been proposed by researchers as the basis for the creation of a new architecture for the Internet, allowing pluralist network environments that support a number of different network protocols simultaneously.

In spite of the benefits provided by network virtualization, there is a series of security issues that need to be considered. Our study revealed a number of security threats, covering the four categories defined by Shirey [16]. The very act of sharing a physical infrastructure among multiple parties is shown to be the source of several of these threats.

This study shows that there have been several efforts to provide security in virtual networks. However, these efforts were not organized in a comprehensible manner. This study provides a systematic overview of the available research results in the field, categorizing work that represents the state of the art and highlighting different approaches for providing security. Additionally, it also evidences imbalances between different sub-areas of security research in network virtualization, which can be used as guidance for future work in this area. Usurpation and access control, for example, are significantly underrepresented in relation to other security countermeasures, and nonrepudiation is not targeted by any publication. Additionally, while a significant body of work exists in the sub-area of availability, only one publication deals with detection and prevention of attacks. Such gaps may represent valuable opportunities for future work.

To summarize, the categorization of security threats and countermeasures presented in this paper simplifies the analysis of which security aspects have not yet been approached and which types of threats need to be mitigated. Furthermore, it makes it easier to identify a number of existing solutions that aim to provide security in virtual networks.

Endnotes

[1]Machine virtualization is available for personal computers, in commonly used operating systems (e.g., Windows, Linux, and Mac OS X).

Competing interests
The authors declare that they have no competing interests.

Authors' contributions
All authors read and approved the final manuscript.

Acknowledgements
The authors would like to thank the anonymous reviewers for their valuable comments and suggestions. This work has been partially supported by FP7/CNPq (Project SecFuNet, FP7-ICT-2011-EU-Brazil), RNP-CTIC (Project ReVir), as well as PRONEM/FAPERGS/CNPq (Project NPRV).

Author details
[1]Institute of Informatics, Federal University of Rio Grande do Sul, Porto Alegre, Brazil. [2]Institute of Computing, University of Campinas, Campinas, Brazil.

References
1. Chowdhury NMMK, Boutaba R (2010) A survey of network virtualization. Comput Netw 54(5):862–876
2. Fernandes N, Moreira MD, Moraes I, Ferraz L, Couto R, Carvalho HT, Campista M, Costa LK, Duarte OB (2011) Virtual networks: isolation, performance, and trends. Ann Telecommun 66(5–6):339–355
3. Anderson T, Peterson L, Shenker S, Turner J (2005) Overcoming the internet impasse through virtualization. Computer 38(4):34–41
4. Bays LR, Oliveira RR, Buriol LS, Barcellos MP, Gaspary LP (2014) A heuristic-based algorithm for privacy-oriented virtual network embedding. In: IEEE/IFIP Network Operations and Management Symposium (NOMS). IEEE, Krakow, Poland
5. Cabuk S, Dalton CI, Ramasamy H, Schunter M (2007) Towards automated provisioning of secure virtualized networks. In: ACM Conference on Computer and Communications Security. New York, USA
6. Yu S, Zhou W (2008) Entropy-based collaborative detection of ddos attacks on community networks. In: IEEE International Conference on Pervasive Computing and Communications. IEEE Computer Society, Washington, DC, USA
7. Oliveira RR, Marcon DS, Bays LR, Neves MC, Buriol LS, Gaspary LP, Barcellos MP (2013) No more backups: Toward efficient embedding of survivable virtual networks. In: IEEE International Conference on Communications. IEEE, Budapest, Hungary
8. LAN/MAN Standards Committee (2006) IEEE Standard for Local and metropolitan area networks – Virtual Bridged Local Area Networks. IEEE Std 802.1Q-2005 (incorporates IEEE Std 802.1Q1998, IEEE Std 802.1u-2001, IEEE Std 802.1v-2001, and IEEE Std 802.1s-2002). http://www.ieee802.org/1/pages/802.1Q-2005.html
9. Rosen E, Cisco Systems I, Rekhter Y, Juniper Networks I (2006) RFC 4364: BGP/MPLS IP Virtual Private Networks (VPNs). http://www.ietf.org/rfc/rfc4364.txt
10. van Cleeff A, Pieters W, Wieringa RJ (2009) Security implications of virtualization: A literature study. In: International Conference on Computational Science and Engineering. IEEE Computer Society, Washington, DC, USA
11. McKeown N, Anderson T, Balakrishnan H, Parulkar G, Peterson L, Rexford J, Shenker S, Turner J (2008) Openflow: enabling innovation in campus networks. SIGCOMM Comput Commun Rev 38:69–74
12. Bari MF, Boutaba R, Esteves R, Granville LZ, Podlesny M, Rabbani MG, Zhang Q, Zhani MF (2013) Data center network virtualization: A survey. Communications Surveys Tutorials, IEEE 15:909–928

13. Zhou M, Zhang R, Xie W, Qian W, Zhou A (2010) Security and privacy in cloud computing: A survey. In: Semantics Knowledge and Grid (SKG), 2010 Sixth International Conference On. IEEE, Beijing, China

14. Hashizume K, Rosado DG, Fernández-Medina E, Fernandez EB (2013) An analysis of security issues for cloud computing. J Internet Serv Appl 4:1–13

15. Scott-Hayward S, O'Callaghan G, Sezer S (2013) Sdn security: A survey. In: Future Networks and Services (SDN4FNS), 2013 IEEE SDN For. IEEE, Trento, Italy

16. Shirey R (2000) RFC 2828: Internet Security Glossary. http://www.ietf.org/rfc/rfc2828.txt

17. Stallings W (2006) Cryptography and Network Security: Principles and Practice. Pearson/Prentice Hall, Upper Saddle River, New Jersey, USA

18. Cavalcanti E, Assis L, Gaudencio M, Cirne W, Brasileiro F (2006) Sandboxing for a free-to-join grid with support for secure site-wide storage area. In: International Workshop on Virtualization Technology in Distributed Computing. IEEE Computer Society, Washington, USA

19. Wolinsky DI, Agrawal A, Boykin PO, Davis JR, Ganguly A, Paramygin V, Sheng YP, Figueiredo RJ (2006) On the design of virtual machine sandboxes for distributed computing in wide-area overlays of virtual workstations. In: International Workshop on Virtualization Technology in Distributed Computing. IEEE Computer Society, Washington, DC, USA

20. Wu H, Ding Y, Winer C, Yao L (2010) Network security for virtual machine in cloud computing. In: Computer Sciences and Convergence Information Technology (ICCIT), 2010 5th International Conference On. IEEE, Seoul, South Korea

21. Cui Q, Shi W, Wang Y (2009) Design and implementation of a network supporting environment for virtual experimental platforms. In: WRI International Conference on Communications and Mobile Computing. IEEE Computer Society, Washington, DC, USA

22. Huang D, Ata S, Medhi D (2010) Establishing secure virtual trust routing and provisioning domains for future internet. In: IEEE Conference on Global Telecommunications, Miami, USA

23. Pignolet Y-A, Schmid S, Tredan G (2013) Adversarial vnet embeddings: A threat for isps?. In: IEEE INFOCOM. IEEE, Turin, Italy

24. Fukushima M, Sugiyama K, Hasegawa T, Hasegawa T, Nakao A (2013) Minimum disclosure routing for network virtualization and its experimental evaluation. IEEE/ACM Trans Netw PP(99):1839–1851

25. Chowdhury NMMK, Zaheer F-E, Boutaba R (2009) imark: an identity management framework for network virtualization environment. In: IFIP/IEEE International Symposium on Integrated Network Management. IEEE Press, Piscataway, USA

26. Fernandes NC, Duarte OCMB (2011) Xnetmon: A network monitor for securing virtual networks. In: IEEE International Conference on Communications. IEEE, Kyoto, Japan

27. Zhang Y, Gao L, Wang C (2009) Multinet: multiple virtual networks for a reliable live streaming service. In: IEEE Conference on Global Telecommunications. IEEE Press, Piscataway, USA

28. Marquezan CC, Granville LZ, Nunzi G, Brunner M (2010) Distributed autonomic resource management for network virtualization. In: IEEE/IFIP Network Operations and Management Symposium, Osaka, Japan

29. Wu Q, Shanbhag S, Wolf T (2010) Fair multithreading on packet processors for scalable network virtualization. In: ACM/IEEE Symposium on Architectures for Networking and Communications Systems. ACM, New York, USA

30. Kokku R, Mahindra R, Zhang H, Rangarajan S (2010) Nvs: a virtualization substrate for wimax networks. In: International Conference on Mobile Computing and Networking. ACM, New York, USA

31. Fernandes NC, Duarte OCMB (2011) Provendo isolamento e qualidade de serviço em redes virtuais. In: Simpósio Brasileiro de Redes de Computadores e Sistemas Distribuídos, Campo Grande, Brazil. (in Portuguese)

32. Yeow W-L, Westphal C, Kozat UC (2011) Designing and embedding reliable virtual infrastructures. SIGCOMM Comput Commun Rev 41(2):57–64

33. Chen Q, Wan Y, Qiu X, Li W, Xiao A (2014) A survivable virtual network embedding scheme based on load balancing and reconfiguration. In: IEEE Network Operations and Management Symposium. IEEE, Krakow, Poland

34. Zhang Q, Zhani MF, Jabri M, Boutaba R (2014) Venice: Reliable virtual data center embedding in clouds. In: IEEE INFOCOM. IEEE, Toronto, Canada

35. Meixner CC, Dikbiyik F, Tornatore M, Chuah C, Mukherjee B (2013) Disaster-resilient virtual-network mapping and adaptation in optical networks. In: International Conference on Optical Network Design and Modeling

36. Roschke S, Cheng F, Meinel C (2009) Intrusion detection in the cloud. In: IEEE International Conference on Dependable, Autonomic and Secure Computing. IEEE Computer Society, Washington, DC, USA

37. Common Vulnerabilities and Exposures (2012) CVE-2012-1516. https://cve.mitre.org/cgi-bin/cvename.cgi?name=CVE-2012-1516

38. Common Vulnerabilities and Exposures (2012) CVE-2012-1517. https://cve.mitre.org/cgi-bin/cvename.cgi?name=CVE-2012-1517

39. Common Vulnerabilities and Exposures (2012) CVE-2012-2449. https://cve.mitre.org/cgi-bin/cvename.cgi?name=CVE-2012-2449

40. Common Vulnerabilities and Exposures (2012) CVE-2012-2450. https://cve.mitre.org/cgi-bin/cvename.cgi?name=CVE-2012-2450

41. Alkmim GP, Batista DM, Fonseca NLS (2013) Mapping virtual networks onto substrate networks. J Internet Serv Appl 3(4):1–15

8

Considering human aspects on strategies for designing and managing distributed human computation

Lesandro Ponciano[*], Francisco Brasileiro, Nazareno Andrade and Lívia Sampaio

Abstract

A human computation system can be viewed as a distributed system in which the processors are humans, called workers. Such systems harness the cognitive power of a group of workers connected to the Internet to execute relatively simple tasks, whose solutions, once grouped, solve a problem that systems equipped with only machines could not solve satisfactorily. Examples of such systems are Amazon Mechanical Turk and the Zooniverse platform. A human computation application comprises a group of tasks, each of them can be performed by one worker. Tasks might have dependencies among each other. In this study, we propose a theoretical framework to analyze such type of application from a distributed systems point of view. Our framework is established on three dimensions that represent different perspectives in which human computation applications can be approached: quality-of-service requirements, design and management strategies, and human aspects. By using this framework, we review human computation in the perspective of programmers seeking to improve the design of human computation applications and managers seeking to increase the effectiveness of human computation infrastructures in running such applications. In doing so, besides integrating and organizing what has been done in this direction, we also put into perspective the fact that the human aspects of the workers in such systems introduce new challenges in terms of, for example, task assignment, dependency management, and fault prevention and tolerance. We discuss how they are related to distributed systems and other areas of knowledge.

Keywords: Human computation; Crowdsourcing; Distributed applications; Human factors

1 Introduction

Many studies have focused on increasing the performance of machine-based computational systems over the last decades. As a result, much progress has been made allowing increasingly complex problems to be efficiently solved. However, despite these advances, there are still tasks that cannot be accurately and efficiently performed even when the most sophisticated algorithms and computing architectures are used [1,2]. Examples of such tasks are those related to natural language processing, image understanding and creativity [3,4]. A common factor in these kinds of tasks is their suitability to human abilities; human beings can solve them with high efficiency and accuracy [1,2].

In the last years, there has emerged a new computing approach that takes advantage of human abilities to execute these kinds of tasks. Such approach has been named *Human Computation* [1,5].

Applications designed to execute on human computation systems may encompass one or multiple tasks. They are called *distributed human computation applications* when they are composed of multiple tasks, and each individual task can be performed by a different human being, called *worker*. In the last years, distributed computing systems have been developed to support the execution of this type of application. They gather a crowd of workers connected to the Internet and manage them to execute application tasks. The precursor of such systems is reCAPTCHA [6]. Currently, there is a broad diversity of distributed human computation applications and distributed systems devoted to execute them, such as: games

---

*Correspondence: lesandrop@lsd.ufcg.edu.br
Federal University of Campina Grande, Department of Computing and Systems, Av. Aprígio Veloso, 882 – Bloco CO, 58.429-900, Campina Grande – PB, Brazil

with a purpose [7], contests sites [8], online labor markets [9], and volunteer thinking systems [10]. In this paper, we focus on online labor markets and volunteer thinking systems.

Online labor markets gather a crowd of workers that have a financial motivation [9]. The precursor of this type of system is the Amazon Mechanical Turk platform (mturk.com). Such plaform reports to have more than 400,000 registered workers [11], and receives between 50,000 and 400,000 new tasks to be executed per day (mturk-tracker.com) at the time of writing. Volunteer thinking systems, in turn, gather a crowd of workers willing to execute tasks without any financial compensation [10]. One of the precursors of this type of system is the Zooniverse citizen-science platform (zooniverse.org). Currently, Zooniverse hosts 21 scientific projects and has over one million registered workers. Only Galaxy Zoo, the largest project at Zooniverse, had 50 million tasks performed by 150,000 workers in a year of operation [12]. Thus, both labor markets and volunteer thinking are large-scale distributed human computation systems.

Because the computing units in human computation systems are human beings, both the design and management of applications tap into concepts and theories from multiple disciplines. Quinn and Bederson conducted one of the first efforts to delimit such concepts and theories [1,5]. They present a taxonomy for human computation, highlighting differences and similarities to related concepts, such as collective intelligence and crowdsourcing. Yuen et al., in turn, focus on distinguishing different types of human computation systems and platforms [3,4]. More recently, Kittur et al. built a theoretical framework to analyze future perspectives in developing online labor markets that are attractive and fair to workers [13]. Differently from previous efforts, in this study, we analyze human computation under the perspective of *programmers seeking to improve the design of distributed human computation applications* and *managers seeking to increase the effectiveness of distributed human computation systems.*

To conduct this study, we propose a theoretical framework that integrates theories about human aspects, design and management (D&M) strategies, and quality of service (QoS) requirements. Human aspects include characteristics that impact workers' ability to perform tasks (e.g., cognitive system and emotion), their interests (e.g., motivation and preferences), and their differences and relations (e.g., individual differences and social behavior). QoS requirements, in turn, are metrics directly related to how application owners measure applications and systems effectiveness. These metrics are typically defined in terms of time, cost, fidelity, and security. Finally, D&M strategies consist of strategies related to how the application is designed and managed. They involve activities such as application composition, task assignment, dependency management, and fault prevention and tolerance.

This framework allows us to perform a literature review that expands previous literature reviews to build a vision of human computation focused on distributed systems issues. We emphasize our analysis on three perspectives: 1) findings on relevant human aspects which impact D&M decisions; 2) major D&M strategies that have been proposed to deal with human aspects; and 3) open challenges and how they relate to other disciplines. Besides providing a distributed systems viewpoint of this new kind of computational system, our analysis also puts into perspective the fact that human computation introduces new challenges in terms of effective D&M strategies. Although these challenges are essentially distributed systems challenges, some of them do not exist in machine-based distributed systems, as they are related to human aspects. These challenges call for combining distributed systems design with theories and mechanisms used in other areas of knowledge where there is extensive theory on treating human aspects, such as Cognitive Science, Behavioral Sciences, and Management Sciences.

In the following, we briefly describe the human computation ecosystem addressed in this paper. Then, we present our theoretical framework. After that, we analyze the literature in the light of our framework. This is followed by the discussion of challenges and perspectives for future research. Finally, we present our conclusions.

2 Distributed human computation ecosystem

The core agents in a distributed human computation ecosystem are: requesters, workers, and platform. *Requesters* act in the system by submitting human computation *applications*. An application is a set of *tasks* with or without dependencies among them. Typically, a human computation task consists of some input data (e.g., image, text) and a set of instructions. There are several types of instructions, such as: transcription of an item content (e.g., reCAPTCHA tasks [6]), classification of an item (e.g., Galaxy Zoo tasks [14]), generation of creative content about an item [15], ranking and matching items [16], etc.

Workers are the human beings who act as human computers in the system executing one or more tasks. They generate the task output by performing the instructions upon the received items. After executing a task, the worker provides its *output*. The application output is an aggregation of the outputs of all their tasks. In paid systems, when a task is performed, the requester may accept the solution if the task was satisfactorily performed; otherwise, she/he can reject it. Workers are paid only when their solutions are accepted. The receiving of tasks to be executed, the provision of their outputs, and the receiving of the payment for the performed tasks occur via a human computation platform.

The *Platform* is a distributed system that acts as a middleware receiving requester applications and managing the execution of their tasks by the workers. Platforms manage several aspects of tasks execution, such as: providing an interface and language for tasks' specification, performing task replication, maintaining a job board with a set of tasks waiting to be performed, controlling the state of each task from the submission up to its completion. Examples of platforms with such characteristics are the online labor markets Amazon Mechanical Turk (mturk.com) and CrowdFlower (crowdflower.com), and the volunteer thinking systems Zooniverse (zooniverse.org) and CrowdCrafting (crowdcrafting.org). Online labor markets also implement functionalities that allow requesters to communicate with workers that performed their tasks, provide feedback about their outputs, and pay for the tasks performed by them.

Some studies have analyzed human computation ecosystem. In general, they focus mainly on proposing a taxonomy for the area [1,3,5,17] and discussing platform issues [18,19]. Quinn et al. [1,5] propose a taxonomy for human computation that delimits its similarities and differences when compared to others fields based on human work, such as: crowdsourcing, social computing, and collective intelligence. Vukovic and Yuen et al. focus on classifying human computation platforms based on their function (e.g., design and innovation), mode (e.g., competition and marketplace platforms), or algorithms [3,17]. Dustdar and Truong [18] and Crouser and Chang [19] focus on hybrid platforms based on the collaboration between machine and human computing units. Dustdar and Truong [18] focused on strategies to provide machine computation and human computation as a service, using a single interface. Crouser and Chang [19] propose a framework of affordances, i.e., properties that are inherent to human and properties that are inherent to machine, so that they complement each other.

Differently from these previous efforts, in the present work we focus on analyzing strategies for designing and managing distributed applications onto human computation platforms. Our main focus is not to survey existing human computation platforms, but to analyze D&M strategies that have been proposed to be used in these kind of platforms. Our analysis is based on a theoretical framework built upon theories and concepts from multiple disciplines dealing with (i) human aspects, such as: Motivation Theory [20], Self-determination Theory [21], Sense of Community Theory [22], Human Error Theory [23], Coordination Theory [24] and Human-in-the-Loop literature [25], and (ii) applications design, applications management and QoS aspects, such as: the great principles of computing [26]; application design

methodologies [27,28]; taxonomies for application management in grid computing [29], web services [30], and organizations [31].

3 Theoretical framework

Theoretical frameworks have several distinct roles [32]. Most important for us, they allow researchers to look for patterns in observations and to inform designers of relevant aspects for a situation. Our framework is designed to assist the analysis of the diverse aspects related to human computation applications. It is organized in three dimensions which represent different perspectives in which it is possible to approach human computation: *QoS requirements, D&M strategies,* and *human aspects.* Each dimension is closely connected to an agent in the human computation ecosystem: QoS requirements are requesters' effectiveness measures; D&M strategies are mainly related to how platforms manage application execution; and human aspects are worker characteristics. Each dimension is composed of a set of factors. Figure 1 provides an overview of the framework.

Considering their relations, it is clear that the dimensions are not independent. The definition of D&M strategies is affected by both the QoS requirements and the human aspects. QoS requirements reflect requester objectives that should guide the design of suitable D&M strategies. Human aspects, in turn, consist in workers' characteristics that delimit a restriction space where D&M strategies may act aiming at optimizing QoS requirements. D&M strategies generate a final output whose quality is a measure of their capacity of optimizing QoS requirements taking into account human aspects. In the following we detail our framework by discussing the theories that support its dimensions and their factors.

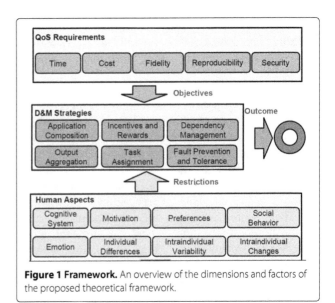

Figure 1 Framework. An overview of the dimensions and factors of the proposed theoretical framework.

3.1 QoS requirements

The QoS requirements dimension encompasses a set of quantitative characteristics that indicate requesters' objectives and how they evaluate application effectiveness. QoS requirements have been mainly addressed in two distinct areas: process management for organizations [33], and QoS for software systems [26]. Based on the literature from these areas, we define QoS requirements in terms of the following factors:

- *Time* refers to the urgency to transform an input into an output. It includes response time, and delays on work queues, and a time limit (deadline) for generating an output;
- *Cost* refers to expenditure on the application execution. It is usually divided into enactment and realization cost. Enactment cost concerns expenditure on D&M strategies, and realization cost, expenditure on application execution.
- *Fidelity* reflects how well a task is executed, according to its instructions. Fidelity cannot be described in a universal formula and it is related to specific properties and characteristics that define the meaning of "well executed" [30]. It is a quantitative indicative of accuracy and quality.
- *Reproducibility* refers to obtain similar output when the application is executed at different times and/or by different group of workers taken from the same population [34].
- *Security* relates to the confidentiality of application tasks and the trustworthiness of resources that execute them.

3.2 D&M strategies

Based on application design and management methodologies in machine-based computation [29,30,35] and in organizations [28,31], we define five factors for the D&M strategies dimension: application composition, incentives and rewards, dependency management, task assignment, output aggregation, and fault prevention and tolerance.

Application Composition. It consists of two major activities: problem decomposition and application structuring. Problem decomposition includes the following decisions: 1) tasks granularity, e.g., generating fewer task that require more effort to be executed (coarse-grained) or generating many small tasks that require less effort to be executed (fine-grained); 2) worker interfaces for the tasks, i.e., the interface design of the web page that shows the instructions of the work to be done.

Application structuring consists in how to compose the application considering possible dependencies between its tasks. As exemplified in Figures 2 and 3, the two major application structuring patterns are *bag-of-tasks* and *workflow*. Bag-of-tasks applications are composed of a

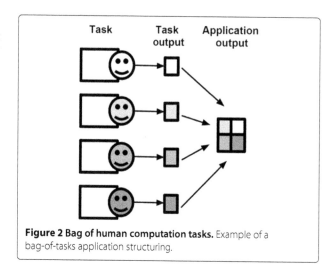

Figure 2 Bag of human computation tasks. Example of a bag-of-tasks application structuring.

set of independent tasks. For example, a group of Human Intelligence Tasks (HITs) in MTurk platform [36]. Workflow applications, in turn, are composed of a set of tasks organized in a sequence of connected steps [37]. Each step is composed by one or more tasks. Independent tasks are usually grouped in the same workflow step. Interdependent tasks, in turn, constitute different workflow steps.

Incentives and Rewards. Incentive are put in place when the participants exhibit distinct objectives and the information about them are decentralized [38]. In human computation systems, requesters and workers may have different interests. For example, some workers may be interested in increasing their earnings, while requesters are interested in which tasks are performed with greater accuracy. Incentive strategies are used to align the interests of requesters and workers [39]. They are usually put in place to incentivize workers to exhibit a behavior and achieve a performance level desired by the requester, which includes executing more tasks, improving accuracy and staying longer in the system. Incentives can be

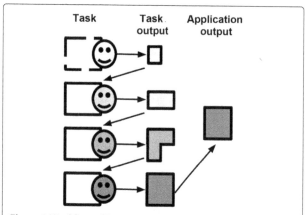

Figure 3 Workflow of human computation tasks. Example of a workflow application structuring.

broadly divided into non-monetary and monetary. Examples of non-monetary incentives are badges provided as a recognition for workers' achievements, and rank leaderboard for the workers to gauge themselves against peers. Monetary incentives are usually associated with a reward scheme, which defines the conditions for a worker to be rewarded, e.g., providing an output identical to the majority of other workers who perform the task. Game theory is an important theoretical guide to incentivize workers' engagament and effort in human computation systems [40,41].

Dependency Management. It focuses on the coordination between interdependent tasks. A framework of dependencies between tasks in human computation is presented by Minder et al. [42]. It is mainly based on the Coordination Theory [24]. Dependencies among tasks can be broadly divided into four levels: serialization, visibility, cooperation, and temporal. Serialization dependencies specify whether tasks in the application require a serial execution. Such dependencies are usually defined in application structure by routing operations, such as: sequence, parallelism, choice and loops. Visibility dependencies define whether the work performed in a task must be visible to the other tasks (e.g., when a task updates a global variable). Cooperation dependencies, in turn, define which tasks hold a shared object at each time and can perform operations on it without restriction. Finally, temporal dependencies specify whether a set of tasks must perform operations in a particular temporal dependency.

Task Assignment. It defines how to choose which worker will execute a task. The strategies can be broadly divided into scheduling, job board, and recommendation. Scheduling is a push assignment; workers receive and execute tasks assigned to them. Scheduling strategies assign tasks to workers trying to optimize one or more QoS requirements. It is usually based on application and/or workers information. Job board, in turn, is a pull assignment; workers use search and browser functionalities to choose the tasks they want to execute. It allows workers to select those tasks they expect to enable them to maximize their metrics, such as: earnings, preferences, and enjoyment. Finally, Recommendation is a hybrid assignment; workers receive a set of tasks and they choose which of them they want to perform. Recommendation is mapped into scheduling when the amount of tasks recommended is 1, and it is mapped into job board when all tasks are recommended.

Output Aggregation. It is concerned with aggregating sets of individual task outputs to identify the correct output or to obtain a better output. It is interchangeably called judgment aggregation and crowd consensus. An aggregation function may be implemented in several ways and it may be executed by a machine or a human. A simple example is that of different task outputs that constitute different parts of the application output; thus, the aggregation is only a merge of task outputs. A more sophisticated aggregation function may ask workers to improve available task outputs and generate an application output. Note that output aggregation is an *offline* procedure, i.e., it is executed after the outputs of all application tasks have already been obtained. There are also *online* procedures which involve failure detection in each task output, as well as strategies to detect and manage cheating workers. We discuss online procedures in fault tolerance strategies.

Fault Prevention and Tolerance. Faults are events which potentially may cause a failure. A failure is a malfunction or incorrect output. Thus, fault prevention consists in avoiding events which may cause failures and fault tolerance consists in identifying and managing failures after they occur. To analyze human error in human computation systems, we join together human error concepts from Human Error Theory [23] and concepts related to the implementation of fault prevention and tolerance in computing system from Human-in-the-Loop [25] and machine-based distributed systems [43] literatures.

To execute a task, a human first constructs a mental plan of a sequence of actions that ends with the conclusion of the task [23]. Three types of failures may occur in this process: *mistakes*, *lapses* and *slips*. Mistake is a failure in constructing a suitable plan to execute the task, then the plan is not correct. Lapses and slips are failures in the execution of a correct plan. Lapses occur when the worker forgets to perform one action of the plan. Finally, slips occur when the worker performs incorrectly an action of the plan. A diversity of faults can generate such failures, for example: lack of knowledge or time to execute the task, and stochastic cognitive variability such as variability of attention.

Fault prevention strategies usually focus on methodologies for design, testing, and validation of tasks instructions, and testing resources capabilities. Fault tolerance, in turn, consists of four phases: failure detection, damage confinement, failure recovery, and fault treatment. Failure detection consists of identifying the presence of a failure, e.g., identifying that a task output is incorrect. Damage confinement aims at determining the boundaries of failures and preventing their propagation, e.g., identifying which tasks outputs are incorrect and preventing that other tasks make use of these outputs. Failure recovery tries to bring the flow of execution to a consistent state, e.g., re-executing tasks that produced incorrect outputs. Finally, fault treatment involves treating faults to prevent the occurrence of new failures.

3.3 Human aspects

In our context, human aspects are human beings characteristics that determine the way they perform tasks. These aspects have been widely addressed in Psychology studies. They can be broadly divided into the following factors: cognitive system [44,45], motivation [20], preferences [46], social behavior [47], emotion [48,49], individual differences [50,51], and intraindividual changes [52].

Cognitive system. Its function includes several processes of task execution, such as information processing, understanding, and learning. It specifies processes' organization on long-term and short-term memory. Long-term memory is where knowledge is stored. In turn, short-term memory is a working memory used to process information in the sense of organizing, contrasting, and comparing [44]. Humans are able to deal with few items of information simultaneously in their working memory, and any interactions between items held in their working memory also require working memory capacity, reducing the number of items that can be dealt with simultaneously [45]. Cognitive overload occurs when tasks processing exceeds working memory capacity.

Motivation. From the motivation theory viewpoint [20], humans are guided by motivation impulses or goals, i.e., the desire to do/obtain new things and to achieve new conditions. Incentive studies explore the way such goals influence human behavior. Considering the self-determination theory [21], motivation is broadly divided into intrinsic and extrinsic. In task execution, intrinsic motivation may consist of workers internal desires to perform a particular task because it gives them pleasure or allows them to develop a particular skill. Extrinsic motivation, in turn, consists of factors external to the workers and unrelated to the task they are executing.

Preferences. Humans exhibit personal preferences [46]. Such preferences are explained on the basis of two types of influences: their own past experiences and the experiences of others which are directly observable by them. As an example of workers preferences in task, consider the case where, after feeling bored several times when executing high-time-consuming tasks, workers always choose to execute only low-time-consuming tasks.

Social behavior. Sociality meanvs group/community organization to perform activities [53]. In general, communities form and persist because the individual takes advantage of them and thereby serve their interests. Sense of Community theory suggests that members develop sense of community based on membership, influence, integration and fulfillment of needs, and shared emotional connection [22]. This behavior may influence the way community members behave and execute tasks in the system.

Emotion. Emotion can be defined as a human complex psychological and physiological state that allows humans to sense whether a given event in their environment is more desirable or less desirable [49]. Emotion concerns, for instance, mood, affection, feeling and opinion. It interacts with and influences other human aspects relevant to task execution effectiveness. For example, it influences cognitive system functions related to perception, learning and reasoning [49].

Intraindividual variability and change. Humans show intraindividual variability and change [52]. Intraindividual variability is a short-term or transient fluctuation characterized by factors as: wobble, inconsistency, and noise. Intraindividual change is a long-term lasting change as a result of learning, development, or aging.

Individual differences. Humans show variability between themselves in several factors [50,51], such as decision making and performance. In this study we focus mainly on individual differences in terms of the following three human competencies: knowledge, skills, and abilities. Knowledge refers to an organized body of information applied directly in the execution of a task. Skill refers to the proficiency in tasks execution, usually measured qualitatively and quantitatively. Abilities are those appropriate on-the-job behaviors needed to bring both knowledge and skills in task execution.

4 Instantiating the framework

Now we turn to map the literature on human computation by using our theoretical framework. This is done through a literature review focused on analyzing: a) how human computation studies on D&M strategies have dealt with human aspects discussed in our framework to satisfy the QoS requirements of requesters; and b) what are the relevant results regarding these human aspects upon which future D&M strategies decisions can be based. Throughout this section, for each D&M factor, we discuss the human computation studies and extract the major implications for system design related to human factors.

4.1 Application composition

Application composition consists of two major activities: task design and application structuring.

Task design impacts on the ability of worker to complete tasks quickly, effectively, and accurately [54]. Poorly designed tasks, which show high cognitive load, can cause fatigue of workers, compromising their understanding of instructions, decreasing their productivity and increasing their errors [55]. This usually occurs because of the limitations of the human working memory. This is the case of tasks where humans are asked to choose the best item among several options [56,57]. To perform this task, humans compare the items and choose the best of them on their working memory. Such kind of task generates a cognitive load, which increases in proportion as the number of items to be compared increases. The higher the cognitive load, the higher error chances. Tasks can also be designed to motivate workers to put more effort in generating correct outputs. Huang et al. show that one way to achieve it is to tell workers explicitly that their work will be used to evaluate the output provided by other workers [58].

Application structuring studies can be broadly divided into static workflows and dynamic workflows. Example of static workflow composition is that used in Soylent [59]. Soylent is a word processor add-in that uses MTurk's workers (mturk.com) to perform text shortening. Soylent implements the Find-Fix-Verify workflow, i.e., find areas of the text that can be shortened, fix and shorten the highlighted area without changing the meaning of the text, and verify if the new text retain its meaning. This task distinction captures human individual differences mainly in terms of the type of tasks workers want to perform, i.e., find, fix, or verify tasks. Static workflows can be optimized. Cascade [60] and Deluge [61] are examples of optimized workflows to taxonomy creation tasks.

Example of dynamic workflow composition is that used in Turkomatic [55]. In Turkomatic, workers compose the workflow dynamically on a collaborative planning process. When a worker receives a task, she/he performs it only if it is simple to be executed; otherwise, the worker subdivides it into two other tasks. A problem occurs when workers generate unclear tasks that will be executed by other workers. Other approach is proposed by Lin et al. [62]. They assume that workflow composition results in different output quality when executed by different groups and they propose the availability of multiple workflows composition with independent difficulty level and dynamically switch between them to obtain higher accuracy in a given group of workers. Finally, Bozzon et al. propose a system that dynamically controls the composition and execution of the application, and reacts to some specific situations, such as: achievement of a suitable output and identification of a spammer [63]. It allows the system to adapt the application to changes in workers characteristics and behavior.

Implications for systems design. We extract two major guidelines from this discussion: 1) application designers must avoid task cognitive overload, in what requiring a small amount of specialized ability, skill and knowledge in a same task can contribute; 2) given that workers in a platform display individual differences, application designers can take advantage of worker diversity by developing applications with different types of tasks, each type requiring a different skill; this may be done either by defining a static composition of tasks that require different skills or by using dynamic composition to adapt to different groups of workers.

4.2 Incentives and rewards

Incentive and reward schemes have been designed to incentivize specific behaviors and maximize requesters'

QoS requirements [39,64,65]. Unfortunately, there is no consensus in the literature on the effect of incentives on worker behavior. Its effect seems to vary with the type of task. In some tasks, increasing financial incentives allows one to increase the amount of workers interested in executing the task [8,66,67], but not necessarily the quality of the outputs [67]. In other tasks, quality may be improved by increasing intrinsic motivations [68]. Incentives also relates to other aspects of task design, for example, some studies show that incentives work better when they are placed in the focal position in task worker interface [69], and task fidelity is improved when financial incentives are combined with a task design that asks workers to think about the output provided by other workers for the same task [70].

Besides defining right incentives, requesters must also define a suitable reward scheme. Witkowski et al. analyze a scheme that pays workers only if his/her output agrees with those provided by others, and that penalizes with negative payment in the case his/her output disagrees. They show that such scheme acts as a self selection mechanism that makes workers with lower quality choose not to participate [71]. Rao et al. show that a reward scheme that informs workers that they will be paid if their outputs are similar to the majority motivates workers to reflect more on what other workers would choose. This generates a higher percentage of correct outputs and the obtained outputs are closer to the correct one [72]. Huang et al. analyze three schemes in a group of workers [73]: (i) individual, in which reward depends only on worker performance; (ii) teamwork, in which workers in the group are paid similarly based on the average of their performance; and (iii) competition, in which workers in the group are opponents and they are paid based on their differences of performance. The effectiveness of these schemes tends to vary with other application settings such as social transparency.

Implications for systems design. We extract two major guidelines from this discussion: 1) given that the effect of incentives on intrinsic and extrinsic motivations appears to be different in different types of tasks, designers must test how combinations of such incentives contribute towards the desired quality in their specific context; 2) task peformance can be improved by using incentives that motivate workers to reflect more on what output other workers would provide for the same task.

4.3 Task assignment

We broadly divided task assignment strategies into scheduling, job board, and recommendation.

Task Scheduling strategies try to optimize some QoS requirements by exploiting information about the affinity between tasks and workers. Scheduling strategies in human computation literature have considered several human aspects. Some strategies consider workers' emotional states allocating tasks that are appropriate to current worker's mood [74]. Heidari and Kearns take into account task difficulty and workers abilities [75]. They analyze the case in which workers can decide between execute one task or forward it. When one worker decides to forward a task, it will be scheduled to a more qualified worker. It generates a forwarding structure on task scheduling that improves outputs' quality. Waterhouse proposes a strategy based on a probabilistic metric of mutual information between workers. The strategy tunes the assignment of tasks to the workers that will increase the amount of information gain [76].

Other thread of scheduling strategies is inspired by the hierarchical structure in today's organizations, exploring individual differences [77,78]. They consider working teams and roles, such as supervisors and workers. Tasks are first assigned to supervisors, who assign them to workers in their team taking into account the qualification and skills of each worker. Skill-based scheduling considers different workers qualification levels and that qualification level increases in the proportion that workers adequately perform more tasks [79]. There are also approaches that use information and contents liked by the worker on social networks to automatically match workers preferences and task requirements [80].

Job Board strategies are used mainly in online labor market platforms, where tasks are usually made available together with their rewards to workers in boards [81]. Job boards allow workers to choose tasks that fit their preferences [82]; thus, task instructions must be clear and attractive to workers [83]. Requesters define job parameters so as to address workers interests and make their tasks attractive to workers. For example, AutoMan adjusts tasks' price and tasks' allocation time to motivate more workers to try executing them [66]. By adjusting these parameters, AutoMan tries to optimize QoS requirements addressing workers' time and financial incentives. Toomim et al. propose a method to characterize workers preferences for some interfaces and tasks [84]. This information is used in future task design.

Task Recommendation strategies recommend tasks to workers according to some affinity criteria [85]. The platforms oDesk (odesk.com) and Elance (elance.com) are based on job boards, but they also make use of a recommendation system to inform workers about new jobs that match their skills. We are not aware of studies that evaluate the effectiveness of such functionalities on these platforms. Yi et al. propose a matrix completion approach to infer workers preferences in pairwise comparison tasks [86]. The method may be useful to improve task recommendation strategies.

In job board and tasks recommendation approaches, it is also required a mechanism that allows requesters to choose which of the candidate workers will perform the task or which solution will be paid. In research and practice, three strategies that explore these dimensions are: *auction*, in which the task is allocated to the worker that charges the lowest value (e.g., odesk.com); *challenge*, in which all workers perform the available tasks, but only the best solution is paid (e.g., topcoder.com [8]); and *registration order*, in which the task is allocated to the first worker that signed up to run it (e.g., mturk.com [87]). To the best of our knowledge, no study was conducted to compare the performance of these approaches and to indicate in what situations each should be used.

Implications for systems design. Two basic guidelines to highlight in this context are: 1) given that most of platforms are based on job boards and that in this environment the effectiveness of a task relies on its ability to gain attention of suitable workers, requesters must provide task descriptions with information that allows workers to easily identify if the task match their skills, preferences and interests; 2) requesters must avoid generating too restrictive tasks in order to take advantage of the diversity and larger quantities of workers that job boards and recommendation strategies give access to.

4.4 Dependency management

We focus on analyzing the dependency management strategies that take into account human aspects, while ensuring temporal, serialization, visibility, and cooperation dependencies. Most studies address only temporal dependencies, in which a set of tasks must be performed in a particular order (e.g., [36,77]) or in a synchronous way (e.g., [88,89]).

Serialization dependency studies in human computation have focused maily on applications with loop or without loop. Example of human computation applications without loops are those that deal with planning activities [90]. Such applications usually include a sequence of steps such as: decomposition of the problem into small tasks, execution of each task and aggregation of these partial task outputs to obtain the final output as a result to the problem. This is the case of Turkomatic [55], CrowdForge [91], CrowdPlan [90], and combination of creative design [92]. Application with loops, in turn, include some iterative processes [36] as in Find-Fix-and-Verify [59] and Iterative Improvement [93].

Visibility dependency is common in working group. It usually needs a shared environment that unobtrusively offers up-to-date group context and explicit notification of each user's action when appropriate. Mao et al. [89] and Zhang et al. [94] address visibility dependencies in human computation applications. In their studies, workers try to achieve a global goal. This goal can be, for example, a collaborative itinerary planning [94], a collaborative graph coloring [89]. In these cases, workers can see outputs generated to correlated tasks. Such type of task is usually related to agreement or consensus and the visibility decision may impact both worker behavior as well as the time required to obtain an output [88].

Cooperation dependencies are also related to working group. Mobi [94] and TurkServer [89] allow one to implement applications that contain cooperative tasks. Zhang et al. show that the unified view of the task status allows workers to coordinate and communicate more effectively with one another, allowing them to view and build upon each other's ideas [94]. Platforms such as MTurk maintain workers invisible and not able to communicate with each other. Turkopticon is a tool that allows one to interrupt such invisibility, making possible workers to communicate among themselves [95].

Implications for systems design. The major guideline regarding dependency management is that designers must consider that some degree of visibility and communication between workers may be positive for application performance in terms of time and accuracy. It seems that workers should be allowed: 1) to see the status of tasks that are interdependent with his/her task in order to synchronize its execution with any global task constraint; and 2) to communicate with other workers that are executing tasks interdependent with his/her task in order to improve cooperation.

4.5 Output aggregation

There are a range of output aggregation strategies in human computation, most of them are already discussed by Law and von Ahn [96] and Nguyen et al. [97]. We focus on discussing studies that account for human aspects.

An example of comparable outputs aggregation strategy is majority vote [36,66], in which the output of the application is the most frequent task output. This strategy assumes that the majority of the workers assigned to any task are reliable. Majority vote does not perform properly when the error chance in task execution is high. Sheng et al. investigate the impact of the number of task executions on output accuracy and shows that quality of the output is improved by using additional workers only when the workers accuracy is higher than 0.5 [98]. They propose a repeated-labeling technique that selects data points for which application quality should be improved by the acquisition of multiple task outputs.

Diverse studies have been devoted to aggregating a set of outputs and obtaining an accurate output taking into account workers expertise and task characteristics. Whitehill et al. consider that an output accuracy depend on the difficulty of the task and expertise of the worker [99]. They proposed Generative Model of Labels, Abilities, and Difficulties (GLAD) which estimates these parameters using Expectation Maximization (EM) probabilistic models and evaluate tasks output in a way that

experts' outputs count more. Hovy et al. propose Multi-Annotator Competence Estimation (MACE) which uses EM to identify which annotators are trustworthy and considers this information to predict outputs [100]. Wang et al. propose a recursive algorithm to improve the efficiency of compute EM models in these contexts [101]. Dalvi et al. propose a technique to estimate worker reliabilities and improve output aggregation [102]. The strategy is based on measuring agreement between pairs of workers.

Another output aggregation challenge arises in unstructured outputs, e.g., open-ended [56,59] and image annotation tasks [103]. In this case, a way to find the best output is to apply a vote-on-the-best strategy in which workers evaluate the quality of each output or they choose which of them exhibits the highest quality [104]. It exploits individual differences, given that some workers are better at identifying the correct outputs than producing them themselves [56]. When the set of options is too large, it may be difficult for workers choose the best item. An alternative in this case is to develop a second human computation application in which few items are compared in each task and the best item is chosen by tournament (e.g., [56,57]). Other peculiarity of unstructured outputs is that even poor outputs may be useful. For example, other workers can aggregate such poor outputs, and generate a new better output [55]. The quality of the aggregation can also be improved by using estimations of the difficulty level of tasks and skills of workers [103].

Implications for systems design. When developing output aggregation strategies, designers must weigh at least three parameters that impact on the quality of the final output: 1) task cognitive load; 2) the amount of different workers that provided task outputs, i.e., redundancy degree; and 3) the accuracy of each worker that provided the outputs. As in the literature, the value of each of parameters can be obtained in a statistical evaluation, considering that the accuracy of the final output tends to be higher with more accurate estimation of these parameters.

4.6 Fault prevention and tolerance

The prevention of faults in task instructions can be done by using offline and/or online pilot tests [87]. Offline tests are conducted with accessible people that can provide feedback on issues and improvements in the tasks instructions. Online tests, in turn, are driven onto a platform, and they are more realistic than offline tests. In this case, workers may not be accessible to provide feedback about the task instructions, but their outputs can be analyzed to identify problems.

The prevention of undesired workers is usually done by using qualification tests [87]. They consist in requiring the execution of a gold standard test that certifies whether the worker has the skills and qualifications required to perform application tasks. Only workers who perform accurately are considered qualified. A downside of this approach is not considering changes in workers behavior after executing the test. Malicious workers usually change their behavior over time [105]. CrowdScape is a system that allows requesters to select workers based on both task output quality and workers' behavioral changes [106].

Studies also have been devoted to fault tolerance which consists in four phases: failure detection, damage confinement, failure recovery, and fault treatment.

Failure detection has been made by using: 1) conformance voting, which allows one to detect poorly executed tasks; and 2) timing, which allows one to detect worker evasion, i.e., the worker is assigned to perform a task, but gives up executing and do not deallocate the task. In conformance vote, one worker or a group of workers evaluate whether a task output is correct. When the output is not correct, the task needs to be re-executed by another worker [55]. Timing, in turn, defines a maximum time that a task can remain allocated to a worker; it is expected that a worker provides an output up to this time. If that time expires without an output being provided, the task is deallocated and made available to another worker [59].

Damage Confinement is usually made by using error recovery techniques in each task or workflow step. It prevents that damages propagate to the next workflow step. This propagation occurs, for example, in workflow derailment problems [104], which arises when an error in the task executions prevents the workflow conclusion.

Failure Recovery has been made by using majority voting, alternative, and human assessment. These strategies exploit human individual differences by using redundancy of workers. If different and independent workers provide the same output to a task, it increases the confidence that the task is being performed in accordance with its instructions [107]. In majority voting, several workers perform the same task in parallel and the most frequent output is considered correct. In alternative strategies, in turn, a worker executes the task and, if an error occurs, the task is executed again by another worker [55]. In these redundancy-based strategies, the impact of the redundancy degree on output accuracy is highly dependent on the type of task. Increasing the redundancy of workers does not necessarily increase the confidence that the correct output will be obtained [108]. Furthermore, the perception of redundancy by the workers may have a negative effect on their motivation and work quality. The more co-workers working in the same task are perceived by workers, the lower their work quality [109]. This occurs because workers demotivate thinking that their effort does not count for much.

Finally, in human assessment strategies, the outputs generated by a worker are evaluated by others. This can be implemented in two ways: arbitration and peer review. In arbitration, two workers independently execute the tasks and another worker evaluates their outputs and solve disagreements. In peer review, the output provided by each worker is reviewed by another worker. Hansen et al. show that in text transcribe tasks, the peer review strategy is significantly more efficient, but not as accurate for certain tasks as the arbitration strategy [110].

Fault Treatment has been made by fixing problems in task design, and by eliminating or reducing the reputation of unskilled or malicious workers. For example, TopCoder [8] maintains a historical track of the number of tasks each worker chooses to execute, but did not conclude. This track is used to estimate the probability that the worker chooses tasks and do not execute it. Ipeirotis et al. propose to separate systematic errors from bias due to, for example, an intraindividual variability such as distraction [111]. This distinction allows also a better estimation of accuracy and reputation of the worker. Such estimation may be used to prevent assigning to a worker tasks for which he/she is not qualified or that he/she will not complete the execution. Another important aspect in fault treatment is to provide feedback to workers about his/her work [112]. It helps workers to learn how to accurately execute the task (intraindividual changes) and avoid errors due to lapses (intraindividual variability) [111].

Implications for systems design. The three major guidelines extracted from this discussion are: 1) designers must test the task worker interface and check workers skills/reputation; to this end pilot tests and qualification tests can be applied; 2) redundancy is the basis of fault tolerance strategies, but requesters must generate tasks that maximize the number of workers capable of executing it, increasing the potential of redundancy of the task; and 3) requesters must provide workers assessment and feedback in order to allow them to learn from tasks they perform incorrectly.

5 Challenges and perspectives

In the last section, we analyzed the human computation literature and its implication for design in the light of our theoretical framework. Now we turn to discuss challenges and perspectives in D&M strategies. Although our list is by no means exhaustive, it offers examples of topics in need of further work and directions that appear promising.

5.1 Relations between dimensions of the framework

Table 1 synthesizes the contributions on the relationships between D&M strategies and human aspects identified in the last section. As shown, there are several relationships for which we could not find any study. This state of affairs indicates a large amount of research still to be conducted after mapping the impact of human aspects

Table 1 Human aspects factors addressed in D&M strategies

	Application composition	Incentives and rewards	Dependency management	Task assignment	Output aggregation	Fault tolerance
Cognitive System	[54-57]			[75]	[99,103]	[111]
Motivation		[8,58,64-67,69,71,72]		[66]		[67,68,109]
Preferences	[59]			[81-85]		
Social behavior		[70,73]	[88,89,94,95]	[80]		[66]
Emotion				[74,113]		[111]
Individual differences	[55,59,62]			[8,76-78]	[55,56,59,98-100,102]	[55,59,104,106,110]
Intraindividual Variability						[106,111,112]
Intraindividual changes				[79]		[105,112]

on D&M effectiveness. Two other issues that still require further understanding are: 1) adequate combinations of D&M strategies; and 2) the impact of D&M strategies on workers' cognition and behavior.

It is intuitive that one D&M strategy may impact on the effectiveness of another. For example, by generating a fine-grained application composition to account for the human cognitive system, one may generate undesired effects: 1) designing tasks too susceptible to cheater workers, which reduces the effectiveness of fault tolerance strategies; or 2) generating a large number of tasks with a too high number of dependencies among them, which may reduce parallelism in task execution and impact on dependency management. More empirical research on how to adequately combine D&M strategies in distributed human computation is still required.

Besides the requesters' perspective that tries to understand how to take advantage of human aspects to achieve QoS requirements, studies must also identify possible side-effects of the strategies on workers cognition and behavior. Two cognitive effects that may be relevant to consider are: *Framing effect* – workers may generate different outputs based on how a task is designed–, and *Hawthorne effect* – workers may alter their behavior when they know that they are being observed. Two behavioral effects are collusion, an agreement between workers to act similarly (e.g., planning collusion against requesters which submit poorly designed tasks [55]), and sabotage, workers change their behavior to take advantage of the system (e.g., inhibiting competitors in a "maximum observability" audition [8]). Also, there is room for studies focused on workers and on the fair relationship between workers and requesters [114].

5.2 Exploring the Interdisciplinarity of D&M strategies improvement

Application composition. The main human aspects factors that have been addressed in application composition are cognitive system and motivation/incentives. By taking

into account such factors in the context of task execution, human computation application composition is clearly related to the disciplines: *ecological interface* [115], and *goal setting* [116]. Ecological interface principles are grounded on how the human cognitive system works and its effects on information understanding and processing. Such principles may support the development of task designs to avoid cognitive overload and improve task execution effectiveness. Goal setting studies, in turn, may help better defining both task instructions and the way their outputs will be evaluated by the requester. Knowledge of such topics and reasoning about their relationships to human computation can help in the formulation of new strategies.

Task assignment. Studies on task assignment have mainly taken into account: preferences and individual differences. Two other disciplines that take into account these aspects in task assignment are *person-job fit* [117] and *achievement motivation* [118]. The domain of person-job fit research consists on tasks characteristics, worker characteristics, and required outcomes. It emphasizes the fit and matching of workers and tasks in the prediction of both worker and organizational outcomes. Achievement motivation is a motivation for demonstrating high rather than low ability. This motivation influences the tasks a human chooses to perform, i.e., his/her preferences. According to this concept, individuals select tasks they expect to enable them to maximize their chances of demonstrating high ability and avoiding demonstrating low ability. These concepts may inspire tasks scheduling and task recommendation strategies in human computation.

Dependency management. Ensuring tasks dependencies and still extracting the greatest potential (optimizing QoS requirement) of a crowd of workers is one of the main challenges of dependency management strategies. Similar challenge has been addressed in at least two other disciplines: *work teams* [119] and *Groupware* [120]. Both disciplines focus on group behavior and performance.

Work team studies usually focus on group work in an organization not necessarily performed through a computer system. Groupware is generally associated with small groups working collaboratively through a computer system. Experiences on how human aspects are addressed in these disciplines may inspire solutions that consider these factors in human computation.

Output aggregation. Two important areas related to output aggregation are *Judgment Aggregation* [121] and *Social choice theory* [122]. Judgment aggregation is the subject of a growing body of work in Economics, Political science, Philosophy and related disciplines. It aims at aggregating consistent individual judgments on logically interconnected propositions into a collective judgment on those propositions. In these situations, majority voting cannot ensure an equally consistent collective conclusion. Social choice theory, in turn, is a theoretical framework for analysis of combining individual preferences, and interests to reach a collective decision or social welfare. According to this theory any choice for the entire group should reflect the desires/options of the individual to the extent possible. The studies that have been conducted in these disciplines seem to be related to human computation output aggregation [123,124]. A better mapping of their similarity and differences may help in the reuse and development of new output/judgment aggregation strategies.

Fault prevention and tolerance. Besides preventing and tolerating faults, one should also consider how to evaluate system QoS in the presence of human faults. For example, fault tolerance is mainly based on task redundancy, but defining the appropriate level of redundancy is a challenging task. Maintaining a low level of redundancy may not recover failures and maintaining a high level of redundancy can lead to a high financial cost or high volunteer effort to run the entire application. This kind of study has been conducted in other disciplines such as: *human aspects evaluation* [125] and *performability* [126]. Human aspects evaluation is an assessment of the conformity between the performance of a worker and its desired performance. Performability, in turn, focuses on modeling and measuring system QoS degradation in the presence of faults. Experiences on performability and human aspects evaluation may be useful to address QoS requirements in the presence of worker faults.

6 Conclusions

In this paper, we analyzed the design and management of distributed human computation applications. Our contribution is three-fold: 1) we integrated a set of theories in a theoretical framework for analyzing distributed human computation applications; 2) by using this theoretical framework, we analyzed human computation literature putting into perspective the results in this literature on how to leverage human aspects of workers in

D&M strategies in order to satisfy the QoS requirements of requesters; and 3) we highlighted open challenges in human computation and discussed their relationship with other disciplines from a distributed systems viewpoint.

Our framework builds on studies in different disciplines to discuss advances and perspectives in a variety of immediate practical needs in distributed human computation systems. Our literature analysis shows that D&M strategies have accounted for some human aspects to achieve QoS requirements. However, it also shows that there are still many unexplored aspects and open challenges. Inevitably, a better understanding of how humans behave in human computation systems and a proper delimitation of the human aspects involved is essential to overcome these challenges. We hope our study inspires both discussion and further research in this direction.

Competing interests

The authors declare that they have no competing interests.

Authors' contributions

LP, FB, NA, and LS jointly designed the theoretical framework used to contextualize and discuss the literature in this survey. LP drafted most of the manuscript and conducted the bulk of the review of the literature. FB, NA and LS did a smaller portion of the review of the literature and revised the manuscript in several interactions. All authors read and approved the final manuscript.

Acknowledgements

Lesandro Ponciano thanks the support provided by CAPES/Brazil in all aspects of this research. Francisco Brasileiro acknowledges the support received from CNPq/Brazil in all aspects of this research.

References

1. Quinn AJ, Bederson BB (2011) Human computation: a survey and taxonomy of a growing field. In: Proceedings of the SIGCHI Conference on Human Factors in Computing Systems (CHI). ACM, New York, pp 1403–1412
2. Savage N (2012) Gaining wisdom from crowds. Commun ACM 55(3):13
3. Yuen M-C, Chen L-J, King I (2009) A survey of human computation systems. In: Proceedings of the International Conference on Computational Science and Engineering (CSE), vol. 4. IEEE Computer Society, Washington, DC, pp 723–728
4. Yuen M-C, King I, Leung K-S (2011) A survey of crowdsourcing systems. In: Proceedings of the International Conference on Privacy, Security, Risk and Trust (PASSAT). IEEE Computer Society, Washington, DC, pp 766–773
5. Quinn AJ, Bederson BB (2009) A taxonomy of distributed human computation. Technical report, University of Maryland
6. Von Ahn L, Maurer B, McMillen C, Abraham D, Blum M (2008) recaptcha: Human-based character recognition via web security measures. Science 321(5895):1465–1468
7. von Ahn L, Dabbish L (2008) Designing games with a purpose. Commun ACM 51(8):58–67
8. Archak N (2010) Money, glory and cheap talk: analyzing strategic behavior of contestants in simultaneous crowdsourcing contests on topcoder.com. In: Proceedings of the International World Wide Web Conference (WWW). ACM, New York, pp 21–30
9. Ipeirotis PG (2010) Analyzing the amazon mechanical turk marketplace. XRDS 17(2):16–21
10. Ponciano L, Brasileiro F, Simpson R, Smith A (2014) Volunteers' engagement in human computation astronomy projects. Comput Sci Eng PP(99):1–12

11. Ross J, Irani L, Silberman M, Zaldivar A, Tomlinson B (2010) Who are the crowdworkers?: shifting demographics in mechanical turk. In: Proceedings of the ACM SIGCHI Conference on Human Factors in Computing Systems, Extended Abstracts (EA). ACM, New York, pp 2863–2872

12. Ball NM (2013) Canfar+ skytree: Mining massive datasets as an essential part of the future of astronomy. In: American Astronomical Society Meeting Abstracts, vol. 221. American Astronomical Society, Washington, DC

13. Kittur A, Nickerson JV, Bernstein M, Gerber E, Shaw A, Zimmerman J, Lease M, Horton J (2013) The future of crowd work. In: Proceedings of the ACM Conference on Computer-Supported Cooperative Work and Social Computing (CSWC). ACM, New York, pp 1301–1318

14. Lintott CJ, Schawinski K, Slosar A, Land K, Bamford S, Thomas D, Raddick MJ, Nichol RC, Szalay A, Andreescu D, Murray P, Vandenberg J (2008) Galaxy Zoo: morphologies derived from visual inspection of galaxies from the Sloan Digital Sky Survey. Mon Notices R Astronomical Soc 389:1179–1189

15. de Araújo RM (2013) 99designs: An analysis of creative competition in crowdsourced design. In: Proceedings of the First AAAI Conference on Human Computation and Crowdsourcing (HCOMP). AAAI, Palo Alto, pp 17–24

16. Marcus A, Wu E, Karger D, Madden S, Miller R (2011) Human-powered sorts and joins. Proc VLDB Endow 5(1):13–24

17. Vukovic M (2009) Crowdsourcing for enterprises. In: Congress on Services - I. IEEE Computer Society, Washington, DC, pp 686–692

18. Dustdar S, Truong H-L (2012) Virtualizing software and humans for elastic processes in multiple clouds – a service management perspective. IJNGC 3(2):109–126

19. Crouser RJ, Chang R (2012) An affordance-based framework for human computation and human-computer collaboration. IEEE Trans Vis Comput Graph 18(12):2859–2868

20. Maslow AH (1943) A theory of human motivation. Psychol Rev 50:370–396

21. Deci EL, Ryan RM (1985) Intrinsic Motivation and Self-determination in Human Behavior. Plenum Press, New York

22. McMillan DW (1996) Sense of community. J Commun Psychol 24(4):315–325

23. Reason J (1990) Human Error. Cambridge University Press Cambridge [England], New York

24. Malone T (1994) The interdisciplinary study of coordination. ACM Comput Surv 26(1):87–119

25. Cranor LF (2008) A framework for reasoning about the human in the loop. In: Proceedings of UPSEC. USENIX Association, Berkeley, pp 1–15

26. Denning PJ (2003) Great principles of computing. Commun ACM 46(11):15

27. Georgakopoulos D, Hornick M, Sheth A (1995) An overview of workflow management: from process modeling to workflow automation infrastructure. Distrib Parallel Databases 3(2):119–153

28. Kiepuszewski B, Hofstede AHMT, Bussler C (2000) On structured workflow modelling. In: CAiSE. Springer-Verlag, London, pp 431–445

29. Yu J, Buyya R (2005) A taxonomy of workflow management systems for grid computing. J Grid Comput 3(3):171–200

30. Cardoso J, Miller J, Sheth A, Arnold J (2002) Modeling quality of service for workflows and web service processes. J Web Semant 1:281–308

31. Kumar A, Van Der Aalst WMP, Verbeek EMW (2002) Dynamic work distribution in workflow management systems: How to balance quality and performance. J Manage Inf Syst 18(3):157–193

32. Grudin J, Poltrock S (2012) Taxonomy and theory in computer supported cooperative work. In: Handbook of Organizational Psychology. Oxford University Press, Oxford, pp 1323–1348

33. Van der Aalst W, van Hee KM (2004) Workflow Management: Models, Methods, and Systems. Cooperative Information Systems Series. Mit Press, Cambridge, Massachusetts, United States

34. Paritosh P (2012) Human computation must be reproducible. In: Proc. of CrowdSearch, pp 20–25

35. Cirne W, Paranhos D, Costa L, Santos-Neto E, Brasileiro F, Sauvé J, Silva FA, Barros CO, Silveira C (2003) Running bag-of-tasks applications on computational grids: The mygrid approach. In: Proceedings of the International Conference on Parallel Processing. IEEE Computer Society, Washington, DC, pp 407–416

36. Little G, Chilton LB, Goldman M, Miller RC (2010) TurKit: Human Computation Algorithms on Mechanical Turk. In: Proceedings of the ACM Symposium on User Interface Software and Technology (UIST). ACM, New York, pp 57–66

37. Dorn C, Taylor RN, Dustdar S (2012) Flexible social workflows: Collaborations as human architecture. Internet Comput IEEE 16(2):72–77

38. Laffont J-J, Martimort D (2009) The Theory of Incentives: the Principal-agent Model. Princeton University Press, Princeton, New Jersey

39. Scekic O, Truong H-L, Dustdar S (2013) Incentives and rewarding in social computing. Commun ACM 56(6):72–82

40. Ghosh A (2013) Game theory and incentives in human computation systems. In: Michelucci P (ed) Handbook of Human Computation. Springer, New York, pp 725–742

41. Jain S, Parkes DC (2009) The role of game theory in human computation systems. In: Proceedings of the ACM SIGKDD Workshop on Human Computation (HCOMP). ACM, pp 58–61

42. Minder P, Bernstein A (2011) Crowdlang - first steps towards programmable human computers for general computation. In: Proceedings of the ACM SIGKDD Workshop on Human Computation (HCOMP)

43. Jalote P (1994) Fault Tolerance in Distributed Systems. Prentice-Hall, Upper Saddle River

44. Simon HA (1990) Invariants of human behavior. Annu Rev Psychol 41(1):1–19

45. Sweller J, Merrienboer JJGV, Paas FGWC (1998) Cognitive architecture and instructional design. Educ Psychol Rev 10:251–296

46. Kapteyn A, Wansbeek T, Buyze J (1978) The dynamics of preference formation. Econ Lett 1(1):93–98

47. Alexander RD (1974) The evolution of social behavior. Annu Rev Ecol Evol Syst 5(1):325–383

48. Gross JJ (1998) The emerging field of emotion regulation: An integrative review. Rev Gen Psychol 2(3):271–299

49. Dolan RJ (2002) Emotion, cognition, and behavior. Science (New York, N.Y.) 298(5596):1191–1194

50. Parasuraman R, Jiang Y (2012) Individual differences in cognition, affect, and performance: Behavioral, neuroimaging, and molecular genetic approaches. NeuroImage 59(1):70–82

51. Stanovich K, West R (1998) Individual differences in rational thought. J Exp Psychol Gen 127(2):161–188

52. Ram N, Rabbitt P, Stollery B, Nesselroade JR (2005) Cognitive performance inconsistency: Intraindividual change and variability. Psychol Agin 20(4):623–633

53. Coleman J (1990) Foundations of Social Theory. Harvard, Cambridge, Massachusetts, United States

54. Khanna S, Ratan A, Davis J, Thies W (2010) Evaluating and improving the usability of mechanical turk for low-income workers in India. In: Proceedings of the ACM Annual Symposium on Computing for Development (ACM DEV). ACM, New York, pp 1–10

55. Kulkarni A, Can M, Hartmann B (2012) Collaboratively Crowdsourcing Workflows with Turkomatic. In: Proceedings of the ACM Conference on Computer-Supported Cooperative Work and Social Computing (CSWC). ACM, New York, pp 1003–1012

56. Sun Y-A, Roy S, Little G (2011) Beyond independent agreement: A tournament selection approach for quality assurance of human computation tasks. In: Proceedings of the AAAI Workshop on Human Computation (HCOMP). AAAI, Palo Alto, CA, USA, pp 113–118

57. Venetis P, Garcia-Molina H, Huang K, Polyzotis N (2012) Max algorithms in crowdsourcing environments. In: Proceedings of the International World Wide Web Conference (WWW). ACM, New York, pp 989–998

58. Huang S-W, Fu W-T (2013) Enhancing reliability using peer consistency evaluation in human computation. In: Proceedings of the ACM Conference on Computer-Supported Cooperative Work and Social Computing (CSWC). ACM, New York, pp 639–648

59. Bernstein MS, Little G, Miller RC, Hartmann B, Ackerman MS, Karger DR, Crowell D, Panovich K (2010) Soylent: a word processor with a crowd inside. In: Proceedings of the ACM Symposium on User Interface Software and Technology (UIST). ACM, New York, pp 313–322

60. Chilton LB, Little G, Edge D, Weld DS, Landay JA (2013) Cascade: Crowdsourcing taxonomy creation. In: Proceedings of the SIGCHI Conference on Human Factors in Computing Systems (CHI). ACM, New York, pp 1999–2008

61. Bragg J, Mausam, Weld DS (2013) Crowdsourcing multi-label classification for taxonomy creation. In: Proceedings of the First AAAI Conference on Human Computation and Crowdsourcing (HCOMP). AAAI, Palo Alto, pp 25–33

62. Lin CH, Mausam, Weld DS (2012) Dynamically switching between synergistic workflows for crowdsourcing. In: Proceedings of the AAAI Conference on Artificial Intelligence (AAAI). AAAI, Palo Alto, pp 87–93

63. Bozzon A, Brambilla M, Ceri S, Mauri A (2013) Reactive crowdsourcing. In: Proceedings of the International World Wide Web Conference (WWW) International World Wide Web Conferences Steering Committee (IW3C2), Geneva, pp 153–164

64. Singla A, Krause A (2013) Truthful incentives in crowdsourcing tasks using regret minimization mechanisms. In: Proceedings of the International World Wide Web Conference (WWW). International World Wide Web Conferences Steering Committee (IW3C2), Geneva, pp 1167–1177

65. Singer Y, Mittal M (2013) Pricing mechanisms for crowdsourcing markets. In: Proceedings of the International World Wide Web Conference (WWW). International World Wide Web Conferences Steering Committee (IW3C2), Geneva, pp 1157–1166

66. Barowy DW, Curtsinger C, Berger ED, McGregor A (2012) Automan: a platform for integrating human-based and digital computation. SIGPLAN Not 47(10):639–654

67. Mason W, Watts DJ (2009) Financial incentives and the "performance of crowds". In: Proceedings of the ACM SIGKDD Workshop on Human Computation (HCOMP). ACM, New York, pp 77–85

68. Rogstadius J, Kostakos V, Kittur A, Smus B, Laredo J, Vukovic M (2011) An assessment of intrinsic and extrinsic motivation on task performance in crowdsourcing markets. In: Proceedings of the International Conference on Weblogs and Social Media (ICWSM). AAAI, Palo Alto, pp 321–328

69. Chandler D, Horton JJ (2011) Labor allocation in paid crowdsourcing: Experimental evidence on positioning, nudges and prices. In: Proceedings of the AAAI Workshop on Human Computation (HCOMP). AAAI, Palo Alto, pp 14–19

70. Shaw AD, Horton JJ, Chen DL (2011) Designing incentives for inexpert human raters. In: Proceedings of the ACM Conference on Computer-Supported Cooperative Work and Social Computing (CSWC). ACM, New York, pp 275–284

71. Witkowski J, Bachrach Y, Key P, Parkes DC (2013) Dwelling on the negative: Incentivizing effort in peer prediction. In: Proceedings of the First AAAI Conference on Human Computation and Crowdsourcing (HCOMP). AAAI, Palo Alto, pp 190–197

72. Rao H, Huang S-W, Fu W-T (2013) What will others choose? how a majority vote reward scheme can improve human computation in a spatial location identification task. In: Proceedings of the First AAAI Conference on Human Computation and Crowdsourcing (HCOMP). AAAI, Palo Alto, pp 130–137

73. Huang S-W, Fu W-T (2013) Don't hide in the crowd!: Increasing social transparency between peer workers improves crowdsourcing outcomes. In: Proceedings of the SIGCHI Conference on Human Factors in Computing Systems (CHI). ACM, New York, pp 621–630

74. Morris R (2011) The emergence of affective crowdsourcing. In: Proceedings of the CHI Workshop on Crowdsourcing and Human Computation. ACM, New York, NY, USA

75. Heidari H, Kearns M (2013) Depth-workload tradeoffs for workforce organization. In: Proceedings of the First AAAI Conference on Human Computation and Crowdsourcing (HCOMP). AAAI, Palo Alto, pp 60–68

76. Waterhouse TP (2013) Pay by the bit: An information-theoretic metric for collective human judgment. In: Proceedings of the ACM Conference on Computer-Supported Cooperative Work and Social Computing (CSWC). ACM, New York, pp 623–638

77. Noronha J, Hysen E, Zhang H, Gajos KZ (2011) Platemate: crowdsourcing nutritional analysis from food photographs. In: Proceedings of the ACM Symposium on User Interface Software and Technology (UIST). ACM, New York, pp 1–12

78. Schall D, Satzger B, Psaier H (2012) Crowdsourcing tasks to social networks in bpel4people. World Wide Web 17(1):1–32

79. Satzger B, Psaier H, Schall D, Dustdar S (2011) Stimulating skill evolution in market-based crowdsourcing. In: BPM. Springer-Verlag, London, pp 66–82

80. Difallah DE, Demartini G, Cudré-Mauroux P (2013) Pick-a-crowd: Tell me what you like, and i'll tell you what to do. In: Proceedings of the International World Wide Web Conference (WWW). International World Wide Web Conferences Steering Committee (IW3C2), Geneva, pp 367–377

81. Chilton LB, Horton JJ, Miller RC, Azenkot S (2010) Task search in a human computation market. In: Proceedings of the ACM SIGKDD Workshop on Human Computation (HCOMP). ACM, New York, pp 1–9

82. Lee U, Kim J, Yi E, Sung J, Gerla M (2013) Analyzing crowd workers in mobile pay-for-answer qa. In: Proceedings of the SIGCHI Conference on Human Factors in Computing Systems (CHI). ACM, New York, pp 533–542

83. Jacques JT, Kristensson PO (2013) Crowdsourcing a hit: Measuring workers' pre-task interactions on microtask markets. In: Proceedings of the First AAAI Conference on Human Computation and Crowdsourcing (HCOMP). AAAI, Palo Alto, pp 86–93

84. Toomim M, Kriplean T, Pörtner C, Landay J (2011) Utility of human-computer interactions: toward a science of preference measurement. In: Proceedings of the SIGCHI Conference on Human Factors in Computing Systems (CHI). ACM, New York, pp 2275–2284

85. Ambati V, Vogel S, Carbonell JG (2011) Towards task recommendation in micro-task markets. In: Proceedings of the AAAI Workshop on Human Computation (HCOMP). AAAI, Palo Alto, pp 80–83

86. Yi J, Jin R, Jain S, Jain AK (2013) Inferring users' preferences from crowdsourced pairwise comparisons: A matrix completion approach. In: Proceedings of the First AAAI Conference on Human Computation and Crowdsourcing (HCOMP). AAAI, Palo Alto, pp 207–215

87. Chen JJ, Menezes NJ, Bradley AD, North T (2011) Opportunities for crowdsourcing research on amazon mechanical turk. In: Proceedings of the CHI Workshop on Crowdsourcing and Human Computation. ACM, New York, pp 1–4

88. Kearns M (2012) Experiments in social computation. Commun ACM 55(10):56–67

89. Mao A, Parkes DC, Procaccia AD, Zhang H (2011) Human Computation and Multiagent Systems: An Algorithmic Perspective. In: Proceedings of the AAAI Conference on Artificial Intelligence (AAAI). AAAI, Palo Alto, pp 1–6

90. Law E, Zhang H (2011) Towards large-scale collaborative planning: Answering high-level search queries using human computation. In: Proceedings of the AAAI Conference on Artificial Intelligence (AAAI). AAAI, Palo Alto, pp 1210–1215

91. Kittur A, Smus B, Khamkar S (2011) Crowdforge: Crowdsourcing complex work. In: Proceedings of the ACM Symposium on User Interface Software and Technology (UIST). ACM, New York, pp 43–52

92. Yu L, Nickerson JV (2011) Cooks or cobblers?: crowd creativity through combination. In: Proceedings of the SIGCHI Conference on Human Factors in Computing Systems (CHI). ACM, New York, pp 1393–1402

93. Dai P, Mausam, Weld DS (2010) Decision-theoretic control of crowd-sourced workflows. In: Proceedings of the AAAI Conference on Artificial Intelligence (AAAI). AAAI, Palo Alto, pp 1168–1174

94. Zhang H, Law E, Miller R, Gajos K, Parkes D, Horvitz E (2012) Human computation tasks with global constraints. In: Proceedings of the SIGCHI Conference on Human Factors in Computing Systems (CHI). ACM, New York, pp 217–226

95. Irani LC, Silberman MS (2013) Turkopticon: Interrupting worker invisibility in amazon mechanical turk. In: Proceedings of the SIGCHI Conference on Human Factors in Computing Systems (CHI). ACM, New York, pp 611–620

96. Law E, von Ahn L (2011) Human Computation: An Integrated Approach to Learning from the Crowd. In: Synthesis Lectures on Artificial Intelligence and Machine Learning Series. Morgan & Claypool, San Rafael, CA, United States

97. Nguyen QVH, Nguyen Thanh T, Lam Ngoc T, Aberer K (2013) An Evaluation of Aggregation Techniques in Crowdsourcing. In: Proceedings of the International Conference on Web Information Systems Engineering (WISE). Springer, New York, pp 1–15

98. Sheng VS, Provost F, Ipeirotis PG (2008) Get another label? improving data quality and data mining using multiple, noisy labelers. In: Proceedings of the ACM SIGKDD International Conference on Knowledge Discovery and Data Mining (KDD). ACM, New York, pp 614–622

99. Whitehill J, Ruvolo P, fan Wu T, Bergsma J, Movellan J (2009) Whose vote should count more: Optimal integration of labels from labelers of unknown expertise. In: Advances in Neural Information Processing Systems. Curran Associates, Inc., Red Hook, pp 2035–2043

100. Hovy D, Berg-Kirkpatrick T, Vaswani A, Hovy E (2013) Learning whom to trust with mace. In: Proceedings of the Conference of the North American Chapter of the Association of Computational Linguistics, Human Language Technologies (NAACL-HLT). Association for Computational Linguistics, Stroudsburg, pp 1120–1130

101. Wang D, Abdelzaher T, Kaplan L, Aggarwal CC (2013) Recursive fact-fnding: A streaming approach to truth estimation in crowdsourcing applications. In: Proceedings of the International Conference on Distributed Computing Systems (ICDCS). IEEE Computer Society, Washington, DC, pp 530–539

102. Dalvi N, Dasgupta A, Kumar R, Rastogi V (2013) Aggregating crowdsourced binary ratings. In: Proceedings of the International World Wide Web Conference (WWW). International World Wide Web Conferences Steering Committee (IW3C2), Geneva, pp 285–294

103. Salek M, Bachrach Y, Key P (2013) Hotspotting - a probabilistic graphical model for image object localization through crowdsourcing. In: Proceedings of the AAAI Conference on Artificial Intelligence (AAAI). AAAI, Palo Alto, pp 1156–1162

104. Kulkarni A (2011) The complexity of crowdsourcing: Theoretical problems in human computation. In: Proceedings of the CHI 2011 Workshop on Crowdsourcing and Human Computation. ACM, New York, pp 1–4

105. Vuurens J, Vries APD, Eickhoff C (2011) How Much Spam Can You Take? An Analysis of Crowdsourcing Results to Increase Accuracy. In: Proceedings of the ACM SIGIR Workshop on Crowdsourcing for Information Retrieval (CIR). ACM, New York, pp 48–55

106. Rzeszotarski J, Kittur A (2012) Crowdscape: interactively visualizing user behavior and output. In: Proceedings of the ACM Symposium on User Interface Software and Technology (UIST). ACM, New York, pp 55–62

107. Kochhar S, Mazzocchi S, Paritosh P (2010) The anatomy of a large-scale human computation engine. In: Proceedings of the Acm Sigkdd Workshop on Human Computation (HCOMP). ACM, New York, pp 10–17

108. Amir O, Shahar Y, Gal Y, Ilani L (2013) On the verification complexity of group decision-making tasks. In: Proceedings of the First AAAI Conference on Human Computation and Crowdsourcing (HCOMP). AAAI, Palo Alto, pp 2–8

109. Kinnaird P, Dabbish L, Kiesler S, Faste H (2013) Co-worker transparency in a microtask marketplace. In: Proceedings of the ACM Conference on Computer-Supported Cooperative Work and Social Computing (CSWC). ACM, New York, pp 1285–1290

110. Hansen DL, Schone PJ, Corey D, Reid M, Gehring J (2013) Quality control mechanisms for crowdsourcing: Peer review, arbitration, and expertise at familysearch indexing. In: Proceedings of the ACM Conference on Computer-Supported Cooperative Work and Social Computing (CSWC). ACM, New York, pp 649–660

111. Ipeirotis PG, Provost F, Wang J (2010) Quality management on amazon mechanical turk. In: Proceedings of the ACM SIGKDD Workshop on Human Computation (HCOMP). ACM, New York, pp 64–67

112. Dow S, Kulkarni A, Klemmer S, Hartmann B (2012) Shepherding the crowd yields better work. In: Proceedings of the ACM Conference on Computer-Supported Cooperative Work and Social Computing (CSWC). ACM, New York, pp 1013–1022

113. Picard RW (2003) Affective computing: challenges. Int J Hum-Comput St 59(1–2):55–64

114. Silberman MS, Ross J, Irani L, Tomlinson B (2010) Sellers' problems in human computation markets. In: Proceedings of the ACM SIGKDD Workshop on Human Computation (HCOMP). ACM, New York, pp 18–21

115. Rasmussen J, Vicente K (1989) Coping with human errors through system design: implications for ecological interface design. Int J Man-Mach Stud 31(5):517–534

116. Locke EA, Latham GP (2002) Building a practically useful theory of goal setting and task motivation. A 35-year odyssey. Am Psychol 57(9):705–717

117. Edwards JR (1990) Person-job Fit: A Conceptual Integration, Literature Review, and Methodological Critique. University of Virginia, Charlottesville, Virginia, United States

118. Nicholls JG (1984) Achievement motivation: Conceptions of ability, subjective experience, task choice, and performance. Psychol Rev 91(3):328–346

119. Hackman JR (1987) The design of work teams. In: Lorsch J (ed) Handbook of Organizational Behavior. Prentice-Hall, New Jersey, pp 315–342

120. Karsenty A, Beaudouin-Lafon M (1993) An algorithm for distributed groupware applications. In: Proceedings of the International Conference on Distributed Computing Systems (ICDCS). IEEE Computer Society, New York, pp 195–202

121. Dietrich F, List C (2007) Arrow's theorem in judgment aggregation. Soc Choice Welfare 29(1):19–33

122. Taylor A, Pacelli AM (2008) Mathematics and Politics: Strategy, Voting, Power, and Proof. Springer, New York

123. Mao A, Procaccia AD, Chen Y (2013) Better human computation through principled voting. In: Proceedings of the AAAI Conference on Artificial Intelligence (AAAI). AAAI, Palo Alto, pp 1142–1148

124. Pettit P (2001) Deliberative democracy and the discursive dilemma. Phil Issues 35(s1):268–299

125. Whitefield A, Wilson F, Dowell J (1991) A framework for human factors evaluation. Behav Inform Technol 10(1):65–79

126. Misra KB (2008) Handbook of Performability Engineering. Springer, London

9

Social debt in software engineering: insights from industry

Damian A Tamburri[1]*, Philippe Kruchten[2], Patricia Lago[1] and Hans van Vliet[1]

Abstract

Social debt is analogous to technical debt in many ways: it represents the state of software development organisations as the result of "accumulated" decisions. In the case of social debt, decisions are about people and their interactions. Our objective was to study the causality around social debt in practice. In so doing, we conducted exploratory qualitative research in a large software company. We found many forces together causing social debt; we represented them in a framework, and captured anti-patterns that led to the debt in the first place. Finally, we elicited best practices that technicians adopted to pay back some of the accumulated debt. We learned that social debt is strongly correlated with technical debt and both forces should be reckoned with together during the software process.

Keywords: Software project management; Social debt; Socio-technical decisions; Social software engineering; Case study

1 Introduction

Software engineering success is increasingly dependent on the well-being of development communities [1]. In some of our previous work [2-4], we found many decisions influencing community well-being. For example, changing the organisational structure [5] of the development community (e.g., through outsourcing), changing the development process (e.g., by adopting agile methods), leveraging on global collaboration (e.g., by striking a balance between formal and informal communication across global sites) are all socio-technical decisions, i.e. social and technical at the same time, that influence the state and welfare of developing communities and their members [5]. The social connotation of these decisions, changes the way people work and interact with others - i.e., their organisational and social structure [4]. The technical connotation of these decisions, changes the way in which development tasks are worked out. In agile methods, for example using Kanban boards, a "pull" task-allocation is often used, as opposed to classic "push".

Some socio-technical decisions eventually cause additional cost (e.g., through delays) on software projects and the development community around them. This cost, is not immediately visible and its resolution is often postponed. Also, if the same decisions remain into place, project costs may increase. For example, organisations often employ strict information-filtering protocols to protect industrial secrets when they embark in open-source [6]. This decision, however, might slow down development interactions, causing delays or even inciting fear.

This extra cost is conceptually similar to technical debt [7], i.e., the additional project cost caused by sub-optimal technical decisions. However this extra cost is not necessarily related to code and it is actually "social" in nature, i.e. connected to people and their development organisation. Paraphrasing Cunningham [8] who first introduced technical debt, social debt can be thought as: "not quite right development community - which we postpone making right". In Layman's terms, by social debt, we indicate the additional cost occurring when strained social and organisational interactions get in the way of smooth software development and operation.

While technical debt has received increased attention over the last 10 years, this other form of debt, namely "social debt", has remained latent and relatively unexplored. For instance, software engineering practitioners still lack a way to formalise socio-technical decisions and measure the connected debt.

This article takes one small step forward towards defining and studying social debt by means of an industrial

*Correspondence: damianandrew.tamburri@polimi.it
[1]VU University Amsterdam, Amsterdam, The Netherlands
Full list of author information is available at the end of the article

exploratory case study. The case study was driven by the following research questions: "What are the factors at play around social debt during the software lifecycle? Are there patterns in said factors? Can they be mitigated?"

From our study we learned that, indeed, there is a strong correlation between social debt and sub-optimal characteristics in organisational-social structures behind software development communities. Also, social debt is inextricably related to technical debt in many ways, e.g., uninformed socio-technical decisions generate both social and technical debt in a compounding manner that cannot be trivially "payed back". In addition, our findings suggest the presence of community "smells", i.e., precursors to the emergence of social debt, much like code smells may lead to technical debt, e.g. as shown in [9] by Zazworka et al. Finally, our findings uncovered some "mitigation strategies", i.e., ways in which some community "smells" may be averted and avoid the debt, even if partially.

In summary, this article offers four contributions: (1) a framework to define and interpret social debt; (2) a list of community "smells", intended as socio-technical anti-patterns that may appear normal but in fact reflect unlikeable community characteristics, such as anti-social organisational behaviour across the community, e.g., developers that refuse or delay information sharing; (3) a list of mitigations to said community "smells", as emerging from our case study; (4) a list of lessons learned as part of our case study that further discuss social debt and its implications.

The rest of the article is structured as follows: Section 2 outlines previous work related to the study of social debt. Section 3 outlines our study design, discussing our research methods and materials. Section 4 presents our contribution while Section 5 discusses their implications, pointing out to relevant threats to validity and ways in which they were tackled. Finally, Section 6 concludes the article.

2   State of the art

On of the very first attempts at linking software and the social/organisational processes around it is represented by Conway's Law [10]. According to Conway's law, software mimics (and sometimes is almost isomorphic to) the organisational-social structure around it. Therefore, understanding and supporting this structure, is critical to engineer software better, e.g., fitting dynamic users' needs and their new expectations. This can be useful to, for example, use IT to support governance in global corporations [11].

Nagappan et al. [12] show in practice the influence of organisational structure and other "human" aspects on software quality. This and similar works (e.g. Repenning et al. [13] or Viana et al. [14]) bring evidence that motivates our study of social communities in organisations and the debt (if any) connected to them. This family of studies contributes to social debt by providing evidence of its existence and impact. In addition these studies provide valuable data to identify the orders of magnitude that regulate social debt. Our study is related to results noted by Nagappan et al. [12], in that we confirmed the relation between solid and straightforward software development/operations and well-structured software development social organisations. However, in our case we observed a live organisational and social structure to elicit possible causes and effects for its sub-optimality. While Nagappan et al. establish the causality between organisational structures and software quality, we strived to understand patterns of sub-optimality across said structures, e.g., to allow for preventive action by means of social networks analysis (SNA) [15]. More in particular, we found correlations between sets of organisational-social circumstances and additional cost in software process. Also, we reported the recurrent set of circumstances in which said additional costs occur. While the study by Nagappan et al. serves as motivation and theoretical foundation for our study of social debt, the results in this paper are useful for practitioners embarking on software engineering so that recurrent patterns can be detected and avoided.

Studies on socio-technical congruence, first defined by Cataldo et al. in [16] can support the study of social debt. Socio-technical congruence is the degree to which technical and social dependencies match, when coordination is needed. For example, in [17] Cataldo et al. elaborate socio-technical congruence in formal terms and empirically investigate its impact on product quality. Similar works (e.g. [18]), can be used as starting points to evaluate metrics for social debt. Perhaps socio-technical congruence represents a first rudimental metric for social debt in certain development communities. In our study we did not put any emphasis on measurements, although we offer a rough estimation of the debt we encountered. Our measurement, however, is not based on socio-technical congruence. Nevertheless, the results of our study could be used to evaluate if and how socio-technical congruence can be used as a measurement for social debt and to what degree. Indeed, as part of our results we observed that socio-technical congruence is sufficient to express one third of the possible "debt-effects", i.e., those related to collaboration.

An evolution of the socio-technical stream leads to works such as that of de Souza et al. [19] discuss awareness maintenance mechanisms. These mechanisms are intuitively close to the notion of social debt, since their role is to track and maintain project knowledge with the aim of limiting delays and connected "debt". In relation to this, our work offers means to observe social debt in action and relate it to social constructs and characteristics such as awareness.

Bird et al. in [20] use social-network analysis to investigate coordination among groups of developers with socio-technical dependencies. These lead to using social-networks analysis to elaborate on social debt, studying the very foundations of communities, i.e. their social-network representation. In our work, we did carry some limited form of social-network and organisational analysis. An additional study of our data using socio-technical networks as a construct to structure our data might have revealed additional insights in social debt. This study, however, is out of the scope of this article. Conversely, our results in this paper strive to concretise recurrent set of circumstances into patterns that can quickly be reused in practice to avoid connected nasty consequences.

Works in organisational or socio-technical decision making (e.g. scaling agile methods or offshoring) can provide sample arenas in which social debt emerges. For example, Cusick and Prasad in [21] research the process of understanding if the current organisational layout of a company is performant (or even compatible) with certain decisions (going "offshore" in their case). For more informed decision-making, it is vital to measure the social debt (if any) connected to such decisions. Similarly to [21], many works research the influence of organisational decisions on collaboration and product quality aspects, for example [22,23]. These works support the study of social debt's impact in different scenarios, in terms of end-product quality and evolvability. Our work shares similar goals to the works above in supporting decision-making by means of a social debt framework - to establish the variables around the phenomenon - and recurrent patterns behind its emergence - to avoid or calculate additional costs.

Finally, from a social point of view, many works are indeed related to defining and characterising social debt. First, there is a rich and elaborate body of knowledge concerning social capital, e.g., Meverson in [24]. In Layman's terms, social capital assumes the role of an opposite force to social debt in that it measures and maintains the positive value connected to certain organisational and social structures. In continuum with social capital, social and organisational Labianca et al. in 2008 introduced the notion of social ledger [25], conceptually similar to social debt. Quoting from Labianca et al. "[the effect of] the social liabilities that can result from negative relationships [...] in order to flesh out the entire social ledger [of an organization]".

3 Research design

3.1 Research problem and research question

From sociology literature, quoting from Onions [26]: "social debt of a society represents the set of strained social relationships that emerges as a consequence of debtor-creditor circumstances". In software engineering,

the concept can be used, for example, to represent the lack of trust within a community [27] or the degree to which it is immature or unable to tackle a certain development problem. We sought to characterise and study social debt, pivoting around the following research questions: "What are the factors at play around social debt during the software lifecycle? Are there patterns in said factors? Can they be mitigated?"

3.2 Research methodology

3.2.1 Empirical background

The results in this article are based on a study in a large IT service provider (which we call "Capita" from now on) for the aviation industry. "Capita" has around 3,000 employees in several locations in Germany and around Europe. Also, "Capita" controls several offices in 14 other countries.

The context of our investigation is a large software project featuring the Integration of two very different software products (which we call "Integra" from now on). The community of developers we analysed involves two geographically distributed production sites A and B. Both sites are responsible for the implementation of incoming user requests (e.g., new requirements, revised requirements, bug-reports, etc.) and maintenance of the two products to be integrated (which we call RED and GREEN, from now on). The main organisational difference between the two sites, pointed to us when we first started our investigation, is that responsibilities in the remote site are limited to follow what is decided by product managers in Site A. Product managers are responsible for management, software architecture, requirement elicitation and critical decision making. Also, while RED was a well established product, active for well over 10 years, the GREEN product and people were relatively new.

In our study, the objective of "Capita" was to: (a) clarify the organisational and social problems for the project under inquiry by distilling a clearer organisational picture (i.e., to understand the organisational scenario involving the two sites and their ramifications to other branches of the "Capita", if any); (b) later on, consolidate and generalise our approach for this study for further reuse in other projects. The gathered data was to be analysed and evaluated, highlighting the pros and cons (consistencies, completeness, weakness, strengths, etc.) from a decision-making point of view, highlighting the roles and factors involved in the different groups taking part in the scenario, and trying to find ways to harmonise their collaboration for the benefit of the Integration project. The industrial partner instructed us to possibly describe how the decision making process should be carried out at best and what knowledge elements should be part of the decision making so that resulting organisational and social structure is more sound, well constructed and better fit for the development effort at hand.

3.2.2 Data collection

The data we used to obtain our results is based on 16 semi-structured interviews (with an average of 90 mins per interview) as well as 3 focus-groups (with a duration average of 3 hrs) and two workshops (half-day) to investigate the scenario over a period of 6 months. The study involves a total of 22 people, including: managers, architects, developers, operators, Integration engineers, testers, technological assistants, logistic assistants and product owners. Interviewee selection was carried out to ensure complete coverage of the development/operations community at hand. This criterion made sure that the entire organisational and social scenario was investigated. Nevertheless, to access difficult to reach or hidden populations in our scenario, we adopted "Snowball" sampling, i.e., asking our interviewees "who else should we ask about <a topic>?" [28]. This is typical in scenarios such as ours where fear and similar social factors may obscure key people or information from researchers' view.

Interviews[a] were structured according to procedures and guidelines suggested by Neville-Neil [29]. It should be noted that social debt itself was never mentioned during data elicitation, to avoid bias. In addition, focus-groups were instrumented according to guidelines previously introduced by Morgan et al. [30]. Finally, workshops were structured according to the "Working Group" organisational and social structure in [5]. The aim of the workshops was to provide validation of observations made and refinement where possible, e.g., for unclear or misunderstood concepts. A final workshop was held with all participants present, to further validate our observations after analysis was completed. A report of the study was compiled into a presentation and hand-outs with possible comments. After the presentation, the results were discussed in groups and hand-outs were used for feedback. Following strict non-disclosure agreements, all transcriptions were completely anonymised at the source.

3.3 Analysis methods

The findings presented in this paper were elaborated following a rigorous empirical analysis approach based on several methods and described in the following.

3.3.1 Grounded theory

The results reported in this article were obtained conducting an exploratory case study, according to guidelines proposed in Runeson et al. [31]. We analysed said material using Grounded Theory [32,33]. Our GT approach is structured as follows:

1. **Open Coding** - (4 phases)

a) Pilot study: a set of 3 interviews were randomly selected to generate an initial set of codes by an independent researcher.

b) develop initial theory: based on the pilot study, an initial theory was generated

c) Constant comparison: the pilot study generated an initial set of 39 codes. These were organised into a hierarchy of codes based on emerging relations between concepts. Thus structured, the start-up list of codes was used to code the rest of the interviews. Each interview transcript was analysed line by line with the list of codes. A code was applied if it reflected a concept in a paragraph, i.e., microanalysis [34].

d) Constant memo-ing: along step 3, notes were kept to capture key messages, relations and observations on the study.

2. **Selective Coding** - (2 phases)

a) Axial coding: comparing the concepts coded led us to inductively generate relations among coded concepts (e.g. "Sub-Optimal Organisational Structure" causes "Social Debt", etc.)

b) Aliasing: the definitions of all concepts coded were compared with each other to identify aliases.

3. **Theoretical Coding** - (3 phases)

a) Data arrangement: we captured every portion of text that was coded with a code on a table.

b) Data modelling: the data was represented in a diagram (see Figure 1). The diagram shows all the core concepts (i.e., code-clusters resulting from axial coding, phase (b)) and relations found

c) Theoretical sampling: the diagrams and all the data at hand were analysed and sorted, trying to identify recurrent patterns, underlying relations and hidden meaning. Our observation was aided by standard analysis methods such as weighted frequency analysis (i.e. by analysing the number of times certain concepts showed up against the number of interviews in which they were found) card-sorting (by rearranging the hierarchy of types to let underlying relations show themselves), and conceptual modelling.

Finally, coding was carried out by two independent coders to ensure inter-coder reliability. First, the method was applied by a junior researcher that generated the pilot list of possible codes (39 codes). Second, a post-doc researcher re-coded a fresh version of the entire dataset using the pilot list of codes, resolving issues in concordance with researchers involved.

3.3.2 Causality modelling

To represent causality, we applied the 6C model [35]. The 6C model allows to represent empirical causality by relating six variables: **Cause**, meaning the event or

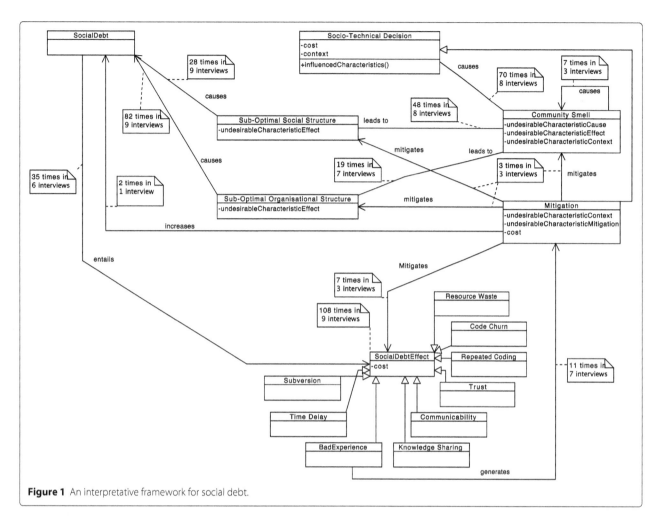

Figure 1 An interpretative framework for social debt.

circumstance that gives rise to a consequence; **Consequence**, meaning the effect produced by a certain cause; **Condition**, meaning the constellation of variables that need to be true in order for a cause to manifest into a consequence; **Context**, meaning the circumstances that form the setting of the causality function; **Covariance**, the set of conditions that produce a mutual variation with cause or effect; **Contingent**, the event or artefact whose value is compromised by the consequences in the causality function. These six variables are to be found among core concepts.

For example, on Figure 2, "Category" represents a community smell. The left-hand side represents the cause for "Category", i.e. the set of circumstances that make "Category" evident and result into the consequences on the right-hand side. In addition to the cause, the smell

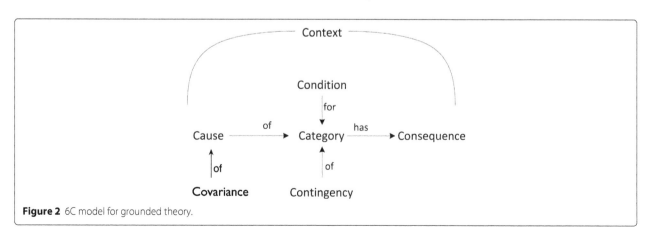

Figure 2 6C model for grounded theory.

"Category" might be subject to a set of conditions (box on top of "Category", see Figure 2). Causes for "Category" exist in the context of the smell (On top of the conditions in Figure 2). Let's assume you might want to do something about the smell by influencing "Category" cause. Certain covariances (or co-evolving factors) might occur (lower-box under "Category" cause). Contingents (lower-box on the right-hand side) represent the value or event influenced by the consequences of "Category", similar to covariances, but for consequences.

From the total set of core concepts extracted during coding, we identified existing causality dependencies for about 20% of concepts found. While in most cases the application of the 6C was straightforward, in some cases we fell short in identifying "Covariance" and "Contingent". This is further discussed in Section 5. When our data did not allow us to apply the 6 Cs, we used a " - " sign in the related figure: there was no core concept in our study that was applicable.

4   Results

4.1   Defining social debt: a framework

As previously noted, the core concepts that define social debt emerging from our study are presented in Figure 1 using a UML notation. The framework depicts the core concepts that play a role in social debt (Classes UML Classes). For example, the "SocialDebt" class. The framework also represents the relations behind said concepts (Associations between UML Classes). For example, the "SocialDebt" class is in causal relationship with the "Sub-Optimal Social Structure" class, in particular with its "undesirableCharacteristicEffect" attribute. Comments represent how often the relations were found in the dataset. For example, the causal relationship between the "SocialDebt" class and the "Sub-Optimal Social Structure" class was found 28 times in 9 interview transcripts. To keep the diagram compact, we did not include the occurrence frequency of core concepts[b].

Based on the definitions and relations for concepts in Figure 1, social debt is defined as **a cumulative and increasing cost in the current state of things, connected to invisible and negative effects within a development community. These effects might need some digging in order to be found since they are connected to undesirable, often implicit characteristics in the organisational and social structure [5] emerging in development communities. These characteristics produce an additional cost, e.g., increase the time needed for development.**

To elaborate a (very rough) estimate for the impact of social debt in "Integra", we proceeded as follows: (a) we counted the sub-optimal characteristics reported in its organisational and social structure over a period of 18 months (114 distinct characteristics); (b) we calculated the average delay (4 hrs) using delays directly reported in our interviews for these characteristics, where possible[c]; (c) multiplied the two values.

According to our calculations, This figure equates to a total of 57 days of extra cost connected to social debt. This number is referred to the closing date of our study. Moreover, evidence from the final rounds of interviews and workshops (around the end of our study) suggest that this estimate was bound to increase, e.g., quoting from the last workshop in our dataset: "I am [still] not aware of any way to provide [direct] feedback to an architect. The only way we are using is by talking and asking around [to strangers]".

In addition, our study revealed a number of characteristics of social debt, also evident in Figure 1:

- **Social Debt is indirectly connected to socio-technical decisions; analysing the latter requires aiming for the former** - As evident from Figure 1 there is no direct relation between socio-technical decisions ("Socio-Technical Decision" class in Figure 1) and the emergence of social debt ("SocialDebt" class in Figure 1). For example in our case study of "Integra" we found a key decision to adopt a new programming language as an Integration bridge between RED and GREEN. This decision seemed good at the time it was taken and was motivated by two reasons: (a) the language's efficiency for the job; (b) the language was shared between RED and GREEN, tentatively helping in the creation of an organisational bridge between the two communities. Eventually, however, the decision caused the addition of new technicians to the organisational and social structure which caused fear factors to emerge in the rest of developers. Consequent condescending behaviour resulted in managers and software architects to issue a project slow-down, for problem-solving. At the end of the study, we confirmed that problems related to that decision were still causing slowdowns. This not withstanding, this property might be related to the exploratory nature of our study. Since we introduced social debt only after the interviews, it would have been impossible for interviewees to point out direct relationships between social debt and socio-technical decisions, if any.

- **Social Debt cannot be ascribed to any one software artefact in the development and operations process, rather, it is an emergent property of the development community itself** - As evident from Figure 1, there are no relations between social debt and any software artefacts. Conversely, there is strong evidence that suggests the effect social debt has on software artefacts, as represented by the relation between the "SocialDebt" class in Figure 1) and the "DebtEffect" sub-classes in Figure 1. For example, in our case study of "Integra" none of the interviewees could point fingers as to who or what was causing trouble (e.g., extra costs or delays) in GREEN or RED and their Integration. There was a perception of problems that pervaded the "Integra" project, and this "hunch" sentiment is constant across our entire dataset. In addition, over 100 "DebtEffects" were reported in 14 interviews as connected to software artefacts as well.

- **Social Debt can be quantified by combining social network analysis of undesirable characteristics with analysing their compounding costs** - As evident from Figure 1 the "SocialDebt" class is strongly correlated to the "Sub-Optimal Social Structure" and "Sub-Optimal organisational Structure" classes. Sub-optimality for these classes is determined by a series of "undesirableCharacteristicEffect" that can be quantified. For example in our case study of "Integra" we found, among others, the following sub-optimal characteristics: "colleague downturn" - people refuse or refrain from helping; "extraneous colleagues" - coworkers do not know each other. Both these characteristics can be measured through social network analysis (e.g., as suggested in [36]); consequently the connected cost may be estimated. This not withstanding, more research is needed to establish and apply the use of SNA for social debt estimation.

- **Social Debt's existence is heralded by organisational and social anti-patterns (i.e., community "smells") which are emerging and recurring across the community** - As evident from Figure 1 the "Socio-Technical Decision" class is in a causal relationship with "Community Smell". Also, according to our evidence, the times at which this causality was reported are antecedent to the emergence of sub-optimal organisational structures. For example in our case study of "Integra" we found a pattern of behaviour recurring in subsequent periods of time and a consequent suboptimal characteristic, "communication delays". We defined this pattern as the "radio-silence" community "smell", that is, a recurring delay (a few hours to half a day) in answering sometimes critical emails or posts. The smell is connected to the previously reported "extraneous colleagues" characteristic. Communication was relying solely on the "kindness-of-strangers" effect. Although the delay may seem small enough, its compounding effect across the community produced a non-trivial delay. An overview of the smells we found is available in Section 4.2.

- **Social Debt can be causing technical debt as well** - For example in our case of "Integra" we found the "replicated-coding" and the "code-churn" technical debt smells [9]. Both smells were emerging from the aforementioned socio-technical decision to adopt a new language as an Integration bridge between the RED and GREEN products as well as a collaboration ground for both communities. As a result of the intended collaboration, people at both ends of the bridge (both in RED and GREEN) replicated pretty much the same functionality (although with different structure) working for re-adaptation of their "end", with consequent waste. Hence, both smells are a "SocialDebtEffect", that is, a negative effect with invisibile socio-technical causes.

- **Social Debt may be mitigated by specific socio-technical decisions ("mitigations")** - For example in our case of "Integra" we found over 50 decisions (or better, instances of "Socio-Technical Decision" class) made to try and "pay back" parts of the accumulated social debt, with mild to very good results. Among these decisions was the decision to adopt a supporting learning community for technicians and staff involved in "Integra". This decision was taken to "pay back" some of the debt connected to the "radio-silence" smell, and succeeded, at least partially. The supporting community increased the social and organisational mesh across the project network and increased mutual social relations such as collaboration, learning and understanding. An overview of the successful mitigations emerging from our study is available in Section 4.3 and mapped to the smells they were addressing.

4.2 Hunches for social debt? Community "smells"!

In essence, community "smells" are sets of organisational and social circumstances with implicit causal relations. These circumstances together are not a problem per se, but if reiterated over time cause social debt, in the form of mistrust, delays, uninformed or miscommunicated architectural decision-making. We found over 70 series of such circumstances in the "Integra" project. 9 such circumstances were recurring over time (i.e., more than 5 times), and reported over the 6-month timespan of our study. Here follow these 9 community "smells":

1. **Organisational Silo effect:** this smell was reported 7 times. In essence, (too) high decoupling development tasks (and related developers) in the community caused lack of communication. Also, high task decoupling lowered developers' mutual awareness [37] and collaboration probably compromised socio-technical congruence [16]. In our scenario these circumstances led to "organisational silos", i.e., sets of loosely dependent development partners wasting resources over the development lifecycle. The *developer silos* smell is shown in Figure 3.

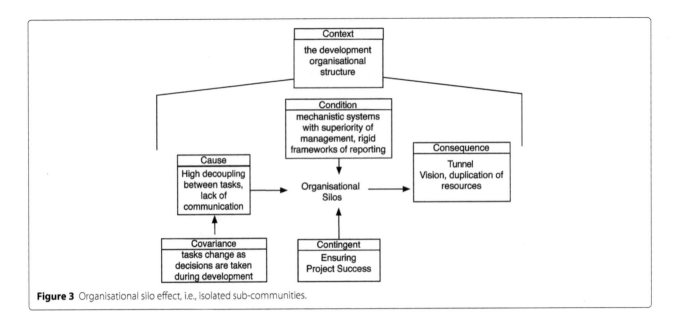

Figure 3 Organisational silo effect, i.e., isolated sub-communities.

Cause: high decoupling between tasks, lack of communication or lack of cooperation in checking task dependencies. *Context:* the entire development and operation community around "Integra". *Conditions:* fine-grained command and control policies for information exchange. Strict superiority management and use rigid frameworks of reporting to control and administer command. *Consequences:* as a consequence of this smell, the community filled with wasted resources (e.g., time) and duplication of code. Also, people in the community reportedly developed a "tunnel vision" with a consequent lack of creativity, lack of cooperation and collaboration. Also, this condition eventually led some developers

to make architecture decisions without the necessary background and premises, quoting from our interviews "they [members of team RED] started taking decisions on their own using different format every time, I could see it from TCR (technical change request) documents". *Covariance:* number of tasks and number of dependencies are proportional to architecture decisions - change or increase to such decisions usually has two effects: (a) number of tasks increase; (b) number of dependencies increase. *Contingent:* this smell produces a risk on ensuring project success.

2. **Black-cloud effect:** this smell was reported 8 times. In essence, this smell was caused by two distinct

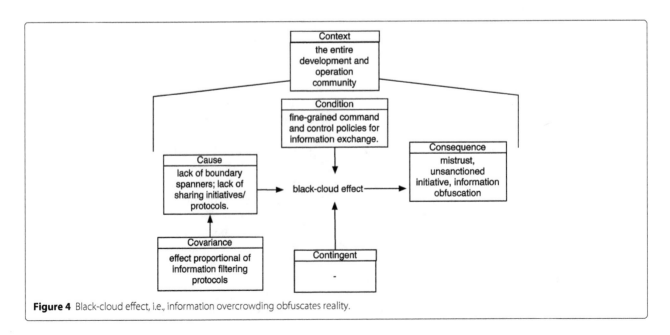

Figure 4 Black-cloud effect, i.e., information overcrowding obfuscates reality.

circumstances taking place at the same time. First, the lack of people able to bridge the knowledge and experience gap between RED and GREEN product teams (i.e., project boundary spanners [38]). Second, the lack of prescribed occasions for knowledge sharing (e.g., daily stand-ups). These two circumstances combined together increasingly created confusion every time knowledge exchange initiatives took place. A "black-cloud" of confusing back-and-forth messages were constantly obfuscating reality. The *black-cloud* effect smell is shown in Figure 4.*Cause:* lack of boundary spanners; lack of sharing protocols. *Context:* the entire development and operation community around "Integra". *Conditions:* fine-grained command and control policies for information exchange. *Consequences:* this smell reportedly created mistrust and people taking "matters and decisions in their own hands", quoting from our interviews. *Covariance:* the effect of this smell is proportional to the number of information filtering protocols (e.g., how many clearance levels) in place to protect information exchange. *Contingent:* -.

3. **Prima-donnas effect:** this smell was reported 9 times. unreceptiveness to change in RED (a legacy product), caused severe isolation problems for people involved. These people become "prima donnas", acting with a seemingly condescending and egotistical behaviour, unable to welcome support from development partners. This compromised the chances of success for "Integra". This scenario led to the emergence of the "Prima Donnas" community smell. Some areas of the development community are still unable or irreceptive towards external influence, cooperation or collaboration. Quoting

from the interviews: "everyone wants to pull the stream towards their own windmill and [everyone will vote] for a decision that simplifies their agenda, uncooperative behaviour [...]". The *prima-donnas* smell is shown in Figure 5. *Cause:* innovation and organisational inertia, stagnant collaboration. *Context:* this smell was having an effect in all interactions between RED and GREEN. *Condition:* -. *Consequence:* seemingly egotistical behaviour, lack of communication and collaboration. *Covariance:* organisational changes increased irreceptiveness to external forces, since every change sparked more fear in prima donna sub-communities. *Contingent:* -.

4. **Leftover-techie effect:** this smell was reported 6 times. Increased isolation of maintenance, help-desk and operations technicians in both RED and GREEN reportedly caused technicians to feel as the "last piece of the ladder" and also the "first ones to deal with all complaints [from clients]". This led to creating mistrust some sort of sharing villainy, i.e., misconduct in sharing results or current status in the unwilling technicians. The *leftover-techies* smell is shown in Figure 6. *Cause:* increased isolation between development and operations people. *Context:* this smell was having an effect in all interactions between RED and GREEN as well as the interactions between all products involved and the (paying) customers. *Condition:* -. *Consequence:* seemingly egotistical behaviour for knowledge and status awareness sharing, lack of communication and general lack of trust. *Covariance:* the more clients the more the negative effect of the smell. *Contingent:* -.

5. **Sharing villainy:** this smell was reported 5 times. Lack of knowledge exchange incentives or face-to-face meetings in "Integra" limited the value

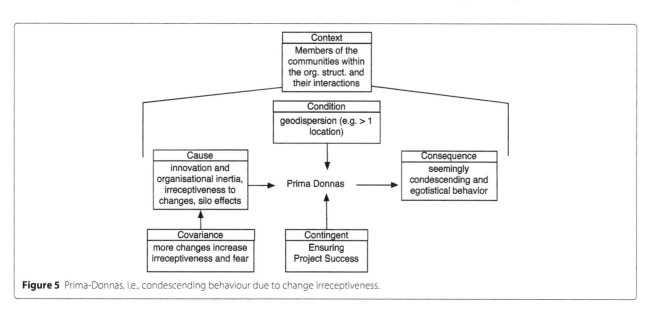

Figure 5 Prima-Donnas, i.e., condescending behaviour due to change irreceptiveness.

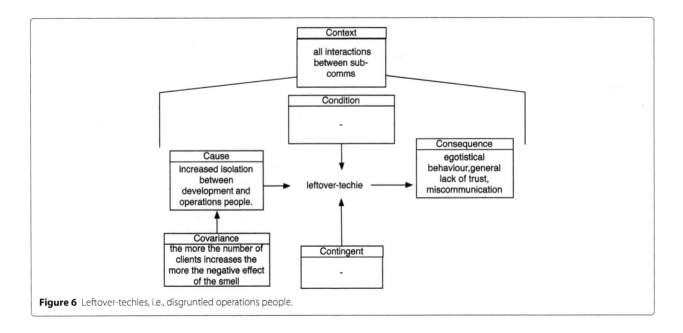

Figure 6 Leftover-techies, i.e., disgruntled operations people.

that developers perceived in sharing their knowledge and experience. Knowledge interaction became a chore, an activity connected more to waste of time and effort, rather than producing evident benefit. This condition limits developers' engagement in knowledge sharing, to a point in which shared information is outdated, unconfirmed or wrong. This scenario leads to the emergence of the "Sharing Villainy" community smell. People do not recognise the importance of sharing good quality knowledge carefully, e.g., by sharing outdated, unchecked updates.

The *sharing-villainy* smell is shown in Figure 7. *Cause:* lack of knowledge sharing incentives as well as activities which promote useful knowledge sharing and synch, e.g., face-to-face meetings. *Context:* this smell negatively affects knowledge exchange and related interactions across the community. For example, people in RED were not motivated enough (e.g., by incentive), enabled (e.g., by buddy-pairing with GREEN) or instructed (e.g., by protocols like agile methods as in GREEN) to communicate with fellow partners overseas, likely disseminate unconfirmed or outdated knowledge, forming the

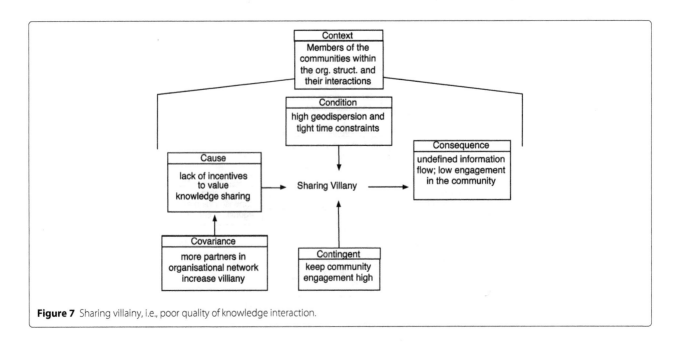

Figure 7 Sharing villainy, i.e., poor quality of knowledge interaction.

ideal conditions for the "Sharing Villainy" smell, as the pattern became recurrent. *Condition: - . Consequence:* undefined information flow and lower engagement in the community, as a consequence of members' detachment. *Covariance: - . Contingent: - .*

6. **Organisational Skirmish:** this smell was reported 7 times. Misalignment between organisational culture in the development unit and the operations unit during "Integra" caused severe managerial issues. For example, different average expertise levels between GREEN and RED reportedly expected dropped productivity up to 50% for weeks at the first attempt to integrate. This scenario leads to an "organisational skirmish" among organisations, each with its own layout and properties. The *Organisational Skirmish* smell is shown in Figure 8. *Cause:* different communication and expertise levels adopted between units involved in the project. *Context:* The skirmish smell was observed during maintenance of RED and GREEN as separate products, but their Integration would likely see the same effect as well. *Condition: - . Consequence:* this smell led to project delay of a few days. *Covariance: - . Contingent: - .*

7. **Architecture hood effect:** this smell was reported 5 times. Architecture decision-makers for "Integra" were far away from both GREEN and RED developers and operators. Also, decisions were taken in an "architecture board" across which it was difficult to find those directly responsible for decisions and their reasoning. This created social strain when decisions were "questioned" by developers or operators in GREEN and RED. In essence, the decision to adopt a software architects' board to speed-up decisions, did in fact increase decision-making but created a "nobody's fault" effect from architects, nobody wanted to take accountability for the decision and lead in its implementation in practice. Also, developers were reportedly blaming the architecture decisions for any technical mishaps during "Integra". The *architecture hood effect:* smell is shown in Figure 9. *Cause:* geographical and socio-technical dispersion of architecture decisions. *Context:* The smell was observed when decisions were being communicated to RED and GREEN. *Condition:* geographical distance between decision makers and others played a major role. *Consequence:* this smell led to uncooperative behaviour across the community. *Covariance: - . Contingent: - .*

8. **Solution defiance:** this smell was reported 9 times. Different levels of experience and different cultural backgrounds divided developers into overly similar subgroups (through homophily). Then, developers divided themselves into factions with completely conflicting opinions concerning socio-technical or technical decisions to be taken. This slowed down "Integra" by up to 2 days and led (in some cases) to "organisational rebellion" (e.g., some developers did not take the decision into account until the last possible minute). The *solution defiance* smell is shown in Figure 10. *Cause:* homophile subgroups. *Context:* The smell was observed when opinions on decisions were being asked to RED and GREEN communities. *Condition:* different experience and cultural backgrounds. *Consequence:* uncooperative behaviour, ignoring decisions. *Covariance:* the more decisions are thrown the more defiance is fostered. *Contingent:* technical debt emerging in the project was reportedly dependent on this circumstance.

9. **Radio-silence:** this smell was reported 16 times. Increasingly formal organisational structure full of

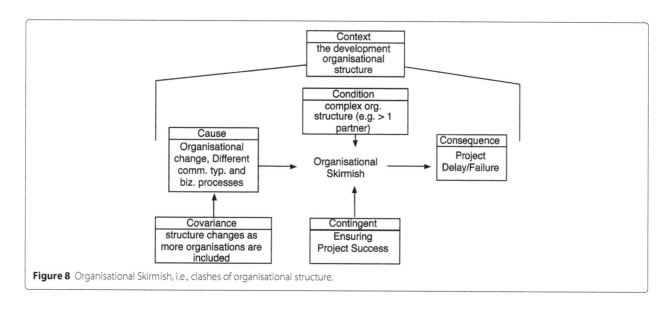

Figure 8 Organisational Skirmish, i.e., clashes of organisational structure.

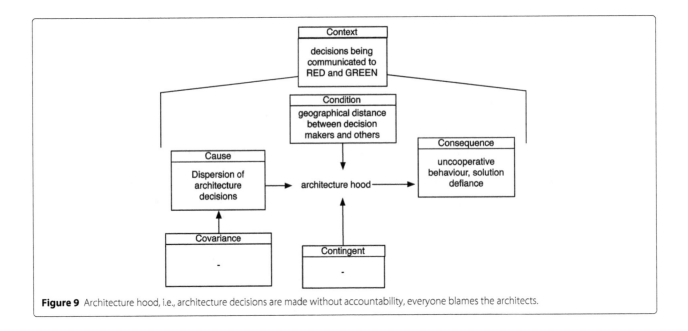

Figure 9 Architecture hood, i.e., architecture decisions are made without accountability, everyone blames the architects.

"regular procedures" forced changes to be retarded, time is lost between people, mostly extraneous between each other, to be notified and certified with. This introduced a fixed recurring delay of 1/2 to 2 days per decision. Also, sometimes people reportedly refrained from asking additional info at all. The *radio-silence* smell is shown in Figure 11. *Cause:* highly formal and complex organisational structure. *Context:* The smell was observed when socio-technical decisions were being communicated to RED and GREEN sub-communities. *Condition:* closed organisational compartments between RED

and GREEN. *Consequence:* time delay. *Covariance:* the more decisions are made the more the delay. *Contingent:* -

4.3   It smells! What can I do? Mitigations!

Not all debts in "Integra" were left unpaid or un-tackled. We found over 26 socio-technical decisions operated with the intent of mitigating, although partially, the effect or debt evident in "Integra". Seven interviewees reportedly belonging to the management board of "Integra" reported over 20 socio-technical decisions operated over the span of 18 months to "pay back the debt". In this paper we report

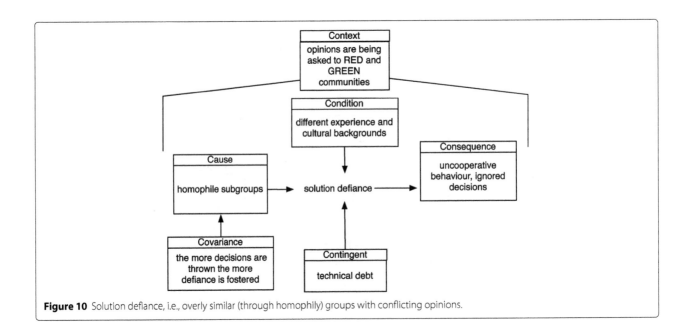

Figure 10 Solution defiance, i.e., overly similar (through homophily) groups with conflicting opinions.

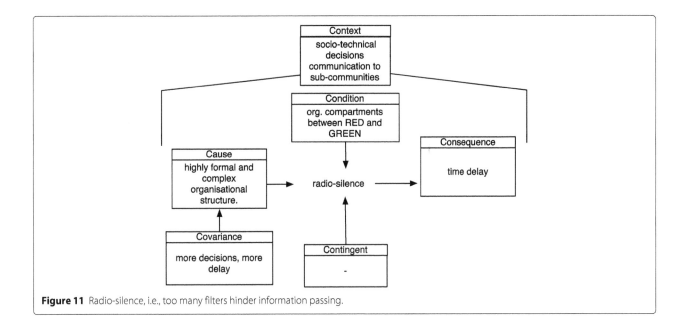

Figure 11 Radio-silence, i.e., too many filters hinder information passing.

only those decisions that reportedly[d] procured a beneficial effect and map these decisions to the relative smell they tried to tackle. Unfortunately, we did not have data to understand to what degree these decisions reduced or hampered the effect of related smells. Also, we found evidence of mitigations that increased social debt rather than the opposite. It is worth mentioning that about 40% of the mitigations adopted did not yield positive outcomes and, in some cases, they made things worse. Also, over 80% of the reported mitigations were generated by "BadExperience" as a malevolent effect connected to social debt (see the relation between "BadExperience" and "Mitigation" in Figure 1).

We found recurring evidence that 6 such decisions procured clear benefits to tackle some community "smells", i.e., "deodorants" for said smells:

1. **Full-circle**: to mitigate the **leftover-techie** smell, managers for "Integra" decided to establish a fixed, dedicated instant-messaging line of communication between operations technicians, managers and key developers, in a manner much consistent with the DevOps trend [39]. This decision indeed greatly hampered further consequences, although not all the connected debt was actually payed back.
2. **Learning-community**: to mitigate the **radio-silence** smell, managers for "Integra" decided to establish an online learning community much similar to the Learning Community type reported in our previous work[5]. All practitioners involved in the project were eventually involved in the community and led by dedicated tutoring and coaching personnel. This

decision reduced almost completely further delays and consequences of the radio-silence smell, either directly (by creating stronger social and organisational bonds between practitioners) or indirectly (some practitioners were learning from the community what they would have otherwise asked to stranger colleagues). Nevertheless, we found evidence that subversive behaviour eventually emerged across the community which suggests the need for ad-hoc community structure and management. More in particular, some community members started using the community to "outsource" part of their work or decisions, for example, quoting from our interviews [members of the learning community] are essentially "[different developers from different products and] from different teams each pulling towards their own direction, pushing their own work, instead of finding a common standard [for community structure and goals]".

3. **Culture conveyors**: to mitigate the **prima donnas** and **sharing villainy** smells, managers for "Integra" decided to appoint some developers both in RED and GREEN as architects (i.e., through promotion). The promotion was subject to the condition that new architects would also disseminate a homogeneous organisational culture harmoniously, with the intent of Integrating the RED and GREEN communities as their respective products were being integrated. This decision reduced smell effects but, reportedly, not as much as originally hoped, considered the expense for the promotions. Although we did not have enough data to investigate further, this decision might have,

in fact, payed back some debt while generating some other, connected to the additional introduced cost (promotion scheme).

4. **Stand-up voting**: to mitigate the **architecture-hood** smell managers for "Integra" decided to establish fixed daily stand-ups also for RED (previously adopting a "waterfall" process model). At the end of the stand-ups practitioners would be asked to vote in an anonymous voting-system either for accepting decisions communicated as part of the meeting or proposing feasible alternatives. This decision indeed reduced greatly the effect of the smell almost to none. Nevertheless, the application of this strategy suggests the continued and consistent presence of mistrust among professionals in both RED and GREEN.

5. **Community-based contingency planning**: to mitigate the **prima-donnas** and **solution defiance** smells, managers for "Integra" decided to: (a) make technical (e.g., architecture) and socio-technical (e.g., social or organisational structure changes) together; (b) use the appointed learning community as a device to generate "contingency plans" in case certain technical or socio-technical decisions lead to warning scenarios. This increased the cohesion of the community and reportedly hampered the effects of the smells.

6. **Social wiki**: to mitigate the **prima donnas**, **solution defiance**, **black-cloud effect**, **sharing villainy** and **organisational silo effect** smells, managers for "Integra" decided to adopt a "social wiki" combining practitioners profiles with the artefacts under their care and the connected documentation. This decision was being implemented at the time our study completed its analysis so we are unsure as to the cost or effect of said mitigation. Nevertheless, we decided to report it as it is consistent with the increasing needs for Enterprise 2.0 and enterprise social networking [40].

5   Discussion

This section discusses our findings and their implication. Also, we report a number of lessons learned from the study. These are general insights that might benefit further research into social debt as well as practitioners at hands with it. Finally, we discuss a few threats to validity we identified for this study.

5.1   On the implications of social debt

In the following, the implications for social debt are emphasised in bold.

In previous work [3] we operated a rough comparison of social debt with the notion and state of the art in technical debt. What resulted were a series of key research questions on the overlaps between social and technical debt.

Among said questions, was the following: "What decisions cause both technical and social debt?". We indadvertedly stumbled upon the answer to this question, that is, **decisions about using technicalities (e.g. introducing new programming language) to influence community aspects as well, might lead to technical and social debt together**. In our scenario we found 7 such decisions. For example, the previously mentioned decision to use a common programming language between RED and GREEN as a collaboration opportunity. Although it seemed a good decision, well motivated and with sound rationale, the decision ultimately led to technical and social debt. All such decisions should be taken into further inquiry by social and technical debt researchers for further study.

Community smells can be clustered in three sets, depending on their context: (1) smells that exist in a community's structure - i.e., that can be observed and have an effect on the structural properties of a community, such as its formality; (2) smells that exist in the community's context - i.e., that can be observed and have an effect on the constellation of properties surrounding the community's operational environment, such as political boundaries or laws; (3) smells that exist in the community members' interactions - i.e., the set of social and technical relations and actions that allow the community to exist, such as meetings. This suggests a framework to structure future research in discovering community smells, but also suggests an intrinsic difficulty to measure social debt in a precise way, depending on non-trivial relations and characteristics with implicit relations.

The three clusters above share a remarkable similarity with the 3C model for communitarian work, previously defined in [41]. The 3C model states that three basic activities drive the operations for software production: (a) *communication* with peers to realise organisational activities; (b) *coordination* of activities and tasks to achieve planned business goals; (c) *cooperation* on tasks that require concurrent and shared work/expertise. Intuitively, smells that exist in community members' interactions hinder *communication*. Similarly, *coordination*, or organisation in context [42], is compromised by smells that exist in the communities' context. Finally, *cooperation*, is compromised by smells existing in communities' structure.

This intuitive similarity has two key implications: (1) the investigation of social debt [3] needs to focus around the three dimensions in the 3C model and, consequently, rotate around community smells in the corresponding clusters; (2) software engineering research focuses on investigating one out of three sets of smells, that of coordination by means of socio-technical congruence [16] - studying the remaining two dimensions could prove valuable to govern development communities, maximising their social worth or managing their social debt [3], if any.

Influencing "smells" without preemptive study is ultimately a trial-and-error exercise. In our case, we found over 10 relatively uninformed socio-technical decisions made to tackle "smells". These did not yield the desired effect and, in 3 cases, reportedly led to worse outcomes. This suggests that a more accurate study of "smells" and mitigations is in order. This study might reveal previously reported "smells" as well as effective ways in which they were tackled under certain conditions. This study might start from the body of literature in software engineering success or failure or, in parallel, from the body of literature in organisations and social networks research.

5.2 Lessons learned

There are several lessons we learned from studying the scenario at hand.

Integrating two products means joining two (or more) communities as well. In our case, many social, organisational and technical decisions were taken along the way to "merge" the two communities involved into one. However, we discovered a number of "ancillary" people, part of other business units, not directly involved in "Integra" that actually played a role in the project (e.g., helpers, information conveyors, etc.). With this we learned that the organisational and social Integration between communities responsible for a certain product is critical and should be carefully planned and orchestrated.

Software practitioners generally associate guilt and fear to the social and organisational investigation of their efforts. We observed this circumstance in many previous studies of similar nature. It may well be connected with the "my boss will not be happy about this" social dynamic, which may cause the connected anxiety. Nevertheless, with this we learned that the tools with which a development community should be studied or "influenced" should be automated and non-invasive, observing people and software artefacts together as well as based on gamification schemes and similar technology.

Many "Contingent" factors for reported smells were missing. We observed this circumstance on 4 out of 9 reported smells. This can suggest that, for instance, the smells are applicable to multiple possible "Contingents" or "Contingents" for negative effects observed were not addressed by practitioners in the first place. This calls for further research to identify and study "Contingent" factors.

Divide-and-conquer may no longer be fit to rule. In our set of 90 organisational, socio-technical or technical decisions, over 80% of these decisions applied a classic software engineering innuendo: *divide-et-impera*. Most of these decisions, however, implied divisions in the product as well as corresponding divisions in the community. While the former may procure benefits, the latter

may compromise everything. With this we learned that a more communitarian formula should be researched for teaching and practicing software engineering. In fact, this observation is corroborated by looking more deeply at the mitigations reported in Section 4.3. All the mitigations reported have the goal of increasing the diversity, connectedness and awareness [43] of a community of people. More research is needed to establish the ways and practices in this theoretical formula. Such research would very well benefit from the study of successful (and failing) open-source communities. These are a clear example of efficient and powerful self-organisation.

5.3 Threats to validity

Based on the taxonomy in [44], there are four potential validity threat areas, namely: external, construct, internal, and conclusion validity.

External Validity concerns the applicability of the results in a more general context. Being this study performed in one organisation, results could be specific to its context. To reapply results and possibly confirm the validity of this study we are planning additional independent exploratory case-studies.

Construct Validity and *Internal Validity* concern the generalisability of the constructs under study, as well as the methods used to study and analyse data (e.g. the types of bias involved). To mitigate these threats, our methods were tailored to use multiple triangulation of data sources. A representative from *"Integra"* verified our interpretations of the data and provided clarifications and corrections where necessary. Partial results and incremental analysis was conducted to gather constant independent feedback by three senior researchers.

Conclusion Validity concerns the degree to which our conclusions are reasonable based on our data. Our conclusions were drawn by an analysis of empirical evidence using known and confirmed methods from literature such as, coding, gap- and taxonomy analysis. The approach and instruments that we used to gather such evidence were presented and validated in previous work [2,4,45].

6 Conclusions and future work

In this paper we discuss and elaborate on the notion of social debt that was originally introduced in [3]. To investigate social debt in action we conducted a case study in industry. To answer our primary research questions, namely, "What are the factors at play around social debt during the software lifecycle? Are there patterns in said factors? Can they be mitigated?", this article offers four key contributions.

First, a framework to define and interpret social debt. This can be used in practice to identify the variables that govern social debt, e.g., for more informed decision-making.

Second, a list of community "smells". These are socio-technical anti-patterns that may apparently look normal but reflect unlikeable community characteristics, such as anti-social organisational behaviour across the community, e.g., developers that refuse or delay information sharing. These patterns can be used in practice to "sense" the precursors of social debt in much the same way code smells fathom technical debt.

Third, a list of mitigation strategies to community "smells", as emerging from our case study. These can be used in practice to reduce the negative effects connected to some "smells".

Fourth, a list of lessons learned as part of our case study that further discuss social debt and its implications. These can be used by researchers interested in pursuing further social debt research.

From our study we learned that social debt is a force to be reckoned with, hand in hand with technical debt. This force is connected to sub-optimal characteristics in software development communities. Further research is needed to generate a more systematic approach. For example, the use of community detection and characterisation mechanisms via social networks analysis might be used to understand if social debt can somehow be measured automatically. Also, investigating further the relation between software architectures and "organisational architectures" might reveal patterns that lead to social and technical debt.

In the future, we plan to devise mechanisms to visualise and study the social community structure of development communities, by putting together their socio-technical properties and observable characteristics. In so doing, we hope to discover ways to mine data from software development communities that can lead to the discovery of their sub-optimal characteristics, and, possibly, any connected "smells". Also, we plan to elaborate further on the notion of community "smells" perhaps starting from analysing literature in software engineering (e.g., studying software failure stories). More in particular, we plan to answer the following research questions:

"What software engineering artefacts are affected by community smells?" Much information and data in our dataset concerning software artefacts (e.g., software architecture, requirements, integration requests, etc.) in our investigation scenario remains to be analysed - perhaps this data can be analysed in continuation with the study in this paper, e.g., to understand if community smells have a direct or indirect impact on software itself.

"How can social debt be measured?" Social debt clearly entangles a number of software and lifecycle artefacts, finding measurements for the negative characteristics connected to social debt in said artefacts is the starting point to measure social debt in the first place. This research venue might benefit from research in Mining Software Repositories (MSR) since it involves mining software products to establish causality. However, an exploratory study is needed to establish what should be measured and how.

"Are there community smells previously reported in literature?" Software engineering literature offers empirical research in software failure that could potentially contain a number of community smells. Mapping this portion of software engineering literature could be a valuable tool for practitioners embarking on complex software engineering endeavours involving more than one team or organisation.

7   Endnotes

[a]Interview guide is only available through written request.

[b]Nevertheless, every core concept was found more than 48 times in the entire dataset.

[c]The average of 4 hrs was calculated on 34 sub-optimal characteristics for which our interviewees explicitly gave us a delay - this average was then extended to all sub-optimal characteristics found.

[d]By at least two interviewees.

Competing interests
The authors declare that they have no competing interests.

Authors' contributions
DAT carried out the analysis and wrote a draft report to be submitted to the attention of PK, PL and HVV. DAT also drafted a publishable manuscript and submitted it to all coauthors. All authors helped partially to analysis and contributed during brainstorming and theory-building. HVV and PK provided major edits to the manuscript while PL contributed to study design, provided major edits to the manuscript and co-located editing, reviewing and analysis sessions via Skype. All authors read and approved the final manuscript.

Acknowledgements
The authors would like to thank Dr. Francesco Castri for his invaluable contribution to this study.

Author details
[1]VU University Amsterdam, Amsterdam, The Netherlands. [2]University of British Columbia, Vancouver, Canada.

References
1. Keyes J (2011) Social Software Engineering. Taylor & Francis, Auerbach Series, Boca Raton, FL
2. Tamburri DA, di Nitto E, Lago P, van Vliet H (2012) On the nature of the GSE organizational social structure: an empirical study. doi: 10.1109/ICGSE.2012.25
3. Tamburri DA, Kruchten P, Lago P, van Vliet H (2013) What is social debt in software engineering?. In: Cooperative and Human Aspects of Software Engineering (CHASE), 2013 6th International Workshop On, Washington, DC. pp 93–96. doi:10.1109/CHASE.2013.6614739
4. Tamburri DA, Lago P, van Vliet H (2013) Uncovering latent social communities in software development. IEEE Software 30(1):29–36. doi:10.1109/MS.2012.170
5. Tamburri DA, Lago P, van Vliet H (2013) Organizational social structures for software engineering. ACM Comput Surv 46(1):3

6. Capek PG, Frank SP, Gerdt S, Shields D (2005) A history of ibm's open-source involvement and strategy. IBM Syst J 44(2):249–258

7. Kruchten P, Nord RL, Ozkaya I (2012) Technical debt: From metaphor to theory and practice. IEEE Software 29(6):18–21

8. Cunningham W (1993) The WyCash portfolio management system. OOPS Messenger 4(2):29–30

9. Zazworka N, Shaw MA, Shull F, Seaman C (2011) Investigating the impact of design debt on software quality. In: Proceedings of the 2nd Workshop on Managing Technical Debt. MTD '11. ACM, New York, NY, USA. pp 17–23. doi:10.1145/1985362.1985366. http://doi.acm.org/10.1145/1985362.1985366

10. Conway ME (1968) How do committees invent. Datamation 14(4):28–31

11. Wenger E, McDermott RA, Snyder W (2002) Cultivating Communities of Practice: a Guide to Managing Knowledge. Harvard Business School Publishing

12. Nagappan N, Murphy B, Basili V (2008) The influence of organizational structure on software quality: an empirical case study. In: International Conference on Software Engineering. IEEE, Leipzig, Germany. pp 521–530

13. Repenning A, Ahmadi N, Repenning N, Ioannidou A, Webb D, Marshall K (2011) Collective programming: making end-user programming (more) social 6654:325–330. http://www.bibsonomy.org/bibtex/26e8152bfef95458d1dcec728a4f51c2a/dblp

14. Viana D, Conte T, Vilela D, de Souza CRB, Santos G, Prikladnicki R (2012) The influence of human aspects on software process improvement: Qualitative research findings and comparison to previous studies. In: EASE. pp 121–125

15. Meneely A, Williams L, Snipes W, Osborne JA (2008) Predicting failures with developer networks and social network analysis. In: Harrold MJ, Murphy GC (eds). SIGSOFT FSE. ACM. pp 13–23

16. Cataldo M, Herbsleb JD, Carley KM (2008) Socio-technical congruence: a framework for assessing the impact of technical and work dependencies on software development productivity. In: Proceedings of the Second ACM-IEEE International Symposium on Empirical Software Engineering and Measurement. ESEM '08. ACM, New York, NY, USA. pp 2–11. doi:10.1145/1414004.1414008. http://doi.acm.org/10.1145/1414004.1414008

17. Cataldo M, Mockus A, Roberts JA, Herbsleb JD (2009) Software dependencies, work dependencies, and their impact on failures. IEEE Trans Software Eng 35(6):864–878

18. Kwan I, Schroter A, Damian D (2011) Does socio-technical congruence have an effect on software build success? a study of coordination in a software project. IEEE Trans Software Eng 37(3):307–324. doi:10.1109/TSE.2011.29

19. de Souza CRB, Redmiles DF (2011) The Awareness Network, To Whom Should I Display My Actions? And, Whose Actions Should I Monitor? IEEE Trans Software Eng 37(3):325–340

20. Bird C, Nagappan N, Gall H, Murphy B, Devanbu P (2009) Putting it all together: Using socio-technical networks to predict failures. In: Proceedings of the 2009 20th International Symposium on Software Reliability Engineering. ISSRE '09. IEEE Computer Society, Washington, DC, USA. pp 109–119. doi:10.1109/ISSRE.2009.17

21. Cusick JJ, Prasad A (2006) A practical management and engineering approach to offshore collaboration. IEEE Software 23(5):20–29

22. Jaktman CB (1998) The influence of organisational factors on the success and quality of a product-line architecture. In: Australian Software Engineering Conference. IEEE Computer Society, Washington, DC. pp 2–11

23. Andreou AS (2003) Promoting software quality through a human, social and organisational requirements elicitation process. Requir Eng 8(2):85–101

24. Meverson EM (1994) Human capital, social capital and compensation: The relative contribution of social contacts to managers' incomes. Acta Sociologica 37(4):383–399

25. Labianca G, Brass DJ (2006) Exploring the social ledger: Negative relationships and negative asymmetry in social networks in organizations. Acad Manage Rev 31(3):596–614

26. Muir DE (1962) The social debt: An investigation of lower-class and middle class norms of social obligation. American Sociological Review 27(4):532–539

27. Moe NB, Smite D (2008) Understanding a lack of trust in global software teams: a multiple-case study. Software Process: Improvement and Practice 13(3):217–231

28. Atkinson R, Flint J (2012) Accessing hidden and hard-to-reach populations: Snowball research strategies 33

29. Neville-Neil G (2011) Interviewing techniques. ACM Queue 9(6):30

30. Morgan DavidL., Krueger RichardA. (1993) 1. In: Morgan DL (ed). When to use focus groups and why. SAGE Publications, London. pp 3–19. http://www.bibsonomy.org/bibtex/2ce683d8f889e49e740d81683fdc2c2b9/pkraker

31. Runeson P, Höst M (2009) Guidelines for conducting and reporting case study research in software engineering. Empirical Software Eng 14(2):131–164

32. Corbin J, Strauss A (1990) Grounded theory research: Procedures, canons, and evaluative criteria. Qualitative Sociology 13(1):3–21

33. Schreiber C, Carley KM (2004) Going beyond the data: Empirical validation leading to grounded theory. Comput Math Organization Theory 10(2):155–164

34. Onions PEW (1962) Grounded theory applications in reviewing knowledge management literature. 1–20

35. Glaser BG (1978) Theoretical Sensitivity: Advances in the Methodology of Grounded Theory. Sociology Press, San Francisco, CA

36. Kilduff M, Tsai W (2003) Social Networks and Organizations. SAGE Publications Ltd, London

37. Chisan J, Damian D (2004) Towards a model of awareness support of software development in gsd. IEE Seminar Digests 2004(912):28–33. doi:10.1049/ic:20040309

38. Peng Y, Sutanto J (2012) Facilitating knowledge sharing through a boundary spanner. IEEE Trans Prof Commun 55(2):142–155

39. Labs P (2013) 2013 state of devops report. Technical Report. Available Online

40. Li M, Chen G, Zhang Z, Fu Y (2012) A social collaboration platform for enterprise social networking. In: Gao L, Shen W, Barths J-PA, Luo J, Yong J, Li W, Li W (eds). CSCWD. IEEE, Washington, DC. pp 671–677

41. Swart J, Henneberg SC (2007) Dynamic knowledge nets - the 3c model: exploratory findings and conceptualisation of entrepreneurial knowledge constellations. J Knowledge Manage 11(6):126–141

42. Boella G, van der Torre L (2006) Coordination and organization: Definitions, examples and future research directions. Electron Notes Theor Comput Sci (ENTCS) 150(3):3–20

43. Manteli C, van der Hooff B, van Vliet H (2014) The Effect of Governance on Global Software Development: An Empirical Research in Transactive Memory Systems. Inf Software Technol 56(10):1309–1321

44. Wohlin C, Runeson P, Höst M, Ohlsson MC, Regnell B, Wesslén A (2000) Experimentation in Software Engineering: an Introduction. Kluwer Academic Publishers, Norwell, MA, USA

45. Tamburri DA (2012) Going global with agile service networks. IEEE Conference Proceedings, Washington, DC

10

An approach towards adaptive service composition in markets of composed services

Alexander Jungmann[1*] and Felix Mohr[2]

Abstract

On-the-fly composition of service-based software solutions is still a challenging task. Even more challenges emerge when facing automatic service composition in markets of composed services for end users. In this paper, we focus on the functional discrepancy between "what a user wants" specified in terms of a request and "what a user gets" when executing a composed service. To meet the challenge of functional discrepancy, we propose the combination of existing symbolic composition approaches with machine learning techniques. We developed a learning recommendation system that expands the capabilities of existing composition algorithms to facilitate adaptivity and consequently reduces functional discrepancy. As a representative of symbolic techniques, an Artificial Intelligence planning based approach produces solutions that are correct with respect to formal specifications. Our learning recommendation system supports the symbolic approach in decision-making. Reinforcement Learning techniques enable the recommendation system to adjust its recommendation strategy over time based on user ratings. We implemented the proposed functionality in terms of a prototypical composition framework. Preliminary results from experiments conducted in the image processing domain illustrate the benefit of combining both complementary techniques.

Keywords: Service composition; Service functionality; Service recommendation; Reinforcement learning; Service markets; Image processing; On-the-fly computing

1 Introduction

A major goal of the Collaborative Research Centre 901 "On-The-Fly (OTF) Computing" [1,2] is the automated composition of software services that are traded on markets and that can be flexibly combined with each other. In our vision, a user formulates a request for an individual software solution, receives an answer in terms of a composed service, and finally executes the composed service.

Figure 1 illustrates the very basic idea of OTF Computing. A so-called OTF provider receives and processes a user request. The processing step mainly involves automatic composition of individual software solutions based on elementary services supplied by service providers. The OTF provider responds in terms of a composed service that provides the functionality the user specified.

As an illustrative example, let us assume that someone wants to post-process a holiday photo. The person, however, is not able to use a monolithic software solution (e.g., he does not know how to handle it or a solution is not available at all). Web based platforms such as Instagram [3] provide image processing services that can be applied to an uploaded photo or video. The selection of appropriate services, however, has still to be done manually by the user. Furthermore, the variety of available services is restricted.

Now let us consider a market of image processing services. The person who wants to post-process his photo becomes a customer (henceforth referred to as user) within this market by formulating a request describing what he expects from the execution result. A solution that satisfies the user's request is automatically composed based on image processing services that are supplied by different service providers. In this scenario, the user only has to pay for the actually utilized functionality.

*Correspondence: alexander.jungmann@c-lab.de
[1]Cooperative Computing & Communication Laboratory (C-LAB), University of Paderborn, Fuerstenallee 11, 33102 Paderborn, Germany
Full list of author information is available at the end of the article

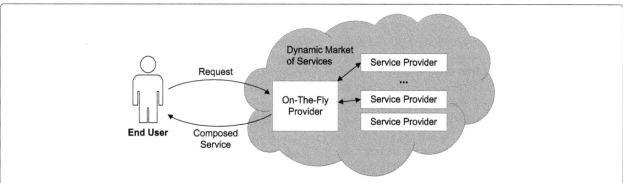

Figure 1 Basic On-The-Fly (OTF) computing concept for generating individual software solutions. An end user formulates a request, which is processed by a so-called OTF provider. An OTF provider automatically generates an individual software solution by asking appropriate service providers for services and by composing those services.

Furthermore, he benefits from the variety of image processing services that are provided by different service providers.

Different major challenges inevitably emerge, when trying to establish automated service composition in such a market environment. Some of them were already introduced in our previous work [4]. In this paper, however, we exclusively focus on service functionality, i.e., the discrepancy between the functionality desired by a user and the actual functionality when finally executing the composed solution. This gap between "what a user wants" and "what a user gets" exists due to

- the necessary trade-off between degree of abstraction and level of detail of the applied composition formalism in order to ensure feasibility,
- the data-dependency and context-sensitivity of service functionality, as well as
- inexpert users, who formulate imprecise requests while additionally having individual preferences that can hardly be described in all details in advance.

The majority of existing composition approaches can be considered as symbolic techniques that base on explicitly given information [5-15]. Alternatively, machine learning techniques are proposed to replace symbolic techniques (cf. Section 6). To overcome the mentioned functional discrepancy, however, we propose to not replace symbolic techniques, but to expand them by machine learning techniques. In our work, a symbolic composition approach is responsible for composing solutions that are correct with respect to formal specifications (service descriptions and user requests). A Reinforcement Learning (RL) based recommendation system, in turn, supports the symbolic approach in deciding between alternative composition steps based on implicit information in terms of user feedback from previous composition processes. When combined, both techniques benefit from each other: The composition algorithm determines (and restricts) the

learning space of the recommendation system, while the recommendation system estimates the quality of the composition strategy. In case of low quality, i.e., in case of an unacceptable gap between "what a user wants" and "what a user gets", the composition algorithm can adjust its behaviour to improve the result for future composition processes (e.g., by choosing an alternative solution). The contributions of this paper are as follows.

1. We emphasize the necessity to develop more fine grained methods for selecting services not only based on their abstract functional properties (and non-functional attributes, as, e.g., done in [16]) but also based on their functionality when executed.
2. We introduce and motivate image processing as appropriate application domain in order to not only consider service composition on the symbolic level, but also on the execution level. Furthermore, we provide an illustrative problem description based on a realistic image processing example.
3. We descriptively explain the conceptual and technical integration of our learning recommendation system into an Artificial Intelligence (AI) planning-based technique - a representative of symbolic composition approaches - in order to meet the challenge of functional discrepancy.
4. Experimental results within the image processing domain include the entire loop of composition, execution and learning, and demonstrate the benefits of combining symbolic approaches with machine learning techniques.

The remainder of this paper is organized as follows. Section 2 introduces and motivates image processing as application domain. It also covers the symbolic approach for automatically composing simple sequences of image filters and emphasizes the problem we are tackling in this paper. Section 3 outlines the functionality of our learning recommendation approach. The conceptual and technical integration is described in Section 4. Experimental results are presented in Section 5. After discussing related work in Section 6, the paper finally concludes with Section 7.

2 Motivation and problem description

In our work, we make an extensive use of image processing examples for investigating and clarifying open challenges as well as developing and evaluating new methods in order to meet these challenges. From the image processing perspective (cf. Section 2.1), we investigate to what extent currently existing service composition techniques facilitate automatic composition of image processing solutions and how to overcome possible shortcomings. In doing so, we obtain new insights in a domain with specific characteristics. This, in turn, enables us to come up with more specialized concepts. These concepts can then be generalized and transferred back to the service-oriented computing (SOC) domain.

From the SOC perspective (cf. Section 2.2), the characteristics of the image processing domain such as

- high variability of existing, simple services,
- demand for complex services providing data-dependent and context-specific functionality,
- availability of executable implementations provided by open source libraries,
- inherent vividness for motivating new challenges and new concepts,

enable us to realize examples of high practical relevance, while the complexity of those examples can be gradually increased. In our experience, increased practical relevance has a highly positive impact on the awareness and acceptance of SOC techniques in general.

2.1 From the image processing perspective

Developing image processing solutions heavily depends on the area of application and the underlying conditions. In embedded systems, e.g., image processing software is usually optimized for specific hardware while the implemented algorithms are often highly specialized for certain tasks. In order to reduce redundant implementation steps, a functional prototype can be realized in advance. In doing so, developers primarily focus on the desired functionality. They determine at an early stage, if and how the underlying image processing task can be solved.

A possible way of solving an image processing task is to follow a component-based approach. Existing algorithms are considered to be distinct components. Components can be interconnected in a loosely coupled manner in order to generate a composition of image processing algorithms. A composition is subsequently executed and evaluated in an application-specific test case. If the evaluation result does not satisfy the requirements, the respective composition is partially refined by adding, removing or adjusting available components. The modified composition is again executed and evaluated. These steps are repeated until either a prototype that provides the desired functionality was realized, or until the task itself is modified, since no feasible solution could be found.

In the end-user domain of photo and video post-processing, users do not implement a complete post-processing approach by programming new software. They use existing algorithms that are provided by monolithic solutions (such as Adobe Photoshop, Corel Photo-Paint, and GIMP) or by web-based solutions (like, e.g., Instagram) and combine them in an arbitrary order. End-users, whether or not being an expert, however, follow a strategy that is similar to the previously outlined way of prototyping. In order to get a solution that satisfies individual preferences, existing algorithms are consecutively applied in a trial and error manner.

Dependent on a user's degree of expertise, this trial and error process can be highly time consuming. Consider, e.g., an end-user, who has a concrete idea of how his holiday photos should look like. If he is a novice, however, he has no idea about which algorithms have to be applied in order to achieve the desired result. As a consequence, he simply tries different algorithms or combinations of algorithms in order to come up with a satisfying result. But even being an expert in image processing does not necessarily mean that you are able to come up with a satisfying solution from scratch. In any case, a composition of concrete algorithms has to be identified, most likely by a trial and error like strategy. Regardless of whether being an expert or a novice, users almost always have to deal with one and the same question: Which composition of available algorithms solves the image processing task as good as possible?

By automating this composition process, both novices and experts can be supported and the effort for finding a satisfying solution can be minimized. In the best case, an optimal solution that perfectly satisfies a user's expectations is identified and the problem is solved fully automatically. However, users can even benefit from non-optimal solutions: The composition information can be used as starting point for manual modifications while the search space for possibly promising modifications was also reduced. In general, the problem of automatically composing image processing software solutions is similar to the service composition problem.

Throughout this paper, we use a simple yet expressive pre-processing use case for illustration and evaluation purposes. Figure 2a shows a photo of a sleeping dog. In order to modify only those parts of the image that belong to the dog's gray muzzle, the associated pixels shall be isolated as good as possible. Figures 2b and 2c show example images that can be achieved by applying a sequence of simple image processing filters.

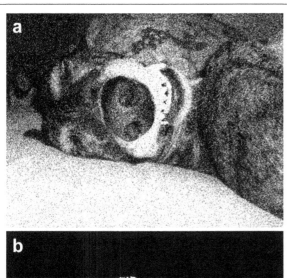

Figure 2 Example for functional discrepancy in the image processing domain. Based on original image **(a)**, desired image **(b)** and undesired image **(c)** were produced by means of two formally equivalent solutions.

2.2 From the service-oriented computing perspective

In order to design image processing services that serve as *loosely coupled*, functional components for the composition process, we adhered to the relevant key principles of SOC [17]. *Statelessness* is achieved by encapsulating existing OpenCV algorithms [18], which do not depend on any state information, but consume a single image and provide a modified version of that image. Since the functionality of

some of these algorithms can be influenced by changing parameters and in order to ensure *autonomy*, we interpret an algorithm with different parameter sets as separate services.

To support *composability* of simple image processing filters, the functionality of our services is formally specified in terms of abstract propositions. In this context, we follow an IOPE (input, output, postconditions, effects) [19] approach to facilitate AI planning techniques. In the most general sense, propositions correspond to attributes of an image that are changed by applying a service.

We specify an image processing service s in terms of the tuple $(i, o, p^+, p^-, e^+, e^-)$, where each element corresponds to a set of propositions. Input i and output o represent signature information (basic input and output data types) of a service. They ensure syntactically correct solutions and a successful execution. Required preconditions p^+, prohibited preconditions p^-, positive effects e^+, and negative effects e^- correspond to semantic information. Semantic information reduces the set of syntactically correct solutions to only those solutions that are really useful.

Table 1 lists four specifications of services that provide functionality for solving our example. Service s_1 converts a multi-channel image into a single-channel image that only contains gray level information. Any existing color information is lost during the conversion step. Service s_2 applies a binary thresholding method. The semantic description ensures, that images are processed only once by a thresholding service. Services s_3 and s_4 realize a blurring functionality for reducing image noise. They can be applied to both single-channel images and multi-channel images. Furthermore, the services can be applied arbitrarily often. However, although having the same formal specification, the services differ in their implemented blurring methods.

We use the same formalism for specifying a request; that is, a request r is defined in terms of tuple $(i, o, pre, post)$, with i and o denoting input and output, respectively, *pre* denoting the preconditions and *post* denoting the postconditions. The request for the desired functionality in our example is defined as

$$
\begin{aligned}
i &= \{\textit{multi-channel}\}, \\
o &= \{\textit{single-channel}\}, \\
pre &= \{\textit{colored}\}, \\
post &= \{\textit{blurred, threshold, gray}\} ,
\end{aligned}
\tag{1}
$$

with i and *pre* describing the original image (Figure 2a) as a multi-channel, color picture, and o and *post* describing the desired image (Figure 2b) as well as the undesired image (Figure 2c) as a single-channel, grayscale picture, which was blurred and additionally modified by a thresholding filter.

Table 1 Specifications of image processing services (simple filters)

Service s_i	Description	Signature		Preconditions		Effects	
		i_{s_i}	o_{s_i}	$p_{s_i}^+$	$p_{s_i}^-$	$e_{s_i}^+$	$e_{s_i}^-$
s_1	Multi-channel to single-channel	*Multi-channel*	*Single-channel*	-	-	*Gray*	*Colored*
s_2	Binary thresholding	*Single-channel*	*Single-channel*	-	*Threshold*	*Threshold*	-
s_3	Gaussian filter	*Single-channel*	*Single-channel*	-	-	*Blurred*	-
		Multi-channel	*Multi-channel*	-	-	*Blurred*	-
s_4	Median filter	*Single-channel*	*Single-channel*	-	-	*Blurred*	-
		Multi-channel	*Multi-channel*	-	-	*Blurred*	-

Figure 3 shows the composition state space based on the specified services and the specified request. An action (edge) corresponds to appending a service to the present sequence of services. States encode attributes of an image. The depicted automaton produces all solutions that are syntactically and semantically correct. The composition problem itself is now to find a path from initial state q_0 to goal state q^*. The identified path is equivalent to the composed solution. That said, the major question we are facing becomes clear: Which path solves the problem the best? That is, which composed solution produces an execution result that approximates the desired solution (Figure 2b) and not a formally equivalent solution such as Figure 2c?

For solving the composition problem on the symbolic level, we applied a forward search algorithm. From the AI perspective, the algorithm can be considered as a tree-search approach [20], which allows different search nodes to correspond to the same state in the composition space. These redundant paths enable our search algorithm to identify solutions that contain loops (e.g., consecutive invocations of blurring filters). In order to decide which action (service) should be chosen next in each

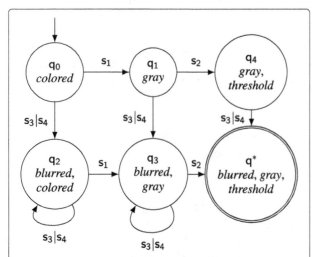

Figure 3 Composition state space for request (1) based on the service specifications listed in Table 1.

state, our learning recommendation system comes into play.

2.3 Possible reasons for functional discrepancy

Before presenting our learning recommendation system, let us take a closer look at some possible reasons for functional discrepancy in our OTF context. For a better understanding, Figure 4 illustrates the so-called OTF Computing process. A user only interacts with an OTF provider. He formulates a request (*Step 1*), gets a response in terms of a composed service (*Step 2*), executes the composed service (*Step 3*) and rates his degree of satisfaction regarding the execution result (*Step 4*).

2.3.1 Abstraction

Functionality of services is usually described by service providers in terms of abstract, functional properties. Desired functionality, in turn, is abstractly described by users. Due to the abstraction, similar services most likely end up with identical formal descriptions, although they provide different functionality when executed. The expressiveness of specification languages might theoretically be high enough to make a difference between similar services. Abstraction, however, is necessary to ensure feasibility of composition processes. Furthermore, the more precise and restrictive functional properties are specified, the higher the probability to exclude solutions that might be desired by users.

2.3.2 Data- and context-dependency

In certain domains, service functionality heavily depends on the concrete data that has to be processed. Although the functional description of a service might be very detailed, there is always a high probability that a service is not or not sufficiently fulfilling the required functionality when executing it with concrete data. It is usually impossible to predict, consider and formalize every possible execution context in advance.

2.3.3 Inexpert users

Users are not necessarily experts in the domain in which they formulate a request. As a consequence, although having the possibility to describe a request on a very

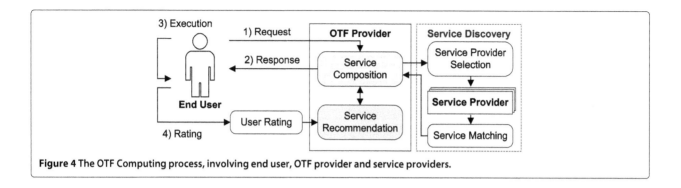

Figure 4 The OTF Computing process, involving end user, OTF provider and service providers.

detailed level, inexpert users are not able to describe all details that are necessary for composing a solution that exactly produces desired execution results. Most of the time, indeed, user requests will likely be imprecise or incomplete. A composition process is able to automatically produce solutions that satisfy a user request. However, that does not necessarily mean that the composed solution also produces execution results that satisfy the user.

2.3.4 Divergent user preferences

In a market of composed services, users with different preferences will occur. As a consequence, although users specify the same request and provide the same data, the actually desired functionality might still differ. Assuming that users rate their satisfaction regarding the result of a composition process, an OTF provider most likely receives divergent feedback for identical requests. An OTF provider has to analyse user feedback in order to group user profiles according to similar preferences. New requests have to be assigned to existing or new groups, so that an OTF provider can compose a service according to the specific preferences of a group. Handling this so-called *concept drift*, however, is beyond the scope of this paper.

3 Learning recommendation system

Recommendation systems are applied to provide users with the most suitable services to their specific interests. Chan et al., e.g., developed a recommendation system that captures implicit knowledge by incorporating historical usage data [21]. In their work, however, generated recommendation values are neither used for automatic service composition, nor do they evolve by learning from history.

In our work, we interpret service composition as sequential application of composition steps such as appending a service to a sequence (cf. Section 2.2). Whenever alternative composition steps occur, our recommendation mechanism supports the composition process in identifying the most appropriate candidate. The recommendation strategy is adjusted over time based on

feedback. For adjusting the decision-making processes, we apply RL [22] techniques.

RL addresses the problem faced by an autonomous agent that must learn to reach a goal through sequential trial-and-error interactions with its environment. RL techniques, however, do not try to reach a particular goal. They try to maximize reward in the long run by identifying optimal actions. Depending on its actions, an agent receives reward values. These values are incorporated into the decision-making process in order to adjust the future action selection strategy.

In our context, the agent corresponds to the OTF provider, who has the goal to compose a solution that satisfies the user. A single action corresponds to a composition step. A sequence of composition steps generates a composed service that can be executed by the user. The reward values an OTF provider receives are provided by users in terms of ratings.

3.1 Independent state models

Reinforcement Learning bases on the major assumption, that the underlying decision-making process does not depend on history, but is memoryless and can be modeled as Markov Decision Process (MDP) [23]. The fundamental assumption behind modelling a sequential decision-making problem as MDP is that the reward function is Markovian [24]. All information needed to determine the reward (and to choose an action) at a given state must be encoded in the state itself, i.e., states have to satisfy the Markov property. In case of the composition state space shown in Figure 3, the Markov property is not fulfilled, since not enough information is encoded in a single state. To decide whether to append a service or not heavily depends on previous composition steps. For that reason, the composition model's state space is automatically transformed into a Markovian state space by augmenting the composition model's states with additional information in terms of the actual composition structure. Roughly speaking, a Markov state encodes a composition model's state's history. As a consequence, the recommendation system can estimate the quality of a service as a function of the previous actions of the search algorithm.

3.2 Markov model based on composition rules

From the recommendation system's perspective, we interpret a service composition step as an application of a composition rule that compactly describes a formally correct modification during the composition process. The syntax of composition rules is identical to the syntax of production rules for specifying a formal grammar. A grammar G is defined by the tuple (N, Σ, P, S), where N denotes a finite set of *non-terminal symbols*, Σ denotes a finite set of *terminal symbols*, P denotes a finite set of production rules, and $S \in N$ denotes a distinguished start symbol. In our context, non-terminal symbols correspond to functionality that still has to be realized, i.e., the remaining path in the search tree from the current node to the goal node. Terminal symbols correspond to concrete services, which cannot be replaced anymore. The start symbol corresponds to the formally specified request. In case of our example, it corresponds to the path from initial state q_0 to goal state q^*.

Note: In this paper, we omit an introduction of the mathematical basis as well as a formal description of the Markov model, but present the basic idea only. A comprehensive formal description of the underlying Markov model was already introduced in our previous work [25,26]. In the paper at hand, we focus on the combination of symbolic approaches and our learning recommendation system.

Table 2 shows the right regular composition grammar for our running example addressed by the forward search algorithm. This grammar is automatically generated by the recommendation system during the search process of the composition algorithm (see Section 4.2 for an example). In terms of composition rules, two formally correct solutions for our example correspond to the following two derivations:

$$V \xrightarrow{r_1} s_1 W \xrightarrow{r_6} s_1 s_4 Y \xrightarrow{r_{11}} s_1 s_4 s_4 Y \xrightarrow{r_{12}} s_1 s_4 s_4 s_2 \tag{2}$$

$$V \xrightarrow{r_1} s_3 X \xrightarrow{r_9} s_3 s_1 Y \xrightarrow{r_{12}} s_3 s_1 s_2 \tag{3}$$

Figure 5 depicts the graphical representation of the Markovian state space, based on the composition grammar defined in Table 2. Nodes correspond to states. Edges correspond to possible actions that can be performed in order realize a transition from one state to another. A single state is equivalent to the current composition structure described in terms of terminal and non-terminal symbols. Performing an action is equivalent to applying a composition rule. Initial states correspond to distinguished start symbols. States without any non-terminal symbols are final states. The annotated quality values $Q(s, r)$ can be interpreted as an estimation of how good it is to apply a composition rule r based on the current composition structure. Roughly speaking, the higher a so-called Q-value, the better the evaluation of an alternative composition rule in a specific state. Adjusting these so-called Q-values based on feedback is up to the applied RL method.

3.3 Incorporating temporal difference learning

According to our idea of OTF Computing, OTF providers do not know in advance which services are available on the market. Hence, also the recommendation system's composition rules must be created at runtime. A complete model of the environment is not available a priori.

In such situations, Temporal-Difference (TD) learning can be used. TD learning is one central concept of RL. It combines the advantages of Monte Carlo methods with the advantages of dynamic programming. Monte Carlo methods allow for learning without relying on a model of the environment. Dynamic programming provides techniques for estimating value functions in terms of Q-values without waiting for a final outcome. Hence, Q-values are already updated during the composition process for adjusting the recommendation strategy in an on-line manner, and not only after a user gave his feedback.

In order to maximize the final reward in the long run, TD learning algorithms try to identify the most appropriate sequence of actions by trial-and-error. A fundamental question in this context is how to choose an action when there are multiple alternatives. If only the action with the highest Q-value is always selected (*exploitation*), the learning algorithm may be stuck in a local maximum. If, in turn, Q-values are not considered at all but actions are always selected randomly (*exploration*), the learning

Table 2 Right regular composition grammar for producing all solutions provided by the automaton in Figure 3

N :	{V, W, X, Y, Z}		
	$V = (q_0, \dots, q^*)$	$W = (q_1, \dots, q^*)$	$X = (q_2, \dots, q^*)$
	$Y = (q_3, \dots, q^*)$	$Z = (q_4, \dots, q^*)$	
Σ :	$\{s_i \mid 1 \leq i \leq 4\}$		
P :	$\{r_i \mid 1 \leq i \leq 14\}$		
	$r_1 = V \rightarrow s_1 W$	$r_2 = V \rightarrow s_3 X$	$r_3 = V \rightarrow s_4 X$
	$r_4 = W \rightarrow s_2 Z$	$r_5 = W \rightarrow s_3 Y$	$r_6 = W \rightarrow s_4 Y$
	$r_7 = X \rightarrow s_3 X$	$r_8 = X \rightarrow s_4 X$	$r_9 = X \rightarrow s_1 Y$
	$r_{10} = Y \rightarrow s_3 Y$	$r_{11} = Y \rightarrow s_4 Y$	$r_{12} = Y \rightarrow s_2$
	$r_{13} = Z \rightarrow s_3$	$r_{14} = Z \rightarrow s_4$	
S :	V		

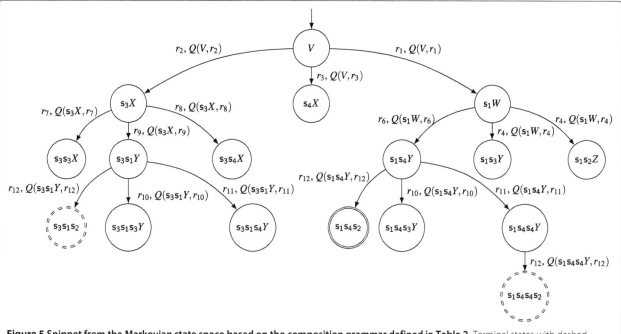

Figure 5 Snippet from the Markovian state space based on the composition grammar defined in Table 2. Terminal states with dashed borders correspond to the solutions (2) and (3), respectively.

behaviour will never converge. There already exist different approaches to cope with this problem in the RL domain, such as the ϵ-greedy strategy or softmax action selection strategy [22].

4 Integration

Figure 6 shows the main components and interaction processes of our combined approach. The service composition component and the service recommendation com-

ponent are two distinct modules that interact with each other in order to generate service-based software solutions that i) are formally correct with respect to user requests and ii) approximate implicit user requirements over time based on user ratings. Without any additional information, the service composition component implements an uninformed search strategy [20]. In combination with the recommendation system as learning evaluation function, the composition component realizes an informed search strategy.

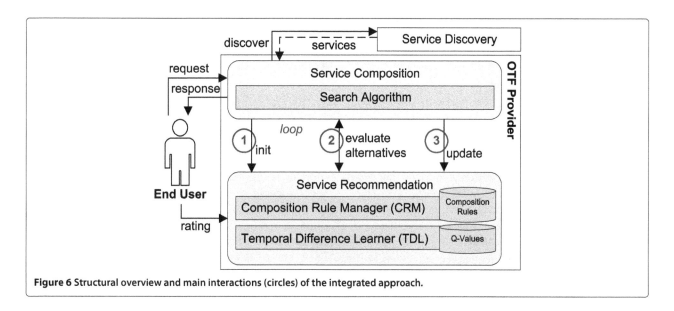

Figure 6 Structural overview and main interactions (circles) of the integrated approach.

4.1 Conceptual overview

The service discovery encapsulates (and currently abstracts) the functionality to discover services in a market. For the remainder of this paper, we assume the service discovery to work in a synchronous manner; that is, services and their descriptions are kept in stock in a local repository, while a discovery request is answered by the service discovery in terms of a message containing all possible candidates for a composition step. In a distributed market environment with multiple service providers, however, the service discovery has to be exchanged by an asynchronous approach, e.g., realized by means of publish/subscribe techniques. Furthermore, an independent matching mechanism such as [27] has to be integrated to ensure that an OTF provider receives only appropriate services from service providers.

The service composition module implements a breadth-first forward search algorithm [20]. It considers only formal specifications in terms of pre- and postconditions (effects). It does not only consider goals that exactly satisfy a user's postconditions, but also goals that are likely to be the actual goal of a user, by accepting states as goal states, that are supersets of the specified postconditions. In contrast to the recommendation module, the composition module is memoryless. Each composition process starts from scratch without relying on knowledge from previous composition processes. In order to identify the most up to date actions (services) during the search process, the composition module interacts with the service discovery.

Technically, the service recommendation module can be interpreted as a learning evaluation function that supports the composition module in deciding what action is best in a specific context. The recommendation module consists of two components: Composition Rule Manager (CRM) and Temporal Difference Learner (TDL). The CRM generates and stores composition rules based on formally correct actions identified by the composition module. Composition rules are generated only once, are aggregated over time, and represent all formally correct modifications that were identified by the composition module so far.

The TDL maintains the learned knowledge in form of state transition values (Q-values) in a Markovian state space. A state in the TDL corresponds to a composition structure, and an action is equivalent to a rule that modifies the composition structure. Whenever the CRM generates a new composition rule, the TDL modifies the state space. The TDL stores a Q-value for each state-action pair. The Q-values are adjusted during the composition process and after a user has rated a solution – according to the implemented learning algorithm and the corresponding Q-value update function (see Section 4.3).

4.2 Automatic rule and state generation

Whenever a new composition process starts, the composition module notifies the recommendation module by means of an initialization message (*Interaction 1* in Figure 6) containing the initial state and the goal state of the composition task. The CRM identifies (or generates) the non-terminal symbol that corresponds to the desired functionality. Subsequently, the TDL marks the respective non-terminal as initial state for the upcoming search process.

After initialization, the search process starts. For each service returned by the service discovery, the composition module sends a request to the recommendation module in order to evaluate how good it is to apply the service in the current context (*Interaction 2* in Figure 6). Each request comprises the search algorithm's current state q_n, the respective service s and the next state $q_{n'}$; we write $(q_n, s, q_{n'})$. Based on this information, the CRM identifies (or generates) a composition rule r. In case of forward search, a rule corresponding to a right regular grammar is constructed (cf. Section 3.2). If the rule is not yet assigned to the current state within the Markov state space, the TDL integrates the rule and the corresponding successor state into its state space and assigns an initial Q-value. The recommendation system returns the ids of the rule and the two corresponding Markov states that reflect the search algorithm's composition step in the TDL state space. After selecting a service, the composition module informs the recommendation module about its decision by transmitting the associated ids of the service's related rule and Markov states (*Interaction 3* in Figure 6). Based on this information, the recommendation module's TDL updates its internal state.

4.2.1 Forward search example

By way of illustration, let us consider our running example. The composition problem is addressed by a forward search algorithm. An initialization message comprising initial state q_0 and goal state q^* is sent to the recommendation module. The CRM cannot identify a corresponding non-terminal symbol. Hence, it introduces a new symbol V as a placeholder for the path from q_0 to q^*; we write $V = (q_0, \ldots, q^*)$. The TDL then sets its initial state to V (cf. Figure 7).

The composition module's forward search now enters its search loop. Three syntactically and semantically valid services s_1, s_3, and s_4 are discovered, resulting in three successor nodes. Two of these successor nodes represent the same state, namely q_2, while the third node represents state q_1 (cf. Figure 8). For each new search node, the composition module formulates evaluation requests. For request tuple (q_0, s_1, q_1), a corresponding composition rule is not yet available. The CRM generates a new composition rule $r_1 = V \rightarrow s_1 W$ with $W = (q_1, \ldots, q^*)$.

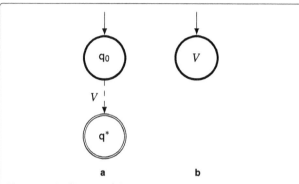

Figure 7 Initialization of the integrated composition process. Search tree **(a)** and TDL state space **(b)** after initialization.

The TDL extends its state space by incorporating rule r_1 for performing a state transition from state V to a new state s_1W.

Analogously, two new composition rules $r_2 = V \rightarrow s_3X$ and $r_3 = V \rightarrow s_4X$ with $X = (q_2, \dots, q^*)$ are generated for tuple (q_0, s_3, q_2) and tuple (q_0, s_4, q_2), respectively, and integrated into the TDL state space. Let us assume that the composition module chooses service s_1 over services s_3 and s_4; that is, it selects node q_1 as next search node. The composition module notifies the recommendation system, so that the TDL can update its internal state from state V to state s_1W by applying r_1.

After two additional iterations, the sequence $\langle s_1, s_4, s_2 \rangle$ was identified as solution for our composition problem (cf. Figure 9). During the composition process, the right regular composition grammar shown in Table 2 was partially generated. While the search tree is discarded, the Markovian state space is preserved. In case of a similar

user request, the grammar as well as the state space will be extended according to new alternative services that are discovered or according to alternative search paths that are explored by the search algorithm.

4.3 Prototypical realization

We implemented the presented concepts in terms of a prototypical composition framework. Figure 10 depicts the structural overview. The *Service Composition* component controls the overall composition process. It implements the forward search algorithm. This algorithm interacts with a *Service Repository* to get the most up to date service specifications and associated executable services that can be applied in the current search state. In this context, a simple matching operator ensures syntactically correct interconnections based on signature information. The *Learning Recommendation System* provides learned knowledge in order to support the composition component. However, the recommendation system *does not* dictate which search node should be visited next. As the name implies, it only *recommends* a node selection strategy based on learned knowledge. In contrast to the recommendation system, the composition component is memoryless. Each search process starts from scratch without relying on knowledge from previous search processes

The CRM generates and maintains composition rules that were identified by the composition component during all search processes so far. The TDL implements the relevant concepts for reinforced learning. Based on the CRM and the behaviour of the composition component, the TDL automatically constructs, extends and maintains a Markovian state space. The TDL also maintains and

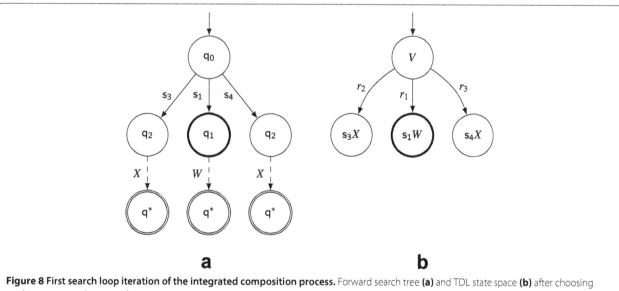

Figure 8 First search loop iteration of the integrated composition process. Forward search tree **(a)** and TDL state space **(b)** after choosing service s_1 over services s_3 and s_4.

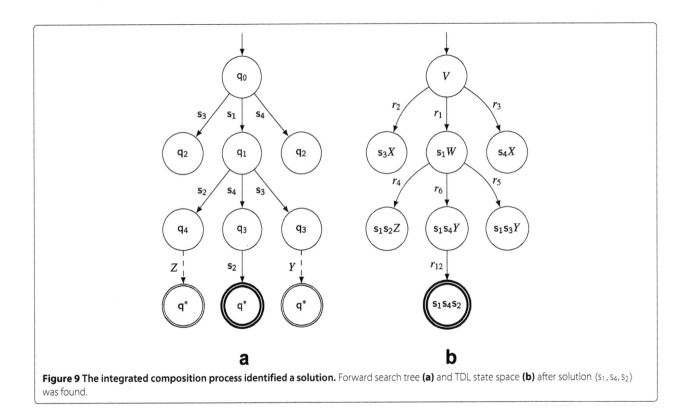

Figure 9 The integrated composition process identified a solution. Forward search tree **(a)** and TDL state space **(b)** after solution $\langle s_1, s_4, s_2 \rangle$ was found.

updates Q-values based on reward given by the *Automatic Evaluation* component after automatically executing a composed solution by means of the *Service Execution* component.

4.3.1 Composition process

First of all, the composition component initializes the recommendation system in order to set its initial state to the corresponding start symbol. Subsequently, the informed search algorithm enters its search loop. Whenever a node is visited the first time, service candidates are requested from the service repository and corresponding child nodes are computed. Subsequently, the

recommendation system rates the candidates by two mechanisms:

1. Each alternative child node is assigned its current Q-value for enabling the search algorithm to select the *globally* best candidate.
2. The complete list of the current node's child nodes is sorted according to the TDL's action selection strategy in order to enable the search algorithm to select the *locally* best alternative. In case of ϵ-greedy, with a probability $1 - \epsilon$, the list of alternatives is sorted in a greedy manner, i.e., alternatives with the highest Q-value are in the first place, whereas

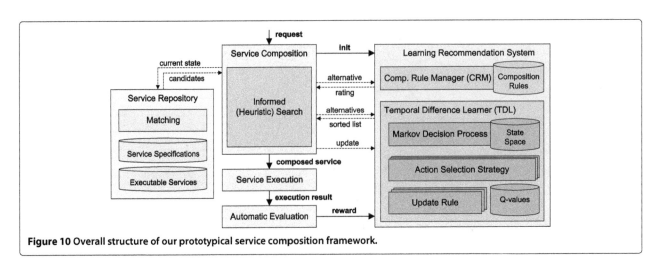

Figure 10 Overall structure of our prototypical service composition framework.

alternatives with the lowest Q-value are in the last place (exploitation phase). With probability ϵ, however, the list of alternatives is randomly shuffled (exploration phase).

After choosing a node (either globally or locally) and entering a new node, the composition module informs the recommendation system to update both the current state in the MDP and the corresponding Q-value. As soon as a formally correct solution was identified, the framework immediately proceeds with execution. Subsequently, the execution result is automatically evaluated by comparing it with the desired result (image). The evaluation result is finally fed back as reward to the recommendation system for a final update of the corresponding Q-value.

4.3.2 Search node selection strategy
As described in the previous section, alternative nodes can be selected by the composition component either globally based on absolute Q-values, or locally by picking a child node from a sorted list. On the one hand, when only selecting globally, the TDL's action selection strategy is completely bypassed. The TDL's action selection strategy, however, is crucial for balancing exploitation of already learned knowledge and exploration of new and possibly better alternatives. On the other hand, when only selecting locally, the search algorithm may be stuck in a branch that does not contain a formally correct solution at all. Only selecting nodes from all globally available nodes enables the algorithm to leave such a branch again. As a consequence, we allow the search algorithm to randomly choose how to select the next search node. The weights κ, ν, and μ for selecting globally greedy, globally randomly, and locally, respectively, have to be adjusted in advance.

4.3.3 Q-Learning as TDL implementation
In our prototype, we integrated Q-Learning to adjust the Q-values over time based on user feedback [28]. Q-Learning is a TD learning algorithm that directly approximates Q-values by means of its update function

$$Q(s_t, r_t) \leftarrow Q(s_t, r_t)$$
$$+ \alpha \left[\gamma \max_r \left[Q(s_{t+1}, r) \right] - Q(s_t, r_t) \right],$$
$$\tag{4}$$

with current state s_t, next state s_{t+1}, current composition rule r_t, next composition rule r_{t+1}, discount factor γ, and learning rate α.

Figures 11b,c,d,e illustrate the actual learning process (with $\alpha = 0.9$ and $\gamma = 0.9$) based on a right regular composition grammar, whereas the search nodes are selected only locally (based on ϵ-greedy). Each figure shows the Markovian state space and the associated Q-values *after* a composition process was completed and a user rating

was incorporated as final reward. Thick arrows indicate the chosen path from initial state to final state. Q-values $Q(X, r_1)$, $Q(s_1 Y, r_2)$, and $Q(s_1 Y, r_3)$ are initialized with 0.

Figure 11b: Service $s_1 s_3$ was composed and executed. During the composition process, composition rule r_3 was chosen randomly. The execution result was rated with value 0.5. The rating value was immediately integrated as final reward by adjusting $Q(s_1 Y, r_3)$.

Note: Final reward is always incorporated unmodified and replaces the Q-value of the lastly applied composition rule.

Figure 11c: The composition process again produced composed service $s_1 s_3$. Composition rule r_3, however, was not selected randomly, but greedily based on $Q(s_1 Y, r_3)$, which was modified in the previous composition process. After selecting r_3 and before transitioning to state $s_1 s_3$, update rule (4) is applied to adjust $Q(X, r_1)$. Q-value $Q(s_1 Y, r_3)$ does not change, since it is equivalent to the rating result, which is the same as before.

Figure 11d: Composition rule r_2 was randomly selected during the composition process. Executing composed service $s_1 s_2$ results in an image that is identical to the desired result image. Hence, the rating value is 1. Q-value $Q(s_1 Y, r_2)$ is immediately updated. During the composition process, however, this value was not yet available. Due to the max operator in the Q-Learning update function, $Q(X, r_1)$ was again updated based on $Q(s_1 Y, r_3)$.

Figure 11e: The composition process operated in a greedy manner again. Furthermore, $Q(X, r_1)$ was updated based on $Q(s_1 Y, r_2)$ this time. As a consequence, the value significantly increased.

By consecutively applying the update rule when moving through the state space and by continually incorporating ratings of consecutive composition processes, user ratings are propagated throughout the state space. In the most general sense, the overall composition process adapts its composition strategy to produce a composed service that approximates the desired functionality, which is implicitly determined by user feedback.

Note: Another TD learning algorithm that could be applied is SARSA [29,30]. The *off-policy* Q-Learning algorithm directly approximates the optimal Q-values – independent of the action that was selected (max operator). The *on-policy* SARSA algorithm, in turn, does always update Q-values based on the selected action.

5 Experiments and results
We conducted several experiments for investigating the difference between a *planning only* (purely symbolic) composition strategy (e_1 in Table 3) and a combined

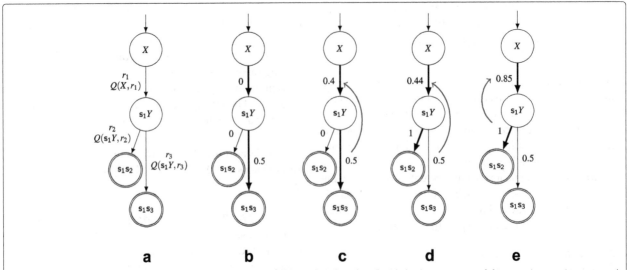

Figure 11 Demonstration of the learning process in terms of Q-Learning. Based on the Markovian state space **(a)**, user ratings are incorporated as feedback and propagated throughout the state space dependent on the action selection strategy during each consecutive composition process **(b)-(e)**.

planning and learning strategy with only local search node selection (e_2 in Table 3). Selecting search nodes only locally is possible in our example, since there exists no branch in which the search algorithm might be stuck. There is always the possibility to find a formally correct solution and to terminate. Furthermore, we experimentally investigated the influence of *additionally selecting search nodes globally* based on Q-values (e_3 in Table 3). To investigate how good the three different strategies can cope with imprecise request specifications, we repeated experiments e_1, e_2, and e_3 for three different request specifications (r_1, r_2, and r_3 in Table 4). Technically, the amount of valid goal states is increased by removing propositions from the request's postconditions.

We implemented the set of services described in Section 2.2 based on OpenCV algorithms [18]. Service s_1 was implemented by exactly one executable service. The functionality for service s_2 was provided by 14 executable services with different thresholding techniques and threshold values. Both service s_3 and service s_4 were each implemented by two executable services with different kernel sizes. Furthermore, we added 10 additional services that realize a morphological filtering functionality: 5

services for dilating, and 5 services for eroding an image. These services serve as optional functionality, that might be selected by the composition algorithm to improve the execution result.

The goal of the composition processes during the experiments was to compose a service that solves our running example; that is, a solution that approximates the desired image (Figure 2b) as good as possible by processing the original image (Figure 2a). Regarding the recommendation system, we chose a typical though static setting for the Q-Learning update function and the ϵ-greedy action selection mechanism; that is, $\alpha = 0.9$, $\gamma = 0.9$, and $\epsilon = 0.1$.

We executed 30 independent simulation runs for each of the nine combinations (experiments × requests). Each simulation run involved 1000 consecutive composition processes. We compare the quality of the composition processes by means of the final reward per composition process (smoothed mean value and 95% confidence interval). Recall: The higher the final reward, the more similar is the automatically produced image to the desired image and consequently the higher the quality of the composed solution.

Table 3 Different search node selection settings

	Search node selection		
	Global, greedy	Global, random	Local
Experiment e_i	κ_{e_i}	ν_{e_i}	μ_{e_i}
e_1	0	1	0
e_2	0	0	1
e_3	1	0	1

Table 4 Requests with different level of precision

	Semantic information	
Request r_i	Pre_{r_i}	$Post_{r_i}$
r_1	Colored	Blurred, gray, threshold
r_2	Colored	Blurred, gray
r_3	Colored	Threshold

5.1 Preliminary results

Across all following figures, red plots correspond to final reward values of the purely planning composition strategy (experiment e_1). Search nodes are always selected randomly from all available candidates. Blue plots represent the results of the combined approach including planning and learning with local search node selection only (experiment e_2). Next search nodes always correspond to the first node in the list of child nodes as provided by the recommendation system. In fact, this setting can be interpreted as an informed depth first search strategy. The green plot represents the results of the combined approach including planning and learning with uniformly distributed weights (experiment e_3) for selecting search nodes either globally, based on their Q-values, or locally, as described before.

Figure 12 shows the results for request r_1; the original request of our running example. Both composition strategies that include learning clearly outperform the purely planning based approach, whereas the strategy including only local node selection performs best in the long run. As expected, the purely planning approach is not able to improve its composition strategy over time. The mean values of the final reward almost always remain between 0.5 and 0.6. Furthermore, the randomness in selecting search nodes is reflected by the confidence interval, which is the widest of all depicted plots. The learning composition strategy with local node selection significantly improves during the first 400 composition processes. The benefit of our combined approach is clearly visible. The benefit is also visible, when regarding the results of the third composition strategy. However, selecting search

nodes also globally has a mostly negative influence to the learning process. Although the composition strategy improves the fastest during the first 170 composition processes, it considerably worsen once in a while during the following composition processes (e.g., between composition process 170 and 190). The relation between local and global search node selection seems to be highly unbalanced – at least for our example. Identifying a good balance (or even trying to do some dynamic balancing) is beyond the scope of this paper. It needs a more thorough investigation, based on examples that do not allow local search node selection only.

Figure 13 shows the results for request r_2; a reduced version of the original request of our running example. We removed the (most likely) most important proposition *threshold* from the postconditions. The effect of this modification is clearly visible, when comparing the results in Figure 13 with the corresponding results in Figure 12. The mean value of the purely planning composition strategy is significantly lower then before (≈ 0.1). The tighter confidence interval indicates, that less different solutions were composed by chance. Again, the second composition strategy performs best. In this scenario, it performs even significantly better than the third composition strategy. However, the results from the previous scenario cannot be achieved. Furthermore, the confidence interval is much wider than before, meaning that more different solutions where chosen by chance. Roughly speaking, the recommendation system lacks the guidance of the search algorithm based on the important *threshold* proposition. The TDL counters this circumstance by increased exploration, which, in turn, guides the search algorithm in identifying

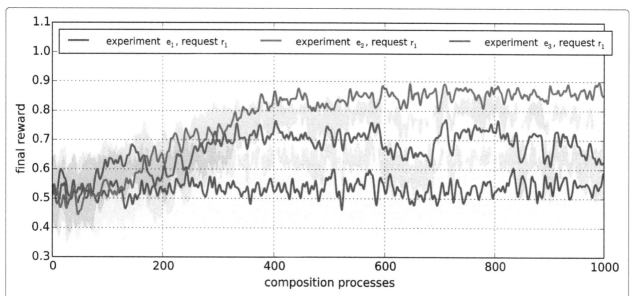

Figure 12 Results of e_1 (red; pure planning with random search node selection), e_2 (blue; planning + learning with local search node selection only), and e_3 (green; planning + learning with global and local search node selection) for request r_1.

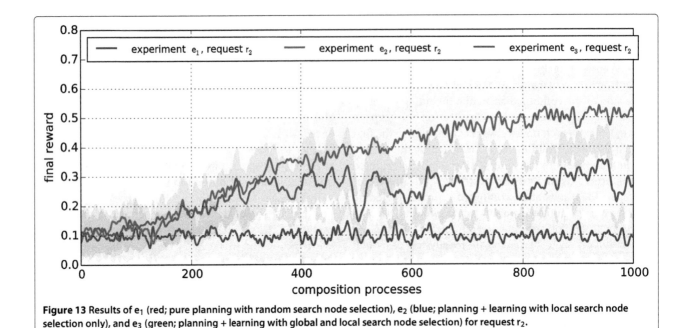

Figure 13 Results of e_1 (red; pure planning with random search node selection), e_2 (blue; planning + learning with local search node selection only), and e_3 (green; planning + learning with global and local search node selection) for request r_2.

better solutions. This reciprocal relationship is exactly what we intended to achieve. It can be interpreted as self-balancing mechanism of the entire approach. However, more experiments are necessary in order to investigate, to which degree the recommendation system can counter missing (formal) specifications. It may even be possible to achieve better results in the long run by (dynamically) adjusting the settings of the TDL module.

Figure 14 shows the results for request r_3; an alternative, reduced version of the original request of our running example. This time, all goal propositions except for proposition *threshold* were omitted. The results are indeed surprising. While the purely planning strategy performs as good as in the r_1 case, the two strategies including learning perform even better. The composition strategy including local and global node selection is even able to catch up to the composition strategy including only local node selection. Now, what general conclusions can be drawn from these – to be honest – unexpected results? First, there might be parts of a formal specification that

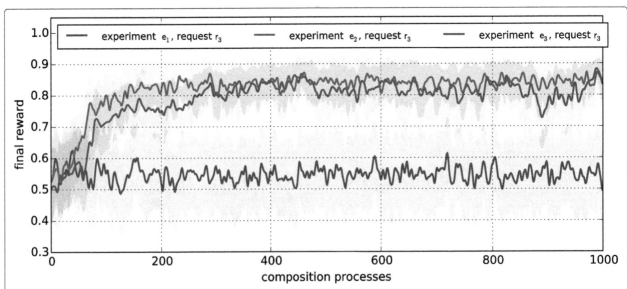

Figure 14 Results of e_1 (red; pure planning with random search node selection), e_2 (blue; planning + learning with local search node selection only), and e_3 (green; planning + learning with global and local search node selection) for request r_3.

are more important than others. This leads to the initial idea of assigning, let's say, statements about the importance or influence to single propositions (e.g., in terms of fuzzy expressions). Second, precise formal specifications are not always the best choice when search algorithms are supported in decision-making by a learning evaluation function.

6 Related work

In the last years, there has been an increasing amount of research on automated service composition incorporating Markov models and RL. However, we are not aware of any approach that combines reinforced learning techniques with symbolic techniques in order to realize adaptive service composition for markets of composed services. Ignoring feedback such as user ratings in the composition process is troublesome, because a user might not be satisfied with a solution even if it is formally correct. The novelty of this paper is the *integration* of automated service composition with a learning recommendation system in order to narrow the gap between "what a user wants" and "what a user gets". To the best of our knowledge, such an integration has not been done before.

The general idea of incorporating Markov models or RL into service composition, however, is not new. Wang et al., e.g., propose an approach that enables composed services to adapt to dynamic environments [31]. By modelling composed services as MDPs, multiple alternative workflows and services are integrated into a composed service. During execution, workflow selection is controlled by a RL mechanism. Similar to our approach, there is no separation between building abstract workflows and concrete, composed services. In contrast to our work, however, the composition process itself is not interpreted as MDP, but the result of the process.

One approach that considers service composition and RL at a time is proposed by Todica et al. [32]. They divide service composition into abstract work-flow generation and service instantiation. RL is then applied to the abstract work-flow generation phase. Their motivation is identical with ours, namely to improve the entire composition process by involving learning from previous attempts. In our work, however, RL is not applied for solving the service composition problem directly, but to support it in terms of a recommendation system during decision making. By doing so, RL is not replacing but extending classical search algorithms or AI planning approaches.

Kun et al. combine a MDP model and Hierarchical Task Networks (HTN) planning to increase flexibility of automatic service composition [33]. Their proposed model enhances HTN planning in order to decompose a task in multiple ways and to identify more than one possible solution. An evaluation mechanism then identifies a composition out of the set of possible solutions that is

optimal with respect to non-functional properties. RL, however, is not applied in their work. In contrast to our work, again, the composition process itself is not modelled as MDP, but the result of the composition process. Similar to the work of Wang et al. [31], the identified solutions are aggregated in a single model. In case of failures, e.g., alternative solutions enhance the probability of a successful execution. In our work, we currently do not compose solutions with alternative execution branches. However, in our opinion, our approach would most likely benefit from it. Similar to collecting knowledge from consecutive composition processes, an extended approach would additionally collect knowledge from consecutive execution processes of a composed service. This information could then be integrated as additional learning samples into our recommendation system. As a consequence, services that, e.g., were not reliable during execution, would be considered less often during future composition processes.

Moustafa and Zhang introduce two RL algorithms for multi-objective optimization of competitive service properties during service composition [34]. Both approaches mainly base on Q-Learning and allow for identifying Pareto optimal solutions. The first approach addresses each service property in a separate learning process. For selecting a distinct service during the composition process, the separate learning processes are coordinated. The second approach is an extended version of the approach that was originally proposed by Dehousse et al. [35]. In comparison to the first approach, the second approach considers a complete vector of all competitive service properties in a single learning process. In our work, we currently do not consider competitive service properties. In fact, we do not consider non-functional (QoS, performance) properties at all. Incorporating multi-objective optimization of functional and non-functional properties, however, is an important and necessary step for our future work.

Two other composition approaches that incorporate Q-Learning are proposed by Wang et al. [36] and Yu et al. [37]. Wang et al. introduce a service composition concept based on a multi-agent Q-Learning algorithm. Agents benefit from the experiences other agents made before. As a consequence, the convergence speed of the overall learning process is improved in comparison to independently learning agents and a single agent, respectively, as it is currently realized in our approach. When dealing with a market environment, however, we won't get out of including a similar mechanism. An OTF provider will most likely receive similar requests at the same time, leading to parallel learning processes that have to be appropriately synchronized. Furthermore, different OTF provider may want to cooperate and share their individually learned knowledge.

The work of Yu et al. [37] places special emphasis on the advantages of Q-Learning (model-free RL) when composing services in a distributed and dynamic environment. Their work confirms our design decision to select TD learning for our market scenario.

Another promising approach towards adaptivity is the dynamic reconfiguration of composed services during runtime, as, e.g., proposed in [38-40]. In our current OTF Computing context, we are separating composition and execution phase, since both processes are embedded in a market environment with strictly regulated interaction processes between users, OTF providers, and service providers. However, in our opinion, dynamic reconfiguration is essential in order to realize our vision of OTF Computing. Experience from consecutive execution processes with pre-defined alternatives or alternatives identified by invoking a composition process from within the execution process has to be aggregated in our recommendation system, e.g., by assembling Q-values from independent Markov models.

7 Conclusion and outlook

In this paper, we presented a service composition approach that integrates planning and learning for coping with functional discrepancy; a challenge that inevitably emerge when dealing with markets of composed services for users. An AI-based composition process represents a symbolic approach that sequentially generates a service-based software solution based on formal specifications.

To narrow the gap between the functionality desired by a user and the actual functionality of the composed solution, a learning recommendation system supports the composition algorithm in decision-making problems that cannot be solved on the symbolic level alone. The recommendation system adapts its recommendation strategy over time based on user ratings from previous composition processes. The entire recommendation process is modelled as MDP. Techniques from RL are then applied to adjust the decision-making processes.

Throughout the entire paper, image processing served as application domain. A running example was used to motivate the problem and illustrate major processes. The running example was also used for conducting experiments and investigate different composition strategies. Preliminary results demonstrate the benefit of combining symbolic approaches and machine learning.

Before being of practical usage, however, several loose ends have to be tied up and open challenges have to be solved; conceptually and technically. For example, until now, in order to concentrate on the main integration of planning and learning, we always assumed a static context; that is, we assumed that identical user requests with identical concrete execution data and identical user preferences are received in a sequential manner.

In reality, our approach has to be able to deal with different scenarios (combinations of imprecise request specifications, different execution data, and varying user preferences) – simultaneously. For instance, identical formal user requests might come along with different execution data or different user preferences. In general, independent as well as interrelated learning processes (and Markov models) have to be coordinated to encounter this so called concept drift.

Furthermore, a mechanism for minimizing the state space explosion problem on the recommendation module's side has to be developed. Consider the composition state space of our running example. Each possible combination produces a new distinct state within the recommendation module, leading to an infinite amount of states in the worst case. A state abstraction approach for representing a set of concrete states by means of a single abstract state is one possible solution to overcome this issue. We are currently working on this issue and will present a possible solution in the near future.

Future work also comprises more extensive experiments (with a significantly bigger and dynamic service pool) in order to investigate the scalability of our approach in combination with a state abstraction mechanism. In this context, we want to enable our composition approach to not only compose sequences of services, but more complex data and control flows. The recommendation system has to be able to represent more complex composition structures in order to consider them in its Markov model. One possible solution is to substitute regular grammars by graph grammars. Last but not least, non-functional properties such as costs, performance values, reputation, and reliability have to be considered during the composition process in order to drive our vision of On-The-Fly Computing forward.

Regarding our future work, we are confident to say, that the image processing application domain provides all necessary ingredients for testing and evaluating developed concepts in realistic scenarios.

Competing interests
The authors declare that they have no competing interests.

Authors' contributions
AJ designed the recommendation system, implemented the proposed approach in terms of a prototype, conceived and carried out the evaluation in the image processing domain, and wrote the manuscript. FM contributed the conceptual design of the proposed approach from the symbolic perspective. Both authors read and approved the final manuscript.

Acknowledgments
This work was partially supported by the German Research Foundation (DFG) within the Collaborative Research Centre "On-The-Fly Computing" (SFB 901).

Author details
[1] Cooperative Computing & Communication Laboratory (C-LAB), University of Paderborn, Fuerstenallee 11, 33102 Paderborn, Germany. [2] Department of Computer Science, University of Paderborn, Warburger Str. 100, 33098 Paderborn, Germany.

References

1. Happe M, Meyer auf der Heide F, Kling P, Platzner M, Plessl C (2013) On-The-Fly Computing: A novel paradigm for individualized IT services. In: IEEE 16th International Symposium on Object/Component/Service-Oriented Real-Time Distributed Computing (ISORC). IEEE Computer Society, Washington, DC, USA. pp 1–10. doi:10.1109/ISORC.2013.6913232
2. (2014) Collaborative Research Center 901 - On-The-Fly Computing. http://sfb901.uni-paderborn.de Accessed 2015-03-08
3. Instagram (2014). http://www.instagram.com Accessed 2015-03-08
4. Jungmann A, Mohr F, Kleinjohann B (2014) Combining Automatic Service Composition with Adaptive Service Recommendation for Dynamic Markets of Services. In: IEEE World Congress on Services (SERVICES). IEEE Computer Society, Washington, DC, USA. pp 346–353. doi:10.1109/SERVICES.2014.68
5. Berardi D, Calvanese D, De Giacomo G, Lenzerini M, Mecella M (2003) Automatic composition of e-services that export their behavior. In: Service-Oriented Computing (ICSOC).Lecture Notes in Computer Science. Springer Berlin Heidelberg, Heidelberg, Germany. pp 43–58. doi:10.1007/978-3-540-24593-3_4
6. Sirin E, Parsia B, Wu D, Hendler J, Nau D (2004) HTN planning for web service composition using SHOP2. Web Semantics: Sci Services Agents World Wide Web 1(4):377–396. doi:10.1016/j.websem.2004.06.005
7. Oh S-C, On B-W, Larson EJ, Lee D (2005) Bf*: Web services discovery and composition as graph search problem. In: Proceedings of the IEEE International Conference on e-Technology, e-Commerce and e-Service (EEE). IEEE Computer Society, Washington, DC, USA. pp 784–786. doi:10.1109/EEE.2005.41
8. Liang QA, Su SYW (2005) And/or graph and search algorithm for discovering composite web services. Int J Web Services Res 2(4):46–64
9. Brogi A, Corfini S (2007) Behaviour-aware discovery of web service compositions. Int J Web Services Res 4(3):1–25. doi:10.4018/jwsr.2007070101
10. Oh S-C, Lee D, Kumara SRT (2007) Web service planner (wspr): An effective and scalable web service composition algorithm. Int J Web Services Res 4(1):1–23. doi:10.4018/jwsr.2007010101
11. Oh S-C, Lee D, Kumara SRT (2008) Effective web service composition in diverse and large-scale service networks. Services Comput, IEEE Trans 1(1):15–32. doi:10.1109/TSC.2008.1
12. Sirbu A, Hoffmann J (2008) Towards scalable web service composition with partial matches. In: Proceedings of the IEEE International Conference on Web Services (ICWS). IEEE Computer Society, Washington, DC, USA. pp 29–36. doi:10.1109/ICWS.2008.69
13. Bartalos P, Bieliková M (2010) Qos aware semantic web service composition approach considering pre/postconditions. In: Proceedings of the IEEE International Conference on Web Services (ICWS). IEEE Computer Society, Washington, DC, USA. pp 345–352. doi:10.1109/ICWS.2010.90
14. Bertoli P, Pistore M, Traverso P (2010) Automated composition of web services via planning in asynchronous domains. Artif Intelligence 174(3-4):316–361. doi:10.1016/j.artint.2009.12.002
15. Wang P, Ding Z, Jiang C, Zhou M (2014) Constraint-aware approach to web service composition. IEEE Trans Syst Man Cybernetics: Syst 44(6):770–784. doi:10.1109/TSMC.2013.2280559
16. Qu L, Wang Y, Orgun MA (2013) Cloud service selection based on the aggregation of user feedback and quantitative performance assessment. In: Proceedings of the IEEE International Conference on Services Computing (SCC). IEEE Computer Society, Washington, DC, USA. pp 152–159. doi:10.1109/SCC.2013.92
17. Erl T (2005) Service-Oriented Architecture: Concepts, Technology, and Design. Prentice Hall, Upper Saddle River, NJ, USA
18. (2014) OpenCV - Open Source Computer Vision. http://opencv.org/ Accessed 2015-03-08
19. Ghallab M, Nau D, Traverso P (2004) Automated Planning: Theory & Practice. Morgan Kaufmann, San Francisco, CA, USA
20. Russell S, Norvig P (2009) Artificial Intelligence: A Modern Approach. 3rd edn.. Prentice Hall, Upper Saddle River, NJ, USA
21. Chan N, Gaaloul W, Tata S (2012) A recommender system based on historical usage data for web service discovery. Service Oriented Comput Appl 6(1):51–63. doi:10.1007/s11761-011-0099-2

22. Sutton RS, Barto AG (1998) Reinforcement Learning: An Introduction. MIT Press, Cambridge, Massachusetts
23. Puterman ML (2005) Markov Decision Processes: Discrete Stochastic Dynamic Programming. Wiley-Interscience, Hoboken, NJ, USA
24. Thiébaux S, Gretton C, Slaney JK, Price D, Kabanza F (2006) Decision-theoretic planning with non-markovian rewards. J Artif Intelligence Res (JAIR) 25:17–74. doi:10.1613/jair.1676
25. Jungmann A, Kleinjohann B (2013) Learning recommendation system for automated service composition. In: Proceedings of the IEEE International Conference on Services Computing (SCC). IEEE Computer Society, Washington, DC, USA. pp 97–104. doi:10.1109/SCC.2013.66
26. Jungmann A, Kleinjohann B, Kleinjohann L (2013) Learning Service Recommendations. Int J Bus Process Integration Manage 6(4):284–297. doi:10.1504/IJBPIM.2013.059135
27. Platenius M-C, Becker S, Schaefer W (2014) Integrating service matchers into a service market architecture. In: Software Architecture. Springer International Publishing, Cham, Switzerland. pp 210–217. doi:10.1007/978-3-319-09970-5_19
28. Watkins CJCH, Dayan P (1992) Q-learning. Machine Learning 8(3-4):279–292
29. Rummery GA, Niranjan M (1994) On-line Q-learning using connectionist systems. Technical report, Cambridge University, Engineering Department
30. Sutton RS (1996) Generalization in reinforcement learning : Successful examples using sparse coarse coding. Proc 1995 Conference Adv Neural Inf Process Syst 8:1038–1044
31. Wang H, Zhou X, Zhou X, Liu W, Li W, Bouguettaya A (2010) Adaptive service composition based on reinforcement learning. In: Service-Oriented Computing. Springer Berlin Heidelberg, Heidelberg, Germany. pp 92–107. doi:10.1007/978-3-642-17358-5_7
32. Todica V, Vaida M-F, Cremene M (2012) Using machine learning in web services composition. In: Proceedings of the Fourth International Conference on Advanced Service Computing. IARIA XPS Press, Wilmington, DE, USA. pp 122–126
33. Kun C, Xu J, Reiff-Marganiec S (2009) Markov-HTN planning approach to enhance flexibility of automatic web service composition. In: Proceedings of the IEEE International Conference on Web Services (ICWS). IEEE Computer Society, Washington, DC, USA. pp 9–16. doi:10.1109/ICWS.2009.43
34. Moustafa A, Zhang M (2013) Multi-objective service composition using reinforcement learning. In: Service-Oriented Computing, Lecture Notes in Computer Science. Springer Berlin Heidelberg, Heidelberg, Germany Vol. 8274. pp 298–312. doi:10.1007/978-3-642-45005-1_21
35. Dehousse S, Faulkner S, Herssens C, Jureta IJ, Saerens M (2009) Learning optimal web service selections in dynamic environments when many quality-of-service criteria matter. In: Machine Learning. InTech Europe, Rijeka, Croatia. pp 207–230. doi:10.5772/6555
36. Wang H, Wang X, Zhou X (2012) A multi-agent reinforcement learning model for service composition. In: Proceedings of the IEEE International Conference on Services Computing (SCC). IEEE Computer Society, Washington, DC, USA. pp 681–682. doi:10.1109/SCC.2012.58
37. Yu L, Zhili W, Lingli M, Jiang W, Meng L, Xue-song Q (2013) Adaptive web services composition using q-learning in cloud. In: Proceedings of the IEEE World Congress on Services (SERVICES). IEEE Computer Society, Washington, DC, USA. pp 393–396. doi:10.1109/SERVICES.2013.33
38. Spanoudakis G, Zisman A, Kozlenkov A (2005) A service discovery framework for service centric systems. In: Proceedings of the IEEE International Conference on Services Computing (SCC). IEEE Computer Society, Washington, DC, USA. pp 251–259. doi:10.1109/SCC.2005.17
39. Zisman A, Spanoudakis G, Dooley J (2008) A framework for dynamic service discovery. In: Proceedings of the 23rd IEEE/ACM International Conference on Automated Software Engineering (ASE). IEEE Computer Society, Washington, DC, USA. pp 158–167. doi:10.1109/ASE.2008.26
40. Bucchiarone A, Marconi A, Mezzina C, Pistore M, Raik H (2013) On-the-fly adaptation of dynamic service-based systems: Incrementality, reduction and reuse. In: Service-Oriented Computing, Lecture Notes in Computer Science. Springer Berlin Heidelberg, Heidelberg, Germany Vol. 8274. pp 146–161. doi:10.1007/978-3-642-45005-1_11

11

Applying *p*-cycle protection for a reliable IPTV service in IP-over-DWDM networks

Ahmed Frikha[*], Bernard Cousin and Samer Lahoud

Abstract

Today, television over Internet protocol (IPTV) has become very popular and service providers must deal with the rapid growth in the number of IPTV customers. Service providers must ensure the reliability of IPTV to satisfy customers' needs, as a network failure could disrupt an IPTV transmission.

Survivable multicast routing is important for providing a reliable IPTV service. Generally, most carriers route multicast traffic using the protocol-independent multicast source-specific mode (PIM-SSM) based on the routing information provided by the interior gateway protocol (IGP). Restoration using the IGP reconfiguration is slow and typically takes from 10 to 60 seconds. To ensure a fast restoration, we consider node and link failure recovery in the Dense Wavelength Division Multiplexing (DWDM) optical layer. The backup path is provided in this layer. Thus, the multicast tree does not change at the IP layer (the logical links do not change) and the restoration time is faster (typically of the order of 50 to 80 ms).

In this paper, we apply *p*-cycles in IP-over-DWDM networks to provide a robust IPTV service. In addition, we propose a novel concept for node protection using *p*-cycles to achieve more efficient resource utilization. We also propose a new algorithm, the node and link protecting candidate *p*-cycle based algorithm (NPCC). This algorithm integrates our new concept for node protection. Extensive simulations show that it outperforms the existing approaches in terms of blocking probability, resource utilization efficiency and computation time rapidity.

Keywords: IPTV service; multicast routing; IP-over-DWDM networks; Reliability; *p*-cycles; node and link protection

1 Introduction

Nowadays, many telecoms companies offer the television over IP (IPTV) service and distribute television channels using backbone networks. An IPTV service requires stringent quality of service constraints (for example, for packet loss, jitter and end-to-end delay) to satisfy customers' needs. Service providers must also ensure the reliability of the IPTV service. A simple link or router failure could disrupt the television content distribution for several seconds, if no protection mechanism is implemented.

IPTV contents could be carried using the IP multicast to save bandwidth capacity. In fact, multicasting enables a single packet to be sent to multiple destinations at once. Although many multicast routing algorithms have been proposed for IPTV services, most of the carriers today implement the protocol-independent multicast source-specific mode (PIM-SSM) [1]. For many

*Correspondence: ahmed.frikha@ahmedfrikha.com
IRISA, University of Rennes 1, Campus universitaire Beaulieu, 35042 Rennes, France

reasons, this protocol is efficient for internet broadcast-style applications such as IPTV. Obviously, PIM-SSM is simple to implement for network operators thanks to the source-specific mode (SSM) [1], which makes this protocol ideal for IPTV. SSM does not require the network to maintain knowledge about which sources are actively sending multicast traffic, unlike the internet standard multicast (ISM) protocol. This advantage makes PIM-SSM more scalable than ISM.

To ensure IPTV reliability, survivable multicast routing must be guaranteed. Moreover, service providers must ensure a fast restoration time for link and router failure recovery. The PIM-SSM protocol uses the routing information provided by the interior gateway protocol (IGP) to compute a multicast tree. Thus, restoration at the IP layer using IGP reconfiguration requires IGP to be aware of the failure, then PIM-SSM can use the new IGP shortest paths to rebuild a new multicast tree using the prune-and-join process. This operation is slow, and typically takes from 10 to 60 seconds [2]. To avoid rebuilding the multicast tree and to ensure a fast restoration, we consider node and link failure recovery at the DWDM layer. The backup path is provided at this layer. This makes restoration time faster as the multicast tree does not change at the IP layer (the logical links do not change).

The p-cycle protection approach was introduced by WD Grover [3] for link failure recovery at the DWDM layer. A p-cycle is cycle-oriented spare capacity preconfigured at the DWDM layer. In Figure 1 we show an example of a p-cycle in an optical network. Note that a p-cycle does not traverse a node or a link more than once. Moreover, a p-cycle is oriented.

The advantage of using p-cycles for protection can be summarized in two main points. First, p-cycles ensure a fast restoration time (typically of the order of 50 to 80 ms) as the protection is done at the DWDM layer and p-cycles are preconfigured [4]. Second, the p-cycle protection approach can achieve an efficient use of the network capacity compared to other protection approaches, such as the one-plus-one (1 + 1) and the one-by-one (1:1) restoration methods. In fact, a p-cycle can protect both on-cycle links and straddling links. An on-cycle link belongs to the p-cycle, and is directed opposite to the p-cycle. In Figure 2, we show an example of an on-cycle link protected using a p-cycle. The on-cycle link is represented using a red line and the protection segment provided by the p-cycle is represented using a dashed green line. In this figure, we see that the p-cycle and the failed link are in opposite directions.

A straddling link does not belong to a p-cycle. However, its extremity nodes are traversed by the p-cycle. The p-cycle provides two protection segments: one protection segment for each directed-link. In Figure 3, we show an example of a straddling link protected using a p-cycle. In this figure, we show the protection segment that protects the directed-link used by the light tree. The protection segment in the opposite direction to the link is not shown

in this figure. This characteristic of p-cycles allows the required backup bandwidth capacity to be reduced.

The p-cycle technique was extended to support node protection in the DWDM layer using the node encircling p-cycle concept (NEPC) [5]. According to this concept, a protecting p-cycle of a given node must link all neighboring nodes of the failed node. This constraint is too strict. The method could discard some nodes that can be protected by the p-cycle but which do not satisfy the constraint. This will affect the efficiency of the p-cycles in terms of capacity saving.

In this paper, we consider link and node failure recovery at the DWDM layer using p-cycles. We extend the node protection concept of the p-cycle approach to achieve more efficient resource utilization. Then, we propose a novel algorithm, the node and link protecting candidate p-cycle based algorithm (NPCC). The NPCC algorithm integrates our proposed concept for node protection. This algorithm ensures node and link failure recovery based on a set of candidate p-cycles to overcome the high computation time problem.

The rest of this paper is organized as follows. In Section 2, we present the IPTV architecture and discuss the restoration mechanisms to ensure a reliable IPTV service. In Section 3, we extend the p-cycle protection concept for protecting nodes in light trees. In Section 4, we present our novel algorithm for combined node and link failure recovery using the novel node protection concept. Extensive simulations and numerical results are presented in Section 5. The conclusions are given in Section 6.

2 IPTV architecture and restoration mechanisms

In this section, we present the main components of the IPTV architecture and we give an example. Then, we discuss the restoration mechanisms, and we highlight the advantages of applying the p-cycle protection approach for IPTV.

2.1 IPTV architecture
The main components of an IPTV architecture are [2-6]:

- A super headend (SHE): The SHE is located in the core network. Also called the IPTV backbone, it collects television content from television networks, such as satellites and off-air distributions. After video processing, encoding and management, the SHE distributes the television content using IP routers to multiple video hub offices (VHOs).
- A video hub office (VHO): A VHO receives IPTV content transmitted by the SHE through the IPTV backbone routers. Then, it combines this content with the local television and the video on demand (VoD) content. The SHE routers, the VHO routers and the links that connect them form the IPTV

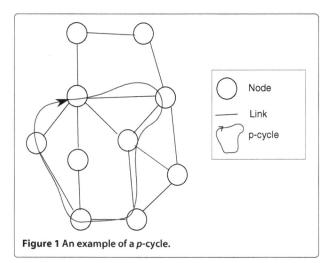

Figure 1 An example of a p-cycle.

Node

Link

p-cycle

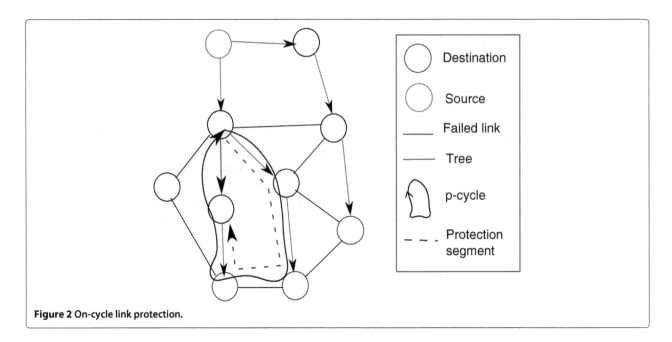

Figure 2 On-cycle link protection.

backbone. Each VHO in turn serves a metro area by transmitting the IPTV content to multiple video serving offices (VSOs).

- A video serving office (VSO): A VSO contains the aggregation routers that aggregate local loop traffic from subscriber homes, i.e., local digital subscriber line access multiplexers (DSLAMs).

A simplified example of an IPTV architecture is illustrated in Figure 4. In this example, the SHE gathers the national channel content from off-air and the international channel content from satellites. Then, it sends this content to multiple video hub offices (VHOs) using IP multicast and through the underlying DWDM layer. IP multicast is very important for saving network bandwidth as it allows a packet to traverse a link once to reach multiple destinations. The example does not show the traversed IP routers that connect the SHE to each VHO. The figure shows a house with a television and a set-top box, which is connected via a residential gateway to a DSLAM, connected in turn to a VSO.

PIM-SSM is largely used for IPTV video distribution with an IPTV backbone. A multicast tree is computed using this protocol based on the routing information

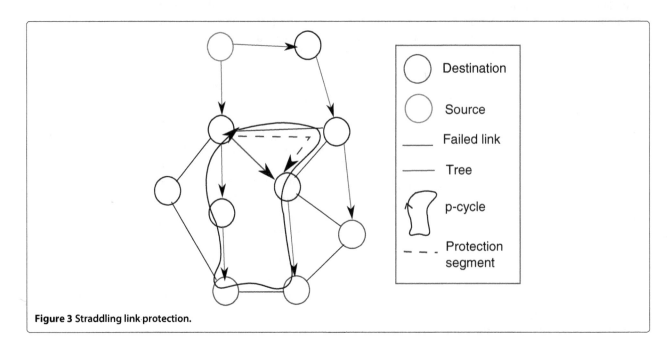

Figure 3 Straddling link protection.

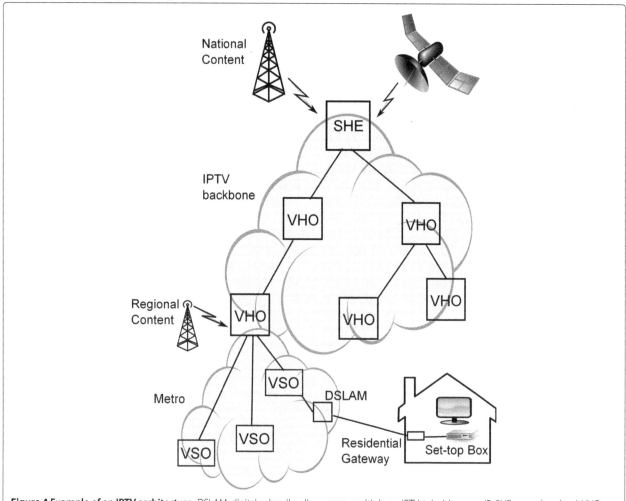

Figure 4 Example of an IPTV architecture. DSLAM, digital subscriber line access multiplexer; IPTV, television over IP; SHE, super headend; VHO, video hub office; VSO, video serving office.

provided by the IGP. The multicast tree is used to deliver IPTV content from the SHE to each VHO. Each television channel is assigned to a unique multicast group.

An IPTV service requires a high bandwidth and stringent quality of service constraints. In particular, IPTV is very sensitive to packet loss, as one lost packet could disrupt video quality. Delay and the jitter are also critical for the quality of an IPTV service. These three quality of service constraints rely on network dependability. A link or node failure could disrupt the IPTV service, if there is no restoration mechanism for the multicast tree.

2.2 Restoration mechanisms

With IGP reconfiguration, after a link or node failure, PIM-SSM must rebuild the multicast tree. But before that, IGP must be aware of the failure and compute the new shortest paths at the level of each router. PIM-SSM will use these new shortest paths to rebuild the multicast tree using the prune-and-join process. This approach is not suitable for a real-time IPTV service as the restoration process takes too much time, typically between 10 and 60 seconds [2]. With multi-protocol label switching (MPLS) fast reroute protection, the restoration time can be reduced to between 50 ms and 100 ms [2]. Backup label-switched paths (LSPs) are pre-established, and stored in the router forwarding tables and this makes fast rerouting possible at the IP MPLS layer.

Other restoration mechanisms have been used in the DWDM layer and can achieve lower restoration times. One-plus-one (1 + 1) and one-by-one (1:1) restoration can be implemented in the DWDM layer. The restoration time for these approaches is less than 20 ms [2]. However, they are not efficient in terms of bandwidth saving, as backup paths cannot be shared. In these approaches, a backup path is dedicated for one and only one working path. The *p*-cycle protection approach, described in the previous section, ensures node and link failure recovery while maintaining a fast restoration time (typically of the order of 50 to 80 ms) [4]. Moreover, this approach achieves an efficient use of the network capacity compared to the other protection approaches.

These restoration mechanisms are proposed for unicast traffic. Some other restoration mechanisms focus on protecting multicast trees against network failures. In 2009, F Zhang and WD Zhong proposed the efficiency-score based heuristic algorithm of node and link protecting p-cycle (ESHN) [7]. Although the ESHN algorithm has a lower blocking probability than the OPP-SDP algorithm [8] and the ESHT algorithm [9] in dynamic multicast traffic, ESHN does not efficiently use the protection capacity provided by a p-cycle, especially when protecting nodes. The ESHN algorithm does not take into consideration all nodes that a p-cycle can protect when selecting a protecting p-cycle. This is due to the two hard constraints imposed by the method used by ESHN for protecting nodes. The first constraint is that a node protecting a p-cycle has to link all one-level downstream nodes of the failed node. The second constraint is that the p-cycle must contain one of the upstream nodes of the failed node in the light tree. Of course these reduce the computation time for the algorithm as they limit the search space for the p-cycles. However, they prevent the ESHN algorithm from achieving the best resource utilization. Furthermore, when the traffic load is high, the computation time for the ESHN algorithm remains high and does not satisfy the IPTV service requirements.

In this work, we focus on the design of a reliable IPTV service. We use link and node failure recovery at the DWDM layer to give a short restoration time. We use p-cycles to ensure efficient use of network capacity. We also extend the node protection of the p-cycle approach to achieve more efficient resource utilization. In Section 3, we provide a detailed study of node protection using p-cycles and we present our proposed concept for protecting nodes in the light tree.

3   Node protection using p-cycles

3.1   Existing approaches for node protection using p-cycles

In this section, we present some existing well-known concepts for node protection using p-cycles. NEPC [5] uses p-cycles for node protection. Figure 5 illustrates an example of node protection using this concept. The p-cycle must traverse all neighboring nodes of the failed node to protect it. The drawback of this concept is that in some cases finding such a p-cycle is not possible. Moreover, some p-cycles that do not meet this constraint could protect the failed node while reserving less spare capacity. The constraint imposed by this concept is too strict and prevents the protection algorithm from achieving good resource utilization.

Some systems that ensure link and node failure recovery in a multicast session simplify the node protection to reduce the computation time. For example, in the ESHN algorithm, the p-cycle has to link: (1) all one-level downstream nodes of the failed node and (2) one of the upstream nodes in the light tree. Figure 6 illustrates a simple example for protecting a node using the ESHN algorithm. In this example, the failed node (or protected node) is represented by a grey circle, the source node by a green circle, the destination nodes by red circles and the multicast tree by a blue line. The p-cycle links the two one-level downstream nodes of the failed node (nodes belonging to the tree) and the source node (the upstream node of the failed node). Thus, the p-cycle satisfies the constraints and can protect the failed node. On node failure, the source node detects the failure and reroutes the multicast traffic through the protection segment (dashed green line). Although this approach relaxes the constraint imposed by NEPC, the protection capacity provided by the p-cycles is still not used efficiently as some p-cycles could protect a node without meeting the first or second constraint of this approach.

3.2   The proposed concept for node protection using p-cycles

In this section, we present our novel concept for protecting nodes in multicast traffic. Before presenting our concept, we will introduce some notation. Let T be a multicast light tree to be protected, s be the source node in T, N_f be an intermediate node in T, and $D = \{d_1, d_2, .., d_i\}$ be the set of destinations in T that are affected when a failure occurs on the node N_f.

Theorem 1. *A p-cycle C_j in the network can protect the node N_f if and only if there exists a protection segment $[N_a, N_e] \in C_j$ such that:*

1. *The node $N_a \in T$, the node $N_e \in T$ and $N_f \notin [s, N_a]$ where $[s, N_a]$ is the segment in T linking the source s to the node N_a.*
2. *$\forall d_k \in D, \exists$ a node $N_k \in [N_a, N_e]$ and $N_k \in]N_f, d_k]$, where $]N_f, d_k]$ is the segment in T linking N_f to d_k.*
3. *$N_f \notin [N_a, N_e]$.*

Proof Once a failure occurs on the node N_f, the multicast traffic is rerouted through the p-cycle C_j to ensure the survivability of the multicast session. The p-cycle must provide a protection segment to deliver the multicast content to all destinations that are affected by the failure of N_f. This segment is denoted by $[N_a, N_e]$.

First, we justify why constraint (1) is required. The extremities N_a and N_e of this segment must be in T. In fact, the node N_a is responsible for injecting the multicast traffic into the protection segment $[N_a, N_e]$ when N_f fails.

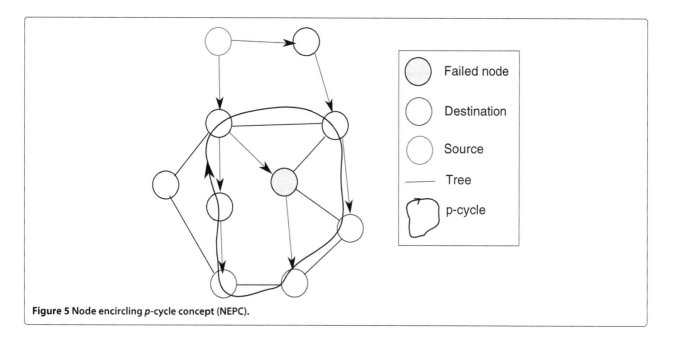

Figure 5 Node encircling *p*-cycle concept (NEPC).

In addition, N_a must not be affected by the failure of N_f, i.e., N_a must continue to receive the multicast traffic even if a failure occurs on node N_f ($N_f \notin [s, N_a]$). The node N_a must split the incoming light signal into two outgoing signals. The first is injected into the protection segment and the second is forwarded to the downstream node of N_a in the light tree T. The node N_e is the last intersection node between T and C_j.

Second, we prove the necessity of constraint (2). To ensure failure recovery, we must make sure that all destinations affected by the failure of N_f continue to receive the multicast traffic through the protection segment $[N_a, N_e]$.

Two scenarios are possible for delivering the multicast traffic to an affected destination d_k. In the first, the segment $[N_a, N_e]$ carries the multicast traffic directly to d_k, i.e., the protection segment traverses the node d_k. In the second scenario, the segment $[N_a, N_e]$ carries the traffic to the destination through an intermediate node N_k. The node N_k must be an upstream node of d_k and a downstream node of N_f in the light tree. This constraint ensures that the failed node N_f does not belong to the segment $[N_k, d_k]$ of the light tree. The node N_k splits the incoming signal into two signals. The first is sent to the next node in the protection segment to ensure that the remaining

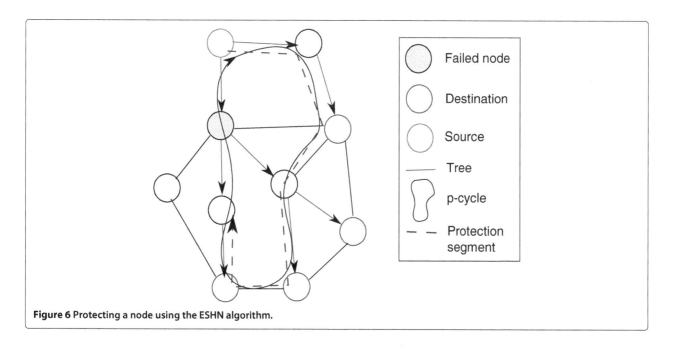

Figure 6 Protecting a node using the ESHN algorithm.

affected destinations will receive the multicast content. The second is forwarded to the downstream node of N_k in the light tree to reach d_k.

Finally, we prove that constraint (3) is necessary. We must make sure that the protection segment is not affected by the failure of N_f. Therefore, the protection segment $[N_a, N_e]$ should not traverse the node N_f.

3.3   Example

In Figure 7, we provide an example of a p-cycle that can protect the node N_f based on our concept. The set of destinations affected by the failure of N_f is $D = \{d_1, d_2, N_e\}$. This p-cycle has two original characteristics that other node protection concepts [5-7] do not have. First, it can traverse the protected node. Second, it does not have to traverse all affected destinations or neighboring nodes of the protected node. The p-cycle provides a protection segment represented with a dashed green line in the figure. The node N_a activates the p-cycle by injecting the multicast traffic into the protection segment $[N_a, N_e]$. This segment carries the traffic to d_2 through the intermediate node N_2, and to d_1 and N_e directly as it traverses them.

4   The proposed protection algorithm

In this section, we present our proposed algorithm NPCC for protecting nodes and links in the DWDM layer to give a reliable IPTV service. Our algorithm deploys the aforementioned concept for node protection using p-cycles.

4.1   Selection of candidate p-cycles

First, the NPCC algorithm enumerates a set of candidate p-cycles in an offline phase, i.e., before any requests have

been received. Using these candidate p-cycles will considerably reduce the computation time for the algorithm. In fact, considering the total p-cycle set when selecting a new p-cycle to be established, is a very slow task, especially when the number of p-cycles in the network is high. Therefore, we select a set of candidate p-cycles to reduce the computation time for our algorithm.

We have defined a new score, the protection capacity (PC), for each p-cycle in the network. We use this score to select a candidate p-cycle set. This score is computed in advance for each unity p-cycle before routing requests. A unity p-cycle is a p-cycle in the network that reserves only one bandwidth unity (e.g., one wavelength) on each traversed link. The PC score of a unity p-cycle C_j, specified by equation (1), is defined as the ratio of the largest amount of link capacity on the network LC_j that C_j can protect over the spare capacity required for setting up C_j. $|C_j|$ is given by the number of links traversed by C_j.

$$PC(C_j) = \frac{LC_j}{|C_j|} \tag{1}$$

A p-cycle with a high PC is useful as it maximizes the amount of protected capacity while reserving less spare capacity. The l p-cycles with highest PC are selected as the candidate p-cycle set, where l is a parameter for the algorithm. The goal in selecting this set is to maximize the capacity that can be protected on the network.

4.2   Flow chart for the NPCC algorithm

Figure 8 is a flow chart for the NPCC algorithm. We will introduce some notation before describing how this

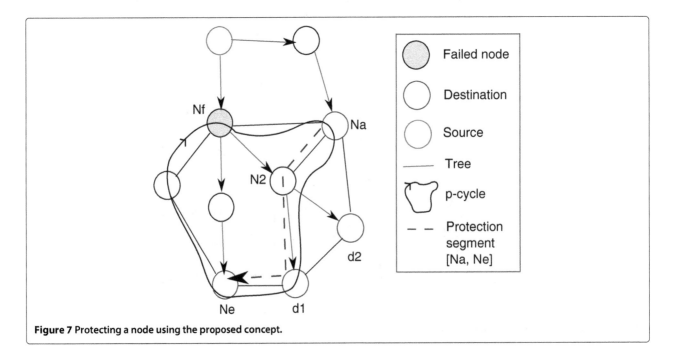

Figure 7 Protecting a node using the proposed concept.

algorithm works. Let us consider a multicast request and its corresponding light tree T. The light tree is constructed using the PIM-SSM [1] multicast routing protocol. Let L denote the set of links in T and N denote an unprotected intermediate node in T. The links in T that can be protected by the existing p-cycles in the network are removed from L and the nodes in T that are protected by the existing p-cycles are removed from N. Note that the existing p-cycles were previously established to protect other light trees in the network. If $L \neq \phi$ or $N \neq \phi$, the algorithm computes new p-cycles to protect the remaining unprotected links in L as well as the remaining unprotected nodes in N.

To select a new protecting p-cycle, the algorithm uses the unity p-cycle procedure, which is based on the efficiency score (ES). In this procedure, we deploy the same ES used in the ESHN algorithm to measure the efficiency of each p-cycle in the candidate p-cycle set. This score adapts the efficiency-ratio-based unity p-cycle heuristic algorithm (ERH) [10] to deal with node and link failures in multicast traffic. This score considers the highest number

of unprotected nodes as well as the highest number of unprotected links in the multicast tree that a unity p-cycle can protect. Let C_j be a unity p-cycle in the network. The ES of C_j is given by equation (2), where $W_{j,L}$ is the highest number of unprotected links in L that C_j can protect, $W_{j,N}$ is the highest number of unprotected nodes in N that C_j can protect, and $|C_j|$ is the spare capacity required for setting up a unity p-cycle C_j. $|C_j|$ equals the number of links traversed by C_j.

$$ES(C_j) = \frac{W_{j,L} + W_{j,N}}{|C_j|} \qquad (2)$$

The ES-based unity p-cycle procedure calculates the ES of each unity p-cycle in the candidate p-cycle set and selects the p-cycle with maximum ES. The set of links protected by the selected unity p-cycle is removed from L and the set of protected nodes is removed from N. This process is iterated until all the links and all the nodes of T are protected, i.e. $L = \phi$ and $N = \phi$. The selected unity p-cycles are configured and the corresponding wavelengths are reserved. Note that the reserved p-cycles may serve to protect subsequent multicast requests. This is why after routing a multicast tree, we compute the set of links in L and the set of nodes in N that can be protected by the existing p-cycles in the network. Finally, the reserved capacity of an existing p-cycle in the network is released when the p-cycle does not protect any working link and nodes in the network.

5 Performance evaluation

In this section, we present the evaluation of our algorithm NPCC, which is proposed for providing a reliable IPTV service. Our method guarantees the recovery from link and node failure at the DWDM layer with a fast restoration time. We compare our algorithm with the ESHN algorithm, which was reported to be the most efficient algorithm for dynamic multicast traffic protection in terms of resource utilization efficiency and blocking probability.

In our simulation, we assumed that request arrival follows a Poisson process with an average arrival rate λ, and the request holding time follows an exponential distribution with an average holding time μ. Hence, the offered traffic load for the network is given by $\lambda\mu$.

We ran simulations on the following well-known and frequently used European optical topologies developed within the COST-266 [11] and COST-239 [12] projects:

- The COST-266 core topology [11] contains 16 nodes and 23 links, with an average nodal degree of 2.88. The total number of p-cycles in this topology is 236 (118 p-cycles in each direction).

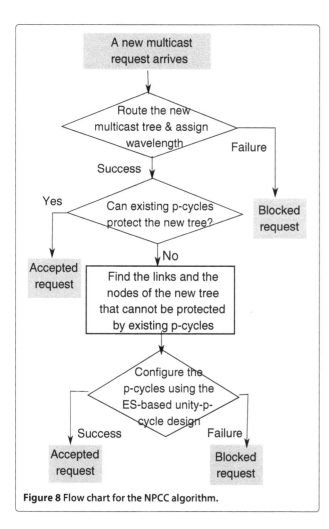

Figure 8 Flow chart for the NPCC algorithm.

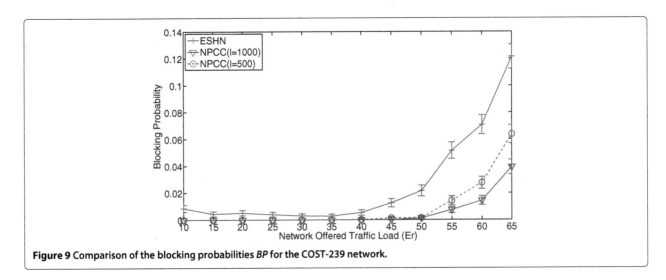

Figure 9 Comparison of the blocking probabilities *BP* for the COST-239 network.

- The COST-239 topology [12] contains 11 nodes and 26 links, with an average nodal degree of 4.727. The total number of p-cycles in this topology is 5,058 (2,029 p-cycles in each direction).

In our study, without loss of generality, we assumed that each link has two fibers. The two fibers transmit in opposite directions; 16 wavelengths are available on each fiber. The source and the destinations of each multicast session are randomly selected (uniform distribution law). We chose the number of destinations in each multicast request $D = 5$, which seems to be reasonable as the total number of nodes in the used topologies is less than 16. We compared the performance of the algorithms using the following performance criteria:

- The blocking probability (*BP*), which is the percentage of requests that cannot be routed or protected among the total number of requests.

- The resource utilization (*RU*), which is the percentage of reserved wavelengths in the network among the total number of wavelength links.

$$RU = \frac{W_R}{E \times W}$$

where W_R is the total number of wavelength links reserved in the network, E is the number of fibers in the network and W the number of wavelengths per fiber.

- The average computation time (*CT*), which is required for routing and protecting a traffic request.

Performance criteria *BP*, *RU* and *CT* were computed according to the traffic load. For each traffic load value, 5×10^5 requests were generated. This number of requests is enough to measure *BP*, *RU* and *CT* with a 95% confidence interval.

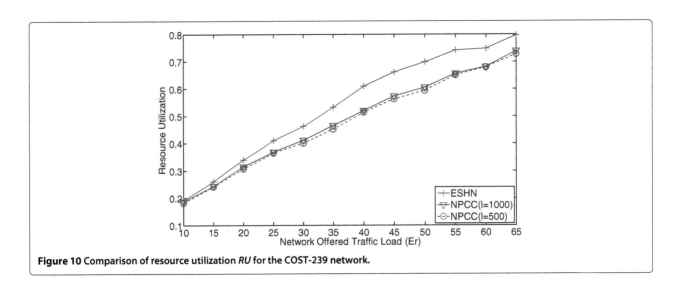

Figure 10 Comparison of resource utilization *RU* for the COST-239 network.

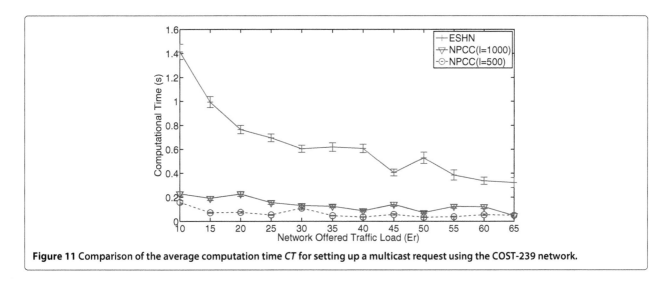

Figure 11 Comparison of the average computation time *CT* for setting up a multicast request using the COST-239 network.

First, we considered the COST-239 topology. The total number of *p*-cycles in this topology is 5,085. We ran the NPCC algorithm with two different values for the number of candidate *p*-cycles, $l = 1000$ and $l = 500$. The blocking probability measured for the COST-239 network is shown in Figure 9. For all the algorithms, the blocking probability increased when the traffic load was high. The NPCC algorithm, with both $l = 1000$ and $l = 500$, outperformed the ESHN algorithm having a lower blocking probability, especially when the traffic load was high. The NPCC algorithm with $l = 1000$ had the lowest blocking probability. When $l = 500$, the blocking probability of NPCC increased but remained lower than that of ESHN. This is because $l = 500$ is very low compared to the total number of *p*-cycles in the COST-239 network (5,058).

Figure 10 shows the resource utilization of the algorithms. When the traffic load increases, the wavelength percentage reserved per link is higher for each algorithm.

The wavelength percentages reserved by NPCC with $l = 1000$ and NPCC with $l = 500$ are very close. This percentage is very low compared with that of the ESHN algorithm, especially when the traffic load is high. For a traffic load equal to 65 erlang, almost 70% of the wavelengths on each link are reserved for the NPCC algorithm and 80% for the ESHN algorithm.

To assess the speed of our proposed algorithm, we looked at the average computation time *CT* for setting up a multicast request. Figure 11 shows the value of *CT* for each algorithm, measured for the COST-239 network according to the network traffic load. As shown in this figure, the NPCC algorithm with $l = 500$ has a shorter computation time than the NPCC algorithm with $l = 1000$ or the ESHN algorithm. This is due to the low number of *p*-cycles considered for the protection ($l = 500$). The average computation time *CT* of the NPCC algorithm with both $l = 500$ and $l = 1000$ is very low compared with that of the ESHN algorithm. The NPCC algorithm

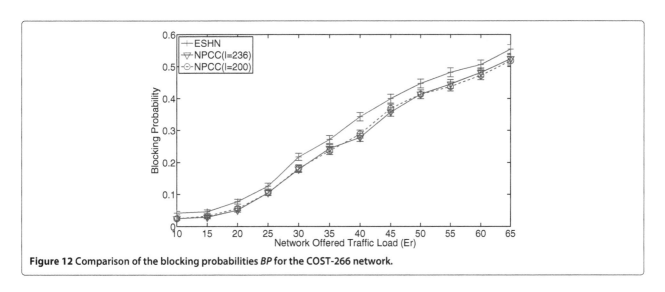

Figure 12 Comparison of the blocking probabilities *BP* for the COST-266 network.

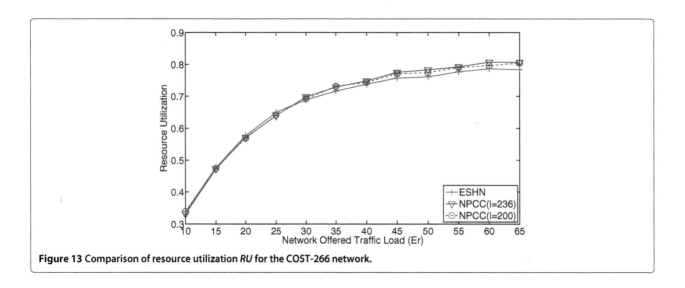

Figure 13 Comparison of resource utilization *RU* for the COST-266 network.

outperforms the ESHN algorithm in terms of blocking probability, resource utilization and computation time.

Now, we consider the COST-266 topology. The total number of *p*-cycles in this topology is 236. We ran the NPCC algorithm with two different values for the number of candidate *p*-cycles, $l = 236$ and $l = 200$. Figure 12 shows the blocking probabilities for the COST-266 network. The connectivity of this topology is very low (2.88). Therefore the blocking probabilities of the algorithms are very high compared with those for the COST-239 topology for the same network traffic load. For all the algorithms, the blocking probability increased rapidly as the traffic load increased. The ESHN algorithm has a higher blocking probability than the NPCC algorithm with $l = 236$ or the NPCC algorithm with $l = 200$. The blocking probability of NPCC with $l = 236$ and the blocking probability of NPCC with $l = 200$ were very close since the values of l were close.

Figure 13 shows the resource utilization of the algorithms for the COST-266 topology. The wavelength percentage reserved by the algorithms was almost the same. The percentage of reserved wavelengths per link increased as the traffic load increased. Note that the resource utilization of the ESHN algorithm was slightly lower than that of our algorithm NPCC when the traffic load was higher than 35 erlang. This is because the blocking probability was high. In other words, the probability of rejecting requests for ESHN increased and no resource had been reserved for the rejected requests. This reduced the resource utilization of ESHN.

6   Conclusion

In this work, we focused on the reliability of an IPTV service. First, we presented the main components of the IPTV architecture, then we discussed existing restoration mechanisms for the IP and DWDM layers. The

restoration methods proposed for DWDM are more efficient and more suitable for IPTV in terms of restoration time. We also highlighted the advantage of applying *p*-cycle protection for producing a reliable IPTV service.

Second, we extended the concept of node protection using *p*-cycles to deal with multicast traffic. Our novel concept allows the protection capacity provided by a *p*-cycle to be used efficiently. We proposed a novel algorithm, NPCC, which uses our concept for node protection. The NPCC algorithm ensures both link and node failure recovery in the DWDM layer for dynamic multicast traffic. This algorithm reduces the computation time for setting up a multicast traffic request by enumerating a set of candidate *p*-cycles based on the *PC* score.

Finally, we compared our proposed algorithm with the ESHN algorithm, which was reported to be the most efficient algorithm for node and link failure recovery for dynamic optical multicast traffic. Extensive simulations showed that the NPCC algorithm had a lower blocking probability and outperformed the ESHN algorithm in terms of resource utilization and computation time.

Abbreviations
BP: blocking probability; CT: computation time; DSLAM: digital subscriber line access multiplexer; DWMD: dense wavelength division multiplexing; ERH: efficiency-ratio-based unity *p*-cycle heuristic algorithm; *ES*: efficiency score; IGP: interior gateway protocol; IP: Internet protocol; IPTV: television over IP; ISM: internet standard multicast; LSP: label-switched path; MPLS: multi-protocol label switching; NEPC: node encircling *p*-cycle concept; NPCC: node and link protecting candidate *p*-cycle based algorithm; PIM-SSM: protocol-independent multicast source-specific mode; QoS: quality of service; RU: resource utilization; SHE: super headend; SSM: source-specific mode; VHO: video hub office; VoD: video on demand; VSO: video serving office.

Competing interests
The authors declare that they have no competing interests.

Authors' contributions
AF carried out the study of the IPTV service reliability, proposed the NPCC algorithm, performed the simulations and wrote the manuscript. BC and SL participated in discussing the idea of algorithm and the selection of

parameters values and reviewed the manuscript. All authors read and approved the final manuscript.

References

1. Bhattacharyya S (2003) An overview of source-specific multicast (SSM). IETF RFC 3569
2. Doverspike R, Ramakrishnan KK, Chase C (2010) Structural overview of ISP networks In: Kalmanek C, Misra S, Yang R (eds) Guide to reliable internet services and applications, Computer Communications and Networks. Springer, London, pp 19–93
3. Grover WD, Stamatelakis D (1998) Cycle-oriented distributed preconfiguration: ring-like speed with mesh-like capacity for self-planning network restoration. In: Proceedings of IEEE International Conference on Communications (IEEE ICC), vol 1, pp 537–543
4. Clouqueur M, Grover WD (2005) Availability analysis and enhanced availability design in p-cycle-based networks. Photonic Netw Commun 10(1): 55–71
5. Doucette J, Giese PA, Grover WD (2005) Combined node and span protection strategies with node-encircling p-cycles. In: Proceedings of the workshop on design of reliable communication networks (DRCN). Ischia (Naples), Italy, pp 213–221
6. Cisco Systems (2006) White paper on optimizing video transport in your IP triple play network. http://www.cisco.com.
7. Zhang F, Zhong WD (2009) Performance evaluation of optical multicast protection approaches for combined node and link failure recovery. J Lightw Technol 27(18): 4017–4025
8. Singhal NK, Sahasrabuddhe LH, Mukherjee B (2003) Provisioning of survivable multicast sessions against single link failures in optical WDM mesh networks. J Lightw Technol 21(11): 2587–2594
9. Zhang F, Zhong WD (2009) p-cycle based tree protection of optical multicast traffic for combined link and node failure recovery in WDM mesh networks. IEEE Commun Lett 13(1): 40–42
10. Zhang ZR, Zhong WD, Mukherjee B (2004) A heuristic method for design of survivable WDM networks with p-cycles. IEEE Commun Lett 8: 467–469
11. Maesschalck SD, Colle D, Lievens I, Pickavet M, Demeester P, Mauz C, Jaeger M, Inkret R, Derkacz BM (2003) Pan-European optical transport networks: an availability based comparison. Photonic Netw Commun 5(3): 203–226
12. Batchelor P, Daino B, Heinzmann P, Weinert C, Spath J, Van Caenegem B, Hjelme DR, Inkret R, Jager HA, Joindot M, Kuchar A, Le Coquil E, Leuthold P, De Marchis G, Matera F, Mikac B, Nolting HP, Tillerot F, Wauters N (1999) Ultra high capacity optical transmission networks. Final report of Action COST 239

12

PortView: identifying port roles based on port fuzzy macroscopic behavior

Guang Cheng[1*] and Yongning Tang[2]

Abstract

Port is a basic parameter in TCP/IP data communication. However, a port by its number has no clear association to the types of applications. Identifying such an association, which is referred to as a port role, provides important information to many network applications such as IDS and traffic shaper, as well as detecting new network services and security attacks. Traditional studies on port role identification are only based on port behavior shown on an individual host, other than jointly viewed macroscopic port behavior embodied by all relevant traffic flows among multiple hosts. Port role identification based on macroscopic behavior can reflect severs or clients to discover new services or attacks in the network. In this paper, we propose a novel port role identification approach called PortView, which is based on fuzzy macroscopic port behavior analysis. In our approach, we design a two-dimensional Macroscopic Port Classification Plane (MPCP) to classify port roles into six role zones using an EM fuzzy clustering algorithm. Comprehensive experiments using real Internet traces from the CERNET network validate that PortView can effectively and accurately identify port role based on its macroscopic port behavior.

Keywords: Port role identification, Macroscopic behavior

1. Introduction

Most current Internet applications are based on TCP or UDP. Traditionally, network applications use fixed port numbers assigned by IANA [1]. Accordingly, TCP and UDP port numbers are directly associated to the types of various network application, e.g. TCP/80 for HTTP etc. TCP and UDP ports identified with 16-bit numbers can be partitioned into three types: (1) Well-known Ports, which are port numbers between 0 to 1023, and closely bound to system specific services and protocols; (2) Registered Ports, which are port numbers between 1024 to 49151, and used by processes of procedures and executed programs of common users; and (3) Private Ports, which are port numbers between 49152 to 65535, and dynamically or temporarily used by client communication processes or executed programs.

Each TCP or UDP port used in a TCP/IP network application implies a communication channel, which can also be exploited by an intruder. Port exploitation based network intrusion are mainly manifested in the following two styles: (1) exploiting common ports, and attacking hosts through known system bugs; (2) planting Trojan horses to victim hosts through backdoor opened by other network vulnerabilities. It is worth noting that port numbers used by various malicious software (e.g., Trojan programs) are widely distributed, which don't only use registered ports. Port scanning is commonly used by an intruder to search for potential targets. Network administrators can monitor their networks by tracking abnormal port roles, such as a client host provides services outwards the public. Many other port related behaviors such as the changes of port in/out degreecan help check whether or not a host behaves normally. In general, port profile is a very important metric for application traffic classification. Correctly identifying server ports among network traffic has great significance for accurately classifying traffic application types.

At present, few studies focus on identifying port roles, i.e., a port belongs to a server or client port. Many network security and management applications, such as port scanning, worm detecting, traffic classification etc., are closely related to port role identification. In this paper, we define and analyze port roles based on their macroscopic traffic behavior. Macroscopic port roles

* Correspondence: gcheng@njnet.edu.cn
[1]School of Computer Science and Engineering, Key Laboratory of Computer Network and Information Integration, MOE, Southeast University, Nanjing, P.R. China
Full list of author information is available at the end of the article

first can be classified into active ports and non-active ports, and then active ports are classified into normal behavior roles and abnormal behavior roles. Abnormal behavior roles are classified into scan attacked ports and service failed ports, and normal behavior ports can be classified into client ports, server ports, or p2p ports etc. For this purpose, we use data mining to classify port roles from massive traffic data automatically. The contributions in this paper can be summarized as the following:

Define port role to distinguish different communication pattern.
Propose a two-dimensional Macroscopic Port Classification Plane (MPCP) that creates a new space for traffic behavior analysis.
Propose an EM fuzzy clustering algorithm to classify port traffic into six behavior zones in MPCP.

The rest of the paper is organized as follows. Firstly, we analyze Macroscopic Port Role in Section 2. We design a two dimensional Macroscopic Port Classification Plane and propose an EM clustering algorithm for fuzzy port behavior analysis in Section 3. Extensive experiments using real Internet traces to validate PortView are shown in Section 4. The related work is presented in Section 5. Finally Section 6 concludes this paper.

2. Macroscopic port role analysis
In this section, we will introduce the definition of Macroscopic Port Role as a new defining traffic characteristic, and use it re-profile several common network applications or behaviors.

2.1 Macroscopic port role
With the intent to define Macroscopic Port Role, we first define several port related parameters.

Let SF_i be a set of flows with source port i such that $\forall f \in SF_i$, $getSrcPort(f) = i$. We denote $n_i=|SF_i|$ as the size of SF_i. Here, $getSrcPort(f)$ is the source port number of the flow f, retrieved via the function $getSrcPort()$. Similarly, $getDstPort()$, $getSrcIP()$ and $getDstIP()$ are the functions to retrieve destination port, source IP and destination IP from the flow f. Accordingly, a flow f is uniquely defined as $f = \{getSrcIP(f), getDstIP(f), getSrcPort(f), getDstPort(f)\}$.

All distinct source IP addresses retrieved from the flows in SF_i, which are related to the source port i, constitutes the source IP set denoted as $SSIP_i$. The number of all distinct source IP addresses with source port i is denoted as $|SSIP_i|$. Similarly, all distinct destination IP addresses retrieved from the flows in SF_i constitute the destination IP set denoted as $SDIP_i$. The number of all distinct source IP addresses with destination port i is denoted as $|SDIP_i|$.

Let DF_j be a set of flows such that $\forall f \in DF_j$, $getDstPort(f) = j$. We denote $m_j=|DF_j|$ as the size of DF_j. All distinct source IP addresses retrieved from the flows in DF_j, which are related to the destination port j, constitute the source IP set denoted as $DSIP_j$. The number of all distinct source IP addresses with destination port i is denoted as $|DSIP_i|$. Similarly, all distinct destination IP addresses retrieved from the flows in DF_j constitutes the destination IP set denoted as $DDIP_j$. The number of all distinct destination IP addresses with destination port i is denoted as $|DDIP_i|$.

Definition 1. For a given port i, its *Macroscopic Port Role* (MPR) observed on a monitored network link during a measurement period T is defined by the 4-tuple port parameters $< SSIP_i, SDIP_i, DDIP_i, DSIP_i >$.

For a source (or destination) port i, if the corresponding $SSIP_i$ and $SDIP_i$ (or $DSIP_i$ and $DDIP_i$) are larger than a threshold, it is called active port. Otherwise, port i is called inactive port. The threshold will be computed by the Port Role Interval Classifying Algorithm in Section 3.4.

In the following, we broadly classify network traffic based on its role into two categories: abnormal and normal network roles. Then, for each category, we re-profile several selected common network applications or network scenarios using MPR analysis to illustrate PortView. It is worth noting that the classification criteria shown in this paper is not the only way to use PortView. The more granular classification criteria are, the more zones we may create in MPCP as discussed later in Section 3.

The different port role of MPR is described from Figures 1, 2, 3, 4, 5. In these figures, the left side of the dotted line means that the *DIP* hosts send some

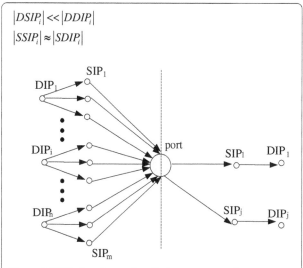

Figure 1 MPR of port scanning. During a port scanning, a scanner attempts to connect to a specific port of a large number of hosts.

$|DSIP_i| \gg |DDIP_i|$
$|SSIP_i| \approx |SDIP_i|$

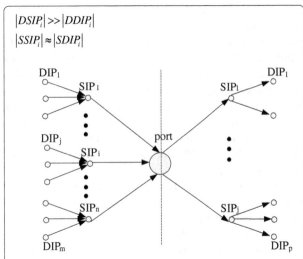

Figure 2 MPR of failed service. In a typical DDoS attack scenario, a large number of DIPs send requests connecting to a specific port i on a few SIPs with destination port i.

$|DSIP_i| > |DDIP_i|$
$|SSIP_i| < |SDIP_i|$

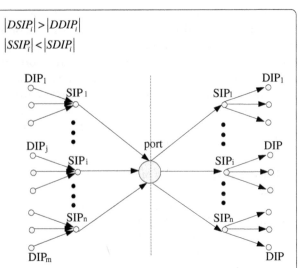

Figure 4 MPR of server application. A service port is the one used by a server listening to the requests from different clients, so the number of servers is usually less than the number of clients.

connection requests to an port i on the SIP hosts. The right side of the dotted line means that SIP hosts with port i send some connection requests to the SIP hosts. These figures show the Macroscopic Port Role.

2.2 MPR of abnormal traffic

In the traffic category of abnormal network role, we study the port role of (1) commonly observed port scanning traffic, and (2) a network service under DDoS attack.

1) *MPR of port scanning:* The MPR of port scanning can be illustrated in Figure 1, which clearly shows that on the left side of the dotted line, a few hosts denoted as *DIP* (Destination IP address) send too many connection requests to an interested port i possibly open on too many hosts denoted as *SIP*

(Source IP address) with destination port i. Thus, we have $|DSIP_i| \ll |DDIP_i|$. Usually only a few *SIPs* (Source IP address) with this port i open response to the connection requests with source port i, as shown on the right side of the dotted line in Figure 1, which can be described with: $|SSIP_i| \approx |SDIP_i|$. Hence, we have the following MPR of port scanning:

$$|DSIP_i| \ll |DDIP_i|$$
$$|SSIP_i| \approx |SDIP_i| \tag{1}$$

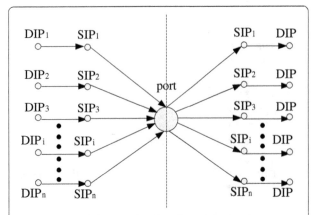

Figure 3 MPR of client application. The port on the client is usually chosen by the operating system dynamically. Different ports are used to communicate with multiple servers.

$|DSIP_i| < |DDIP_i|$
$|SSIP_i| > |SDIP_i|$

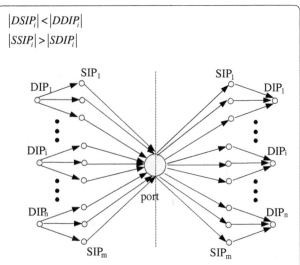

Figure 5 MPR in overlay application. Typically, an overlay node firstly obtains a list of neighbor nodes, and then sends request to each selected node. Hence, in an overlay network which uses a unified service port number to provide service, the communication pattern is that few clients send requests to lots of hosts.

2) *MPR of failed network service:* In a typical DDoS attack scenario, a large number of *DIPs* send requests connecting to a specific port i on a few *SIPs* with destination port i, that implies $|DSIP_i| \gg |DDIP_i|$. For those hosts being DDoS attacked severely, they cannot response interactively. Thus, only a few *SIPs* as shown on the right side of the dotted line in Figure 2 can response to the connection requests with source port i, which implies: $|SSIP_i| \approx |SDIP_i|$. Thus, the MPR of failed service caused by successful DDoS attack can be described as:

$$|DSIP_i| \gg |DDIP_i|$$
$$|SSIP_i| \approx |SDIP_i| \qquad (2)$$

2.3 MPR of normal port behaviors

In the traffic category of normal network behavior, we study the port behavior of (1) client application, (2) server application, and (3) overlay application.

1) *MPR of client application:* In a typical client–server network application, for every monitored network flow $sf_i = (ip_1, ip_2, i, j)$ destined to the host ip_2, a corresponding opposite directional flow $df_i = (ip_2, ip_1, j, i)$ should appear. We denote such a pair of flows $< sf_i, df_i >$ as <in-flow, outflow> pair. In this paper, we denote the MPR of client–server applications as regular port behavior, which can be defined as:

$$|SSIP_i| = |DDIP_i|$$
$$|SDIP_i| = |DSIP_i| \qquad (3)$$

In the most common client–server paradigm (C-S mode), a client with IP address srcIP communicates with a server with IP address dstIP. The port on the client is usually chosen by the client's operating system dynamically. Different ports are used if the same client needs to communicate with multiple servers. However, different clients may happen to choose the same port to communicate to different servers. We show the port behavior in C-S mode in Figure 3, where *SIP* and *DIP* represent client and server hosts respectively. As shown on the left of the dotted line in Figure 4, different SIP addresses with the same port communicate with DIP addresses, while DIP addresses response accordingly. We can see that a given port links a *DIP* to a *SIP*, and different SIP addresses may use the same port to communicate to their connecting DIP addresses. Clearly, the number of SIP addresses is equal to the number of DIP addresses. Thus, we have $|DSIP_i| = |DDIP_i|$. On the right side of the dotted line, we see that the number of

SIP addresses is equal to the number of DIP addresses. Thus, we have $|SSIP_i| = |SDIP_i|$. It is possible that some connecting ports from source IP addresses have not received response from the destination IP addresses. However, even if in such a case, the number of SIP addresses is still equal to the number of DIP addresses since a source IP and a destination IP always emerge in pair in a network flow.

There are further two possible port behavior variations in C-S mode: (1) Different source IP addresses use the same port to communicate to a single destination IP. In this case, the number of source IP addresses is larger than the number of destination IP addresses, namely, $|SSIP_i| \geq |SDIP_i|$. (2) A few source IP addresses send information frequently during the measurement interval. The source port used by a source IP reverses, at the same time, the other source IP uses the same port number to access a different destination IP, the destination IPs which the two source IPs access is random, From the probability theory standpoint, the number of source IPs and destination IPs in flow records in which the client port takes role as a source port are almost equal, namely, $|DSIP_i| \approx |DDIP_i|$. Hence, we have the following observation on the port behavior of C-S mode:

$$|DSIP_i| \approx |DDIP_i|$$
$$|SSIP_i| \approx |SDIP_i| \qquad (4)$$

2) *MPR of server application:* A service port is the one used by a server listening to the requests from different clients. Obviously, the number of servers is usually less than the number of clients. The port behavior of a service port displays that multiple clients marked by *DIP* may send requests to a service port of the servers SIP addresses as shown on the left side of the dotted line in Figure 4. The right side of the dotted line in Figure 4 shows the servers response accordingly from this service port of SIP addresses. Hence, for a service port, there are more srcIPs than dstIPs in its in-flow direction, i.e., $|DSIP_i| > |DDIP_i|$. Since each SIP should answer several clients' requests, the number of srcIPs is less than that of dstIPs in their out-flow direction, i.e., $|SSIP_i| < |SDIP_i|$. Hence, we have the following observation on the port behavior of service port:

$$|DSIP_i| > |DDIP_i|$$
$$|SSIP_i| < |SDIP_i| \qquad (5)$$

In traditional C-S model, a server may have multiple connections to clients. However, a P2P host is limited to provide only one connection to each P2P. Suppose the number of links a server provided is fixed, a P2P host can provide service for more P2P. Hence, we have the following observation on the port behavior of a P2P host:

$$|DSIP_i| >> |DDIP_i|$$
$$|SSIP_i| << |SDIP_i| \qquad (6)$$

3) *MPR of overlay application:* In an overlay network, a node uses a unified service port to provide service to other nodes. Typically, an overlay node firstly obtains a list of neighbor nodes, and then sends request to each selected node. Hence, in an overlay network which uses a unified service port number to provide service, the communication pattern is that few clients send requests to lots of hosts. Figure 5 shows the communication pattern based on a unified port of an overlay network. On the left side of the dotted line of Figure 5, few clients send requests to lots of hosts, i.e., $|DSIP_i| < |DDIP_i|$; On the right side of the dotted line, lots of hosts answer the requests to few clients, i.e., $|SSIP_i| > |SDIP_i|$. Hence, we have the following observation on the port behavior of a unified port in an overlay network:

$$|DSIP_i| < |DDIP_i|$$
$$|SSIP_i| > |SDIP_i| \qquad (7)$$

3. Classifying port role algorithm
3.1 Port role metrics
As discussed in Sec. 2, the Macroscopic Port Role analysis can characterize communication patterns as shown in Eq. 1~Eq. 7. For facilitating MPR based traffic classification, we design a Macroscopic Port Classification Plane (MPCP) with X-Y axes representing two different behavior metrics. Then, we propose a fuzzy port behavior analysis method to divide MPCP into multiple zones with each zone representing different network behavior and corresponding network applications.

Definition 2. Port Exporting Network Activity X_i: for all network flows leaving from port i in a measurement time window, the ratio of the difference between the numbers of related source and destination hosts and the number of all the port i related hosts that send traffic is called port i's Port Exporting Network Activity X_i.

$$X_i = \frac{|SDIP_i| - |SSIP_i|}{|SDIP_i| + |SSIP_i|} \qquad (8)$$

Definition 3. Port Importing Network Activity Y_i: for all network flows destining to port i in a measurement

time window, the ratio of the difference between the numbers of related source and destination hosts and the number of all the port i related hosts is called port i's Port Importing Network Activity Y_i.

$$Y_i = \frac{|DSIP_i| - |DDIP_i|}{|DSIP_i| + |DDIP_i|} \qquad (9)$$

From Definition 2 and 3, $|SDIP_i| - |SSIP_i| < |SDIP_i| + |SSIP_i|$, $|DSIP_i| - |DDIP_i| < |DDIP_i| + |DDIP_i|$. Thus, we have $-1 < X_i, Y_i < 1, i \in [0, 65535]$.

Definition 4. Port Differential Network Activity B_i: for a given port i, the difference between its Port Exporting Network Activity X_i and Port Importing Network Activity Y_i.

$$B_i = X_i - Y_i = \frac{|SDIP_i| - |SSIP_i|}{|SDIP_i| + |SSIP_i|} - \frac{|DSIP_i| - |DDIP_i|}{|DSIP_i| + |DDIP_i|} \qquad (10)$$

Definition 5. Port Accumulative Network Activity A_i: for a given port i, the accumulation of its Port Exporting Network Activity X_i and Port Importing Network Activity Y_i.

$$A_i = X_i + Y_i = \frac{|SDIP_i| - |SSIP_i|}{|SDIP_i| + |SSIP_i|} + \frac{|DSIP_i| - |DDIP_i|}{|DSIP_i| + |DDIP_i|} \qquad (11)$$

Definition 6. Port Overall Network Activity D_i: for a given port i during a measurement time window, the whole numbers of port i's related source and destination hosts. In other word, it is the all number of hosts related to source or destination port i.

$$D_i = |SSIP_i| + |SDIP_i| + |DSIP_i| + |DDIP_i^i| \qquad (12)$$

X_i and Y_i are the basic clustering metrics, which are used to classify port roles into six different zones. A and B are two derived parameters from X and Y, and used directly in the EM clustering algorithm to categorize active ports.

3.2 Fuzzy port behavior
The characteristics of port behavior can be summarized in Table 1. In the following, we introduce Macroscopic Port Classification Plane (MPCP). Then we propose fuzzy port behavior analysis to quantitatively map all earlier discussed network applications or scenarios into the corresponding MPCP zones.

The Macroscopic Port Classification Plane is a 2-dimensional graph, as shown in Figure 6, where X axis represents Port Exporting Network Activity, and Y axis displays Port Importing Network Activity. In the case of normal network behavior, the corresponding Port

Table 1 Port communication behavior

Port status	Basic metrics	Port role	Communication
Normal Port	$X_i \approx Y_i$	Client Port	$\|DSIP_i\| \approx \|DDIP_i\|$ $\|SSIP_i\| \approx \|SDIP_i\|$
		Service Port	$\|DSIP_i\| > \|DDIP_i\|$ $\|SSIP_i\| < \|SDIP_i\|$
		P2P Service Port	$\|DSIP_i\| >> \|DDIP_i\|$ $\|SSIP_i\| << \|SDIP_i\|$
		Overlay Port	$\|DSIP_i\| < \|DDIP_i\|$ $\|SSIP_i\| > \|SDIP_i\|$
Abnormal Port	$X_i \neq Y_i$	Scanning Port	$\|DSIP_i\| << \|DDIP_i\|$ $\|SSIP_i\| \approx \|SDIP_i\|$
		Failed Service Port	$\|DSIP_i\| >> \|DDIP_i\|$ $\|SSIP_i\| \approx \|SDIP_i\|$

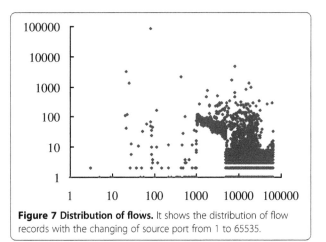

Figure 7 Distribution of flows. It shows the distribution of flow records with the changing of source port from 1 to 65535.

Exporting and Importing Network Activities manifest $X_i \approx Y_i$ (B_i is close to 0) based on Eq. 3. Thus, if the MPR analysis result shows the traffic is spanned along the diagonal area of MPCP (marked as zones 1, 2, 3 and 4 in Figure 7), the corresponding traffic belongs to normal network behavior; otherwise abnormal and the MPR analysis results should show the traffic is either located in zone 5 or 6 in Figure 6. If $-\delta \leq B_i \leq \beta$, $\delta > 0$ and $\beta < 1$, it belongs to normal port behavior. As a failed service port, according to Eq. 1, its Port Exporting Network Activity is less than its Port Importing Network Activity, $X_i < Y_i$. It falls into zone 5. As $B_i < -\delta$, port i falls into zone 5.

According to the analysis of Sec. 3.2 (1), in the case of abnormal network behavior, the corresponding Port Exporting and Importing Network Activities are different: $X_i \neq Y_i$. For scanned port, based on communication relationship as Eq. 1, its Port Exporting Network Activity is more than its Port Importing Network Activity, $X_i > Y_i$. Thus, it is in zone 6, and $B_i > \beta$.

For zone 1, 2, 3 and 4 in the diagonal area, in addition to the condition $-\delta < B_i < \beta$, according to the relationship of client port in Table 1, port i's Port Accumulative Network Activity $A_i \approx 0$, $-\phi \leq A_i \leq \varphi$, and $0 < \phi, \varphi < 1$. Overlay service port is in zone 4, $A_i < -\phi$. Service port is in zone 2, $A_i > \varphi$. For the boundary between zone 2 and 3, according to the classification of service port and p2p port in Table 1, in zone 2, $\varphi < A_i \leq 2 - \gamma$, and in zone 3, $2 - \gamma < A_i < 2$. In conclusion, the range of six zones can be showed in Table 2.

Table 2 shows that in order to classify the 6 roles, we need to determine five arguments δ, β, ϕ, φ, and γ. In the following, we will design a clustering method EM algorithm that can classify the two kinds of distributions.

3.3 EM algorithm for Two classes of distribution
In this section, we will discuss how to determine the boundary arguments for each zone. Observing that each port may play certain role (i.e., projected into certain zone in MPCP) with some probability, we use statistical clustering to determine zone boundaries in MPCP. The basis of

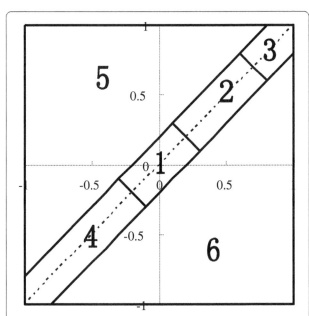

Figure 6 Macroscopic port classification plane. X axis represents Port Exporting Network Activity, and Y axis displays Port Importing Network Activity. The range of six zones can be showed in Table 2.

Table 2 Port behavior zones

Zone ID	Port role	Port zones
1	Client Port	$-\delta \leq B_i \leq \beta, -\varphi \leq A_i \leq \varphi$
2	Service Port	$-\delta \leq B_i \leq \beta, \varphi < A_i \leq 2 - \gamma$
3	P2P Port	$-\delta \leq B_i \leq \beta, 2 - \gamma \leq A_i \leq 2$
4	Overlay Port	$-\delta \leq B_i \leq \beta, A_i < -\varphi$
5	Scanning Port	$B_i < -\delta$
6	Failed Service Port	$B_i > \beta$

statistical clustering is to build a finite mixed statistical model such that it can use k probability distributions to replace k clustering. Since a port may belong to different zones/roles with different probabilities, we define a port role as the MPCP zone it is most likely located (i.e., with the biggest probability distribution).

For two kinds of statistical clustering, if we need to do this on A and B classes, every class is supposed to be normal distribution. Clustering A's expectation and variance are μ_A and σ_A. Clustering B's expectation and variance are μ_B and σ_B. We take samples from the distributions of A and B. The probability of taking A or B is p_A or p_B respectively. Here, $p_A + p_B = 1$. Here, the challenge is how to determine five arguments, μ_A, σ_A, μ_B, σ_B, and p_A (or p_B), by only knowing the MPR analysis result.

Since the distribution that each port follows is unknown initially, we use the fuzzy clustering EM algorithm to classify the port behaviors. In every iterative step of classical k-average clustering algorithm, every port is considered exclusively belonging to a class. Thus, we adopt fuzzy clustering to tackle the challenge of multiple distributions a port may follow. Each port probabilistically belongs to a class. First, every port's class is estimated. Then, compute every port's clustering probability using initial estimated value. These probabilities are used to estimate the argument again. The above process is iteratively conducted for the second time. This method is called Expectation Maximization (EM). First, compute clustering probability, in another word, the expectation's class value; Second, Maximum likelihood the given data's distribution. The following test will show the EM algorithm in detail.

For n port's metric: $x_1, \cdots, x_n$, there are two classes A and B. z is a two-dimensional array. At the very beginning, let z_{Aj} be 1, meaning x_j is in A class; otherwise 0. Let z_{Bj} be 1, meaning x_j is in B class; otherwise 0. Then according to z's value, we can compute k class's argument using the following formula:

$$\mu_A = \frac{\sum_j E(z_{A_j}|x_j)\cdot x_j}{\sum_j E(z_{A_j}|x_j)}, \sigma_A = \frac{\sum_j E(z_{A_j}|x_j)\cdot (x_j - \mu_A)^2}{\sum_j E(z_{A_j}|x_j)}$$

$$\mu_B = \frac{\sum_j E(z_{B_j}|x_j)\cdot x_j}{\sum_j E(z_{B_j}|x_j)}, \sigma_B = \frac{\sum_j E(z_{B_j}|x_j)\cdot (x_j - \mu_B)^2}{\sum_j E(z_{B_j}|x_j)}$$

$$(13)$$

For a port i,

The two class EM classifying method discussed in Eq. (14) can put data into 2 or 3 classes. As in Section 3.1, we provided several metrics that can classify port behaviors, and each time the method uses one dimension metric to do classification. The next subsection will give a detailed port role interval classifying algorithm based on the Eq. (14).

3.4 Port role interval classifying algorithm

In the measuring progress, classifying algorithm first records every port's source IP numbers, source port's destination IP numbers, destination port's source IP numbers, destination port's source IP numbers. After a measuring time period, the role style of the every port's four metric is determined. In measuring data, if the number of a port's related export and import hosts is small, then because of the tiny random difference between the numbers of source and destination hosts, some inactive port will be made with big random difference between port's inward and outward communication metric. At the same time, we care about these active ports with large traffic of the host that influence the network a lot. And we remove these ports with small traffic and have little influence on the network. In order to determine a port is an active port or not, we compute every port's activity metric D. According to the two-class EM algorithm in section 3.3, all the ports are classified into active and inactive ports. Because D is x_1, based on formula (19), we can compute active port's threshold. For all the ports whose activity metric value D_i is bigger than or equal to x_2, they are defined as active ports. Otherwise, they are inactive ports.

For all the active ports, using port's communication difference balance metric B, based on the two-class EM algorithm in section 3.3, we can compute the classification threshold of the normal and the abnormal port. The two-class EM algorithm's two distribution's interval can figure out normal port's range is $[x_1, x_2]$, and abnormal port's range is $(-\infty, x_1), (x_2, +\infty)$. Because port's communication difference balance metric B's range value is $(-2, 2)$, abnormal port's value range is $(-2, x_1), (x_2, 2)$. So we can compute the argument α, β, $\alpha = -x_1, \beta = x_2$ in Table 2.

For all the normal port, using port communication difference accumulation metric A, based on the two-class EM algorithm in section 3.3, we can compute the classification threshold of client port and service port. The two-class EM

$$x_{1,2} = \frac{\mu_A \sigma_B^2 - \mu_B \sigma_A^2}{\sigma_A^2 - \sigma_B^2} \pm \\ \frac{\sqrt{\left(\mu_A \sigma_B^2 - \mu_B \sigma_A^2\right)^2 + \left(\mu_A^2 - \mu_B^2\right)\left(\mu_A \sigma_B^2 - \mu_B \sigma_A^2 - 2\sigma_A^2 \sigma_B^2 \ln(p_B \sigma_A / p_A \sigma_B)\right)}}{\sigma_A^2 - \sigma_B^2}$$

$$(14)$$

algorithm's two distribution's interval can figure out client port's range is $[x_1, x_2]$, and service port's range is $(-\infty, x_1)$, $(x_2, +\infty)$. Because A's value range is $(-2, x_1)$, $(x_2, 2)$, service port's range is $(-2, x_1)$, $(x_2, 2)$. So we can compute the argument $\phi, \varphi, \phi = -x_1, \varphi = x_2$ in Table 2.

Service ports are divided into there kinds: overlay service port, normal service port and P2P service port. Using communication difference accumulation metric A, besides classifying the styles of client port, it can also classify overlay service port. So if it is a overlay port, A's value range is $(-2, -\phi)$. For the range $(\varphi, 2)$, it contains normal and P2P service port. We again use the two-class EM algorithm to classify these two kinds of ports. The result is that service port's range is (φ, x_1), and P2P's service port's value range is $(x_2, 2)$. So we get the argument $\gamma = 2 - x_2$. Based on the method above, we can compute the five arguments in Table 2. So we can classify all the active ports into the six kinds of port roles.

4. Experimental analysis

We will divide port roles as a whole. First, we introduce the experimental traces which are used for interval dividing of port roles. Second, we classify the ports into active ports and inactive ports according to the steps of algorithm in Section 3.4. For active ports, we classify it into normal ports and abnormal ports, and then we classify normal ports into four types of roles: client ports, server ports, P2P ports and overlay ports.

4.1 Experimental traces

Multiple real network traces were selected from the link between CERNET backbone and Jiangsu CERNET network to evaluate PortView. Specifically, we present two representational network traces in this section, namely Trace1 and Trace2. Trace1 was collected on April 10, 2010 with 175 million packets, 117 GB traffic traces, 495,000 flows, and its consecutive observation period is ten minutes. Trace2 was captured on May 4, 2012 with 2.82 million packets, 1.89 GB traffic traces, 17,000 flows, and its observation period is five second. Trace1 is selected to show how PortView performs given relatively rich correlation information among multiple hosts over a longer observation window (10 m). Trace2 is used to validate the agility of PortView given a short observation window (i.e., 5 s). Here, we define PortView agility as its ability to provide port role analysis result over a short time period (e.g., 5 s). Network flows are defined using 4-tuple, i.e. source address, destination address, source port, and destination port in this paper. Trace1 is analyzed from Subsection 4.1 to Subsection 4.3, and the analysis based on Trace2 will be reported in Subsection 4.4.

We can see clearly from Figure 7 that: (1) the number of flows with source port between 1 and 1023 is unevenly distributed; (2) the number of flows with port between 1024 and 5000 is distributed quite uniformly, every source port produces corresponding host amount, the number of host is between 20 and 100; and (3) the flows with port above 5000 is also unevenly distributed.

Figure 8 shows the two-dimensional distribution diagram of port communication difference. We can know from Figure 8 that ports distribute mainly near the origin. According to the Section 3, this type of ports are mainly client ports; In addition, there are a lot of ports which distribute near the diagonal of first quadrant, those ports are server ports, this indicates that most ports belong to normal port. Points in the negative diagonal of third quadrant indicate that the number of IP requesting to this port IP are less than requested port IP amount, this character is similar to scanning, but most of the scanning traffic has no response, that is to say the X-axis coordinate of scanning traffic is close to zero. Because of being in the inner of an overlay, most of requesting traffic has response from a server port of the overlay. There are few points in the third quadrant whose diagonal is near the X-axis, the character is similar to the points which are near the diagonal. Because the requesting traffic is less than the response traffic, points in the fourth quadrant indicate that parts of the traffic of this port are scanning attacks, such as 8088, 7155 and so on.

4.2 Port clustering

According to the activity metric value D of every port, two-class EM algorithm can cluster all 65536 ports into active and inactive ports. The corresponding five metrics $(\mu_A, \sigma_A, \mu_B, \sigma_B, p_A) = (162.426, 720.223, 9.297, 5.789, 0.1)$.

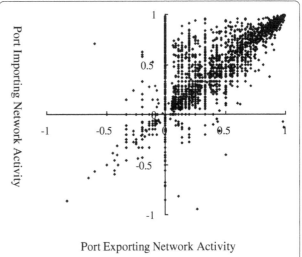

Figure 8 Port differential network activity. Ports distribute mainly near the origin, according to the Section 4, this type of ports are mainly client ports.

Thus we can calculate activity metric value, and classify those ports whose activity value no more than 30 into inactive port, cluster the port whose activity value more than 30 into active port. The number of active ports in this experiment is 5313. In the following, we will analyze 5313 clustered active ports. Figure 9 shows the two-dimensional graph of metric of host difference of 5313 active ports.

We calculate communication difference balance value B of all 5313 active ports, and use two-class EM algorithm to calculate two distribution parameter values $(\mu_A, \sigma_A, \mu_B, \sigma_B, p_A) = (-0.2323, 0.3533, 0.0017, 0.084, 0.17)$. Hence, we can confirm the range of normal ports is $[-0.0547, 0.0596]$, the range of abnormal ports is $(-2, -0.0547)$ and $(0.0596, 2)$. Correspondingly, we can calculate the parameters δ and β in Table 2 as $\delta = 0.0547$ and $\beta = 0.0596$. The number of ports in normal range is 4512, and the number of abnormal ports is 801. Among these ports, there are 176 scanned ports and 625 server failure ports.

We will calculate communication difference cumulative value A of 4512 normal ports, and use two-class EM algorithm to calculate parameter values of client ports and server ports $(\mu_A, \sigma_A, \mu_B, \sigma_B, p_A) = (-0.0039, 0.0363, 1.1873, 0.7509, 0.85)$. Therefore, we can confirm the range of client ports is $[-0.1325, 0.1186]$, the range of server ports is $(-2, -0.1325)$ and $(0.1186, 2)$. Correspondingly, we can calculate the parameters ϕ and φ in Table 2 as $\phi = 0.1325$ and $\varphi = 0.1186$. Among the normal ports, there are 3875 client ports and 637 server ports.

We classify server ports into three types, overlay ports, server ports and P2P ports. We distinguish the type of client ports by communication difference cumulative value A, and classify overlay ports, i.e. the range of A as $(-2, -0.1325)$ are overlay ports, and the amount is 25.

The range of $(0.1182, 2)$ include general server ports and P2P ports, and the amount is 612. In the next, we will use two-class EM algorithm to classify 612 ports with the distribution parameters as $(\mu_A, \sigma_A, \mu_B, \sigma_B, p_A) = (0.6966, 0.4845, 1.8111, 0.1091, 0.45)$. The result is that: the range of server ports is $[0.1186, 1.585]$, the amount is 268; the range of P2P ports is $(1.535, 2)$, and the amount is 344. Thus, we can have the parameter $\gamma = 0.465$ $(2 - \gamma = 1.535)$. We put the experiment result of measured parameter $\delta = 0.0547$, $\beta = 0.1325$, $\varphi = 0.1186$, $\gamma = 0.465$ into interval formula in Table 2. We can get Figure 10, which shows the interval distribution of four type real normal ports corresponding to Figure 6.

In this test, we need use two-class EM algorithm three times to classify ports. The number of port used in the EM algorithm is 65536, 5313, and 4512 in the measured interval respectively. The maximal number of port is less than 65536. We test the cost of port clustering algorithm in the server equipped with CPU P4 Xeron2.4*2, memory 2 GB, hard disk 1.2 TB, NIC 1000 G, and its running time is 850 ms.

4.3 Experimental analysis

As discussed in Section 1, we know that well-known Ports, which range between 0 to 1023, and are closely bound to some specific services. Registered Ports, port numbers range from 1024 to 49151, they are used by processes of procedures and executed programs of common users. Ephemeral Ports, most implementations use port numbers between 1024 to 5000. Reserved Ports: port numbers larger than 5000 are reserved for other services. We can divided 65536 ports into four types: Well-known Ports, Ephemeral Ports, Registered Ports, Reserved Ports. The role of Well-known port is service port. The role of Ephemeral Port is

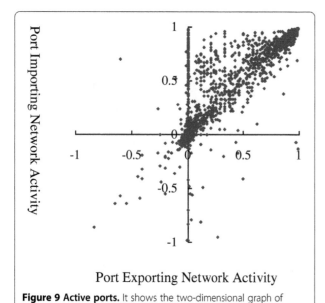

Figure 9 Active ports. It shows the two-dimensional graph of metric of host difference of 5313 active ports.

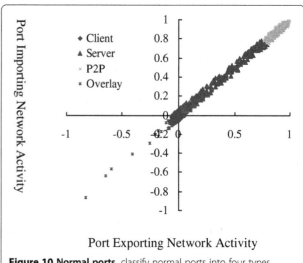

Figure 10 Normal ports. classify normal ports into four types, client ports, overlay ports, server ports and P2P ports.

client port. Registered Ports and Reserved Ports are linked to service port in a local host.

There are 5313 active ports in the experiment. Table 3 gives the relationship between the four port types and the six port roles defined in this paper.

The number of active ports is only 2.14% of the total number of the Well-known ports, which shows that the vast majority of the Well-known port is closed. In Table 3, only seven of the Well-known port is as service port. We can't find any port with client port role in the Well-known port, which also shows that our proposed method can give a correct classification to the client port role. All Ephemeral Ports are active ports, and nearly all Ephemeral Ports are client port role, which is consistent with the definition of Ephemeral Ports.

In the Registered Ports, Service Port and P2P Port account for approximately 50% of the port. Abnormal ports account for another 50%. The result shows that the Registered Ports, port numbers range from 5001 to 49151, is the most common user applications, but also the most vulnerable to attack. Reserved Ports are used nearly.

4.4 Agility validation on PortView

Trace2 was collected only over 5 seconds on May 4, 2012 with 2.82 million packets, 1.89 GB traffic traces, and 17,000 flows. Such a short observation window provides relatively less information to PortView such that we can validate the agility of PortView. We use the activity metric value D to cluster all ports into active and inactive ports. The corresponding five metrics (μ_A, σ_A, μ_B, σ_B, p_A) = (62.34, 325.23, 5.45, 3.08, 0.16). The number of active ports in this experiment is 5215. We calculate communication difference balance value B of all 5215 active Ports. (μ_A, σ_A, μ_B, σ_B, p_A) = (0, 0.527, 0.542, 0.671, 0.55). The number of ports in normal range is 4257, and the number of abnormal ports is 958.

We calculate communication difference cumulative value A of 4257 normal ports. The parameter values of

Table 3 Relationship between the four port types and the six port roles

Port role	Well-known ports	Ephemeral ports	Registered ports	Reserved ports
Total Number of Ports	1024	3977	44151	16384
Client Port	0	3761	29	84
Service Port	7	51	209	2
P2P Port	4	0	340	0
Overlay Port	0	15	9	1
Scanning Port	7	31	135	3
Failed Service Port	4	119	497	5
sum	22	3977	1219	95
Ratio of active ports	2.14%	100%	2.76%	0.58%

client ports and server ports (μ_A, σ_A, μ_B, σ_B, p_A) = (0, 0.0645, -0.0112, 0.1136, 0.85). Among the normal ports, there are 4151 client ports and 105 server ports. This experiment result shows that PortView can perform effectively even only provided a short observation window.

5. Related work

Port based traffic analysis can classify application layer protocols [2,3] used port numbers to analyze the type and trend of traffic application. Wei Li et al. [4] made correlation analysis between metrics related to traffic and application types, and found that, correlation between server ports and application types is the strongest of all the traffic metrics, while that between client ports and application types is very weak, so the discovery of server's port has great significance for improving the accuracy of traffic application classification.

McNutt and De Shon [5] analyzed correlation between ephemeral ports and malicious traffic patterns. Wang [6] analyzed the distribution of ports arger than 1024. Jeff Janies [7] studied the time series model of all the 65536 ports in a host, and described the model of server ports and the ports which were attacked by scanning through the visualization of time series graph. DongJin Lee [8] analyzed the distribution of the UDP to TCP ratio that corresponds to the ports. Allman [9] suggested using different methods to choose ephemeral ports to strengthen the security.

Kuai Xu [10] clustered source ports and destination ports, and calculated source IP entropy distribution, destination IP entropy distribution and source or destination port entropy distribution using information entropy, they classified entropy into low, medium, high three types of value, higher entropy indicated number of different corresponding IPs or ports are larger. We can check if a port is a server port or vulnerability by Kuai Xu's Methodology. Thomas Karagiannis [11] believed that since client may use random ports to connect to server ports, if the port number of an IP address equals the number of related flows, the IP host is a client.

The problem in PortView is essentially similar to the challenges in superspreaders detection to maintain all the flows and the IP addresses existent in the memory during the measurement interval. Such as Snort [12] maintains a record for each active connection and a connection counter for each source IP. Because the number of flows and IP addresses are so huge in the network that these algorithms require a lot of memory to maintain the flows and the IP addresses records, or usually detect the superspreaders in low-speed links. In 2005, Venkataraman [13] proposed two algorithms, one-level filtering algorithm and two-level filtering algorithm, which maintain two hash tables to find superspreaders. These filtering algorithms proposed a t-superspreader IP detection algorithm based on sampling from the set of distinct source destination pairs. In this algorithm, t-superspreader IP is defined as more than tN connections to different destination IP addresses, where N is the number of source-destination IP pairs in the measurement interval.

Some data streaming algorithms have been applied to detect superspreaders. In 2007 Noriaki [14] also proposed a parametric algorithm based on the Bloom Filter to measure the flow numbers. However, they don't compensate for the error brought by the hash collisions, and the memory consumption of the Bloom Filter (BF) is very large, so it is difficult to maintain the BF structure in the SRAM to adapt to the high speed links measurement. In 2003, Cohen [15] introduced a Spectral Bloom Filter (SBF), an extension of the original bloom filter to multisets, allowing the filtering of elements whose multiplicities are below a threshold. In 2005, Qi [16] proposed two algorithms for the detection of super sources and destinations. The first simple algorithm used a standard hash-based flow sampling algorithm, with a bitmap structure to maintain the flow records. The second algorithm uses a two-dimensional bit array to store the flow record and the flow number. In 2009, MyungKeun [17] created a virtual bit vector for each source by taking bits uniformly at random from a common one-dimension bit array instead of the two-dimensional bit array to store the flow record and the flow number.

Some interesting approach uses graphlet. One of the typical works has been proposed in [11] that can capture host behavior using empirically derived patterns. They represent these patterns using graphs, which they call graphlets. Having a library of these graphlets, they then seek for a match in the behavior of a host under examination. A similar work can also be found in [18], which proposed the use of a graph-based structure which is called a graphlet, to capture the interactions among the transport layer protocols, the destination IP addresses and the port numbers. Guillaume Dewaele [19] compared for two given hosts (with the anonymized IP provided in the trace) trace of the computed 9D features and of the associated graphlets.

The EM algorithm also groups the traffic flows into a small number of clusters and creates classification rules from the clusters in some previous works. Nguyen [20] looked at research into the application of Machine Learning techniques to IP traffic classification. In 2004 McGregor et al. [21] applied the EM algorithm to cluster traffic with similar observable properties into HTTP, FTP, SMTP, IMAP, NTP and DNS traffic. The EM algorithm proposed in AutoClass [22] determines the number of clusters and the parameters that govern the distinct probability distributions of each cluster. The EM algorithm in this paper is different from the previous work because we only classify port traffic into six

behavior zones using the EM algorithm rather than some specific traffic applications.

6. Conclusion

Characterizing Macroscopic Port Roles from network traffic provides highly valuable information for various network management tasks. The main purpose of this paper is not to exhaustively list all possible port behaviors, but provides a definition and classification of port roles. In this paper, we firstly classify port roles into six categories, which are scanned ports, failed service ports, client ports, server ports, P2P ports, and overlay ports. Secondly, we propose a port role distribution diagram and define a port behavior measurement metrics to characterize network traffic. A two-class EM fuzzy clustering algorithm is designed to quantitatively determine the classification criteria in the classification distribution diagram. Finally we validate the proposed method based on network traffic captured from a link in the CERNET.

Our contributions include: (1) we research on ports of communication pattern and propose a method to evaluate ports role; (2) we define metrics which can distinguish different ports of communication pattern, and propose a two-class EM fuzzy clustering algorithm, which can achieve fast classifying multi-role of ports; (3) we introduce a new research direction of classifying port role from macroscopic points, which can be used to identify ports type in real-time, discover new applications, and detect new behavior of network attacks.

Competing interest
The authors declare that they have no competing interest.

Authors' contributions
GC created and developed the approach. YT participated in the experiments. GC and YT wrote the manuscript. Both authors read and approved the final manuscript.

Acknowledgment
This work was sponsored by the National Grand Fundamental Research 973 program of China under Grant No. 2009CB320505, the National Nature Science Foundation of China under Grant No. 60973123, the Technology Support Program (Industry) of Jiangsu Province under Grant No. BE2011173, the Qing Lan Project of Jiangsu Province, the Six major talent Summit Project of Jiangsu Province.

Author details
[1]School of Computer Science and Engineering, Key Laboratory of Computer Network and Information Integration, MOE, Southeast University, Nanjing, P.R. China. [2]School of Information Technology, Illinois State University, Normal, IL, USA.

References
1. IANA port numbers. http://www.iana.org/assignments/port-numbers
2. Kim H, Claffy K, Fomenkov M, Barman D, Faloutsos M, Lee K (2008) Internet traffic classification demystified: myths, caveats, and the best practices. In: CONEXT '08: Proceedings of the 2008 ACM CoNEXT Conference. ACM, New York, NY, USA, pp 1–12

3. Labovitz C, Iekel-Johnson S, McPherson D, Oberheide J, Jahanian F, Karir M (2009) Internet Observatory Report. http://www.nanog.org/meetings/nanog47/presentations/Monday/Labovitz_ObserveReport_N47_Mon.pdf

4. Li W, Canini M, Moore AW, Bolla R (2009) Efficient application identification and the temporal and spatial stability of classification schema. Computer Networks 53(6):Pages 790–809

5. McNutt J, Shon MD (2005) Correlations between quiescent ports in network flows. Proceedings of FloCon, Pittsburgh, Pennsylvania, USA

6. Wang H, Zhou R, He Y (2008) An Information Acquisition Method Based on NetFlow for Network Situation Awareness. In: Advanced Software Engineering and Its Applications, 2008. ASEA 2008. IEEE. pp 23–26

7. Janies J, Plots E (2008) A Low-Resolution Time Series for Port Behavior Analysis. In: VizSec '08: Proceedings of the 5th international workshop on Visualization for Computer Security. SpringerVerlag, Berlin, Heidelberg, pp 161–168

8. Lee DJ, Carpenter BE, Brownlee N (2010) Observations of udp to tcp ratio and port numbers. In: Internet Monitoring and Protection (ICIMP), 2010 Fifth International Conference on. IEEE. pp 99–104

9. Allman M (2009) Comments on selecting ephemeral ports. SIGCOMM Comput Commun Rev 39(2):13–19

10. Xu K, Zhang ZL (2008) Supratik Bhattacharyya, Internet traffic behavior profiling for network security monitoring. IEEE/ACM Transactions on Networking (TON) 16(6):1241–1252

11. Karagiannis T, Papagiannaki K, Faloutsos M (2005) BLINC: multilevel traffic classification in the dark, ACM SIGCOMM Computer Communication Review. ACM 35(4):229–240

12. Roesch M (1999) Snort-lightweight intrusion detection for networks. In: Proceedings of the 13th USENIX conference on System administration. pp 229–238

13. Venkataraman S, Song D, Gibbons P, Blum A (2005) New streaming algorithms for fast detection of superspreaders. In: Department of Electrical and Computing Engineering. p 6

14. Kamiyama N, Mori T, Kawahara R (2007) Simple and Adaptive Identification of Superspreaders by Flow Sampling, INFOCOM 2007. In: 26th IEEE International Conference on Computer Communications. IEEE. IEEE. pp 2481–2485

15. Cohen S, Matias Y (2003) Spectral Bloom Filters. In: Proceedings of the 2003 ACM SIGMOD International Conference on the Management of Data. ACM Press, New York, pp pp. 241–252

16. Qi Z, Kumar A, Xu J (2005) Joint Data Streaming and Sampling Techniques for Detection of Super Sources and Destinations. In: Proceedings of the 5th ACM SIGCOMM conference on Internet Measurement. USENIX Association. pp 7–7

17. Yoon MK, Li T, Chen S, Peir JK (2009) Fit a Spread Estimator in Small Memory. In: INFOCOM 2009, IEEE. IEEE. pp 504–512

18. Karagiannis T, Papagiannaki K, Taft N, Faloutsos M (2007) Profiling the End Host. In: Passive and Active Network Measurement. pp 186–196

19. Guillaume D, Yosuke H, Pierre B, Kensuke F (2010) Unsupervised host behavior classification from connection patterns. International Journal Of Network Management 00:1–17

20. T. T Nguyen T, Grenville Armitage A (2008) A survey of techniques for internet traffic classification using machine learning. IEEE Communications Surveys & Tutorials 10:56–76, FOURTH QUARTER

21. McGregor A, Hall M, Lorier P, Brunskill J (2004) Flow clustering using machine learning techniques. In: Proc. Passive and Active Measurement Workshop (PAM2004). Antibes Juan-les-Pins, France, pp 205–214

22. Erman J, Arlitt M, Mahanti A (2006) Traffic Classification Using Clustering Algorithms. In: Proceedings of the 2006 SIGCOMM workshop on Mining network data. ACM. pp 281–286

Permissions

List of Contributors

Morris Riedel
Juelich Supercomputing Centre, Juelich, Germany

Peter Wittenburg
Max-Planck-Institut f ür Meteorologie, Hamburg, Germany

Johannes Reetz
Rechenzentrum Garching, Munich, Germany

Mark van de Sanden
Stichting Academisch Rekencentrum Amsterdam, Amsterdam, Netherlands

Jedrzej Rybicki
Juelich Supercomputing Centre, Juelich, Germany

Benedikt von St. Vieth
Juelich Supercomputing Centre, Juelich, Germany

Giuseppe Fiameni
CINECA, Bologna, Italy

Giacomo Mariani
CINECA, Bologna, Italy

Alberto Michelini
INGV, Rome, Italy

Claudio Cacciari
CINECA, Bologna, Italy

Willem Elbers
Max-Planck-Institut f ür Meteorologie, Hamburg, Germany

Daan Broeder
Max-Planck-Institut f ür Meteorologie, Hamburg, Germany

Robert Verkerk
Stichting Academisch Rekencentrum Amsterdam, Amsterdam, Netherlands

Elena Erastova
Rechenzentrum Garching, Munich, Germany

Michael Lautenschlaeger
Deutsches Klimarechenzentrum, Hamburg, Germany

Reinhard Budig
Deutsches Klimarechenzentrum, Hamburg, Germany

Hannes Thielmann
Deutsches Klimarechenzentrum, Hamburg, Germany

Peter Coveney
University College London, London, UK

Stefan Zasada
University College London, London, UK

Ali Haidar
University College London, London, UK

Otto Buechner
Juelich Supercomputing Centre, Juelich, Germany

Cristina Manzano
Juelich Supercomputing Centre, Juelich, Germany

Shiraz Memon
Juelich Supercomputing Centre, Juelich, Germany

Shahbaz Memon
Juelich Supercomputing Centre, Juelich, Germany

Heikki Helin
CSC - IT Center for Science, Espoo Finland, Finland

Jari Suhonen
CSC - IT Center for Science, Espoo Finland, Finland

Damien Lecarpentier
CSC - IT Center for Science, Espoo Finland, Finland

Kimmo Koski
CSC - IT Center for Science, Espoo Finland, Finland

Thomas Lippert
Juelich Supercomputing Centre, Juelich, Germany

Abrar Ullah
School of Computer Science, University of Hertfordshire, College Lane, Hatfield AL10 9AB, UK

Hannan Xiao
School of Computer Science, University of Hertfordshire, College Lane, Hatfield AL10 9AB, UK

Trevor Barker
School of Computer Science, University of Hertfordshire, College Lane, Hatfield AL10 9AB, UK

Mariana Lilley
School of Computer Science, University of Hertfordshire, College Lane, Hatfield AL10 9AB, UK

Xinghui Zhao
School of Engineering and Computer Science, Washington State University, 14204 NE Salmon Creek Ave., 98686 Vancouver, WA, USA

Nadeem Jamali
Department of Computer Science, University of Saskatchewan, 110 Science Place, S7N 5C9 Saskatoon, SK, Canada

Maarten Decat
iMinds-DistriNet, KU Leuven, 3001 Leuven, Belgium

Bert Lagaisse
iMinds-DistriNet, KU Leuven, 3001 Leuven, Belgium

Wouter Joosen
iMinds-DistriNet, KU Leuven, 3001 Leuven, Belgium

Alex Norta
Tallinn University of Technology, Akadeemia Tee 15A, 12618 Tallinn, Estonia

Lixin Ma
Tallinn University of Technology, Akadeemia Tee 15A, 12618 Tallinn, Estonia
University of Shanghai for Science and Technology, Shanghai, China

Yucong Duan
Hainan University, Haikou, China

Addi Rull
Tallinn University of Technology, Akadeemia Tee 15A, 12618 Tallinn, Estonia

Merit Kõlvart
Tallinn University of Technology, Akadeemia Tee 15A, 12618 Tallinn, Estonia

Kuldar Taveter
Tallinn University of Technology, Akadeemia Tee 15A, 12618 Tallinn, Estonia

May El Barachi
College of Technological Innovation, Zayed University, Khalifa City B, P.O. Box 144534, Abu Dhabi, United Arab Emirates

Nadjia Kara
Department of Software and IT Engineering, University of Quebec, 1100 Notre-Dame, West, Montréal, Quebec, H3C 1 K3, Canada

Sleiman Rabah
Faculty of Engineering and Computer Science, Concordia University, 1515 St. Catherine W, Montreal, Quebec, H4G 2 W1, Canada

Mathieu Forgues
Ericsson Canada, 8400 Blvd, Décarie Montréal, Québec, H4P 2 N2, Canada

Leonardo Richter Bays
Institute of Informatics, Federal University of Rio Grande do Sul, Porto Alegre, Brazil

Rodrigo Ruas Oliveira
Institute of Informatics, Federal University of Rio Grande do Sul, Porto Alegre, Brazil

Marinho Pilla Barcellos
Institute of Informatics, Federal University of Rio Grande do Sul, Porto Alegre, Brazil

Luciano Paschoal Gaspary
Institute of Informatics, Federal University of Rio Grande do Sul, Porto Alegre, Brazil

Edmundo Roberto Mauro Madeira
Institute of Computing, University of Campinas, Campinas, Brazil

Lesandro Ponciano
Federal University of Campina Grande, Department of Computing and Systems, Av. Aprígio Veloso, 882 – Bloco CO, 58.429-900, Campina Grande – PB, Brazil

Francisco Brasileiro
Federal University of Campina Grande, Department of Computing and Systems, Av. Aprígio Veloso, 882 – Bloco CO, 58.429-900, Campina Grande – PB, Brazil

Nazareno Andrade
Federal University of Campina Grande, Department of Computing and Systems, Av. Aprígio Veloso, 882 – Bloco CO, 58.429-900, Campina Grande – PB, Brazil

Lívia Sampaio
Federal University of Campina Grande, Department of Computing and Systems, Av. Aprígio Veloso, 882 – Bloco CO, 58.429-900, Campina Grande – PB, Brazil

Damian A Tamburri
VU University Amsterdam, Amsterdam, The Netherlands

Philippe Kruchten
University of British Columbia, Vancouver, Canada

Patricia Lago
VU University Amsterdam, Amsterdam, The Netherlands

Hans van Vliet
VU University Amsterdam, Amsterdam, The Netherlands

Alexander Jungmann
Cooperative Computing & Communication Laboratory (C-LAB), University of Paderborn, Fuerstenallee 11, 33102 Paderborn, Germany
Department of Computer Science, University of Paderborn, Warburger Str. 100, 33098 Paderborn, Germany

Felix Mohr
Department of Computer Science, University of Paderborn, Warburger Str. 100, 33098 Paderborn, Germany

Ahmed Frikha
IRISA, University of Rennes 1, Campus universitaire Beaulieu, 35042 Rennes, France

Bernard Cousin
IRISA, University of Rennes 1, Campus universitaire Beaulieu, 35042 Rennes, France

Samer Lahoud
IRISA, University of Rennes 1, Campus universitaire Beaulieu, 35042 Rennes, France

Guang Cheng
School of Computer Science and Engineering, Key Laboratory of Computer Network and Information Integration, MOE, Southeast University, Nanjing, P.R. China

Yongning Tang
School of Information Technology, Illinois State University, Normal, IL, USA

Printed in the USA
CPSIA information can be obtained
at www.ICGtesting.com
JSHW051440221024
72173JS00006B/1534